Illustrated

Hawaiian

Dictionary

by *Kahikāhealani Wight*

illustrated by *Robin Yoko Racoma*

BESS PRESS

3565 Harding Avenue
Honolulu, HI 96816
BessPress.com

Design: Carol Colbath
Typesetting: Island Graphics

Library of Congress Cataloging-in-Publication Data

Wight, Kahikahealani.
    Illustrated Hawaiian dictionary /
Kahikahealani Wight ; illustrations by
Robin Yoko Racoma.
            p.   cm.
    Includes illustrations.
    1-57306-239-1
    1. Hawaiian language – Dictionaries –
English. 2. English language – Dictionaries –
Hawaiian. I. Racoma, Robin Yoko, ill. II. Title.
PL6446.W53 2005 499.419-dc20

Reprint 2022
Printed in China

Contents

Preface

Our aim in creating the *Illustrated Hawaiian Dictionary* has been to create a reference that includes words and definitions most commonly used by beginning students of the language. We have limited the number of words (approximately 2,500 entries in each language) for ease of use by beginning learners of all ages. The meanings are those most often heard in simple daily conversation. Example sentences include lines from well-known Hawaiian songs, *'ōlelo no'eau* (wise sayings), historical references, and current topics of concern to the Hawaiian community, such as the debate about sovereignty.

In planning this book, we quickly became aware of one problem: the difficulty of establishing a one-to-one correspondence between English and Hawaiian words. There is often not just one Hawaiian word that translates an English one. Similarly, many Hawaiian words have several possible English translations that are not necessarily connected with each other in Western thinking. This difficulty in establishing a one-to-one correspondence is partly due to Hawaiian's shorter alphabet, which has only seven consonants plus the *'okina* (glottal stop, considered to be a letter of the Hawaiian alphabet) and partly due to the poetic nature of Hawaiian oral expression, which celebrates a multiplicity of meanings or symbols incorporated into one word.

Therefore, you should be aware that we have included a limited number of meanings for most Hawaiian words, selecting those that are most commonly used today, based on our experience as Hawaiian teachers and students. Alternative meanings are listed in parentheses for most words. However, for some Hawaiian words that have a multitude of possible English translations, we have indicated that there are "many other meanings"; in that case you may want to refer to the Pukui and Elbert *Hawaiian Dictionary* for a full list of possible English meanings.

So also for translation of English words into Hawaiian: we have chosen Hawaiian words that seem to be used most often in Hawaiian conversation to translate the English. You should be aware, however, that there may be other equally valid ways to say the same thing in Hawaiian. Do your grandparents use a different word when they speak Hawaiian? Remember that Hawaiian native speech is a rare and precious gift still passed on in oral tradition, and should be a source of learning for all.

Parts of Speech

Hawaiian does not often assign a particular grammatical function or part of speech to a word. For example, *hoaka* means "a crescent, brightness" (nouns), "to cast a shadow, to drive away or ward off" (verbs) and "shining, glittering" (adjectives)—and these are only a few of the meanings listed for this word in Pukui and Elbert's *Hawaiian Dictionary*. Most Hawaiian words used as adjectives (placed after the noun they modify) can also be used as adverbs (placed after the verb they modify). *No'eau*, meaning skilled or clever, is used as an adjective in the phrase *hana no'eau* (skilled activity, art or craft). This same word is used as an adverb in the following sentence: *Ulana no'eau ka wahine i ka lauhala.* (The woman skillfully weaves the *hala* leaves.) To avoid "pigeon-holing" Hawaiian words, restricting their meanings in ways that run counter to Hawaiian thinking, we have decided not to label parts of speech except where needed for clarity.

Plurals and Pronouns

Hawaiian plurals and pronouns need a brief explanation, since they are markedly different from English plurals and pronouns. Hawaiian pluralizes in two ways: singular nouns with "the" (*ke* or *ka*) pluralize by replacing *ke* or *ka* with *nā*: *ka lole* = the dress, *nā lole* = the dresses.

In all other situations, simply add *mau* before the noun: *kā'u pēpē* = my baby, *ka'u mau pēpē* = my babies.

Hawaiian follows other Polynesian languages in pronoun usage. Unlike English, Hawaiian does not distinguish the sex of the person being referred to: *'o ia* can mean either "he" or "she."

Hawaiian also includes dual pronouns, referring to two people, such as *'olua* (you two).

Perhaps most confusing is the use of four words in Hawaiian for "we," including two words for duals (*kāua* = you and I, *māua* = my buddy and I) and two for three or more people (*kākou* = all of us, *mākou* = my buddies and I). Note that *māua* and *mākou* do not include the person being addressed. See the pronoun chart below for reference.

Pronoun Chart

singular	dual (2 people)	plural (3 or more)
au (I, me)	*kāua* (you and I)	*kākou* (us, we all)
	māua (she/he and I)	*mākou* (us, not you)
'oe (you)	*'olua* (you 2)	*'oukou* (you all)
'o ia (he/she)	*lāua* (they 2)	*lākou* (they all)

For dual and plural pronouns, possession of an object is indicated by adding either *ko* or *kā* before the pronoun. Is the item possessed something you cannot help having, a birthright (such as land, ancestors, parents, siblings, feelings, parts of your body)? Is it something you can get into (such as cars, clothes, buildings)? In both instances, use *kō*:

> *kō lākou hale* = their (3) house
> *kō kāua mau kāma'a* = our (your and my) shoes

If, on the other hand, the item possessed is something you can acquire (such as spouses, children, grandchildren, jobs, tools, money, food, drink), use kā:

> *kā lāua mea 'ai* = their (2) food
> *kā mākou kālā* = our (us 3, not your) money

As you become more familiar with the language and Hawaiian thinking, the use of *ko* and *kā* will become clearer.

Singular possessive pronouns combine *ko* or *kā* and the pronoun to form one word. You never say <u>kō au</u> *inoa*, but <u>ko'u</u> *inoa* (my name). Likewise, <u>kā 'o ia</u> *hana* becomes <u>kāna</u> *hana* (her/his job, activity). See the possessive pronouns chart for reference.

Possessive Pronoun Chart

singular	dual (2 people)	plural (3 or more)
ka'u/ko'u (my)	*kā kāua/ko kāua* (our, your and my)	*kā kākou/ko kākou* (our, us all)
	kā māua/ko māua (our, her/his and my)	*kā mākou/ko mākou* (our, not your)
kāu/kou (your)	*kā 'olua/ko'olua* (your) (your all)	*kā 'oukou/ko 'oukou*
kāna/kona (his, her)	*kā lāua/ko lāua* (their)	*kā lākou/ko lākou* (their all)

Spelling

Hawaiian is being revived as a spoken language as a result of the extraordinary dedication of Hawaiian families who have supported the development of Hawaiian language preschools and a growing Hawaiian Immersion program under the Department of Education. New words are being created for science (astronaut = *kela lani*, lit. sky sailor) and new technologies (compact discs = *cēdē, sēdē*). A few old words are being shortened for use in spoken Hawaiian (*pā'ani kinipōpō peku wāwae*, which means "football game, to play football," has being shortened to *pōpeku*). A new reference guide to the latest Hawaiian words is *Māmaka Kaiao,* published by Hale Kuamo'o, University of Hawai'i-Hilo.

While all of us involved in Hawaiian education are thrilled to witness the growth of interest in learning the language, we are aware of the challenges presented by changes in spelling and the use of diacritical marks (*'okina* and *kahakō*). The spellings in this dictionary reflect current usage; however, be aware that you will see variant spellings as you learn more and as the language grows in daily usage.

The Role of Hawaiian Culture

We have chosen to use common *'ōlelo no'eau* (wise sayings) and familiar lines from Hawaiian songs as examples of word usage as often as possible, because wise sayings and songs are an integral part of Hawaiian language and help introduce readers to the poetic nature of Hawaiian thinking. We have identified as many song composers as possible, because they are the skilled poets of our culture. Songs listed as traditional often are older chants that have survived as songs or have been put to melody in modern times.

Translations of the song lines are our own except for a few lines taken from *Nā Mele o Hawai'i Nei, 101 Hawaiian Songs,* by Elbert and Mahoe. We have also included well-known place names on various islands, as well as other names, such as those of winds and rains, since these are another important part of Hawaiian cultural knowledge.

We hope our dictionary will contribute to the practical use of Hawaiian as a living language and provide explanations of basic cultural concepts that clarify areas of difference between Hawaiian and English, such as Hawaiian family terms or the importance of *kalo* (taro) as a symbol for the deep connection Hawaiians feel to our land.

May it also be a first step toward understanding the beauty and subtlety of Hawaiian expression of feelings, which is such as integral part of our language and culture.

E a'o aku, a'o mai i ola nō ka 'ōlelo 'ōiwi o ka 'āina!

Teach and learn so that the native language of the land lives on!

Acknowledgments

No book is ever the work of any one person, no matter whose name is on the cover. In this case, many people worked diligently over many months to help bring the *Illustrated Hawaiian Dictionary* to life.

Robin Racoma provided beautiful illustrations and waited a long time to see them used.

Early contributors included Kau'i Keola of the Hawaiian Immersion program and Hana Pau and friends from the Hawaiian Studies department at Kamehameha Schools.

Hawaiian language students Dr. Houston Wood of the University of Hawai'i-Mānoa English department and Yuka Kimura of Japan helped with editing and feedback, as did Hawaiian language instructors 'Iwalani Koide and Lālepa Koga.

Tracking down song composers proved to be a challenge. Mahalo to Ku'uipo Kumukahi, Gerry Santos, and Ainsley Halemanu for their ongoing *kōkua*.

Thanks to the people at Bess Press for their patience as we figured out how to do it best. Carol Colbath provided the wonderful design. Revé Shapard spent many hours editing through revision after revision, with the assistance of Jeela Ongley.

Tia Ballantine Berger deserves special credit for her many contributions, including thought-provoking commentary and sharp editing skills. *Mahalo piha, e Tia.*

Mahalo iā 'oukou pākahi a pau.

Thanks to each and every one.

Abbreviations

adj	adjective
ant	antonym
approx	approximately
cap	when capitalized
fig	figuratively
lit	literally
n	noun
pl	plural
syn	synonym
v	verb

Pronunciation Guide

Hawaiian consonants are said the same as they are in English, except for *w*, which is usually pronounced like *v* after *i* and *e*.

Vowel sounds:

a, ā	like *a* in *was: (olonā)*
e	like e in *red: (he‘e)*
ē	like *a* in *baby: (nēnē)*
i, ī	like *e* in *me: (imu, kī)*
o, ō	like *o* in *go: (kalo, kō)*
u, ū	like *oo* in *moon: (hula, pā‘ū)*

Hawaiian words are usually stressed on the next-to-last syllable, unless there is a single line over a vowel. This line is called a macron or *kahakō*. It shows that the vowel should be said with stress, or longer and stronger.

Sometimes two vowels go together: *ai, ao, au, ei, eu, oi, ou*. The vowel sounds are rolled together as you say them, with the first one being stronger.

The mark like an upside-down apostrophe (') is called an *'okina*. It marks a glottal stop. It shows that there is a break in the word, as when you say the English *oh-oh*.

Hawaiian-English

a 1. belonging to, of. [*ka puke a Melia*, Melia's book] 2. and (used primarily between sentences). [*Ua holoi ʻo Lahela i nā pā **a** ua kāwele ʻo Kele iā lākou.* Lahela washed the dishes **and** Kele wiped them.] Also used before article *he* (a, an) and before object markers *i / iā* [*he kāne **a** he wahine,* a man **and** a woman] [*Kelepona aku ʻo ia i ke kauka a iā ʻUlulani.* She phones the doctor **and** ʻUlulani.] Note: *A me* also means "and," but is used primarily within a sentence to indicate a second subject or object. [*Ua holoi ʻo Lahela **a me** Kele i nā puna **a me** nā pahi.* Lahela **and** Kele washed the spoons **and** the knives.] 3. until, up to. [*E kali ana māua **a** hōʻea mai ke kaʻa hoʻolimalima.* We (he and I) will wait **until** the taxi arrives. (*a hiki i* = up until, up to, toward [lit., until arrived at]) [*mai Hauʻula **a hiki i** Haleʻiwa,* from Hauʻula **to** Haleʻiwa]

ā jaw. (*ā luna* = upper jaw) (*ā lalo* = lower jaw) [*ʻEha nō ko kaʻu kaikamahine **ā lalo** i ka niho huʻi.* My daughter's **lower jaw** is very painful due to a sore tooth.]

ʻā 1. fiery, burning. 2. turned on (refers to appliances [lit fire]). [*Ua **ʻā** ka lolouila.* The computer is **on.**] (*ka hale ʻā* = the burning house) (*hoʻā* = to turn on machine, electricity, to light fire) [*E **hoʻā** i kāu pipa.* **Turn on** your beeper.]

aʻa 1. rootlet. (*ke aʻa hala* = the *hala* roots) 2. muscle, nerve, vein, artery. (*aʻa koko* = vein, artery [*lit.* blood rootlet]) (*aʻa lolo* = nerve [*lit.* brain rootlet])

‘a‘a 1. to dare, challenge. [*E waiho i ka hilahila i ka hale, e* **‘a‘a** *i ka hula.* (*‘ōlelo no‘eau*) Leave embarrassment at home, **dare** to dance.] 2. volunteer. 3. intrepid, bold. [*He mau wāhine* **‘a‘a** *kēlā mau ho‘okele.* Those navigators are **intrepid** women.]

‘a‘ā 1. to burn, glow, blaze. [**‘A‘ā** *ka pele.* **Lava** glows.] 2. lava, rough type. [*‘Ōkupe ka malihini i ka* **‘a‘ā**. The newcomer trips on the **rough lava rock**.]

‘a‘ahu costume, garment, clothing. [*He pū nui ko kāna mo‘opuna* **‘a‘ahu** *Heleuī.* His (Her) grandchild's Halloween **costume** is a big pumpkin.]

‘a‘ai 1. erosion. 2. to erode. 3. malignant. (*ma‘i ‘a‘ai* = cancer) [*He* **ma‘i a‘ai** *ko ko Anuhea kupuna kāne.* Anuhea's grandfather has **cancer**.]

‘a‘aka 1. grumpy, surly, cranky. 2. wrinkled, peeling.

‘a‘ala fragrant, sweet-smelling. [*He pua* **‘a‘ala** *ka pīkake.* The *pīkake* is a **fragrant** flower.]

‘a‘ali‘i 1. native plant, symbol of independent people of Ka‘ū. [**‘A‘ali‘i** *kū makani.* (*‘ōlelo no‘eau*) The **‘a‘ali‘i** that stands up to the wind. (Ka‘ū folks are known to be intolerant of rulers who abuse commoners.)]

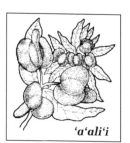
‘a‘ali‘i

‘ae 1. yes. [*Hau‘oli ‘oe?* **‘Ae**, *hau‘oli nō au.* Are you happy? **Yes**, I'm really happy.] 2. to agree, consent. [**‘Ae** *ko ka‘u ipo mau mākua i ko māua male ‘ana.* My sweetheart's parents **agree** to our (his and my) marrying.]

‘a‘e to trespass, break *kapu* or violate law, to tread on, step over (*fig.* oppressed). [*Mai komo i ka heiau i ho‘ola‘a hou ‘ia o* **‘a‘e** *‘oukou i ke kapu.*

Don't enter the religious site that has been rededicated or else you may all **violate** the sacredness.]

aea to come up from under water, to surface. [*Lu'u iho ka lawai'a a **aea** a'e.* The fisherman dives down and then **comes to the surface.**]

'ae'a 1. wandering, shiftless, unstable. (*nā hōkū 'ae'a* = the wandering stars; Hōkūpa'a = North Star, "fixed" star that doesn't move across the sky) (*'ae'a hauka'e* = homeless wanderer [an insult in ancient days]) (*kanaka 'ae'a* = tramp)

'ae kai edge of sea, place where land and sea meet.

aha what. [*He **aha** kēia? He i'a kēia.* **What** is this? This is a fish.] Note: A variation of this basic question is used to ask for specific type or brand name: *He **aha** ke 'ano o* (what is the type/nature of/brand name) + article + noun. [*He **aha** ke 'ano o kēia honu? He 'ea ke 'ano o kēia honu.* **What kind of** turtle is this? This kind of turtle is a tortoiseshell turtle.] Note that asking for a personal name (proper noun) requires use of another question word, namely *'o wai* (who). [*'O wai ka inoa o kēia honu? 'O "Pewa" ka inoa o kēia honu.* **What** is the name of this turtle? "Fin" is the name of this turtle.]

'aha 1. meeting, community. 2. general name for cordage made of coconut fiber, sennit. ('Aha'ōlelo = Congress [*lit.* federal legislature; syn. *'Aha'ōlelo lāhui*]) (*'ahahui* = organization) (*'aha mele* = concert)

ahi fire. (*ahi kao lele* = fireworks) (*kinai ahi* = fire extinguisher or firefighter) (*kāhea pau ahi* = fire alarm) (*pau ahi* = destroyed by fire)

'ahi tuna fish.

'ahia question word asking "how many?" (a less commonly used variation of *'ehia,* used in an idiomatic phrase asking "Which of day of the

week is it?" [*lit.* what number night?]). [*'O ka Pō
'ahia 'o nehinei? 'O ka Pō'ahā 'o nehinei.* **What**
(number) day of the week was yesterday?
Yesterday was Thursday.]

ahiahi evening, time when fires were lit.

'ahi'ahi to slander.

'āhina gray. (syn. *'āhinahina, hinahina, hina*)

'āhinahina Hawaiian silversword, indigenous plant
found on Maui and
Hawai'i islands.

'āhiu wild, untamed (*fig.* shy
or unsocial). [*He pilikia
nui ka pua'a **'āhiu** ma ka
wao nahele.* **Wild** pigs are
a big problem in the rain
forest.]

'āhinahina

aho 1. fishing line, lashing, cord, kite string. 2. breath
(syn. *hanu*). 3. to breathe (syn. *hanu*). (*paupauaho*
= out of breath) 4. idiomatic phrase: *E aho* + verb,
"It's better (to do . . .). [*E aho ka 'ai 'ana i ka
'īnika.* **It's better** to eat spinach.]

ahonui 1. patience. [*Ke mālama 'oe i nā luāhine a
me nā 'elemākule, 'o ke **ahonui** ka mea pono.*
When you take care of the elderly women and
men, **patience** is the proper thing.] 2. patient.
(*ahonui 'ole* = impatient)

ahu 1. pile, mound, mass, cairn. 2. shrine, altar.

ahulau epidemic. [*Nui nā Hawai'i i hala i nā **ahulau**
i kēlā kenekulia aku nei.* Many Hawaiians died
in **epidemics** in the last century.]

ahupua'a traditional land division encompassing a
piece of land from mountains to sea (*lit.* pig
mound, pile of stones where pig image or offering marked boundary of land division).

'ahu'ula feather cloak, a symbol of high rank worn
by male chiefs. [*He **'ahu'ula** mamo ko*

Kamehameha ʻekahi.
Kamehameha I had a
mamo-**feather cloak**.]

ʻahuʻula

ahuwale prominent, in clear
view, obvious.

ai 1. sexual intercourse. (syn.
hana ai, hana ei) (*nā
maʻi hana ei* = sexually
transmitted diseases) 2.
to have sexual relations.

ʻai 1. food, especially plant or vegetable; sometimes
refers specifically to poi or taro. (*ka ʻai me ka iʻa*
= fish and poi) [*Ua lawa mākou i ka pōhaku, ka
ʻai kamahaʻo o ka ʻāina.* Rocks, the astonishing
food of the land, are enough for us. (song,
"Kaulana Nā Pua," by E. Prendergast)] 2. score,
points in a game. [*He aha ka ʻai pōpaʻilima?*
What's the volleyball **score**?] 3. to eat, taste, bite.
[*Mai, mai e ʻai.* Come, come in and **eat**. (traditional greeting; all passersby were welcomed to
eat and rest)]

ʻāʻī neck. (*lei ʻāʻī* = neck *lei*, necktie)

aia there. [*aia i ka uka aʻo Piʻihonua,* **there** in the
uplands of Piʻihonua (song, "Kimo Henderson
Hula," by H.D. Beamer)] Note: *Aia* is essential in
Hawaiian to indicate location in time or space,
but is often not translated into English. Both *ʻō*
and *laila* are used to mean "over there." *ʻŌ* is
used to indicate a general direction; *laila* is used
when the exact location is already known. [*Ua
kipa aku ʻolua i Kahana? Mālie ʻo* **laila**. Have
you (two) visited Kahana? It's peaceful **over
there**.] (*ma ʻō a ma ʻaneʻi* = everywhere [*lit.* over
there and over here])

aia i hea where. [*Aia i hea ka hālāwai ma kēia lā?
Aia ka hālāwai ma ka hōkele hou.* **Where**'s the
meeting today? The meeting is in the new hotel.]

'aiana 1. clothes iron. 2. to iron.

'ai'ē 1. debt. 2. to owe.

'aiha'a hula style with low stance.

'aihue 1. thief, theft. 2. to steal. [*Ua* **'aihue** *'ia ko kona 'ohana ka'a ma ka pāka.* Her family's car was **stolen** at the park.]

'aikalima (from English) ice cream.

'aila 1. oil, fat. 2. greasy, oily, fatty. (*'aila iki* = low fat) (*'aila hamo* = massage oil, ointment, salve)

'aina kakahiaka

'aina meal. (syn. *pā'ina* [also means party, to eat, to party]) (*'aina ahiahi* = dinner) [*E 'ai kākou i ka* **'aina ahiahi** *ma ka hale 'aina 'o Wisteria!* Let's eat **dinner** at the Wisteria restaurant!] (*'aina awakea* = lunch) (*'aina kakahiaka* = breakfast)

'āina land, earth (*lit.* that which feeds spiritually and physically, implying sacredness of land). (*ke aloha 'āina* = patriotism, love of the land) (*'āina hānau* = native land, birthplace; *one hānau, lit.* birth sands, is also frequently used) (*'āina ho'opulapula* = Hawaiian Homestead land) (*'āina nui* = mainland) (*'āina puni 'ole* = continent) (*'āina panoa* = desert) (*nā 'āina 'ē* = foreign lands)

a i 'ole or (*lit.* and if not). [*Hiki iā ia ke hula* **a i 'ole** *ho'okani 'ukulele?* Can she dance hula **or** play the ukulele?]

āiwaiwa mysterious, inexplicable. [*He mea* **āiwaiwa** *ka huaka'i pō.* The night marchers are a **mysterious** thing.]

aka 1. shadow. 2. reflection, image. (*ili i ke aka* = to cast a shadow)

akā but. [*Huhū ka 'ōhua,* **akā** *mālie ke kalaiwa ka'a* *'ōhua*. The passenger is angry, **but** the bus driver is calm.] (*akā na'e, akā nō na'e* = however) [*Ua hao mai ka makani; akā na'e 'a'ole nui loa nā 'ale o ka moana*. The wind was blasting; **however**, the ocean swells weren't really big.]

'aka'aka 1. laughter. [*Ua hū ka 'aka'aka*. **Laughter** burst out.] 2. to laugh. [*Mai 'aka'aka mai ia'u!* Don't **laugh** at me!]

'aka'akai onion. (*'aka'akai lau* = green onion) (*'aka'akai poepoe* = round onion)

akāka clear, luminous, distinct, intelligible. [*Akāka wale ko lāua wehewehe 'ana*. Their (two) explanation is **clear**.]

'ākala 1. native plant, the bright pink Hawaiian raspberry. 2. pink color. [*He hōkele 'ākala 'o ka Royal Hawaiian*. The Royal Hawaiian is a **pink** hotel.]

akamai 1. smartness, cleverness, skill. 2. smart, clever, skilled. [*Nani ke akamai o nā kūpuna!* Our ancestors were very **skilled**!] [*Malia paha e lilo ana ka makana i ka moho akamai*. Maybe the prize will become the **clever** contestant's.]

'ākau 1. right (direction). [*'O wai kēnā ma ka 'ao'ao 'ākau ou ma ke ki'i?* Who's that on your **right** side in the picture?] 2. north. [*Aia 'o Hawai'i ma ka Pākīpika 'ākau*. Hawai'i is in the **north** Pacific.]

ake 1. liver. (*akemāmā* = lungs) 2. to yearn for, want, desire, wish. [*Ake nui nō ka lāhui Hawai'i e 'ōlelo Hawai'i*. The Hawaiian nationality really **wants** to speak Hawaiian.]

ākea 1. width, breadth. 2. broad, wide, spacious, public. [*He kumulā'au ākea ka 'ōhai*. The monkeypod is a **wide** tree.]

'ākea 1. starboard. 2. outer hull of double hulled canoe (*wa'a kaulua*).

akeakamai 1. science, philosophy. 2. scientist, philosopher, lover of wisdom. [*He mau *akeakamai* *ko kākou mau kūpuna.* Our ancestors were **lovers of wisdom**.]

'āke'ake'a 1. obstruction. 2. interfere, block.

akemāmā lungs.

'ākepa bird; one of the wide variety of Hawaiian honeycreepers, currently endangered.

'aki to nibble, nip, snap. [**'Aki** *ka manini i ka limu. Manini* fish **nibble** seaweed.]

'ako 1. to pluck a flower. [*A he pua 'oe, ua* **'ako** *'ia.* You are a flower that has been **plucked**. (song, "Pāpālina Lahilahi," composer unknown)] 2. to trim or cut, as hair.

'ākoakoa to gather together, assemble. [*Ma ka papekema i* **'ākoakoa** *ai ka 'ohana.* It was at the baptism that the family **gathered**.]

'āko'ako'a coral head.

aku 1. bonito fish, prized for delicious flavor. [*'Oiai 'o kēia ka lā hope o ka makahiki, e kū'ai mai kāua i ke* **aku** *a e ho'omākaukau i ka i'a maka.* Since this is the last day of the year, let's (you and me) buy **aku** and prepare sashimi (raw fish).] 2. [directional, away from speaker] word added after verb to clarify direction of action, sometimes essential to meaning: *lawe aku* = to take; *lawe mai* = to bring; *kū'ai aku* = to sell; *kū'ai mai* = to buy. [*E hele* **aku** *'oukou!* (You all) go **away**!]

akua 1. god. [*'O Kūkā'ilimoku ko Kamehameha* **akua** *kaua.* Kūkā'ilimoku was Kamehameha's war **god**.] 2. spirit, ghost, supernatural being. [*Mai maka'u i nā* **akua** *lapu!* Don't be afraid of **ghosts**!] 3. image, idol. [*Nui nā ki'i* **akua** *hou ma ka Pu'uhonua 'o Hōnaunau.* There are lots of new **images** at the Hōnaunau City of Refuge.]

ala 1. path, trail, road. (*alahele* = trail, pathway; *alaloa* = freeway; *alanui* = street, road) 2. to wake up, rise up. (*ho'āla* = to wake someone) [*E* **ala**

*mai! E **ho'āla** kāua iā Papa!* **Wake** up! Let's
wake up Daddy!]

'ala scent, smell (*fig.*
esteemed). [*Moani ke*
'ala o ka laua'e. The
scent of the *laua'e* fern is
borne on the breeze.]
Note: exception to *ke/ka*
rule: *ke 'ala.*

alahele

alahele trail, pathway.

ālai 1. obstruction, block,
hindrance. 2. to obstruct,
block. [*ālai 'ia a'ela e Nounou,* **blocked** by
Nounou (chant, "Kūnihi ka Mauna")]

a laila and then, next. [*Ho'i ka wilikī i ke ke'ena. A*
laila, inu kope 'o ia ala. The engineer returns to
the office. **And then,** she (over there) drinks coffee.]

alaka'i 1. leader, guide. (*alaka'i mele* = song leader)
2. to lead, guide. [*Ke **alaka'i** nei ke kāpena i nā*
koa ma ka paikau. The captain is **leading** the soldiers in the military parade.]

'alalā 1. scream, yell. 2.
Hawaiian crow, currently
near extinction. 3. to
scream, yell. ('Alalākeiki
= channel between Maui
and Kaho'olawe)

alaloa freeway, highway.

'alamihi common black crab.

'alaneo clear, unclouded
sky, calm, serene.

'alalā

'alani orange fruit, orange color.

'alani Pākē tangerine.

alanui street, road. [*Noho ko'u 'Anakala a me ko'u*
*'Anakē ma ke **alanui** 'o Pāhoa ma Kaimukī.* My
Uncle and Aunt live on Pāhoa **Street** in Kaimukī.]

'ālapa 1. athlete. [*He **'ālapa** kaulana 'o Sid Fernandez*. Sid Fernandez is a famous **athlete**.] 2. athletic, active.

alapi'i staircase, ladder. [*Ua pi'i a'e nā mō'ī Kalākaua i ke **alapi'i** koa.* The Kalākaua monarchs ascended the *koa* **staircase**.] (*alapi'i mele* = musical scale)

'alawa to glance quickly (thus to see instinctively or insightfully).

ale to swallow. [*Ua **ale** ke kanaka ma'i i ka huaale.* The patient **swallowed** the pill.]

'ale ocean swell, wave. [*ka 'iwa hehi **'ale*** ('ōlelo no'eau), the *'iwa* bird who steps on the crests of the **ocean swells**]

'ale'ale stirring, rippling. (*Wai'ale'ale* = rippling fresh water)

'alekohola alcohol. (syn. *lama* = rum, in Hawaiian used to represent all types of alcohol) [*'A'ole au e inu **lama**.* I will not drink **alcohol**. (temperance song, 1800s)]

alelo tongue. [*Mai kīko'o 'olua i ko 'olua mau **alelo!*** Don't you two stick out your **tongues**!]

'alemanaka calendar. [*Kū'ai aku nā 'Ahahui Kiwila Hawai'i i ka **'alemanaka** mahina Hawai'i kahiko.* The Hawaiian Civic Clubs sell the old Hawaiian moon **calendar**.]

ali'i

ali'i 1. chief, ruler. 2. royal, noble. [*He mau hale **ali'i** ko Honolulu.* Honolulu has **royal** palaces.]

'ālina scar. [*He **'ālina** lō'ihi ko kona 'ōpū.* His stomach has a long **scar**.]

alo 1. front of body, face; presence. [*he **alo** a he **alo**,* **face** to **face**] 2. (*fig.*) reference to wife.

aloali‘i royal court (*lit.* in the presence of royal chiefs). [*Hiki ke ‘ike ‘ia kekahi* **aloali‘i** *ma ka ho‘okūkū hula ‘o Merrie Monarch.* A **royal court** can be seen at the Merrie Monarch hula contest.]

aloha 1. love, greetings. [**Aloha** *nō au i kou maka.* I **love** your eyes. (song, "Aloha Nō Au I Kou Maka," by Leleiōhoku)] 2. regret, sympathy, compassion, grace. 3. farewell. 4. to love. 5. beloved. [*e Hawai‘i* **aloha** *ē,* oh **beloved** Hawai‘i (song, "Hawai‘i Aloha")] 6. too bad, how sad. [*Ua hala ko lākou makuahine?* **Aloha!** Their (three or more) mother died? **How sad!**] variations: *aloha nō, aloha ‘ino* Note: *Aloha* has many other meanings. (*aloha ‘āina* = patriotism [*lit.* love for the land]) (*Aloha nō au iā ‘oe* = I love you) (*Aloha a hui hou kāua!* = Goodbye until you and I meet again!)

‘alohi 1. brilliance, splendor, brightness. [*ke* **‘alohi** *o ka pō Māhealani,* the **brightness** of the night of the full moon] 2. bright, shiny.

alu to cooperate, work together. [*E* **alu** *like mai kākou, e nā ‘ōiwi o Hawai‘i.* Let's **work together**, natives of Hawai‘i. (song, "Alu Like," by H. Apoliona)]

‘alu to bend, stoop, sag, slacken. (*kī hō‘alu* = slack key, Hawaiian style of guitar playing)

alualu to run, chase after, run for political office. [**Alualu** *‘o Fasi i ke ke‘ena kia‘āina.* Fasi **runs** for governor.]

‘alu‘alu loose, baggy. (*keiki ‘alu‘alu* = premature baby)

ama outrigger float. [*E hāpai i ke* **ama**! Lift up the **outrigger float**!]

‘**Amelika** America. (‘Amelika ‘Ākau = North America) (‘Amelika Hema = South America) (‘Amelika Hui Pū‘ia = United States of America)

'ami 1. joint or hinge. 2. hula step with hip rotation.
ana 1. measurement, design, pattern, model. [*Nani kēia* **ana** *kapa kuiki.* This quilt **pattern** is pretty.] (*anapuni* = circumference) (*anawaena* = diameter) 2. cave. [*Ki'eki'e ka puka o ke* **ana** *'o Kāne ana.* The entrance to Kāne ana **cave** is tall.] 3. to measure, survey, evaluate. (Kalaniana'ole = the immeasurable chief [one whose rank is so high it can not be measured]) (*anawela* = thermometer) [*Ke pi'i a'e nei ka wela ma ke* **anawela**? *Ke kahe nei ko'u hou.* Is the temperature rising on the **thermometer**? My sweat is pouring off.]
ana 'āina 1. surveyor. 2. to survey land. [*Ua* **ana** *'āina lākou i ke alahao.* They **surveyed** the train track.]
'anae mullet fish. (*'ama'ama* = immature mullet)
'ānai 1. friction. 2. to rub, scrub, grind, polish. [*E* **'ānai** *i ka pōhaku a nemonemo.* **Rub** the stone until it is smooth.]
anaina audience, crowd. [*Ua ho'ōho ke* **anaina**. The **audience** cheered.]
'anakala uncle (used to respectfully address any older man as well as family members).
'anakē aunt (used to respectfully address any older woman as well as family members).
anana fathom, measurement of six feet (a traditional unit of measurement: the distance between the tips of the longest fingers of a man extending arms out to the sides). [*'Ekolu* **anana** *ka hohonu o ke kai ma 'ane'i.* The sea is three **fathoms** deep here.] Note: other traditional measurements: *'iwilei* (measurement from collarbone to tip of middle finger extended), *ha'ilima* (distance from elbow to end of finger), *kīko'o* (measurement from end of thumb to end of index finger), *muku* (like *anana*, but the measurement of one arm extends to the elbow only)

'ane'ane nearly, almost. [**'Ane'ane** *make loa ka
'alalā.* The Hawaiian crow is **almost** extinct.]

'ane'i here (location). [*Aia kāna mau puke ma
'ane'i?* Are his books over **here**?] (*ma 'ō a ma
'ane'i* = everywhere [*lit.* there and here]) [*Kū'ai
hele lāua **ma 'ō a ma 'ane'i**.* They (two) shop
everywhere.]

'ānela (from English) angel. [*'A'ole au he **'ānela**, he
kanaka wau.* (*'ōlelo no'eau*) I'm not an **angel**, I'm
a human being (therefore I make mistakes).]

'ane make loa endangered (*lit.* nearly extinct). [**'Ane
make loa** *ke kāhuli.* The *kāhuli* tree snail is
endangered.]

aniani 1. glass (material). (*makaaniani* = eye- glasses) (*pilimaka* = contact lenses) 2. mirror. (*aniani
kū* = standing mirror) 3. transparent, obvious.

ano awe, reverence, peacefulness. (*hō'ano* = holy, to
sanctify, revere)

'ano 1. type, kind. [*He pakalana ke **'ano** o kēnā pua.*
That **type** of flower (by you) is a *pakalana.*] Note:
He aha ke 'ano o is used to ask for type or brand
name. [*He aha ke 'ano o kēlā wa'a? He wa'a
kaukahi kēlā.* **What kind of** canoe is that? That's a
single hull canoe.] [*He aha ke 'ano o kona kalaka? He Chevy kona kalaka.* **What kind of** truck
does he have? His truck is a Chevy.] 2. personality, mood. [*He aha kou **'ano**?* What's wrong with
your **personality**? 3. used before adj. to mean "sort
of." [*Pehea ke kula? **'Ano** maika'i ke kula.* How's
school? School's **okay (sort of good)**.]

'ano'ano seed. [*E 'ōkupu a'e ana kēia **'ano'ano** hē'ī?*
Will this papaya **seed** sprout?]

'ano 'ē odd, strange, unusual. [**'Ano 'ē** *ka hana a
kēlā malihini.* That newcomer's behavior is **odd**.]

'ano hana method, technique. [*He aha ke **'ano hana**
a ka māka'ikiu kaulana?* What is the **method** of
the famous detective?]

anu 1. cold, coldness. 2. a cold (illness). [*He **anu** ko kā 'olua mo'opuna wahine?* Does your (two) granddaughter have a **cold**?]

anuanu cold. [***Anuanu** 'o uka.* The uplands are **cold**.]

ānuenue rainbow. [*Pi'o ke **ānuenue**.* The **rainbow** arches overhead.] (*ānuenue kau pō* = night rainbow)

anuhea fragrance of the mountain forests, cool and sweet.

ānuenue

'ānunu 1. greed. 2. greedy. [*palapala **'ānunu** me ka pākaha,* **greedy** document with extortion (song, "Kaulana Nā Pua," by E. Prendergast)] (syn. *'ānulu, nunu*)

'ānu'u step. [*Ua 'ōkupe ka 'elemakule i ka **'ānu'u** hope o ke alapi'i.* The old man stumbled on the last **step** of the staircase.]

ao 1. light, daylight. [*a ao ka pō,* all night] 2. wisdom, enlightenment. 3. dawn. 4. cloud. 5. world, earth. [*Ko kēia ao, ko kēlā ao.* Those of this **world**, those of that **world**. (Doxology)] (*ao holo'oko'a* = universe) 5. to dawn. [*Ua wana'**ao**/Ua kaiao.* Day has **dawned**.] 6. to regain consciousness.

a'o to learn (*a'o mai*), to teach (*a'o aku*). [*Ua **a'o** 'ia mai mākou ē, he mea nui ka malihini.* We have **learned** that a visitor is an important person. (greeting chant taught in Pūnana Leo school)]

'aoa to bark, howl. [*Ke **'aoa** nei nā 'īlio hae?* Are the fierce dogs **barking**?]

'ao'ao 1. side. [*E aloha aku 'oukou i ka luna 'auhau ma ka **'ao'ao** 'ākau o Kilinahe.* You all greet the tax collector on the right **side** of Kilinahe.] 2. page. [*Aia ka ha'awina ma ka **'ao'ao***

'umikūmāiwa. The lesson is on **page** nineteen.]
3. hemisphere. [*Aia 'o Aotearoa ma ka* **'ao'ao**
hema o ka honua. New Zealand is in the southern **hemisphere** of the world.]

'a'ohe none, to have none, to be none. [**'A'ohe** *āna
hana.* She **doesn't have** a job.]

'a'ole no, not. [**'A'ole** *nahenahe ko ke kāpena leo.*
The captain's voice is **not** soft and sweet.]

'apa to delay, waste time, keep others waiting. (*ka
mili'apa* = slowpoke) [*Na wai i 'imi i* **ka mili'apa**
i ka pi'i kuahiwi? Who was it that looked for the
slowpoke on the hike?]

'āpala (from English) apple. [*'Ono māua i ka pai*
'āpala *me ka 'aikalima.* We (she/he and I) have a
craving for **apple** pie and ice cream.]

'āpana piece, section. [*I* **'āpana** *pai pika nāna, ke
'olu'olu.* Bring him a **piece** of pizza, please.]

'apapane a native bird of the honeycreeper family
with black and red feathers that were used for
featherwork.

'Apelila (from English) April.

apo 1. circle, hoop, bracelet, ring, circuit. (*apo hele* =
orbit of stars, planets) [*He* **apo hele** *lō'ihi ko 'Iao?*
Does Jupiter have a long **orbit**?] 2. to clasp,
embrace, reach around, hug.

'apo to grab, catch, hug; *fig.*
to perceive, understand.
[*Ua* **'apo** *koke 'o ia nei i
ko'u mana'o.* This one
here (she/he) quickly
caught my meaning.]

'apo'apo 1. fit, palpitation,
attack. 2. to have an
attack, fit.

apolima bracelet. [*Pipi'i ke

apolima

apolima *kula Hawai'i.* A Hawaiian gold **bracelet**
is expensive.]

'**āpono** to approve, consent, ratify, to pass a bill. [*E* '*āpono ana 'o Alu Like i kā lāua palapala noi kālā.* Alu Like will **approve** their (two) grant application.]

'**āpuka** 1. fraud, embezzlement, embezzler, deceit. [*Ua lilo kāu kālā i ke kanaka '**āpuka**?* Did your money become the **embezzler**'s?] 2. to cheat, defraud, deceive.

au 1. period of time, era, age, passage of time. (*i kēia au hou* = in this modern era [these days] (*i ke au kahiko* = in ancient days) 2. ocean current, tide, movement. [*He **au** ikaika ko Makapu'u.* Makapu'u has a strong **current**.] 3. to flow, float, move. 4. I, me (*wau* = variant spelling, pronunciation)

āu your (1), yours (*ke kāwele āu, kāu kāwele* = your (1) towel

a'u 1. marlin, swordfish. 2. my, mine. [*ke kopa holoi lole a'u,* **my** laundry detergent]

'*au* 1. handle, stem, stalk, long bone of arm, leg. [*Auī! Wela nō ke '**au** o kēia ipuhao!* Ouch! The **handle** of this pan is really hot!] Note: exception to *ke/ka* rule: *ke 'au.* 2. to swim, travel by sea, usually to a specific destination. [*Ke '**au** nei ke kelamoku i ko Palani mokupe'a.* The sailor is **swimming** to Palani's sailboat.]

'*au'a* to hold back, refuse to part with. [*E '**au'a** 'ia e kama i kona moku.* **Refuse**, child, **to part with** your land. (opening line of ancient chant, "'Au'a 'ia," advising Hawaiians to hold on to their heritage)]

'**auamo** 1. pole across shoulder used to carry burdens, using nets suspended from each end. 2. to carry burden.

'**auana** to wander from place to place, ramble, drift. (*hula 'auana* = modern style hula, probably so called because *hula kahiko*, ancient hula, has stricter rules)

auane'i by and by, later on. [*E kāwele 'oe i kou lauo-ho o ma'i auane'i.* Dry your hair off or else you'll be sick **later on.**]

'au'au to take a bath or swim. [*'Au'au anei nā keiki ma mua o ka 'aina ahiahi?* Do the children **take a bath** before dinner?] (*'au'au kai* = to swim in the ocean; sometimes used to distinguish swimming from taking a bath)

auē too bad, gosh, oh dear, wow (used for a wide variety of situations for problems of minor and major importance; many variations, such as *auē nō ho'i ē!* [oh, for goodness sake!]) (gives extra emphasis). [*Inu 'olua a 'ona ma ka hopenapule? Auē nō ho'i 'olua ē!* You (two) drink until drunk on the weekend? **Oh for goodness sake** you folks!]

'auhau taxes, tariff, levy, charge. [*'O nehinei ka lā uku 'auhau. 'Ano 'ūlōlohi 'oukou!* Yesterday was the day to pay **taxes.** You all are a little late!]

'auhea where (often used as a poetic way of calling the attention of the person/s being addressed; frequent opening line of songs) [*'Auhea wale 'oe, e ku'u pua?* **Where** are you, my beloved flower? (*fig.* pay attention, beloved) (song, "Pua Lilia," by A. Alohikea)]

'auhuhu bush used for fish poison.

auhuli to overturn, over-throw; to till.

auī exclamation of pain.

'aui to turn aside, deviate, decline.

'auinalā afternoon (approx. 2 - 6 p.m.; *lit.* the declining of the sun).

'Aukake (from English) August.

'auinalā

'auli'i dainty, trim, cute, neat. [*Auli'i ko kāna*

kaikamahine pāʻū hula. His daughter's hula skirt is **neat**.]

'**auloa** long limbed.

'**aumakua** family guardian spirit embodied in animal form, such as *manō* (shark), *pueo* (owl), *moʻo* (lizard), *puhi* (eel). (pl. '*aumākua*) '*Aumākua* are usually considered to be restricted to a specific type or individual animal, also to a specific place frequented by the family. [*ʻO ka ʻio kou* **'aumakua**? Is the Hawaiian hawk your **guardian spirit**?]

'**aumoana** 1. sailor. 2. to travel on the open sea.

aumoe midnight, late night. [*Hiaʻā au i ke* **aumoe**. I'm an insomniac at **midnight**.]

'**aumoku** fleet of ships. ('*auwaʻa* = canoe fleet)

'**āuna** flock, large group. (*he ʻāuna manō* = a school of sharks)

aupuni government, kingdom, nation. [*No ka mea, nou ke* **aupuni**, For thine is the **kingdom** (line from "Ka pule a ka Haku," the Lord's prayer)] (*ke aupuni pekelala* = the federal government) (*aupuni moku ʻāina* = the state government) (*aupuni a ka lehulehu* = democracy) (*aupuni mōʻī* = monarchy)

'**auwae** chin. [*He ʻumiʻumi ko ko Kāna Kaloka* **'auwae**. Santa Claus's **chin** has a beard.] ('*auwae puʻu* = discouraged)

'**auwai** canal, ditch, sewer (commonly refers to ditch used to divert water from stream to irrigate taro patch). [*Kahe mau ka wai i nā* **auwai** *kahiko o ka papa loʻi ʻo Kānewai*. Does water continue to flow in the old **ditches** of the taro patch flats called Kānewai?]

awa harbor, channel through reef, port. [*ke* **awa** *lau o Puʻuloa*, the many-channeled **harbor** of Puʻuloa (Pearl Harbor)]

'**awa** plant whose root is chewed or mashed into a

narcotic drink important in ceremonies and used throughout Polynesia. Since it numbs the mouth, *ʻawa* is used as a medicine for toothache.

ʻawaʻawa 1. bitter, sour taste (*fig.* unpleasant, harsh or disagreeable). [*I mua e oʻu mau pōkiʻi a inu i ka wai* **ʻawaʻawa**, *ʻaʻohe hope e hoʻi ai.* Go forward my younger brothers and drink the **bitter** waters (of battle), there is no way to retreat. (Kamehameha's words to his warriors at the battle of ʻIao on Maui)] 2. bitterness, sourness (*fig.* anguish, tragedy).

awakea noon time, midday. (*aloha awakea* = noon greetings, said generally between 10 a.m. and 2 p.m.)

awakea

ʻawapuhi wild ginger, a "pest plant" that takes over and destroys native plant habitats; also, its sweetly scented flower much prized for leis. [*kuʻu lei* **ʻawapuhi** *melemele*, my yellow **ginger** *lei*]

awāwa valley. [*Uluwehi ke* **awāwa** *ʻo Moanalua.* Moanalua **Valley** is lush with greenery.]

ʻawapuhi

ʻaweʻawe 1. tentacles of octopus. [*ʻEwalu* **ʻaweʻawe** *o ka heʻe.* The octopus has eight **tentacles**.] 2. runners of vine.

ʻawelika (from English) average. [*ʻEhia kālā ka* **ʻawelika** *o kāna uku kaulele?* How much money is the **average** of his overtime pay?]

ʻāweoweo a red fish with big eyes. (*alauwā* = young ʻāweoweo)

ʻāwīwī 1. quick, fast. 2. quickly. [*Holo* **ʻāwīwī** *ke kūkini o ke au kahiko.* The king's runners of the ancient days ran **quickly**.] (syn. *wikiwiki*)

e 1. particle used to address someone/something, usually not translated into English. [*E Hawai'i, e ku'u one hānau ē,* **(oh)** Hawai'i, my birth sands (song, "Hawai'i Aloha," by L. Lyons)] 2. particle used in front of infinitive form of a verb [*Komo 'o Mike Hawai'i i Gold's Gym* **e** *ho'oikaika kino i kēlā lā kēia lā.* Miss Hawai'i enters Gold's Gym **to** exercise every day.] 3. particle used in passive sentence to indicate who performed the action. [*Ua huki 'ia ko ke keiki kolohe pepeiao* **e** *kona 'anakē.* The naughty child's ear was pulled **by** her Aunty.] 4. particle; first word of a command, directly before a verb, usually not translated into English. [*E honi aku iā Tūtū, e ka pēpē.* Kiss grandpa/grandma, baby.]

ē 1. particle used at the end of a formal address, usually not translated into English. [*E ke ali'i hanohano* **ē, o** distinguished chief] 2. particle used to add emphasis as in the exclamation *auē nō ho'i ē!* (oh, for goodness sake!).

'ē 1. strange, foreign. [*nā 'āina* **'ē, foreign** lands] 2. before, previously. [*Ua lohe* **'ē** *mākou i ka nūhou.* We (us all, not you) have **already** heard the news.] 3. yes (informal speech). [*Auē! Lepo kēia limu, 'eā?* **'ē 'ē 'ē.** Gosh! This seaweed is dirty, right? **Yah, yah, yah.**]

ea 1. sovereignty, rule. [*Imi nā kānaka maoli i ke* **ea.** The native people of Hawai'i seek **sovereignty.**] 2. life force, breath, gas, vapors. [*Ua mau ke* **ea** *o ka 'āina i ka pono.* State motto, usually translated "The **life** of the land is perpetuated in righteousness" (however, other interpretations are possible).] 3. plastic. [*Nui nā 'eke ea ma KTA.* KTA has lots of **plastic** bags.]

'ea 1. hawksbill turtle, one type of sea turtle found in Hawai'i, formerly prized for its shell. 2. general term for infections, infectious diseases. [*He ma'i 'ea ke anu.* A cold is an **infectious disease**.] 3. melody of song. [*Nani ke 'ea o "Makalapua."* The **melody** of "Makalapua" is pretty.] 4. isn't that so?/right? added to the end of a sentence. [*Momona kēia kokoleka, 'ea?* This chocolate is sweet- tasting, **isn't that so?**] 5. spray.

'eā 1. song refrain, "tra la la." [*Nani wale nā hala 'eā 'eā o Naue i ke kai 'eā 'eā.* So beautiful are the *hala* **tra la la** of Naue by the sea **tra la la**. (song, "Nā Hala o Naue," by J. Kahinu)]

e'e to board plane, boat; to climb, mount. (*hikie'e* = low sofa [*lit.* can climb on]) (*kai e'e* = tidal wave)

'e'ehia 1. awe, reverence, fear. 2. awe-inspiring, solemn, overcome with terror or reverence. [***E'ehia** ka hū 'ana o ka pele ma ka pō.* The spouting of lava in the dark is **awe-inspiring**.]

'e'epa 1. extraordinary, peculiar, abnormal. 2. a name for legendary people with unusual powers, such as Nā Mū.

'eha 1. pain, hurt. [*He 'eha koni ko ko'u iwi 'ao'ao pohole.* My bruised rib has a throbbing **pain**.] 2. sore, painful. [***'Eha** kou wāwae moku, 'eā?* Your cut foot is **sore**, yah?]

'ehā four, a sacred number. In ancient Hawai'i, the counting system was based on 4's. Terms used today to indicate great numbers are derived from this traditional way of counting: *kāuna* = four; *ka'au* = forty; *lau* = four hundred; *mano* = four thousand; *kini* = forty thousand, many; *lehu* = four hundred thousand, very many.

'ēheu wing. [*Ma lalo kou 'ēheu ko mākou maluhia a*

mau loa aku nō. Beneath your **wings** be our peace forever more. ("Queen's Prayer," by Liliʻuokalani)]

ʻehia 1. question word asking "how many?" [**ʻEhia** *kenikeni a nā moʻopuna e hoʻolilo ai ma ke kāni-wala?* **How many** dimes (change) do the grand-children have to spend at the carnival?]

ehu 1. dust. [*Nui ka* **ehu** *ma Kahoʻolawe.* There's lots of **dust** on Kahoʻolawe.] 2. spray. 3. pollen.

ʻehu 1. dust. 2. spray. 3. pollen. 4. dark red hair seen in some Hawaiians; also any color hair other than black; note: only *ʻehu* (not *ehu*) is used for this meaning.

eia (idiom) here is (person, thing). [**Eia** *kāu mau makana.* **Here are** your prizes (presents).] [**Eia** *ka pane a ke aloha.* **Here is** love's answer. (song, "E Waiʻanae," by R. Ngum)] (here, in this place = *ʻaneʻi*) (ant. *aia*, there is, there in that place) (*Eia nei* = "dearie," used to politely address someone whose name you don't know) (*Eia aʻe…* = Here comes…) (*eia hou* = furthermore)

ʻeiwa nine. (syn. *iwa*) (*kanaiwakūmāiwa* = 99 [ten times 9 plus 9])

ʻeka (from English) acre. [**ʻEhia** *mau* **ʻeka** *ma kēia kīhāpai?* How many **acres** are there in this field?]

ʻeke bag. [*Piha kēia mau* **ʻeke** *i ka ʻōpala i kiloi ʻia aku mai nā kaʻa aku i ke kapa alanui.* These **bags** are full of garbage that was thrown out of cars onto the sides of the streets.]

ʻeke kālā

ʻeke kālā wallet, purse.

ʻeke kua backpack.

ʻekolu three. [**ʻEkolu** *a lāua hānaiāhuhu.* They (two) have **three** pets.]

'eku to root, as a pig.

'ele'ele 1. black color. 2. dark.

'elele delegate, messenger. [*He* **'elele** *'o Kūhiō i ka 'Aha'ōlelo lāhui.* Kūhiō was a **delegate** to Congress.]

'elelū cockroach. [*He mū lepo ka* **'elelū***.* The **cockroach** is a dirty bug.]

'elemakule (plural: *'elemākule*) old man.

'ēlemu rear end, buttocks.

'elepaio native bird (*fig.* gossip).

'elepani (from English) elephant.

'eleu lively, nimble, energetic, alert. [**'Eleu** *maoli nō kā Mililani 'īlio pēpē.* Mililani's puppy is really **lively**.]

'elepaio

'eleweka (from English) elevator.

'eli to dig. [*Ke* **'eli** *nei ka mahi'ai i ka māla 'ai.* The farmer is **digging** in the vegetable garden.]

'elima five.

'elua two.

emi 1. inexpensive, cheap. 2. to lessen, reduce. [**Emi** *nā lau 'ai ma ka mākeke mahi'ai.* Vegetables are **inexpensive** at the farmer's market.] (*kū'ai emi* = sale) (*ho'ēmi kino* = diet, to diet)

'emo delay, wait.

'emo 'ole suddenly, instantly, without delay. [**'Emo 'ole***, ua kani ke kelepona.* **Suddenly**, the telephone rang.]

'ena'ena red hot, glowing.

'enuhe caterpillar, an *'aumakua* for some Hawaiians.

eo 1. to be defeated by something/someone. This meaning requires *i/iā* + victor following subject, signifying by whom one will be defeated. [*E* **eo** *ana 'o Kāna Lui* **iā** *'Iolani i ka pōpeku.* St. Louis

will be **defeated by** ʻIolani in the football game.]
2. to win. [*Ua eo kā lāua kimi.* Their (two) team
won.] (*Lanakila* is most often used for "victory,
to win.")

eō 1. to answer, to call. 2. response when name is
called, "present." "I'm here." [*E Pāpā? Eō.*
Daddy? Yes, **I'm here.**]

ʻeono six. (syn *ono*) (*kanakolukūmāono* = 36 [10 x 3
plus 6])

ʻepane (from English) apron, coverall.

ʻeu naughty, playful, mischievous.

ʻeuʻeu exciting, rousing, animating. (*hōʻeuʻeu* = to
incite, encourage)

ʻewa 1. crooked, out of shape. 2. a traditional direction used instead of "west" on Oʻahu as one of
four directions: *ma uka* (toward mountains), *ma
kai* (toward sea), *ʻewa* (west), Diamond Head
(east); based on the name of a town on Oʻahu.

ʻewalu eight. (*nā kai ʻewalu* = the eight seas [for the
eight channels between the eight main islands,
thus a poetic reference to all Hawaiʻi])

ēwe 1. birthplace, rootlet, those related by lineage. 2.
afterbirth. [*Ma lalo o ke kumu niu e kau ai
mākou i ke ēwe.* Under the coconut tree is where
we should place the **afterbirth**. (The traditional
custom of placing a newborn's afterbirth in a
sacred place is still followed in some families.)]

hā 1. breath, life force, spiritual power (exchange of
breath and *hā* is traditional greeting called *honi*).
2. four (syn. *'ehā*). 3. stalk of plant.

ha'aha'a 1. humility, minimum. 2. low, humble,
unpretentious. [*'O au me ka **ha'aha'a**.* **Humbly**
yours. (a common salutation in letters)] (*ke kula
ha'aha'a* = elementary school)

ha'aheo 1. pride, vanity. [*E mau ana ka **ha'aheo**.*
The **pride** will endure. (song, "E Mau Ana Ka
Ha'aheo," by H. Apoliona)] 2. haughty, proud.
[***Ha'aheo** māua 'o Pāpā i kā 'oukou mau māka
maika'i.* Dad and I are **proud** of your (three or
more) good grades.]

ha'alele to leave, resign, abandon.

ha'alulu 1. to shake, quiver, tremble. 2. nervous,
shaky. [***Ha'alulu** ka 'ōlapa ma mua o ka hō'ike
hula.* The dancer is **nervous** before the hula
show.]

ha'anui to boast (syn. *kaena*).

hā'awe 1. burden, backpack. 2. to carry a burden on
the back. [*Mai **hā'awe** i kēnā 'auamo, e ka hoa!*
Don't **carry** that burden, friend! (Don't take on
that responsibility.)]

hā'awi to give, grant, offer. [*E **hā'awi** kāua i kāna
makana iā ia.* Let's you and me **give** him his
present.] (*hā'awi pio* = give up) [*Mai **hā'awi** pio!*
Don't **give up**!] (*hā'awi wale/hā'awi lokomaika'i*
= to give freely)

ha'awina lesson, assignment, monetary award or
allotment, contribution, dream (many meanings).
[*He mau **ha'awina** kāu ma kāu mau papa like*

'ole? Do you have **assignments** in all your different classes?]

hae 1. flag. (*Ku'u hae aloha* = my beloved flag [Hawaiian flag quilts sewn in protest against the overthrow of the monarchy often had this motto]) 2. to bark, growl (dog), chirp noisily (mynah bird). 3. to tear

hae

(related to *hahae*, to tear). 4. wild, fierce, savage, furious.

haehae to tear to bits.

haele to go, come; used instead of *hele* in poetic language, especially in reference to large numbers of people going or coming.

hā'ena red hot, burning red. (syn. *'ena, 'ena'ena* [*fig.* anger, rage]) [*'Ena'ena 'o **Hā'ena** i ka 'ehukai.* (*'ōlelo no'eau*) **Hā'ena** is red hot due to the sea spray. (a play on words celebrating the place named Hā'ena; also connotes danger)]

hāhā 1. *kahuna hāhā*, a type of medical practitioner who diagnosed illness by feeling the body. 2. to grope, feel with the hands. [***Hāhā** ka makapō i ke pihi 'eleweka.* The blind person **feels** the elevator button.]

hahae to tear, strip, as *hala* leaves.

hahai to follow, pursue, chase. [*Huli a **hahai** mai ia'u.* Turn and **follow** me. (hymn, "Kanaka Waiwai," by J. Almeida)]

hai to sacrifice. (*mōhai* = sacrificial offering; *hai kanaka* = human sacrifice)

ha'i 1. to break. 2. to say, tell. [***Ha'i** 'o Ke Aolama i ka nūhou.* Ke Aolama (Hawaiian language news program on radio) **tells** the news.] (*ho'oha'i* = confess, confession)

hāiki restriction, limitation. 2. narrow, pinched.
[***Hāiki*** *kēia lumi.* This room is **narrow**.] [*He
mana'o* **hāiki** *ko ka po'e na'aupō.* Ignorant people are **narrow**-minded.]

haili 1. fond memory. (*haili aloha* = beloved memory)
2. spirit, ghost. (*haili moe* = premonition) [*Kōkua
ka* **haili moe** *i ka ho'okele.* **Premonitions** help a
navigator.]

ha'ilima distance from elbow to end of finger (*lit.*
break arm).

hailona divination.

ha'ina 1. statement, answer, solution. 2. song refrain.

hainakā (from English) handkerchief. (*hainakā pepa*
= facial tissue)

hāinu to give drink.

ha'i 'ōlelo 1. speech, sermon. 2. speaker. 3. to
preach.

haipule 1. church service. [*Aia kekahi hana* **haipule**
*ma Mauna 'Ala no ka ho'omaka 'ana i ka mahina
'ōlelo Hawai'i.* There's a **church service** at Mauna
'Ala for the beginning of Hawaiian Language
month.] 2. to worship (pre-missionary:
ho'omana). 3. religious, devout, pious.

haka 1. platform, shelf,
perch. 2. hole, open
space. 3. medium, psy-
chic. 4. (from English)
heart shape. (*pua haka* =
anthurium flower)

hakahaka 1. empty space,
vacancy. (*pani hakahaka*
= substitute) 2. vacant. (*e
ho'opihapiha i nā haka-
haka* = fill in the blanks)

haka

hakakā 1. fight, quarrel. 2. to fight, quarrel. [*'Oiai kā
kākou mau kāne e* **hakakā** *nei, e kāko'o kākou
wāhine kekahi i kekahi.* Although our husbands

are **fighting** now, let's us women support each other.]

hakakau shelf. [*'Ehia* **hakakau** *o ka waihona lole kahiko?* How many **shelves** does the old closet have?]

hakakē crowded, entangled, overlapping. [**Hakakē** *nā lālā o ke kumuhau.* The branches of the *hau* tree are **overlapping**.]

hakanū silent, sullen, struck dumb. [**Hakanū** *ke anaina i kā Kaipo oli.* The audience was **struck dumb** by Kaipo's chant.]

hākeakea pale, whitish.

haki 1. to break (syn. *ha'i*). [*Ua* **haki** *'ia ko ka wa'a pe'a kia e ka makani e hao mai ana.* The sailing canoe's mast was **broken** by the wind that was blasting.] 2. broken, cut off. (*haki wale* = fragile, easily broken) (*hakina* = fraction)

hākilo to stare at, observe closely.

hakina fraction.

hākōkō 1. wrestling. 2. wrestler. [*Kaulana 'o Akebono i ka* **hākōkō** *Kepanī i kapa 'ia 'o sumo.* Akebono is famous in Japanese **wrestling**, which is called "sumo."]

haku 1. boss, overseer, lord. (*haku 'āina, haku hale* = landlord) 2. to create, compose music or literature. [*Na Lili'uokalani i* **haku** *iā "Aloha 'oe."* It was Lili'uokalani who **composed** "Aloha 'oe."] (*haku mele* = poet, composer) (*haku puke* = author) 3. to braid, arrange. (*lei haku* = type of *lei* in which several types of plant material are braided together)

hala

hala 1. sin, fault. 2. pandanus tree, whose leaves are woven into hats, bags, etc., known as *lauhala* (leaf of the *hala*). 3. to sin. 4. to pass by, to pass away (euphemism for *make*). [*Ua hala ē ka Pu'ulena.* (*'ōlelo no'eau*) It's too late (*lit.* the Pu'ulena wind has already **passed by**).] 5. passed away, dead. [*'Ane'ane e* **hala** *kā kona hoanoho hānaiāhuhu.* His neighbor's pet is almost **dead**.]

hāla'i calm, peaceful.

hala kahiki pineapple (*lit.* foreign *hala*, because the fruit of the *hala* resembles pineapple).

hālau 1. meeting house. 2. hula school or troupe. Note: In ancient Hawai'i, *hālau* were open-sided sheds used to store canoes and as a workplace for canoe carving. They evidently became gathering places where hula and other group activities took place. 3. large, numerous.

hālāwai 1. meeting. 2. horizon. (syn. *kūkulu, 'alihi-lani*) [*mai ka ho'oku'i a ka* **hālāwai**, from the zenith to the **horizon** (line from an *'aumakua* chant recorded by David Malo)]

hale any building, house (see types listed below). (*hale 'aina* = restaurant; *hale ali'i* = palace; Hale Ali'i 'o 'Iolani = 'Iolani Palace; *hale hō'ike'ike* = museum; *hale ho'okolokolo* = court-house; *hale ipu kukui* = lighthouse; *hale ka'a* = garage; *hale keaka* = the-ater; *hale ki'i 'oni'oni* = movie theater; *hale kilo lani, hale kilo hōkū* = astronomical observato-ry; *hale kinai ahi* = fire

hale ali'i

station; *hale kū'ai* = store; *hale kula* = school house; *hale māka'i* = police station; *hale pa'ahao* = jail, prison; *hale pe'a* = tent; *hale o Papa* = women's *heiau*; *hale pule* = church; *hale wai-hona puke* = library) *halelū* psalm (Bible).

hāleu toilet paper. (syn. *pepa hāleu, hēleu*)

hali'a 1. fond remembrance, especially of loved one. [*he* **hali'a**, *he hā'upu e hali 'ia mai*, a **remembrance**, a memory that is borne this way (song, "Pūpū o Ni'ihau," by M. Kanahele)] 2. to recollect, to recall.

halihali to transport. (*ka'a halihali 'ōpala* = garbage truck) (*mea halihali 'ōpala* = garbage men)

hāli'i 1. a covering, spread. 2. to spread out as tablecloth or blanket.

hālike alike, similar. (*ho'ohālike* = to compare) [*Mai* **ho'ohālike** *mai 'oe ia'u me kāu ipo mua.* Don't **compare** me with your former sweetheart.]

Hāloa 1. name of first taro, older brother of first human with same name. [*Na* **Hāloa** *mākou Hawai'i.* We Hawaiians come from **Hāloa**. (Since Hāloa was the name of the first taro as well as the first man, taro is considered to be the respected elder sibling to humans.)] 2. far-reaching, long.

hāmale (from English) 1. hammer. 2. to hammer.

hāmama opened. (*hāmama ka puka* = the door is opened) (*ka pu'uwai hāmama* = open-hearted, kind and loving)

hāmau 1. silence. 2. silent. [*E* **hāmau***!* Be **silent**! (harsher command than *kulikuli* or *pa'a ka waha*)]

hamohamo to rub, pat, pet. [**Hamohamo** *'o Manu i kāna lāpaki.* Manu **pets** her rabbit.] (*'aila hamohamo* = massage oil)

hana 1. work, job, activity. 2. bay (syn. *hono*) 3. to work, do an activity, make something. [*He aha kāu* **hana**? What are you **doing**?] (*hana ho'ohanohano* = ceremony, ritual; *hana ho'ohau'oli* = hobby; *hana ho'ohiwahiwa* = celebration to honor someone; *hana hou* = do it

again, say it again; *hana*
ʻino = to abuse, injure,
cruel, wicked; *hana*
keaka = skit, theatrical
play; *hana lepo* = dirty
work, excrement, to
excrete [euphemism for
kūkae]; *hana lima* =
hand made, manual;

hana mana = miracle, supernatural; *hana noʻeau*
= art, crafts; *ka hana a ke aloha* = lovemaking;
limahana = laborer; *pau hana* = work is finished
[happy hour])

hānai 1. foster child. 2. to raise, rear, feed. [*Na wai
kā i **hānai** iā ia?* Who **raised** her for heaven's
sake?] 3. adopted. (*hānaiāhuhu* = pet, to care for
as a pet)

hanakuli 1. noise. [*Nui ka **hanakuli** ma ka ʻaha
mele.* There's lots of **noise** at the concert.] 2.
noisy.

hanana incident, occurrence. [*Ma ka **hanana** ʻelua,
ua piholo ka waʻa.* On the second **occurrence**,
the canoe swamped.]

hānau to give birth. (*lā hānau* = birthday) [*ʻO ka lā
hea kona **lā hānau**? ʻO ka lā iwakāluakūmālua o
ʻAukake kona **lā hānau**.* Which day is her **birthday**? The 22nd of August is her **birthday**.]
(*Hauʻoli Lā Hānau* = Happy Birthday)

hānau ʻia to be born. [*Ua **hānau ʻia** ko koʻu hoaaloha kupuna kāne ma Niʻihau.* My friend's grandfather was **born** on Niʻihau.]

hanauna generation. [*ʻO ka **hanauna** i koho e hoʻōla
hou i kā kākou ʻōlelo makuahine, ʻo koʻu **hanauna** ia.* The **generation** that chose to revive our
mother tongue, that's my **generation**.]

hanawai 1. to irrigate. 2. to menstruate.

hāneʻe to collapse, slide, cave in. [*Ua **hāneʻe** ka*

uapo i ke ōla'i. The bridge **collapsed** in the earthquake.]

hanini to spill, overflow. [*Hanini ka waiū i kāu kī'aha, e ke kaikamahine.* The milk in your glass **spilled**, girl.]

hānō asthma.

hanohano 1. dignity. 2. honored, noble, glorious. (*ho'ohanohano* = to honor)

hanu breath, to breathe, smell, inhale. (*hanu pilo* = bad breath) (*hanu i loko* = inhale) (*hanu i waho* = exhale)

hānupa 1. choppy sea. 2. surging, swollen.

hao 1. iron, general term for metal. 2. to blast, strike with force as wind or rain. [*Hao mai ka makani.* The wind is **blowing fiercely**.]

ha'o to long for, miss. [*Ha'o kā Kau'inohea ipo iā ia.* Kau'inohea's sweetheart **misses** her.] [*Ha'o au iā 'oe.* I **miss** you.]

haole Caucasian, previously used to denote non-Hawaiians of any race.

hapa 1. part, portion. 2. of mixed blood. [*He hapa Hawai'i kā lāua mo'opuna.* Their (two) grandchild is **part** Hawaiian.] (*hapahā* = one fourth) [*He hapahā koko Pākē kou?* Are you a **quarter** Chinese?] (*hapakolu* = one third) (*hapalua* = one half) [*'O ka hapalua hola 'ehiku kēia.* It's **half** past seven.] (*hapa loa* = small portion)

hāpai 1. to carry, lift, raise. [*Hāpai hao 'o Keanu.* Keanu **lifts** weights.] 2. pregnant.

hapaiki minority. [*'A'ohe koko Hawai'i o ka hapanui o ko Hawai'i po'e. He hapaiki wale nō nā 'ōiwi.* The majority of Hawai'i's people don't have Hawaiian blood. The native people are a **minority**.]

hapanui majority.

hāpapa 1. to extend out, grope, experience, feel. 2. reef, coral flat, rock stratum. [*ma 'ō aku o ka hāpapa,* beyond the **reef**] (syn. *laupapa, papapa*) *hāpuʻu* native fern tree.

hau 1. tree with lightweight wood used for canoe *ama*, bark for cordage, sap and flowers for medicine. 2. ice. 3. dew (syn. *kēhau*). (*hau kea* = snow) (*haukalima* = ice cream)

hau

haukapila (from English) hospital. (syn. *hale maʻi*)

hāʻukeʻuke purple sea urchin, considered a delicacy, also used for medicine.

haukohi shave ice.

haulani 1. to plunge, as a canoe; to surge, as the sea. 2. restless, constantly moving.

hāʻule 1. loss, failure, defeat. 2. to fall, drop, to lose, fail, to die. [*Ke **hāʻule** kekahi mānaleo, hāʻule pū kekahi ʻike Hawaiʻi.* Whenever a native speaker **passes away**, some Hawaiian knowledge is lost.] (*kau hāʻule lau* = fall semester)

haukohi

haumāna student.

haumia 1. uncleanliness, filth. 2. obscene. (*hoʻohaumia* = to pollute) [*Mai **hoʻohaumia** i ke kai!* Don't **pollute** the sea!]

hauna 1. foul smelling, stinky. 2. bad odor, especially rotting fish. (*hohono* = body odor; stinky smell) [***Hauna** ka ʻōpala, akā **hohono** ko ka pēpē kaiapa.* The garbage **smells rotten**, but the baby's diaper **smells stinky**.]

haunaele riot, brawl.

hauʻoli 1. happiness, joy. 2. happy, glad, joyful. (*Hauʻoli Lā Hoʻomanaʻo* = Happy Anniversary)

haupia coconut pudding.

hāʻupu to remember, recollect, recall. [*He **hāʻupu**, he mana*ʻ*o koʻu iā ʻoe.* I **remember** you. (song, "Pūpū o Niʻihau," by M. Kanahele)

Hawaiʻi 1. name of island chain and largest island in archipelago (from *"Hawa iki,"* little Hawa; Hawa iki is a legendary homeland of Polynesians; its exact location is unknown). 2. Hawaiian. [*ʻAʻole ka pīkake he pua **Hawaiʻi** maoli.* The *pīkake* isn't a native **Hawaiian** flower.]

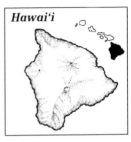

hāwanawana 1. to whisper. 2. whispering. [*ke kai **hāwanawana**,* the **whispering** sea]

hāwāwā unskilled, awkward, clumsy. (syn. *hemahema*). [***Hāwāwā** ka hoʻopaʻa ʻana ke hoʻomaka ʻoe.* Beating time for dancers is **clumsy** when you begin.]

hāweo glowing.

he a, an. [*He manu laha ʻole ka ʻio.* The Hawaiian hawk is **a** rare bird.] To pluralize, add *mau* after *he*. [*He **mau** manakō Hayden kēnā mau huaʻai.* Those fruits (by you) are Hayden mango**es**.]

hē grave. [*Ma ka pā ilina Pākē ma Mānoa i ʻeli ʻia ko Gongon **hē**.* Grandpa's **grave** was dug in the Chinese cemetery in Mānoa.]

hea 1. to call, to name. [***Hea** aku mākou, eō mai ʻoe.* We **call out**, answer us. (a common line in last verse of name chants, requesting a response from the person/god honored)] 2. which. [*Ma ka ʻaoʻao **hea** ʻoe i heluhelu ai i ke kaʻao?* **Which** page did you read the story on?] 3. where. [*Aia i **hea** ko ko ʻoukou makua kāne keʻena?* **Where** is your (three or more) father's office?]

heahea 1. a type of welcoming chant. 2. to call out frequently and hospitably, to welcome.

he'e 1. octopus. 2. to slide, slip, surf, flee, drip. (*'auhe'e* = to flee in battle)

he'e nalu 1. surfing. 2. to surf. (*he'e nalu makani* = wind surfing)

he'e wale 1. miscarriage. 2. to miscarry.

he'e nalu

heha lazy, indolent. [*Heha Waipi'o i ka noe.* Waipi'o is **laid back** in the mist. (song, "Heha Waipi'o," by S. Li'a)]

hehe'e 1. landslide. (syn. *hiolo*) 2. to melt, dissolve, liquefy.

hehena insane, possessed, raving mad. [*He kanaka hehena ke kāpena?* Is the captain a **possessed** person?]

hehi 1. to step on, stamp, trample. [*Ho'omana'o 'oukou i ka inoa o ke kanaka mua loa i hehi i ka papa mahina?* Do you all remember the name of the first person who **stepped** on the surface of the moon?] (syn. *ke'ehi*) (*hehi wāwae* = to pedal) 2. to break a *kapu*.

hei 1. net, snare, stratagem, ruse. 2. string figures. 3. to make string figures. [*Hei 'o Tui i kēlā lā kēia lā.* Tui **makes string figures** each and every day.]

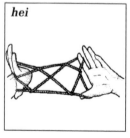

hei

hē'ī papaya.

heiau sacred site of traditional Hawaiian religion, with different types, many of which still exist on each island.

heihei 1. competitive race, such as canoe, foot, horse race. [*Na wai i lanakila i ka* **heihei** *holo wāwae?* Who won the foot **race**?] 2. to race. (*ho'oheihei* = to entrap, to enchant, to mend net)

hekau anchor.

heke best, greatest. [*Moloka'i nō ka* **heke**. ('*ōlelo no'eau*) Moloka'i indeed is the **greatest**.] (*ipu heke* = hula implement made up of two gourds joined together; *heke* is the top gourd)

hekili thunder (*fig.* passion, rage). [*'Ōlapa ka uila, ku'i ka hekili.* Lightning flashes, thunder booms. (familiar line in chants)]

hele to come (*hele mai*), to go (*hele aku*), to move. (*hele wāwae* = to walk) (*ho'ohele i ka 'ilio* = to walk the dog) (*hele loa* = to go with no hope of return) (*hele wale* = to go without purpose)

helehelena features, face. [*Lahilahi kona* **helehelena**. Her **features** are smooth and delicate.]

helele'i 1. to fall (rain, teeth, hair, tears). [*Ke* **helele'i** *nei ka ua ma uka?* Is rain **falling** now up in the mountains?] 2. falling rain, tears, etc. (*ho'ohelele'i* = to scatter, sow)

helikopa (from English) helicopter. [*Nui ko ka* **helikopa** *hanakuli ma ka wao nahele.* There's lots of **helicopter** noise in the wilderness.]

helu 1. number. 2. to count, compute. (*helu 'ai* = score, point [games], to keep score). [*He aha ka* **helu** *'ai i kēia manawa?* What's the **score** now?] (*heluna* = sum, total amount) [*'Ehia kālā ka* **heluna**? How much money is the **total amount**?]

heluhelu to read.

hema left, south. [*E huli* **hema** *ma ka huina alanui.* Turn **left** at the intersection.] [*Ulu ke kope ma Kona* **Hema**. Coffee grows in **South** Kona.]

hemahema awkward, clumsy, unskilled. [**Hemahema** *ka lele 'ana o ka nai'a pēpē.* The baby dolphin's leaping is **awkward**.]

hemo loose, unfastened. [*E helele'i ana paha ko kā 'Iwalani kaikamahine niho* **hemo** *i kēia pō.* 'Iwalani's daughter's **loose** tooth may fall out tonight.]

hemolele 1. perfection, virtue, goodness. 2. perfect, holy, pristine. [*Kaua'i* **hemolele** *i ka mālie ('ōlelo no'eau),* Kaua'i **pristine** in calmness]

henehene 1. to laugh at, ridicule. (*ho'ohenehene* = to tease, laugh at) 2. teasing, giggling, mocking. [**Henehene** *kou 'aka, kou le'ale'a paha.* Your laugh is **teasing**, you're having fun. (song, "He Mea Ma'a Mau Ia," by J. Almeida)]

henoheno lovable.

hewa 1. mistake, fault, sin, guilt. 2. wrong, sinful, guilty. [*Pololei a i 'ole* **hewa** *kāna i pane ai?* Is what he answered right or **wrong**?] (*ho'ohewa* = to complain, find fault)

hī 1. diarrhea. 2. hiss, flow.

hia delight, desire.

hia'ā 1. insomnia, insomniac. [**Hia'ā** *nā 'elemākule.* The old men are **insomniacs**.] 2. sleepless.

hia'ai pleased with, delighted. [**Hia'ai** *nā 'ōpio i ko lākou launa 'ana me nā keiki ma ka Pūnana Leo.* Young people are **delighted** when they get together with the children at Pūnana Leo (Hawaiian Immersion preschools).]

hialoa well trained, skilled.

hiamoe sleep. (*hiamoe iki* = nap) (*ho'ohiamoe* = to put to sleep) [*Ma mua o ko ka mākua* **ho'ohiamoe** *'ana i kāna pēpē, heluhelu lāua i ka puke.* Before the parent **puts** his baby **to sleep**, they (two) read books.]

hiapo first-born child.

hiehie attractive, distinguished. [*kūlana* **hiehie** *ma ka hanohano,* **attractive** and honored position (song, "Nā Pua Lei 'Ilima," by K. Zuttermeister)]

hihi to spread, entangle, intertwine. (*ho'ohihi* = to be enchanted by someone, "smitten") (*lā'auhihi* = vine)

hihia 1. entanglement, difficulty. [*Loa'a ka* **hihia** *me ka hukihuki ma waena o La'akea a me kēlā kaikua'ana ona.* There is **difficulty** and disagreement between La'akea and that older brother of his.] 2. entangled in problems.

hīhīmanu stingray.

hi'i to carry in the arms, as a child.

hi'ipoi to tend, feed, cherish. [*E* **hi'ipoi** *i ka po'ohala.* **Cherish** the family traditions.]

hīhīmanu

hiki 1. can, to be able to. [**Hiki** *iā ia ke 'ōlelo Hawai'i?* **Can** he speak Hawaiian?] 2. to reach a destination. [*E* **hiki** *ana anei ka wa'a pe'a i Nāwiliwili ma mua o ka nāpo'o 'ana o ka lā?* Will the sailing canoe **reach** Nāwiliwili before sunset?] (*hiki nō* = okay, can) (*hiki wale* = easy) (*a hiki i* = until, to, toward) [*E holo wāwae ana kāua mai Kalāheo* **a hiki i** *Keālia.* We (you and I) are going to run from Kalāheo **to** Keālia.]

hikie'e a large, low couch (*lit.* can climb up on).

hikina east. [*mai ka* **hikina** *a i ke komohana,* from **East** to West]

hiki 'ole impossible.

hikiwawe quickly, early, promptly. [*Ua hō'ea* **hikiwawe** *nā 'ōhua i ke kahua mokulele.* The passengers arrived **early** at the airport.]

hikie'e

hilahila shy, ashamed, embarrassed.

hili to braid, plait, string, whip, hit with a stick. [*Ke ho'omaka nei kēlā kāne ala e hili i ko kona lio huelo.* That man over there is starting to **braid** his horse's tail.] [*E **hili** 'olua i ka 'elelū!* (You two) **hit** the cockroach **with a stick!**]

hilina'i to trust, believe, rely on, lean on. [***Hilina'i** au iā 'oe.* I **trust** you.]

hilo 1. first night of Hawaiian moon calendar, new moon. 2. to twist, braid.

hīmeni (from English) 1. hymn, song. 2. to sing. [*Ma kēia Lāpule a'e ana nā hoahānau e **hīmeni** ai i ka **hīmeni** i kapa 'ia 'o Iesu nō ke Kahu hipa.* It's next Sunday that the congregation will **sing** the **hymn** that is called "Iesu Nō ke Kahu hipa."]

hina 1. to fall over, topple. 2. fall over, prostrate.

Hina goddess of the moon, of things feminine, known throughout the Pacific. As wife to Kū, Hina represents forest plants that grow low to the ground (Kū represents those plants that grow upright). Those who gather forest plants traditionally leave offerings for and request permission of Kū and Hina. [*'O **Hina** ka wahine noho mahina.* **Hina** is the woman who lives in the moon.]

hinahina

hinahina 1. gray color. 2. native beach plant used for leis. 3. silversword plant (syn. *'āhinahina*).

hīna'i basket or container used to store food, fish traps (*pōhīna'i* = basketball)

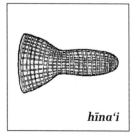

hīna'i

hine splendid, gaudy.

hini delicate, weak.

hinu grease, oil.

hinuhinu bright, shiny. (syn. *'alohi, 'ōlino, hulali*) (*ho'ohinuhinu* = to shine, polish) [*Ke* **ho'ohinuhinu** *nei ka 'ōlapa i nā pūpū kūpe'e*. The dancer is **polishing** the *kūpe'e* shells.]

hiō 1. to lean, slant. [*Ua* **hiō** *aku ka mea pā'ani pōpa'ilima a 'ane'ane hina iho*. The volleyball player **leaned** over until he almost toppled over.] 2. leaning, slanting, diagonal.

hi'ohi'ona features of face or landscape. [*Kama'āina 'o Kihalani i nā* **hi'ohi'ona** *'āina o Kekaha*. Kihalani is familiar with the **features** of the landscape of Kekaha.]

hipa (from English) sheep. [*Ua hānai* **hipa** *lākou ma Ni'ihau*. They raised **sheep** on Ni'ihau.] (*kahu hipa* = shepherd)

hīpu'u knot. [*E nāki'i i ka* **hīpu'u** *i ka lopi*. Tie a **knot** in the thread.]

hi'u tail of fish. (*wahine hi'u i'a* = mermaid) [*Pū ka* **hi'u**. The **tail** sounds (to break wind).]

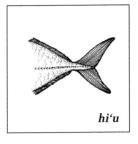

hi'u

hiwa black color of prized offerings to gods. [*'O ka pua'a* **hiwa** *ka mōhai kūpono*. A **black** pig is the appropriate sacrifice.]

hiwahiwa precious, beloved, favorite. [*Ke keiki* **hiwahiwa** *a ke akua*. The precious son of God (Christmas hymn, "Mele Kalikimaka Iā Kākou," composer unknown).]

hoa friend, companion. Note: *ke hoa*, exception to *ke/ka* rule.

ho'ā to turn on electrical appliance, light fire. [*E* **ho'ā** *mua 'oe i ka lolouila. Auē, ua 'ā ka lolouila!*

First, **turn on** the computer. Oops, the computer is on!]

hoaaloha friend. [ʻ*O kou* **hoaaloha** *hou kēia? ʻAe, ʻo Keonaona koʻu* **hoaaloha** *hou.* Is this your new **friend**? Yes, Keonaona is my new **friend**.] (*hoa hana* = colleague, fellow worker; *hoa hānau* = cousin or member of church congregation; *hoa kula* = schoolmate, classmate; *hoa noho* = roommate, neighbor; *hoa paio* = enemy, combatant)

hoʻāhewa to criticize, blame, disapprove. [*Mai* **hoʻāhewa** *ʻoe i kāu moʻopuna wahine. E paka iā ia.* Don't **blame** your granddaughter. Constructively criticize her.] (syn. ʻ*imi hala, hoʻohalahala*)

hoʻāhu to save money. [*Inā ʻoe e* **hoʻāhu** *i kāu kālā, he uku paneʻe kāu?* If you could **save money**, would you get interest?]

hōʻaiʻē 1. credit, loan, charge account. 2. to borrow, lend.

hōʻailona symbol, sign. [*He mau* **hōʻailona** *hoʻokū kaʻa ko ke alanui.* The street has some stop **signs**.]

hoʻāla to wake someone up. (*uaki hoʻāla* = alarm clock)

hōʻala to perfume.

hoʻānuʻunuʻu to undulate (sway up and down).

hōʻāʻo 1. experiment. 2. to try, experiment.

hōʻauʻau to bathe someone. [*Ke* **hōʻauʻau** *nei ka makuahine hou i kāna pēpē.* The new mother is **bathing** her baby.]

hoe 1. paddle, oar. 2. to paddle. (*hoe uli* = steering paddle) (*hoe waʻa* = to paddle, paddler)

hoe

hōʻea to arrive someplace.

hōʻeha to do harm, hurt someone or something.

hoʻēmi to reduce.

hōʻeuʻeu to stir up, excite, encourage. [*Ke **hōʻeuʻeu** nei ke kāpena moku kolo i nā mea luʻu kai.* The tugboat captain is **encouraging** the divers.]

hōhē 1. coward, cowardice. 2. cowardly.

hohoa round tapa beater.

hohono 1. body odor, bad smell. 2. stinky-smelling (refers to body odors only; other offensive smells are *hauna*).

hohoa

hohonu deep, profound. [***Hohonu** ka manaʻo o nā mele kahiko.* The meaning of ancient chants is **profound**.] (*ke kai hohonu* = the deep ocean)

hoʻi 1. chant used as *hālau hula* leaves the stage. 2. to return, go back, to come back (*hoʻi mai*). [***Hoʻi mai** ke aloha me nā aliʻi.* Love **goes back** with the chiefs. (ancient chant, "Hoʻi Ke Aloha i Niʻihau")]

hoihoi interesting. [***Hoihoi** nō ka hana kuʻi ʻai ke nānā aku.* Pounding poi is a really **interesting**-looking, entertaining activity.]

hōʻailona

hoʻihoʻi to return something to someone. [*Pono māua e **hoʻihoʻi** i kā Tūtū ʻumeke.* We two (she/he and I) have to **return** Tūtū's calabash.] (Lā Hoʻihoʻi Ea = Restoration Day, July 31, a traditional holiday celebrating Admiral Thomas's restoration of Hawaiian sovereignty in 1843)

hōʻike 1. show, demonstration, exam. [*Aia ka **hōʻike** hula ʻo Kodak ma Kapiʻolani Pāka ma kēlā pule* *kēia pule.* The Kodak hula **show** is at Kapiʻolani Park every week.] (*hale hōʻikeʻike* = museum) 2. to show, demonstrate, reveal.

hōʻikeʻike 1. display, exhibit. 2. circus.

hōʻiliʻili to collect, gather. [*ʻO ka* **hōʻiliʻili** *poʻoleka kāna hana hoʻohauʻoli.* Collecting stamps is his hobby.]

hoka 1. to "lose out." 2. disappointed. [*ʻAʻole ʻoukou i hele i ka ʻaha mele ʻo Hoʻomau?* **Hoka!** You folks didn't go to the Hoʻomau concert? You **lost out**.]

hōkele (from English) hotel. [*Kaulana ka* **hōkele** *ʻākala ʻo ka Royal Hawaiian.* The pink **hotel** the Royal Hawaiian is well known.]

hoki mule.

hōkio 1. small gourd whistle. 2. to whistle.

hoku a night of the full moon in the Hawaiian moon calendar. [*ʻAuhea ʻoe, mahina ʻo* **Hoku**? Where are you, **Hoku** moon? (song, "Mahina o Hoku," by L. Awa and A. Namakelua)]

hōkū

hōkū star.

hōkūhele planet (syn. *hōkū ʻaeʻa; hōkū lewa*). [*Hiki iā mākou ke ʻike i ka* **hōkūhele** *ʻo Venuse ma ke ahiahi.* We all (not you) can see the **planet** Venus in the evening.]

Hōkūleʻa Arcturus, guiding star for navigators to Hawaiʻi and name of the double-hulled voyaging canoe that began the rediscovery of Hawaiian wayfaring (*lit.* star of gladness/clear star).

hōkūlele shooting star.

Hōkūpaʻa North Star (*lit.* star that doesn't move).

hōkū puhi paka comet.

hola time of day, hour, o'clock. [*'O ka* **hola** *'ehia kēia? 'O ka* **hola** *'eiwa kēia.* What **time** is it? It's nine **o'clock**.]

holo to run, sail, travel, ride, swim. [**Holo** *ke koholā ma ke kai 'o Pailolo ma ka ho'oilo.* Humpback whales **swim** in the Pailolo channel in the wet season.]

holoholo to ride around for fun, "cruise."

holoholona animal (*lit.* that which runs).

holoi to wash, erase, clean. [*Mai* **holoi** *i kou maka. E* **holoi** *i kou mau lima!* Don't **wash** your face. **Wash** your hands!] (*kopa holoi lauoho* = shampoo)

holokai to sail.

holo lio to ride a horse.

holomua to make progress, improve, go forward. [*Ke* **holomua** *nei ka lāhui.* The Hawaiian nation is **making progress**.]

holo'oko'a 1. entire, whole, all. [*E 'ai 'ia ana ka i'a manini* **holo'oko'a**. The **entire** *manini* fish will be eaten. 2. entirely.

holopeki to trot, to jog.

holopono to succeed. [**Holopono** *nā kula kaia-puni.* The Hawaiian immersion schools **succeed**.]

hōlua

holo wāwae to run (*lit.* to travel by foot).

holu 1. to sway (palms), to ripple (water, waves). 2. bumpy (ride).

hōlua ancient royal sport of sledding down grassy slopes, also name of the sled.

honu

hone 1. honey. 2. sweet and soft sounds. [*kou leo*

hone, your **sweet** voice]

honi 1. traditional greeting in which people touched noses and exchanged breath. 2. to kiss, to smell. [*E* **honi** *kāua wikiwiki.* Let's **kiss** quickly. (song, "E Honi Kāua Wikiwiki," by C. E. King)]

hono bay. (syn. *hana*) (Honolulu = calm bay)

honu general name for Hawaiian turtle and specifically green sea turtle, not the *ʻea,* or tortoiseshell turtle.

honua earth, world. (syn. *ao*) [*Nani kēia* **honua** *holoʻokoʻa.* This entire **earth** is beautiful.]

hoʻo prefix often added to verbs or adjectives to change meaning of root word, adding the thought of making it happen. For example, *kipa* = to visit; <u>*hoʻokipa*</u> = to welcome guests, extend hospitality. *Launa* = friendly, sociable, to socialize; <u>*hoʻolauna*</u> = to introduce people. *Maʻa* = used to, skilled at; <u>*hoʻomaʻamaʻa*</u> = to practice. Note: *Hoʻo* changes to *hō* before an *ʻokina* and a vowel: *ʻeha* (sore, painful) becomes *hōʻeha* (to hurt, harm); however, if there is no *ʻokina* before the vowel, the *kahakō* is added over the vowel: *ala* (to wake up, arise) becomes *hoʻāla* (to wake someone else up). A few words with the prefix *hoʻo* are listed below. To find other words beginning with *hoʻo,* look under the alphabetical entry for the root word, for example, under *maikaʻi* for *hoʻomaikaʻi.*

hoʻohaʻi 1. confession. 2. to confess. 3. flirt. 4. to cause to break. 4. to bend, sway.

hoʻohalahala to criticize.

hoʻohālike 1. example. 2. to compare.

hoʻohauʻoli to have fun.

hoʻohenehene to tease.

hoʻoheno 1. to cherish, love. 2. expression of affection. [*He* **hoʻoheno** *ke ʻike aku ke kai moana nui lā.* It's an **expression of affection** to be seen, the broad ocean. (song, "Ka Uluwehi O Ke Kai," by

E. Kanaka'ole)] 3. affectionate, cherished.

ho'ohiki to promise, to swear an oath. [*Ke **ho'ohiki** nei au e mālama i ka honua.* I **promise** to take care of the Earth.]

ho'ōho to exclaim, shout. [***Ho'ōho** ka lehu-lehu i ka pā'ani pōhīna'i.* The public **shouts** at basketball games.]

ho'oholo to decide. [*Ke **ho'oholo** nei ke kōmike.* The committee is **deciding** now.]

ho'ohui to mix, combine, join, add. [*Mai **ho'ohui** i ke kakalina me ka 'aila o pilikia auane'i.* Don't **mix** gasoline and oil or (you'll have) trouble later on.]

ho'ohui 'āina annexation. [*'A'ole i 'ae nā 'ōiwi i ka **ho'ohui āina**.* The native people did not agree to the **annexation**.]

ho'ohuoi to suspect, surmise.

ho'oili 1. inheritance. 2. to land on shore, to load freight, to transfer. 3. to bequeath, leave in will, inherit. 4. to fall upon, as blessing or curse. [*Ua **ho'oili** mai kēia 'oihana ko'iko'i.* This important career **fell upon** my shoulders.]

ho'oilina heritage, inheritance, heir. [*He **ho'oilina** ko 'oukou, he **ho'oilina** ha'aheo.* You all have an **inheritance**, a proud **heritage**. (song, "Ha'aheo," by P. Vaughn)] (*ho'oilina mō'ī* = heir to the throne)

ho'oilo wet season, rainy months, one of two yearly seasons. (*moe kau a ho'oilo* = to have passed away [*lit.* to lie down during the hot and wet seasons])

hō'oio (also **'oio**) 1. to show off. 2. conceited.

ho'okae 'ili racial prejudice.

ho'okahi one of something.

ho'okele

(*ho'okahi kālā* = one dollar)

ho'okāhuli aupuni to overthrow the government.

ho'okalakupua magic.

ho'okamani hypocrite.

ho'okano 1. show off. 2. conceited.

ho'okele steersman (*fig.* leader of any enterprise, especially business).

ho'okō to fulfill command, carry out duty. [*Ua **ho'okō** ka 'ōhua i ko kona haku mau kauoha.* The servant **carried out** his employer's orders.]

ho'oku'i 1. to hit, pound, collide (*fig.* to hurt feelings). [*Ua **ho'oku'i** ke kalaka kinai ahi i ke kalaka halihali 'ōpala.* The fire truck **hit** the garbage truck.] 2. zenith, highest vertical part of sky. [*E nā 'aumākua mai ka **ho'oku'i** a ka hālāwai.* Oh the guardian spirits from the **zenith** to the horizon. (line from a chant for *'aumākua* recorded by David Malo)]

ho'okupu

ho'okūkū contest, competition. [*He **ho'okūkū** oli ko ka **ho'okūkū** hula i kapa 'ia 'o Prince Lot?* Does the hula **competition** called Prince Lot Hula Festival have a chanting **contest**?]

ho'okupu offering. [*Nui nā **ho'okupu** i waiho 'ia ma ka lua pele 'o Halema'uma'u.* Many **offerings** were left at Halema'uma'u crater (Pele's "home").]

ho'olā'au 1. to insist, urge persistently. 2. continuously.

ho'olaha to spread abroad, publish, advertise. (*ho'olaha mana'o* = propaganda)

ho'olale to hurry, rush, hasten, incite. [*No ke aha 'oe e **ho'olale** mai?* Why are you **rushing** here?

(song, "Hōkio," by K. Pukui and M. Lam)]

ho'olulu 1. to be calm. 2. to wait for transportation.

ho'omaha to rest, vacation. (*wā ho'omaha* = vacation) [*I hea ana 'olua e* **ho'omaha** *ai i ka* **wā ho'omaha** *Kalikimaka?* Where are you (two) going to **vacation** during Christmas **vacation**?]

ho'omaha loa retirement.

ho'omāke'aka 1. to make a joke. 2 funny. (*mea ho'omāke'aka* = joker, clown)

ho'omalimali to flatter. [*Ho'omalimali ke kālepa i ke kanaka waiwai.* The merchant **flatters** the rich person.]

ho'onāukiuki to cause irritation, provoke, annoy.

ho'ouna to send. [*Pono 'oe e kū'ai i nā kāleka po'oleka e* **ho'ouna** *aku i kou mau hoaaloha.* You have to buy postcards to **send** to your friends.]

hope 1. last. 2. after, behind. (*Hope Pelekikena* = Vice-President) (*hope loa* = very last) [*'O kēia kona lā* **hope loa** *ma kāna hana.* This is his **very last** day at his job.] (ant. *mua loa* = very first)

hopena result, consequence, ending. [*E 'ike ana 'oe i ka* **hopena** *ma hope!* You'll experience the **consequences** (of your actions) later on!]

hopenapule weekend.

hopohopo 1. anxiety, uncertainty. 2. to worry. 3. anxious, fearful, nervous. [*Hopohopo kāu kime ma mua o ka pā'ani pōhili?* Is your team **nervous** before the baseball game?]

hopu to catch, arrest, seize. [*Ua* **hopu** *ka māka'ikiu i ka mea pōā hale.* The detective **caught** the one who robs houses (burglar).]

hopuna 'ōlelo sentence. [*Mai kākau i ka hua 'ōlelo wale nō! E kākau iho i ka* **hopuna 'ōlelo** *holo'oko'a.* Don't just write the word! Write down the entire **sentence**.] (syn. *māmala 'ōlelo*)

hou 1. perspiration. [*Kahe ka* **hou** *o ka lae.* I'm
sweating (*lit.* the **sweat** of the brow flows).] 2. to
push, shove. 3. new, fresh. 4. again. (*hana hou* =
do it again) (*a hui hou* = till we meet again)

hū 1. spinning top. 2. to overflow, to spout up (liquids, lava). [*Ke* **hū** *a'e mai ka pele mai Hualālai
mai, maka'ala 'o Kona a me Kekaha.* When lava
spouts up from Hualālai, Kona and Kekaha are
alert and watchful.] 3. to grunt, or hum.

hua egg, fruit, offspring. (*hua ale* = pill) (*hua helu* =
number) (*hua moa* = egg) (*hua 'ōlelo* = word)
(*hua palapala* = letter of alphabet) (*hua waina* =
grape) (*hua li'ili'i* = berry)

hu'a bubble, suds, foam.

hua 'ai fruit.

huahua'i to boil, bubble up, gush forth (liquids,
lava). 2. sexual orgasm.

huaka'i trip, voyage, parade. (*huaka'i pō* = night
marchers [spirits said to roam at night]) (*huaka'i
hele* = continuous travel) (*ka'i huaka'i* = parade)

hue gourd, water container.

hu'e to remove, uncover,
expose, open oven. [*Iā
lākou i* **hu'e** *ai i ka imu,
ua māpu mai ke 'ala o
ka pua'a mo'a.* When
they **uncovered** the *imu*,
the scent of cooked pig
was borne on the wind.]

huewai

huehue acne, pimples.

huelo tail of an animal. [*He
huelo mānoanoa ko kēnā pōpoki.* That cat by
you has a thick **tail**.]

huewai water container, water gourd. [*Nani ke
kīnohinohi ma* **nā huewai** *mai Ni'ihau a me
Kaua'i mai.* The designs on the **water gourds**
from Ni'ihau and Kaua'i are beautiful.]

huhū 1. anger, wrath. 2. angry. (*huhū wale* = peevish, cantankerous)

hui 1. society, club, partnership, cluster of fruit such as bananas. [*'O Ānuenue ko mākou **hui** wa'a.* Ānuenue is our canoe **club**.] 2. to join, meet. (*hui pū* = to unite, mix, combine) (*hui malū* = secret club, fraternity)

huī hello.

huihui 1. constellation. [*'O Nāhiku* (*lit.* the seven) *a me Nā Koa* (*lit.* the soldiers) **nā huihui** *a'u i 'ike mua ai.* The Big Dipper and Orion are the **constellations** I've seen before. 2. cluster, collection.

hu'ihu'i cool, chilly, numbing. [*Ua **hu'ihu'i** nā koloaka i nā poke hau āna i ho'okomo ai i nā kī'aha.* The sodas are **chilled** due to the ice cubes he put into the drinking glasses.]

huikala to forgive.

huikau confused, mixed up, confusing. [***Huikau** nā ilāmuku o ka hui holo lio ma ke ka'i huaka'i.* The marshals of the riding units were **confused** in the parade.]

huinakolu

huila wheel. (*noho huila* = wheelchair)

huina 1. sum, total. 2. geometric shape (with attached number). (*huinakolu* = triangle; *huinahā loa* = rectangle; *huinahā like* = square; *huinalima* = pentagon; *huina alanui* = intersection) (*huina loa'a* = profit)

hula

huki 1. to pull. 2. fit of any kind, convulsion, stroke. [*Ua loa'a ka 'elemakule i ka **huki**?* Did the old man have a **stroke**?]

hukihuki 1. quarrel, disagreement. 2. to pull frequently, to jerk. 3. to disagree, quarrel. [**Hukihuki** *mau nā kaikaina ona.* His younger brothers are always **quarreling**.]

hula Hawaiian dance, dancer or chant used to dance.

hulahula dance of non-Hawaiian origin.

hulali shining. [*A he nani lā ke* **hulali** *nei a he nani maoli nō.* It's a true beauty that is **shining** forth. (song, "Royal Hawaiian Hotel," by H. Robins)]

huli 1. taro top, used to replant. 2. to turn, change. 3. to seek, search for, investigate. (*hulikua* = to turn one's back, refuse to help) (*huli hele* = to search everywhere)

hulō (from English) hurrah! [*Hoʻōho ka lehulehu* "**Hulō! Hulō!** The crowd shouted "**Hurrah! Hurrah!**"]

hulu 1. feather. (*hulu manu* = bird feather) (*humuhumu hulu manu* = featherwork)   2. esteemed (especially older relative), choice. (*nā hulu kūpuna* = the esteemed ancestors)

huluhulu 1. body hair, fur. 2. hairy.

hume to tie on *malo.*

humuhumu to sew, stitch. [**Humuhumu** *nā limahana i ko lākou mau lole makalike.* The laborers **sew** their uniforms.]

humuhumunukunukuāpuaʻa *humuhumu* fish with snout like a pig (the state fish of Hawaiʻi), a *kinolau* (body form) of Kamapuaʻa.

huna 1. grain, minute particle, crumb. 2. hidden, secret.

hūnā to hide, conceal. (*hoʻohūnā* = to hide, conceal something) [*Ua* **hoʻohūnā** *ʻia paha ka leka maiā ia mai?* Was the letter from him perhaps **hidden**?] (*peʻe* = to hide oneself)

hune 1. poor, destitute. 2. fine, tiny.

hunehune minute, very fine. (*hune one* = fine-grained sand)

hūnōnakāne son-in-law.

hūnōnawahine daughter-in-law. [*He **hūnōnawahine** lokomaika'i ko ko'u makuahūnōaiwahine.* My mother-in-law has a generous-hearted **daughter-in-law**.] (*makuahūnōaikāne* = father-in-law)

hūpē mucus from nose. [*hūpē kole* (*lit.* running nasal discharge): considered to be an insult]

hūpō stupid, ignorant.

i 1. in, on, at, to. [*Komo hewa ka luna hoʻoponopono i ka ʻāina hoʻopulapula.* The administrator trespassed **on** Hawaiian Homes land.] 2. object marker for indirect or direct object (*iā* is used before pronouns and personal names). [*Kipa aku ʻo ia iā Kamuela, kona hoakula ma Lānaʻi ma ka Pōʻahā.* He visits Kamuela (Samuel), his classmate on Lānaʻi, on Thursdays.] 3. within descriptive sentence, marks cause of condition. [*Wela ke one i ka lā.* The sand is hot **due to** the sun.] 4. first word of phrase used to indicate when an activity occurred (note that there are several other ways to translate "when"). [*I ko ke kauka ʻapoʻapo ʻana , ua kāhea aku ka mea maʻi "E kōkua mai!"* **When** the doctor was having a fit, the patient called out "help!"]

ʻī to say (used frequently in the Hawaiian Bible). [*Ua ʻī akula ke akua iā Moke...*God **said** to Moses....]

ia 1. that (replaces *kēlā*). [*He kuapā ko ʻUalapuʻe, Molokaʻi. He mau pāpaʻi ko ia kuapā.* ʻUalapeʻe, Molokaʻi has a fish pond. **That** fish pond has crabs.] 2. it (sometimes *ia mea*, that thing). [*He peni hou kā Mamo. He peni ʻulaʻula ia.* Mamo has a new pen. **It**'s a red pen.] 3. she/he (usually *ʻo ia*) [*Lelele aʻe ka pailaka a kīkoʻokoʻo hoʻi ia i kona mau wāwae.* The pilot jumps up and down and **she** also stretches her legs.]

iā used in place of *i* as object marker before proper nouns and pronouns. [*Haʻo ʻolua iā Keolalani, ʻaʻole anei? Kamaʻāina māua iā ia.* You (two) miss Keolalani, isn't that so? We (she and I) know him.]

'ia passive tense marker (follows directly after verb). [*Ua haku 'ia ka mele e ko Hawai'i mō'ī hope loa.* The song **was** composed by Hawai'i's last monarch.]

i'a 1. fish or any marine creature, including seaweed. 2. Milky Way. [*Ua huli ka I'a.* It's past midnight (*lit.* the **Milky Way** has turned).] (*i'a maka* = raw fish, sashimi) (*i'a 'ula'ula* = goldfish)

'iako outrigger boom attaching *ama* float to canoe.

Ianuali (from English) January.

'Iao Jupiter or morning star. (*kaiao* = the dawn)

Iāpana Japan. [*'Ōlelo Kepanī ko Iāpana.* **Japan**'s people speak Japanese.]

ia'u to me, at me (objective case). [*E ho'olohe mai ia'u.* Listen **to me**.]

'ie 1. vine that grows around trees, a symbol for Laka. (syn. *'ie'ie*) 2. aerial rootlet of this vine, used to weave baskets, helmets, images. 3. basket, con-

'ie

tainer. (*'ie 'ōpala* = wastebasket) (syn. *kini 'ōpala*) (*'ie lawe* = fish trap)

i'e kuku tapa beater.

'iewe 1. placenta. 2. afterbirth. 3. those descended from a common ancestor. (syn. *ēwe*) [*Ke kanu 'ia nei ko kāna hiapo 'iewe ma lalo o ke kumuniu e ia.* His first-born child's **afterbirth** is being buried under the coconut tree by him.]

ihe spear, dart. [*'O nā ihe ka mea i 'ō'ō 'ia i ke ali'i.* **Spears** were the things thrown at the chief.] (*ihe pahe'e* = short spear; *ihe pakelo* = lance)

'īhepa imbecile, mental incompetent. (syn. *lōlō, hepa*) *ihi* to strip, peel bark or fruit.

'ihi'ihi sacred, majestic. [***'Ihi'ihi** 'o Kamāmalu.* Kamāmalu was **majestic**.] Note: There were two royal ladies named Kamāmalu. This example is a reference to a favorite wife of Liholiho (Kamehameha II) who was known for her large size (over six feet tall) and regal bearing. She accompanied her husband to England where they both contracted measles and died within a few weeks. (*'ihi lani* = chiefly splendor)

iho 1. directional down (added after verb). [*Ke inu **iho** nei ke kanaka makewai i ka wai hua 'ai 'alani.* The thirsty person is drinking **down** orange juice.] 2. axle of wheel, axis of earth, core of fruit. 3. to descend.

ihoiho 1. candle, torch. 2. core of tree.

ihu nose, snout, beak, bill. (*ihu wa'a/manu ihu* = bow of canoe)

'i'i 1. tremolo, vibration of chanting voice. [*Kaulana kēia wahine oli i ko kona **'i'i** ikaika.* This female chanter is well known for her strong **tremolo**.] 2. small, stunted, dwarf.

'ī'ī sour, rancid, moldy.

'i'ika 1. to wince, shrivel, contract. 2. wincing with pain. [*'Oiai he piwa kona, **'i'ika** kona maka.* Since he has a fever, his face **winces with pain**.]

'i'ini 1. yearning, desire. [*'O ia ku'u **'i'ini** pu'uwai.* He is my heart's **desire**.] 2. to desire, crave.

'i'iwi native bird, honey-creeper with red feathers used for capes; a symbol of Hawai'i island (whose color is red) and of native Hawaiians (perhaps because of the word's similarity to *'ōiwi*, meaning native).

'i'iwi

ikaika 1. strength, force, energy. 2. strong, powerful. (*hoʻoikaika* = to put out great effort) (*hoʻoikika kino* = to exercise, strengthen the body)

Ikalia 1. Italy. 2. Italian.

ʻike 1. sight, knowledge. 2. to see, recognize, know, understand, experience, feel, know sexually. [*Ua* **ʻike** *ʻia ke anu o Mauna Kea.* The cold of Mauna Kea was **experienced**.] (*ʻike kumu* = basic or fundamental knowledge; *ʻike loa* = to know well; *ʻike maka* = eyewitness, to experience personally; *ʻike pāpālua* = second sight, especially psychic knowledge; *ʻike pono* = to see clearly, certain knowledge)

ʻikena 1. view, sight, scenic point. 2. knowledge, vision.

iki small, little. [*He mea* **iki**. You're welcome (*lit.* it's a **small** thing; one response to "*mahalo*").] (*ke kamaiki* = the small child)

ikiiki (syn. *ikīki*) 1. very humid, hot weather. 2. hot and sticky, humid. [*ʻOiai he pō* **ikiiki** *ia, ua lele mai nā makika.* Since it was a **humid** night, mosquitoes flew around.]

Ikiiki name of month in Hawaiian moon calendar (during May and June, when hot, humid weather can occur).

ʻīkoi 1. core of some fruit such as breadfruit or apple. 2. float on fishnet.

ʻikuwā 1. clamor, din. 2. to make a loud noise. 3. noisy, loud.

ʻIkuwā name of month of Hawaiian moon calendar (during rainy season of October and November, when storms abound with thunder, high surf).

ila birthmark.

i laila there (used only after the specific place has been named). [*Ua kipa aku māua ʻo kaʻu wahine i Hāʻena a ua nanea* **i laila**. My wife and I visited Hāʻena and relaxed **there**.]

i lalo on bottom, under. (*e noho i lalo* = sit down)

ilāmuku marshall, sheriff.

ili 1. to turn over, to run over with car. 2. stranded. 3. aground (as a ship). [*Ua **ili** ka moku 'o Kīlauea ma ka 'āpapa.* The ship Kīlauea ran **aground** on the reef.] (*ili ke aka* = to cast a shadow) 4. to inherit, inheritance. (*ili 'āina* = inheritance of land)

'ili 1. skin, scalp (human), bark of tree, peel of fruit, hide of animal, surface of sea. (*'ili pāpa'a* = sunburned skin) [*He **'ili pāpa'a** ko ka malihini.* The newcomer has **sunburned skin**.] (*'ili puakea* = light skin, Caucasian) (*'ili holoholona* = leather) (*ka 'ilikai* = the surface of the sea, horizontal) 2. land division within an *ahupua'a*. 3. strap of any kind, reins, belt. (*'ili kuapo* = seat belt)

'iliahi sandalwood.

'ilihune 1. poverty (*lit.* tiny skin), the poor. [*'A'ohe mea 'ai a 'a'ole nui ke kālā a ka po'e **'ilihune**.* The **poor** have no food and little money.] 2. poor.

'ili'ili 1. pebble, stones used for hula. 2. house foundation. (*hō'ili'ili* = to gather, collect)

'Ilikini American Indian.

'ilima native plant used for *lei*, herbal medicine, symbol for island of O'ahu. [*Ola i ka pua o ka **'ilima**.* (*'ōlelo no'eau*) Live due to the **'ilima** flower. (wise saying indicating the extensive use of the *'ilima* as an herbal medicine)]

'ilima

ilina grave, tombstone. (*pā ilina* = cemetery)

'īlio dog. (*'īlio hae* = fierce dog, wolf, jackal)

'iliwai 1. surface of freshwater stream, pond. 2. carpenter's level.

ilo 1. maggot. 2. young shoot. 3. to germinate, sprout. (*ho'oilo* = to cause germination, rainy season)

'īloli 1. emotional disturbance, longings, cravings, and other unpleasant side effects of pregnancy. 2. spotted, daubed with color, speckled.

i luna on top, above. (*e kū i luna* = stand up)

'imi to look for, hunt, search. (*'imi a loa'a* = search for until found; *'imi hala* = to find fault with, blame; *'imi hana* = to seek work, to stir up trouble; *'imi 'ike* = to seek knowledge; *'imi kālā* = to seek money, to earn a living; *'imi loa* = distant traveler [*fig.* great knowledge], to seek far; *'imi na'auao* = to seek knowledge, education; *'imi 'ōlelo* = to slander, lie, cause trouble by gossiping; *'imi pono* = endeavor)

'imo to wink, twinkle. (*e 'imo kou maka* = wink your eye) (*hōkū 'imo'imo* = twinkling star)

imu underground oven. (syn. *umu*) (Kaimukī = oven for baking *tī*; the *tī* root was baked, yielding a delicious sweet)

imu

i mua (command) go forward!

inā if. [**Inā** *'olua i inu i ka wai, 'a'ole 'olua makewai.* **If** you two had drunk water, you wouldn't be thirsty (now).]

ināhea when (used only in questions referring to past actions). [**Ināhea** *i pae ai ka mokulele?* **When** did the plane land?]

inaina 1. anger, hatred. 2. to hate.

'inamona relish made with *kukui* nut.

'īnana animated, stirring with life.

'īnea 1. suffering, hardship, distress. 2. to suffer. [*Nui ka* **'īnea** *o ko kāu wahine makua kāne i ka ma'i pu'uwai, 'a'ole anei?* Your wife's father really **suffered** with heart disease, isn't that so?]

i nehinei yesterday. [**I nehinei** *i puka ai kāna keiki* *mai ka Pūnana Leo mai.* It was yesterday that her child graduated from Pūnana Leo (Hawaiian language preschool).]

'Īnia (from English) 1. India. 2. East Indian.

'īniha (from English) inch.

'īnika 1. (from English) ink. 2. spinach.

'iniki 1. to pinch, nip. 2. sharp, piercing (wind, love pangs). [*E* **'iniki** *niki mālie.* Pinch gently. (traditional song, "'Iniki Mālie")]

'inikua (from English) insurance. (*'inikua ola* = life insurance; *'inikua pau ahi* = fire insurance; *palapala 'inikua* = insurance policy)

'ino 1. storm, harm, evil. [*E pale aku i ka* **'ino**. Keep away hurt and **harm**. (common line in prayers)] 2. to harm, hurt. 3. stormy, bad, wicked, sinful. (*he lā 'ino* = a stormy day, a bad day) 4. spoiled, contaminated, poor quality. 5. an intensifier as in *nui 'ino*, a great many.

inoa name. (*inoa kapakapa* = nickname) (*inoa 'ohana* = family name, last name) [*'O wai kou* **inoa 'ohana**? What's your **last name**?] (*inoa pō* = a name received in a dream)

inu to drink. (*inu lama* = to drink alcohol) (*mea inu* = beverage, drink)

'io Hawaiian hawk, found only on Hawai'i island, a symbol of royal rank due to its high flight. (*'Iolani* = heavenly hawk, name of several monarchs and the royal palace in Honolulu)

'i'o 1. flesh, meat, muscle. (*'i'o hipa* = mutton; *'i'o pua'a* = pork; *'i'o pipi* = beef; *'i'o pale niho* = gums) 2. true, genuine, real. (*mana'o'i'o* = faith [*lit.* true thought])

'iole rat, rodent, mouse. (*'iole pua'a* = guinea pig)

'i'o pale niho gums.

ipo sweetheart, lover. [*'O wai ko kāu* **ipo** *inoa*? What's your **sweetheart**'s name?] (*ho'oipoipo* = to make love) *ipu* 1. gourd, in old Hawai'i, an all-purpose container used for food and water. 2. hula implement. (*ipu 'ai maka* = watermelon) (*ipu 'au'au* = wash basin; syn. *ipu holoi*) (*ipuhao* = pan, pot [*lit.* iron container]; *ipu heke* = gourd

ipu

drum, two gourds attached together; *ipu kī* = teapot; *ipu kī'o'e* = dipper; *ipu kukui* = lamp, lighthouse; *ipu kuni 'ala* = incense burner; *ipu pāwehe* = gourd calabash decorated with tapa designs, found primarily on Ni'ihau and Kaua'i; *ipu wai* = water container)

'iu lofty, sacred. (*'iulani* = the heavenly uplands, the heavenly sacred one, a distant land of the gods. Ka'iulani is the name of the last heir to the Hawaiian throne, Lili'uokalani's niece. A renowned beauty, she died a few years after the overthrow, apparently brokenhearted at the United States's refusal to restore the monarchy.)

'iu'iu majestic, lofty, very high.

Iulai (from English) July.

Iune (from English) June.

iwa nine. (syn. *'eiwa, 'aiwa*)

'iwa frigate bird (*fig.* thief, since this seabird is known for stealing fish from other birds)

'iwa

'iwa'iwa maidenhair fern.

iwakālua twenty.

iwi 1. bone. 2. shell of *'opihi*, shellfish. 3. midrib of coconut or *tī* leaf. (*iwi ā* = jawbone; *iwi 'ao'ao* = rib; *iwi hilo* = thigh bone, femur; *iwi kanaka* = human bone, skeleton; *iwi kuamo'o* = spine, backbone, close relative of chief who served as his personal attendant; *iwilei* = collarbone, measurement from collarbone to tip of middle finger extended; *iwi ʻō* = wishbone; *iwi poʻo* = skull, head bone)

ka the. Note: <u>Ka</u> is used with most Hawaiian words; <u>ke</u> is used before words that begin with k, e, a, and o. [*'A'ala* **ka** *pua pīkake.* **The** *pīkake* flower is fragrant.] [*He mea nui* **ke** *ea i kānaka maoli.* Sovereignty is **the** important thing to the native people of Hawai'i.]

kā 1. beater for knee drum, usually made of dried *tī* leaves. [*ke* **kā** *pahu niu,* the knee drum **beater**] 2. to strike, dash, hurl. 3. to bail water from a canoe. [*Kā nā liu.* **Bail** out the bilges.] 4. exclamation expressing surprise, frustration, disgust (usually pronounced "tsā!"). 5. particle indicating possession. [**kā** *kāu kāne kālā,* your husband**'s** money] [*He kālā* **kā** *kāu kāne.* Your husband **has** money.] [**kā** *lākou mau puke makemakika,* **their** (3) math books] [*He puke makemakika* **kā** *lākou.* They **have** math books.] (Kahi'ukā = the striking tail [name of shark at Pearl Harbor, brother of Ka'ahupāhau, the female *ali'i* shark of Hawai'i])

ka'a 1. car, vehicle. (*ke ka'aahi* = train, railroad; *ke ka'a ho'olima* = taxi, rental car; *ke ka'a lawe ma'i* = ambulance; *ke ka'a lio* = carriage; *ke ka'a 'ōhua* = bus) 2. to roll, twist, revolve. 3. rocking, twisting, tumbling. [*ka 'uala* **ka'a**, the **tumbling** sweet potato]

ka'ahele to make a tour, travel around. (syn. *ka'apuni*)

kā'ai sennit container for chief's bones. [*Na wai i lawe aku i nā* **kā'ai**? Who took the *kā'ai*?]

ka'akua 1. extreme dizziness. 2. to lean back in pain, roll over backwards.

kā‘alo to pass by. (syn. *mā‘alo*)

ka‘ama‘i chronic illness. [*‘O ka mimi kō ke **ka‘ama‘i** ma‘amau o nā Hawai‘i.* Diabetes is the most common **chronic illness** of Hawaiians.]

ka‘ana to divide, share. [*E **ka‘ana** like kākou i nā i‘a.* Let's **divide** up the fish.]

ka‘ao tale, legend, myth (considered to be made up, as opposed to *mo‘olelo*, which are considered to be true stories). [*pīpī holo **ka‘ao*** (*lit.* sprinkled the **tale** runs on); traditional phrase to indicate end of a story]

ka‘apuni to make a tour, go around, surround. [***ka‘apuni** o Maui e ‘ike i nā wai ‘ehā,* **going around** Maui to see the four waters (the four well-known places whose names start with *wai,* indicating freshwater streams there: Waikapu, Wailuku, Waiehu, Waihe‘e) (song, "Nā Wai Kaulana," by A. Namakelua)]

ka‘au forty (part of traditional counting system, based on fours: 4, 40, 400, etc.).

ka‘awale separate, separated, not in use, free. [*Ua **ka‘awale** ka pa‘a male.* The married couple are **separated.**] (*ho‘oka‘awale* = to separate) (*manawa ka‘awale* = free time)

kae contraction of "*ka mea e,*" the one who should, will. [*‘O Nainoa **kae** alaka‘i i nā ho‘okele.* Nainoa is **the one who should** lead the navigators.]

kae treated with contempt, scorn. (*ho‘okae* = to despise, treat with contempt, scorn) (*ho‘okae ‘ili* = racial prejudice) [*Loa‘a ka **ho‘okae ‘ili** ma Hawai‘i nei?* Is there **racial prejudice** here in Hawai‘i?]

ka‘e 1. brink, border, curb. 2. to sulk, fuss, swear. 3. sullen, cross.

kā‘e‘a‘e‘a expert, hero, champion.

kā‘e‘e 1. hand net. 2. to scoop with a hand net. 3. to strain food. [*Kā‘e‘e ‘o Keola i ka hua ‘ai na ka*

pēpē. Keola **strains** the
fruit for the baby.]

kā'e'e

kā'eke'eke hula implement,
pieces of bamboo held
vertically and pounded
on the floor; different
lengths of bamboo pro-
duce higher or lower
pitch.

ka'ele empty and hollow, as a bowl or a canoe (syn.
'olohaka [unlike *ka'ele*, *'olohaka* implies emptiness due to deficiency]).

kā'elo soaked.

Kā'elo name of month during wet season of
December and January in traditional Hawaiian
calendar.

kaena to boast, brag. [***Kaena** ke kā'e'a'e'a i kāna
hana mokomoko*. The champion **boasts** about his
wrestling.]

kā'eo full, referring to calabash (*fig.* full of knowledge). [*ka 'umeke **kā'eo** ('ōlelo no'eau)*, the **full**
calabash (a knowledgeable person)]

kaha 1. grade, mark, punctuation. (*kahaapo* = parentheses, brackets) 2. to mark, draw, scratch, slice
open fish or animal. [*E **kaha** 'oe i ka i'a*. **Slice
open** the fish.] (*kahanalu* = body surfing, to body
surf)

kāhāhā 1. exclamation of surprise, wonder. 2. surprising, astonishing. 3. to be surprised. [***Kāhāhā**
nā luāhine i ka lohe 'ana i ka 'ōpio i oli le'a ai*.
The old ladies were **surprised** when they heard
the youth joyfully chanting.]

kahakaha 1. marking, lines, stripes. 2. striped. [*He
i'a **kahakaha** kāna*. She has a **striped** fish.]

kahakai beach. [*E uhaele kākou i **kahakai***. Let's all
(lots of people) go to the **beach**.] Note: Unlike
English nouns, Hawaiian nouns require "noun

announcers," such as demonstratives (this, that, the) or possessive pronouns (their, my, our). *Kahakai* is one of a handful of words that do not follow this rule: *ke kahakai* is used only before the name of the beach. [*Laukanaka ke kahakai ʻo Hanauma.* The **beach** named Hanauama is crowded with people.]

kahakai

kaha kiʻi 1. artist. 2. to draw or paint pictures. (*kaha kiʻi hale* = architect)

kahakō long mark over vowel to indicate elongation of sound. (*pohō* = waste time, no use doing something; *poho* = palm of hand, pouch)

kahakū to trespass, go where one pleases.

kahamaha to interrupt. (syn. *mauʻaʻe*) [*Mai kahamaha mai iā mākou.* Don't **interrupt** us.]

kahaone sandy beach.

kahapeʻa to make a cross or X.

kāhaʻu to lessen, diminish, as a storm or an illness. [*Ke kāhaʻu nei ka ʻeha konikoni o kona wāwae moku.* The throbbing pain of his cut foot is **diminishing**.]

kahawai

kahawai stream, river.

kahe to flow (liquids). [*Kahe ka wai ma ke kahawai.* Water **flows** in the stream.] (*kahe ka hou* = to sweat, perspire) [*Kahe ka hou o ko nā limahana lae i ke kanu ʻana iho i nā kumuniu.* The laborers **sweat** when they plant the coconut trees.]

kāhea to call out, cry out, greet, name. [*Ua kāhea aku kūpuna i nā malihini "Mai, mai e ʻai."* The

elders **called out** to newcomers, "Come, come
and eat."]

kāhehi to stumble, misstep.

kāheka tidepool. [*Nui nā pe'ape'a ma ke **kāheka**.*
There are a lot of starfish in the **tidepool**.]

kāhela 1. wide expanse of land or sea. [*He **kāhela**
ka 'ikena mai Pukalani aku.* The view from
Pukalani is a **vast expanse of land**.] 2. hula step
and beat of gourd. 3. prone, flat, to lie spread out.

kahelelani small shell of various colors, often used
in Ni'ihau shell *lei*, named for an ancient chief of
Ni'ihau.

kahi 1. place (contraction of *ka* + *wahi*). [*'O Miloli'i
kahi i pi'i ai ke kai e'e ma ka lā 'elima o
Pepeluali.* Miloli'i is the **place** where the tidal
wave rose up on February 5th.] 2. one (the number). (syn. *'ekahi, 'akahi*) (*kahi, lua, kolu* = one,
two, three) 3. to cut, comb, shave, scrape sides of
poi bowl. (*kahi 'umi'umi* = barber, to shave
beard)

kahiau to give generously without thought of return.

Kahiki 1. ancestral Polynesian homeland toward the
East. [*Pele mai **Kahiki** mai,* Pele from the ancestral homeland (Pele is a latecomer to Hawai'i)] 2.
any foreign country, place outside of Hawai'i.

kahiko old, ancient. [*i ke au **kahiko**,* in **ancient**
days]

kāhiko 1. finery, adornment. [*Wailele hune nā pali,
kou **kāhiko** nō ia.* Waterfalls spray the cliffs, it
indeed is your **adornment**. (song, "Moloka'i
Waltz," by M. Kane)] 2. decorated, adorned.

kahikolu trinity. [*'O ke **kahikolu** ka makua, ke keiki
a me ka 'uhane hemolele.* The **trinity** is the
father, son and holy ghost.]

kāhili feather standard, a symbol of an *ali'i*, carried
in processions in front of a royal entourage. [*'O
ke **kāhili** 'ele'ele ka hō'ailona no Kalaniana'ole.*

The black **feather standard** is a symbol for Kalaniana'ole.]

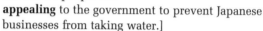
kāhili

kāhoahoa to appeal, intercede. [*Ke **kāhoahoa** nei ko Moloka'i i ke aupuni e hō'ole i ka hui Kepanī e lawe aku i ka wai.* Moloka'i's people are **appealing** to the government to prevent Japanese businesses from taking water.]

kāholo 1. hula step. 2. to hurry, speed. 3. swift, hasty.

Kaho'olawe island formerly used as a bombing target by the U.S. military. It was returned to the state of Hawai'i in 1994.

Kaho'olawe

kahu guardian, keeper, administrator, church pastor. (*kahu ma'i* = nurse) (*kahu mālama* = caretaker, custodian) (*kahu waiwai* = executor of will, trustee)

kahua 1. foundation, base, location, site. 2. any broad, flat field. (*kahua hānai pipi* = ranch; *kahua holoholona* = zoo; *kahua ho'omoana* = campground; *kahua kula* = school campus; *kahua mokulele* = airport; *kahua pā'ani* = stadium, playing field; *kahua waihona 'ōpala* = garbage dump)

kahu hipa shepherd ['*O Iesu ko'u **kahu hipa**, 'a'ole o'u mea e nele ai.* (Halelū 23) The Lord is my **shepherd**, I shall not want. (Psalm 23)]

kāhuli 1. native Hawaiian tree snail (currently close to extinction, but once collected for its brilliantly colored shells). [***Kāhuli** aku, **kāhuli** mai.* Turn under, turn up. (The tree snail frequently turns under leaves.) (traditional song, "Kāhuli Aku Kāhuli Mai," music by J. Kamanā)] 2. to change. 3. to capsize, overthrow. (*hoʻokāhuli aupuni* = to overthrow the government)

kahuna expert in any craft or field of knowledge, priest (many different kinds, including *kahuna lāʻau lapaʻau*, herbal medicine doctor; *kahuna kālai waʻa*, canoe carver).

kahunapule minister, priest.

kai 1. sea, sea water, current, tide. (*kai holo* = current; *kai huki* = undertow; other phrases for the rising and receding of the tide include *kai maloʻo* = low tide; *kai piha* = high tide; *kai hoʻi* = ebbing tide; *kai ulu* = full tide, rising sea) [*Aia ke **kai maloʻo** ma ka hola ʻekolu.* **Low tide** is at 3 oʻclock.] 2. sauce, gravy, dressing. 3. contraction of *ka mea i*, "the one who." [*ʻO McGuire **kai** huakaʻi pū i ʻEnelani me ke kuini Kapiʻolani.* McGuire is **the one who** journeyed to England with the queen Kapiʻolani.]

kai

kaʻi 1. a type of hula chant used for entrance onto the stage. 2. to lead, direct, walk in procession. (*kaʻi huakaʻi* = parade, procession, to walk in a parade)

kaiaka 1. water fluid, thinned down. 2. (from English) kayak .

kaiao 1. dawn. (syn. *wanaʻao, pukana lā* [sunrise]) 2. to enlighten.

kaiapa (from English) diaper. [*Pulu ko ka pēpē **kaiapa**.* The baby's **diaper** is wet.]

kaiapuni Hawaiʻi Hawaiian immersion program.

kaiaulu community, neighborhood. [*Mālie wale ko Nā'ālehu* **kaiaulu**. Nā'ālehu's **community** is calm and peaceful.] (*kula nui kaiaulu* = community college)

kai e'e tidal wave (*lit.* mounting seas).

kaikaina younger sister of female, younger brother of male. [*'O kēlā mea he'e nalu ko Malu* **kaikaina**? Is that surfer Malu's **younger brother**?]

kaikamahine girl, daughter (pl. *kaikamāhine*). (*kaikamahine 'ohana* = niece) [*Auē ke akahai o kāna mau* **kaikamāhine 'ohana**! Gosh how gentle his **nieces** are!]

kaiko'eke brother-in-law of male, sister-in-law of female. (*kaiko'eke kāne* = brother-in-law of female) (*kaiko'eke wahine* = sister-in-law of male)

ka'ikōkō bedridden, extremely old. [*E ola a kolopupū a* **ka'ikōkō**. Live until you crawl around and **have to be carried in a net**. (a familiar line in chants and prayers asking for long life)]

kaikua'ana older sister of female, older brother of male. [*'O wai ko kou kupuna wahine* **kaikua'ana**? What is your grandmother's **older sister**'s name?]

kaikua'ana

kaikuahine 1. sister of a male. 2. female cousin of a male.

kaikunāne 1. brother of a female. [*'A'ohe ona* **kaikunāne**. She doesn't have a **brother**.] 2. male cousin of a female.

kaila (from English) 1. style. 2. stylish, in fashion. [*Hō ka nani!* **Kaila** *kou lole!* How pretty! Your clothes are **stylish**!]

kā'ili 1. to snatch, grab, take by force. (Kūkā'ilimoku

= Kū, snatcher of land divisions, Kamehameha I's war god.) 2. to gasp for breath.

ka'ina sequence, order, succession. [*He **ka'ina** ko kāu hana ho'oma'ema'e hale?* Do you clean house in any particular **order**?]

ka'inapu up and down motion, tossing of ship or prancing of horse. [***Ka'inapu** ko kēlā wahine holo lio lio 'eleu i ke ka'i huaka'i.* The woman rider's lively horse is **prancing** in the parade.]

kainō, kainoa expresses the idea "I assumed, but I was wrong." [***Kainō** paha ua pa'a kou mana'o i 'ane'i.* **I believed mistakenly** that your thoughts were fixed on me. (song, "Alekoki," by L. Alohikea)]

kaiolohia calm sea (*fig.* peace of mind). [*'O ke **kaiolohia** ka pahuhopu.* **Peace of mind** is the goal.]

kaka to rinse, clean. [*Ma hope o ka wehe 'ana i ka pahapaha a me ka 'ōpū, e **kaka** i ka i'a.* After removing the gills and the stomach, **rinse** off the fish.]

kaka'a to roll, turn over, revolve (wheels, gears in machine). [***Kaka'a** nā kia a holo ka mīkini.* The gears **revolve** and the machine runs.]

kakahiaka morning, approximately 6 to 10 a.m. (*kakahiaka nui* = early morning, between 12 p.m. and 6 a.m.)

kakahiaka

kaka'ikahi few, scarce. [***Kaka'ikahi** nā mānaleo Hawai'i.* Hawaiian native speakers are **scarce**.]

kakalina gasoline.

kakani 1. to chatter, talk continuously. 2. noisy, squeaking, crunchy. [***Kakani** ka 'ai 'ana i ka 'ōpelu i palai 'ia.* Eating fried 'ōpelu sounds **crunchy**.]

kākā'ōlelo traditional style of oratory, orator.

kākau 1. to write. (*kākau 'ōlelo* = secretary) (*kākau nūpepa* = reporter) 2. tattoo. (syn. *kākau 'ili*) [*He* **kākau** *'ili ko ke kāne Kāmoa ma ke kīkala.* The Samoan man has a **tattoo** on his hips.] 3. to tattoo.

kākau inoa to register, sign up (sometimes shortened to *kau inoa*). [*Kū laina nā haumāna e* **kākau inoa** *i nā papa like 'ole.* The students stand in line to **register** for all kinds of classes.]

kakekake 1. to jerk, fidget, interfere. 2. to shuffle cards.

kāki'i to strike at, aim at. [*Ua* **kāki'i** *ke kupu'eu i kona hoa paio i ka lā'au pālau.* The hero **aimed** his war club at his enemy.]

kākini 1. dozen. 2. stocking.

kāki'o mange, impetigo.

kāko'o 1. support, aid. 2. to support, aid, assist. [**Kāko'o** *kona 'ohana i ke kupuna kāne i hele a huikau a 'auana aku.* His family **supports** the grandfather who became confused and wandered away.]

kākou we all, us all (three or more). Note: *Kākou* includes everyone present, as in the greeting "*aloha kākou*" (hello to all of us); *mākou* also means we, us (three or more), but excludes the person addressed.

kala 1. (from English) crayon, color. (syn. *waiho'olu'u*) 2. to color. [*E* **kala** *i kēnā ki'i.* **Color** in that (near you) picture.] 3. to loosen, free, forgive, excuse. (*E kala mai ia'u* = I'm sorry, excuse me) 4. rough in texture, like a shark's skin.

kālā money, dollars. [*'Ehia āu* **kālā**? *He iwakālua a'u* **kālā**. How much **money** do you have? I have twenty **dollars**.]

kālā'au hula implement and type of hula using sticks that are hit against each other or those of another dancer.

kālai to carve, cut, hew. (*kālai ki'i* = image carver) (*kālai wa'a* = canoe carver)

kālai 'āina 1. politics. 2. political (based on traditional practice of giving all lands to new ruler to allocate to his supporters and ranking chiefs [*lit.* carving up the land]).

kalaiwa (from English) to drive. [*Ua kalaiwa mamao ko'u hoaaloha i ke alanui mālua-lua.* My friend **drove** far down the bumpy road.]

kalaka (from English) truck.

kalakala rough, harsh, rude. (syn. *kīko'olā*) [*He hana kalakala ka maha'oi.* Being overly aggressive is **rude** behavior.] (*pepa kalakala* = sandpaper)

kalakoa (from English) calico, variegated in color.

kalakupua magic.

kalana county. [*He luna kā Lehua kāne no ke kalana o Maui.* Lehua's husband is a supervisor for Maui **county**.]

kālani gallon.

kalauna (from English) clown. (syn. *mea ho'omāke'aka*)

kalaunu (from English) crown. [*Eia kou lei kalaunu*. Here is your royal **crown**. (song, "E Nihi Ka Hele," by D. Kalākaua)]

kalaunu

kāleka (from English) card, postcard. (*kāleka Kalikimaka* = Christmas card)

kālele 1. support. 2. to trust, depend on. 3. stress.

kalena taut, stretched.

kālena (from English) talent. [*He kālena ko Ka'upena no ke oli 'ana.* Ka'upena has a **talent** for chanting.]

kālepa trader, salesman, merchant. [*Kū'ai aku ke kālepa i ke ka'a.* The **salesman** sells cars.]

Kaleponi (from English) California. [*Kipa aku i Kaleponi he 'āina anu.* Visit **California**, a cold land. (song, "E Nihi Ka Hele," by D. Kalākaua)]

kālewa 1. to float in the wind. 2. to peddle goods. [*Kālewa 'o Nālani i ka 'ohe hano ihu i ka mākeke.* Nālani **peddles** nose flutes at the open air market.]

kali to wait, hesitate. (syn. *alia*) [*E kali iki!* Wait a little!]

Kalikimaka (from English) Christmas. (Hau'oli Lā Kalikimaka = Happy Christmas)

kalima (from English) cream. (*kalima hamo* = ointment) (*'aikalima/haukalima* = ice cream)

kalipa (from English) slipper.

kalo taro, main food of ancient Hawai'i and a symbol of the Hawaiian's family connection to nature and the earth.

kāloke (from English) carrot.

kālua to cook in underground oven, *imu*. [*Ke kālua 'ia nei ka pelehū me ka pua'a.* The turkey is being **cooked** in the underground oven with the pig.]

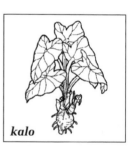

kalo

kama child. [*E kama i ka huli au,* Oh **child** in the changing times (ancient chant "'Au'a 'Ia," urging Hawaiians to hold on to their heritage and land)] (*kama lele* = orphan) (*kama kahi* = only child)

kāma'a shoe. [*'A'ole mākou komo i ke kāma'a i loko o ka hale. E wehe 'oukou i ko 'oukou mau kāma'a ma waho.* We (three, not you) don't wear **shoes** in the house. Take off your (all) **shoes** outside.]

kama'āina 1. native born, local person. 2. familiar, acquainted with. [**Kama'āina** *paha 'oe i ka 'ao'ao Ko'olau o ka mokupuni nui?* Are you perhaps **acquainted with** the windward side of the Big Island?]

kamaehu firmness of resolution.

kamaha'o wonderful, astonishing, surprising. [*Pō la'i e, Pō* **kamaha'o**. Peaceful night, **Wonderful** night. (translation of song "Silent Night" by Stephen and Mary Desha)]

kamahele 1. main branch. 2. strong, far-reaching.

kāma'i to prostitute. (syn. *ho'okamakama* = prostitution, prostitute)

kamaiki child. (*lit.* little child).

kama'ilio to talk, converse.

kāmaka sodomy. (*ho'okāmaka* = homosexuality)

kāmākoi to fish with pole.

kamali'i children (implies children of *ali'i*). (*kamali'i wahine* = princess) (*kamali'i kāne* = prince)

kāmākoi

kamanā carpenter.

kamani 1. native tree with fragrant blossoms. 2. smooth, polished. (*ho'okamani* = hypocrite; to act as a hypocrite)

kāmau to keep on, persevere. (*kāmau kī'aha* = to lift glass, share a drink)

kamawae difficult to please, finicky. [**Kamawae** *kona 'ai 'ana.* He's a **finicky** eater.]

Kāmoa 1. Samoa. 2. Samoan.

kamu (from English) chewing gum.

kana numerical prefix equivalent to 10 x, used for all numbers from 30 - 99. (*kanakolu* = 30 [*kana* = ten times, *kolu* = 3 (from *'ekolu*), or 10 x 3]; *kanahā* = 40; *kanalima* = 50; *kanahikukūmāhiku* = 77)

kāna 1. (*cap.*) saint. (Kāna Kaloka = St. Nick, Santa Claus). 2. his/her or he has/she has. [*He pā mea ʻai kāna mai Masu's mai.* **She/he has** a plate lunch from Masu's.] (*kāna hana* = his/her work)

kanaka human being, person. (pl. *kānaka*)(*kanaka maoli* = native Hawaiian; syn. *ʻōiwi, kupa*) (*kanaka makua* = adult, mature person) (*kanaka nui* or *maka nui* = VIP)

kanakē (from English) candy.

kanalima fifty.

Kanaloa god of the sea.

kānalua 1. to doubt, distrust. 2. doubtful, uncertain, undecided. [*ʻAno kānalua ke kauka inā e ola ana ke kanaka maʻi.* The doctor is rather **doubtful** that the sick person will live.]

kānana 1. sieve, strainer. 2. to strain, as *ʻawa*.

kanapī (from English) centipede.

kānāwai 1. law, code, statute, rule. 2. to obey a law, to learn from experience. [*Ua kānāwai kānaka maoli i kūʻē i ke aupuni.* The native people who opposed the government **learned from experience**.] 3. legal.

kāne male, husband, man. (*kāne wahine make* = widower) (*wahine kāne make* = widow)

Kāne name of major god of old, a creator god symbolized in fresh water as *Kāne i ka wai ola,* Kāne of the waters of life.

kani 1. sound of any kind. 2. to sound, cry out, roar. [*Kani ka pila!* Let the instrument **sound** (play music!).] (*hoʻokani pila* = to play an instrument)

kaniʻahē to giggle, laugh softly.

kanikau lamentation, chant of mourning.

kanikē 1. tolling sound of bell, clock. 2. to toll bell, clock. (*kanikō* = long drawn-out peal of a bell)

kaniʻuhū 1. sorrow, grief. [*Nui ko ke kāne wahine make kaniʻuhū i ka lohe ʻana i ke kanikau.* The

widower's **sorrow** was intense when he heard the
mourning chant.] 2. to sigh, moan. (syn. *'uhū, 'ū*)

kanu to plant, bury. [*Ho'omau kona 'ohana i ka loina
kahiko i ke **kanu** 'ana i kekahi kumuniu me ka
piko o ka pēpē.* Her family continues the ancient
custom of **plant-ing** a coconut tree with the umbilical cord of the baby.] (*mea kanu* = plant)

kanuwika (from English) sandwich.

kao 1. dart, spear (fishing), skyrocket. 2. goat. 3. to
throw javelin, dart.
(*ahikao* = fireworks)

kao

kaomi 1. to push, press. [*E
kaomi i ke pihi.* **Press** the
button.] 2. to suppress
thought, emotion;
restrain. [*Ho'ā'o ke kanaka maoli e **kaomi** i kona
huhū i ka hana kaulike
'ole.* The native Hawaiian
tries to **restrain** her anger at the injustice.]

kaona 1. hidden meaning in Hawaiian poetry. 2.
(from English) town, downtown. [*Ua kipa aku ke
kua'āina i ke **kaona**.* The country person visited
the **town**.]

kapa 1. tapa, Hawaiian cloth made from the bark of
trees such as *wauke,
māmaki.* 2. clothing
made of this cloth, often
scented and elaborately
dyed and decorated. 3.
edge, border. [*Ua kū a'e
ka pueo ma **kapa** alanui.*
The owl appeared on the
edge of the street.] (*kapa
'ia* = to give a name, to be
called or named) [*E **kapa** 'ia ana kona inoa 'o
Kawehi.* Her **name will be called** Kawehi.]

kapa

kāpae to set aside, skip, delete, "pass" in card game.
  [*'Oiai lākou e **kāpae** ana i ka pā'ani hua 'ōlelo, e
  pā'ani pū kāua ma hope.* Although they are **skip-
  ping** the word game, let's you and me play later.]

kapakahi lopsided, crooked. [*Kūlanalana ka 'ōpio i
  ka pi'i 'ana a'e i ke alapi'i **kapakahi**.* The young
  person totters when he climbs up the **crooked**
  staircase.]

kapakē to splash, as raindrops in water. (syn. *pakī*)
  [*Kapakē nā pakapaka ua.* The raindrops **splash**.]

kāpala 1. printing, stamping as decorating tapa
  cloth. 2. to blot, stain, print tapa with carved
  bamboo stamp (*'ohe kāpala*).

kapalili trembling, throbbing with emotion. (*kapalili
  ka pu'uwai* = the throbbing heart) Note:
  Emotional agitation is compared to the fluttering
  of the *kalo* leaf in the wind.

kapalulu roaring, crackling, whirring sounds. (*manu
  kapalulu* = quail)

kapa moe blanket of ancient Hawai'i consisting of
  five pieces of tapa, the top piece decorated and
  sometimes dyed.

kāpekepeke 1. to walk unsteadily. 2. insecure. (*fig.*
  uncertain, doubtful) (*pili kāpekepeke* = uncertain
  relationship)

kāpena (from English) captain. [*'O Kāwika
  Kapahulehua ke **kāpena** mua o ka Hōkūle'a.*
  Kāwika Kapahulehua was the first **captain** of the
  Hōkūle'a.]

kāpī to sprinkle with salt.

kāpi'i curly, person with curly hair (*fig.* warrior,
  attendant to a chief). (syn. *pi'ipi'i*)

kapikala (from English) capital, capitol.

kāpili to build, put together, mend, repair, unite.
  [*Hiki ke **kāpili** hou 'ia nā 'āpana hune o ke pola
  i hā'ule a nahā?* Can the fine pieces of the bowl
  that fell and cracked be **mended**?]

kapu 1. taboo, prohibition, sacredness. [*Ua noa ke kapu*. The **prohibition** has been lifted.] 2. forbidden, sacred, consecrated. [*Kapu ka heiau*. The sacred site is **consecrated**.]

kapuahi fireplace, stove. (*kapuahi ea* = gas stove; *kapuahi uila* = electric stove)

kapua‘i foot (measurement). [*‘Ewalu kapua‘i ka lō‘ihi o ka moena lauhala*. The length of the *lauhala* mat is eight **feet**.] (*kapua‘i kuea* = square foot)

kapu‘au‘au bathtub.

kapukapu 1. dignity, regal appearance. 2. dignified, regal. [*Kapukapu nā maka o Hāli‘ilua lā, lana mālie*. **Regal** are the eyes of Hāli‘ilua, floating calmly. (traditional song, "Hāli‘ilua Lā")]

kāpulu careless, slovenly, gross, disgusting. (Note: *Mōkākī* also means messy and disheveled; however; it doesn't imply carelessness as *kāpulu* does.)

kau 1. season, time. (*kauwela* = summer; *kau hā‘ule lau* = fall, autumn; *kau kupu lau* = spring; *kau ho‘oilo* = rainy season, winter) (*no nā kau a kau* = forever and always) 2. to place, put, perch. 3. a chant of sacrifice to a deity. 4. to board ship, vehicle. [*Ke kau nei nā kelamoku ma luna o ka mokuahi*. The sailors are **boarding** the ship.] (*kau ma luna o* = to board transportation) (*kau kānāwai* = legislator)

kāu you (1) have, yours. [*He aha kāu hana?* What are **you** doing? What is your job?] [*He hana kāu?* Do **you have** a job?] Note: *Kou* has the same meaning, but is used to indicate possession of things one cannot control (chiefs and gods, land, lineage, emotions, name), transportation or things one can wear or enter into (clothes, buildings).

ka‘u my, I have. [*ka‘u papa heluhelu*, **my** reading class] [*Heluhelu au i ka‘u puke i ke ahiahi*. I read

my book in the evening.] Note: *Ko'u* has the same meaning, but is used to indicate possession of things one cannot control (chiefs and gods, land, lineage, emotions, name), transportation or things one can wear or enter into (clothes, buildings).

kaua war, battle. (Kalākaua = the day of battle) (*kaua kūloko* = civil war)

kāua we, us (two) (speaker and person spoken to only). When answering the telephone, say "*aloha kāua.*" Note: *Māua* also means we (two), but excludes the person being addressed.

kauā 1. in ancient days, outcast or slave class. 2. servant. [*He* **kauā** *ko kona kupuna wahine kaikua'ana no Lili'uokalani.* His grandmother's older sister was a **servant** for Lili'uokalani.]

Kaua'i island famous for the natural beauty of the Nā Pali coast and Waimea Canyon.

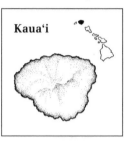

Kaua'i

kaualakō to drag something. (syn. *kauō*)

kauhale home, in ancient Hawai'i a cluster of houses, each used for a separate purpose.

kauhua 1. desire. 2. pregnancy.

kauhale

kauila native tree with hard wood used for weapons, sorcery.

kauka doctor. (*kauka niho* = dentist) (*kauka holoholona* = veterinarian)

kaukahi to stand alone.

kauka'i to depend on. [**Kauka'i** *ka ho'okele 'oihana ma kāna kākau 'ōlelo.* The CEO **depends on** his secretary.]

kaukani thousand. [*'Elua haneli* **kaukani** *kānaka hapa Hawai'i.* (There are) two hundred **thousand** part-Hawaiians.]

kaukau 1. chant of mourning. 2. lower chiefly rank.

kaula rope, cord, string. (*kaula hao* = chain) (*pā kaula hao* = chain link fence) (*kaula 'ili* = lasso)

kaula

kāula prophet, *kahuna* able to predict the future.

kaula'i 1. to dry in sun (clothes, fish). 2. dried in sun (clothes, fish). [*'Ono ka he'e* **kaula'i**. **Dried** octopus is delicious.]

kaulana 1. famous, well known. 2. to become famous. [*E* **kaulana** *ana ka wa'a kaulua 'o Hawai'iloa?* Will the double-hulled canoe Hawai'iloa **become famous**?] 3. resting place, setting of sun.

kaulele to take flight. (*ahikaulele* = rocket)

kaulike 1. equality, justice. 2. equal, just, fair.

kaulike 'ole 1. injustice. 2. unequal, unjust, unfair. [**Kaulike 'ole** *ka uku a ka wahine.* Women's pay is **unequal**.]

kaulua 1. double-hulled canoe. 2. pair.

kaumaha 1. weight, heaviness. 2. heavy. [**Kaumaha** *kēia pahu.* This box is **heavy**.] 3. sad, depressed. [*Ke ma'i kou kupuna kāne,* **kaumaha** *ho'i 'o ia?* When your grandfather is ill, is he also **depressed**?]

kaumaha

kāuna number four in ancient counting, four of something. (*lau* = four hundred; *mano* = four thousand; *kini* = forty thousand; *lehu* = four hundred thousand; all are used figuratively to indicate many, very numerous)

kauna'oa native vine, orange in color, *lei* of Lāna'i.

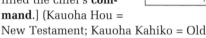
kauna'oa

kauoha 1. command, order, testament. [*Ua ho'okō ka 'ōhua i ke **kauoha** a ke ali'i.* The servant fulfilled the chief's **command**.] (Kauoha Hou = New Testament; Kauoha Kahiko = Old Testament) 2. to order, command.

kaupale boundary, barrier.

kaupalena 1. limit, deadline. [*'O ka lā 'ehā o Iune ke **kaupalena** no ke kālewa 'ana aku i nā laulau.* The fourth of June is the **deadline** for peddling the *laulau*.] (*kaupalena hānau* = birth control) 2. to limit, set a deadline, mark a border.

kaupoku ceiling, roof.

kauwela summer.

kāwele 1. towel, napkin. 2. kind of chant and hula step. 3. to wipe, dry. [*Na lāua e **kāwele** i nā pā.* They two are the ones who should **wipe** the dishes.]

kāwili to mix food, stir, blend. [*E **kāwili** i ke kōpa'a me ka palaoa.* **Mix** the sugar with the flour.]

ke 1. the (used before words beginning with k, e, a, o). [*Hanohano **ke** kahunapule.* **The** minister is distinguished.]

kea white, clear. (Mauna Kea = White Mountain [because it sometimes has snow])

ke'a cross, crucifix. (*fig.* to hinder, obstruct)

keaka theater. (*hana keaka* = theatrical play, skit)

ke'e crooked, bent. (syn. *kīke'eke'e*) (*ho'oke'e* = to make a turn) (*ke'eke'e* = zigzag)

ke'ehi 1. to stamp, step, tread. (syn. *hehi*) 2. stirrup.

ke'ena 1. office, room. (*ke'ena hale* = apartment) (*ke'ena kauka niho* = dentist's office)

keha 1. pride, dignity. 2. proud, dignified, majestic. (*kehakeha* = majestic, dignified)

kēhau dew, mist, dew drop.

kēia this (this person or thing). [*He haumāna 'ōlelo Hawai'i **kēia**. This* is a Hawaiian language student.] (*i kēia mua aku* = in the future)

keiki child, boy. (*keiki papakema* = godchild) (*keiki 'ohana* = nephew) (syn. *keiki hanauna*)

keiki kāne son, boy.

kekahi a, one, another. [*Hākeakea **kekahi** kalo. Uliuli **kekahi** kalo. **One** of the taro is pale. **Another** taro is dark.*] Note: If used before *mau*, means some, several: *kekahi kini* means a can, one of the cans, another can; *kekahi mau kini* means some cans, several cans. (*i kekahi manawa* = sometimes) [*Pā'ani kenika **kekahi** mau haku 'āina **i kekahi manawa**. **Some** of the landlords play tennis **sometimes**.*]

kekele degree of various kinds, including latitude, music, academic, temperature. [*'Ehia **kekele** ka wela o kēia lā? What's the **temperature** today?*] (*kekele loea* = master's degree) (*kekele kauka* = Ph.D.) [*Ua puka aku nei ka wilikī. Ua loa'a ke **kekele** iā ia. The engineer just graduated. She received her **degree**.*]

Kēkēmapa (from English) December.

keko monkey, ape. [*He mau **keko** nā keiki li'ili'i ma ke kahua pā'ani. The little children are **monkeys** on the playground.*]

kekona second (time). [*'Ehia mau **kekona** o ka hola? How many **seconds** does an hour have?*]

kela 1. excelling. 2. to excel, reach high above. (*ho'okela* = to surpass, outdo, excel) (*ho'okelakela* = to flaunt, show off, overbearing, conceited)

kēlā that (far away from speaker, person spoken to).
    [*ʻO ko Ikaika waʻa peʻa* **kēlā**? Is **that** Ikaika's sail-
    ing canoe?] (*kēlā mea kēia mea* = each and every
    one, everything)

kelakela majestic.

kelakona (from English) dragon.

kelalole tailor.

kelamoku sailor.

kele watery, swampy, greasy, fat. (*waokele* = rain for-
    est) (*hoʻokele* = to navigate, navigator [*fig.* to con-
    duct business])

keleawe general name for metals, brass, copper, tin.

kelekalapa (from English) telegraph.

kelepona (from English)
    telephone.

kena quenched (thirst).
    [*ʻAʻole i* **kena** *kona
    makewai i ka inu koloa-
    ka.* Her thirst wasn't
    quenched from drinking
    soda.] (*hoʻokena* = to
    quench thirst)

kelepona

kēnā 1. that (near person
    spoken to). [*He aha ke ʻano o* **kēnā** *peni?* What
    kind of pen is **that** (by you)?] 2. to command,
    order.

keneka (from English) cent. (*hoʻokahi keneka* = one
    cent)

kenekoa (from English) senator.

kenekulia (from English) century. (*i kēlā kenekulia
    aku nei* = in the last century)

kenikeni (from English) pocket change, dime or ten
    cents. Note: *Keneka* (cents) and *kenikeni* (ten) are
    both used to indicate pocket change or loose
    coins. *Koena* (*lit.* left over) is used for change
    from a purchase.

keʻokeʻo 1. white, clear. 2. muslin.

keonimana (from English) gentleman. [*He **keoni-mana** kona 'ano.* His character is that of a **gentleman**.]

kepa notched wedge used to repair calabashes.

Kepakemapa (from English) September.

kepakepa a style of chant in which rapid speech is used.

Kepanī (from English) Japanese. (*ka 'ōlelo Kepanī* = Japanese language) (*Iāpana* = Japan)

Kepania (from English) 1. Spain. 2. Spanish.

kēpau resin, gum, paste. (*'ulu kēpau* = breadfruit paste)

kepolō (from English) devil. [*E komo ana paha 'olua i nā 'a'ahu **kepolō** no ka pō Heleuī?* Are you two maybe going to put on **devil** costumes for Halloween night?]

keu remaining, excessive, spare, more, most, too much. [*He **keu** 'oe a ke kolohe!* You are the **most** mischievous!]

kewe 1. convex, concave, crescent. [***Kewe** ka mahina ma ka pō Hilo.* The moon is **crescent** on the night of Hilo.] 2. crane, boom. [*He **kewe** nui ko ka uapo.* The wharf has a big **crane**.]

kī 1. *tī* plant. 2. key. 3. tea. [*I **kī** a i 'ole i kope nāu?* Would you like **tea** or coffee?] 4. to shoot gun. 5. to spout up, spurt out.

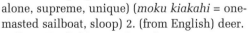

kī

kia 1. pillar, post, prop, mast of ship. (*kiakahi* = person of fixed purpose, alone, supreme, unique) (*moku kiakahi* = one-masted sailboat, sloop) 2. (from English) deer. 3. (from English) gear of machine.

kia'āina governor (*lit.* prop of the land).

kī'aha cup, mug, pitcher, drinking glass.

kia'i 1. guard, watchman, caretaker. 2. to guard, watch. (*kia'i kai* = coast guard)

kia'i kino bodyguard.

kia'i ola lifeguard.

kia'i pō night watchman.

kia manu 1. bird catcher. 2. to catch bird with sticky sap or gum from breadfruit, *pāpalakēpau* and other trees.

kī'amo 1. stopper, plug. 2. sanitary napkin.

kīau to gallop, walk lightly and swiftly.

kiawe 1. tree with wood used to smoke meat. 2. to stream, as rain, to sway.

ki'ei to peek, peer through door, crevice.

ki'eki'e 1. height, tallness. 2. high, lofty. (*kula ki'eki'e* = high school)

kiele gardenia. [*'A'ala nō ke **kiele**. The **gardenia** is very fragrant.]

kīhā 1. to belch, burp. 2. to rise and pitch, as a canoe in heavy seas. [**Kīhā** *nā wa'a i ke kōā 'o Kaiwi.* The canoes **rise and pitch** in the Kaiwi Channel (channel between Moloka'i and O'ahu, crossed each year in what many consider the world's greatest canoe race).]

kīhāpai 1. field, farm, garden, small land division. [*He 'āina momona ko māua **kīhāpai**. Our (his and my) **farm** is fertile.] 2. parish of a church, department of a business.

kīhau 1. frugal. 2. sparingly. [*'Ai **kīhau** 'o ia nei me he manu lā.* This one eats **sparingly**, like a bird.]

kihe 1. sneeze. 2. to sneeze. [*Kihe a maoli ola.* **Sneeze** and live. (blessing after someone sneezes, like *Gesundheit*; often shortened to *ola*)]

kīhei shawl, cloak, cape.

kīhei pili bed covering made of two sheets sewn together.

kīhele to "cruise" around town, go here and there.

kīhene bundle of *ti* leaves used to carry flowers, etc.

[*wāhine **kīhene** pua,* the women with **bundles** of flowers (song, "Makalapua," by Konia/Holt)]

kihi outside corner of house, tip, extremity.

kihikihi 1. curves, zigzag. 2. a fish with yellow and black bands.

kī hōʻalu (*lit.* slackened key) slack key style of guitar playing, so called because strings are slackened in tuning.

kiʻi 1. picture, photo, statue, image, doll. (*kiʻi akua* = idol, image of god) (*kiʻi hoʻohenehene* = caricature) (*kiʻi hoʻoweli* = scarecrow) (*kiʻi ʻoniʻoni* = movie, moving picture) (*kiʻi pōhaku* = petroglyph) (*kiʻi pēpē* = doll) 2. to go and get, fetch. [*E **kiʻi** i nā kikiki ma mua o ka hola ʻehā.* **Get** the tickets before 4 o'clock.]

kiʻi

kīkā (from English) cigar, cigar flower, guitar. [*Hoʻokani ʻo Lokelani i ke **kīkā.*** Lokelani plays the **guitar.**]

kīkaha to soar, glide as bird, to detour, deviate. [***Kīkaha** ka ʻiwa, he lā mālie.* (ʻōlelo noʻeau) The frigate **soars**, it's a calm day.]

kīkaha

kīkala hip, hip bone.

kīkeʻekeʻe curving, zigzag, crooked (road or path). [***Kīkeʻekeʻe** ke alanui i Haleakalā.* The road to Haleakalā is **crooked.**]

kīkēkē to rap, knock. [*I ke kulu aumoe i **kīkēkē** ai kekahi kanaka ma ka puka o ka hale.* It was at midnight that someone **knocked** on the door.]

kīkepa woman's garment, worn under one arm, over opposite shoulder.

kīkī 1. to shoot. (*kīkī wai* = to hose, shoot water with hose) 2. spouting up, shooting as lava, water. (Waikīkī = spouting fresh water [previously known for the many freshwater springs in the area and for the development of extensive taro patches and fishponds])

kīkiʻi to lean back, tilt, extend.

kikiki (from English) 1. to cheat. 2. ticket (syn. *likiki*).

kiko 1. dot, spot, punctuation mark, freckle. 2. dotted, freckled. (*kiko hoʻōho* = exclamation mark; *kiko hoʻomaha* = comma; *kiko nīnau* = question mark; *kiko pau* = period)

kikokiko 1. to type, peck. 2. spotted, freckled.

kīkoʻo 1. measurement from end of thumb to end of index finger. 2. to extend, stretch, stick out. [*Mai kīkoʻo i ke alelo!* Don't **stick out** your tongue!] 3. to pay out funds. (*pila kīkoʻo* = check [*lit.* bill extending credit])

kīkoʻolā sarcastic, rude, impertinent.

kikowaena center of circle, headquarters.

kikowaena kūʻai shopping center, mall. [*Pono paha ʻoe e nānā i nā lole kaila hou ma ke kikowaena kūʻai.* You should perhaps look at the new-style clothes at the **shopping center**.]

kilakila 1. tall, strong, poised, majestic. 2. majestically. [*Kū kilakila ʻo Haleakalā, kuahiwi nani o Maui.* Haleakalā, beautiful mountain of Maui, stands **majestically**. (song, "Kilakila ʻo Haleakalā," by A. Namakelua)]

kilihune fine, light rain, wind-blown spray.

kiliʻopu contented, absorbed in pleasant activity like lovemaking. [*Ua kiliʻopu māua i ka nahele.* We had a **pleasant** time in the forest. (song, "Kuʻuipo I Ka Heʻe Puʻu One," composer unknown)]

kilo stargazer, reader of omens, astrologer. (*kilo hōkū* = astronomer) (*kilo moana* = oceanography, oceanographer) (*kilo ʻuhane* = spiritualism, spiritualist)

kilohana top, decorated sheet of traditional tapa bed covering (*fig.* the best, top quality).

kiloi to throw away. [*Mai poina e* **kiloi** *aku i ka ʻōpala!* Don't forget to **throw away** the garbage!]

kilu ancient game in which romantic favors were granted to the winner.

kime (also **kimi**) (from English) team. [*Lanakila mau ke* **kime** *ikaika i nā pāʻani pōpeku.* The strong **team** always wins the football games.]

kimeki (from English) cement. [*Hoʻohana ʻia nā palaka* **kimeki** *ma ke kahua hale.* **Cement** blocks are used for house foundations.]

kīmō to smash to pieces, break into bits.

kīmopō to assassinate, waylay in the dark (*fig.* any underhanded act).

Kina (from English) 1. China. 2. Chinese. (syn. Pākē)

kīnā 1. blemish, blotch, defect. 2. crop loss due to natural disaster. [*Ke kupu aʻe kekahi* **kīnā**, *he pōpilikia no ke aupuni ʻilihune.* When **crop loss** occurs, it's a calamity for poverty-stricken governments.]

kinai to quench fire. (*kalaka kinai ahi* = fire truck) (*kinai ahi* = firefighter) [*ʻO ke* **kinai ahi** *kae pinana i ke alapiʻi a loaʻa ka pōpoki ma luna o ke kumuʻulu.* The **firefighter** is the one who could climb the ladder to get the cat on top of the breadfruit tree.]

kalaka kinai ahi

kini 1. forty thousand. 2. multitude, many. 3. (from English) tin, can, gin (alcohol). [*ʻO kēnā* **kini**

kupa kāna ʻaina awakea. That **can** of soup (by you) is his lunch.] (*kini ʻōpala* = garbage can)

kinikini 1. marbles 2. very many.

kinipōpō ball used in sports, recently shortened to *pō* in names of games. (*pōhili* = baseball; *pōpaʻilima* = volleyball; *pōhīnaʻi* = basketball; *pōpeku* = soccer, football)

kino 1. body, form, shape. (*kino aka* = spirit of a living person; *kino wailua* = corpse, spirit of a dead person) (*kinolau* = body form [*lit.* many bodies]; supernatural beings such as Māui and Pele could change shape at will; the *kukui* leaf, *humuhumunukunukuāpuaʻa* fish, *ʻāmaʻu* fern, and pig are some of Kamapuaʻa's *kinolau*) 2. physical self.

kinohi genesis, beginning. (*mai kinohi mai* = from the beginning)

kīnohi decorated, ornamented.

kīoe small surfboard.

kīʻoʻe 1. ladle, dip, cup. 2. to ladle, scoop. [*E **kīʻoʻe** i ka pipi kū.* **Ladle** out the beef stew.]

kīʻohuʻohu misty, misty place. (syn. *noe*) [*Kīʻohuʻohu pinepine ʻo Lānaʻi City i ke kakahiaka.* Lānaʻi City is frequently **misty** in the morning.]

kiʻo wai puddle. (syn. *loko wai*)

kipa to visit. [*E **kipa** aku ana ko Kanani mau malihini i ka Hale Aliʻi ʻo Hānaiakamalama.* Kanani's houseguests are going to **visit** Queen Emma's summer palace.] (*hoʻokipa* = to greet, welcome, entertain) (*ka hale hoʻokipa malihini* = the house which welcomes guests [line in many songs])

kipaku to send away, expel, discharge. [*E **kipaku** ʻia ana lākou ʻehā mai ka pūʻali koa aku.* The four of them will be **discharged** from the military.]

kīpapa pavement, to pave (ancient stories tell of Kīpapa Gulch, Oʻahu, being named for the numerous bodies stacked up in battles there).

kīpē bribe, bribery. [*Ua loaʻa ke* **kīpē** *i ke kālai ʻāina?* Did the politician get the **bribe**?]

kipi 1. rebellion, rebel. [*He* **kipi** *kaulana ʻo Wilikoki.* Wilcox is a well-known rebel. (Robert Wilcox is renowned for his role in a short-lived rebellion in 1895 that sought to restore the monarchy, although his flamboyantly princely manner may have obscured the credit due to other leaders such as Bertelman and Widemann.)] 2. to revolt, rebel. 3. rebellious.

kipikua pick-axe.

kipona mixed, mingled colors or texture. (*lei kipona* = a style of Niʻihau shell *lei* or flower *lei* with different shells or colors)

kī pū to shoot or fire a gun. [*Mai* **kī pū***!* Don't **shoot**!]

kīpuka 1. clearing in a lava flow where original vegetation grows. 2. lasso. (syn. *kaula ʻili*) (*kīpuka ʻili* = lariat, lasso) 3. short shoulder cape.

kīpuka

kīpulu fertilizer, mulch.

kiu to spy, observe secretly. (*mākaʻikiu* = detective)

kiwi 1. horn of animal, curved object. 2. bent, curved (*lio lae kiwi* = unicorn)

kīwila (from English) civil, civic, civilian. [*kūʻai hewa i ka pono* **kīwila** *aʻo ke kanaka,* wrongful selling of the **civil** rights of the people (song, "Kaulana Nā Pua," by E. Prendergast)]

kō

kō 1. sugarcane. 2. to fulfill, come to pass, to become pregnant. 3. towed,

dragged, long, as vowels with *kahakō* mark.
(*kōpa'a* = sugar) (*mahikō* = sugar plantation)
(*ho'okō* = to carry out orders, fulfill commands)

koa 1. soldier, warrior. 2. native tree with beautiful
hard wood prized for furniture, bowls, canoes
(*fig.* long lived, like the *koa* tree). 3. brave, courageous.

kōā (sometimes spelled *kōwā*) 1. space between
objects. 2. channel. ['*O 'Alenuihāhā kekahi* **kōā**
maka'u. '*Alenuihāhā* is one of the dangerous
channels.] 3. separated.

ko'a 1. coral, coral head. 2.
fishing shrine, fishing
grounds.

koa'e tropic bird, bird with
long tail living in cliffs.
Koa'e 'ula has a red tail;
koa'e ke'oke'o has a
white tail.

ko'a

kō'ala to broil meat.

koali 1. morning glory, some varieties used in medicines. 2. to swing. (*lele koali* = to jump rope,
swing)

koana space, spacing between rows of stitching on
quilt, width of *lauhala* leaf in weaving.

koe 1. remainder, surplus, leftovers. 2. to remain,
exclude. 3. not yet, almost. (*koena* = remainder,
leftovers, change from paying) [*Eia ke* **koena**.
Here's the **change**.] (*koe wale* = except for)
[*Maika'i ke kula*, **koe wale** *kēia, nui ka
ha'awina*. School is good, **except for** this, there's
lots of homework.]

ko'e worm of any type.

kō'eha'eha 1. heat, sultriness (*fig.* mental or physical
discomfort, distress). 2. uncomfortably hot.
[**Kō'eha'eha** '*o 'Ewa nei i ke kauwela*. Here in
'Ewa it's **uncomfortably hot** in summer.]

ko'eko'e cool, damp, insipid, tasteless.

kōelepālau dessert made with sweet potatoes and coconut milk.

kohana barren, naked, alone. (syn. *'ōlohelohe*) (*kū kohana* = to stand alone)

kohe 1. vagina. 2. crease, groove.

kōheoheo 1. to fall through air. 2. poisonous. [*Kōheoheo ka lā'au make.* Insecticides are **poisonous**.]

kōhi 1. to gather. 2. to restrain, hold back. 3. fatty, rich food.

koho 1. guess, choice, selection. 2. to guess, choose. (*koho mua* = first choice, first guess, hypothesis) (*koho pāloka* = election, to elect [*lit.* choose ballot])

koholā whale, humpback. (*palaoa* = sperm whale)

kohu 1. resemblance, appearance, likeness. 2. alike, similar. 3. attractive, pleasing, in good taste. (*kohu like* = similar, alike) (*kohu 'ole* = inappropriate, improper) (*kohu mea* = it seems as if) [*Kohu mea, he 'opihi kēia kaikamahine.* **It seems as if** this little girl is an *'opihi* (always clinging).] (*ho'okohu* = to take a fancy to, have a crush on, to appoint, authorize, presumption, pretense) [*'O Samuel Wilder King ke kia'āina i ho'okohu 'ia.* Samuel Wilder King was the governor who was **appointed**.]

koi 1. requirement. 2. fishing pole. 3. to urge, implore, require, insist on. [*E koi ana nā alaka'i hula iā 'oukou e ho'oma'ama'a.* The hula leaders are going to **require** you folks to practice.]

ko'i

ko'i adze, axe. [*Ke kua iho nei 'o Kaipo lāua 'o*

*Makoa i ke kumukoa i ke **koʻi**? Kāhāhā!* Kaipo and Makoa are cutting down the koa tree with an **adze**? Astonishing!]

koʻiawe light rain, rain shower. [*he **koʻiawe** ka huila wai,* water wheel's **shower** (song, "Huila Wai," by Liliʻuokalani)]

koihonua genealogical chant for *aliʻi* family.

koʻikoʻi 1. stress, weight, responsibility. (*hoʻokoʻikoʻi* = to emphasize in speech, to burden) 2. urgent, prominent, important, harsh, severe. [*He mea **koʻikoʻi** ka hoʻihoʻi ʻana mai i nā iwi o kūpuna i lawe aku ʻia.* Returning the bones of ancestors that were taken away is an **urgent** matter.]

koi pohō 1. suit for damages. [*Na ka hui ʻoihana kahiko e uku i ka hoʻopaʻi ma ke **koi pohō**?* Will the old corporation pay the fine in the **suit for damages**?] 2. to sue for damages.

kōkala thorns of *lauhala*, pineapple.

kō kānāwai law enforcement. [*ʻO ke **kō kānāwai** kā kāu moʻopuna wahine ʻoihana?* Is **law enforcement** your granddaughter's career?]

koke 1. quick. 2. near, quickly, soon, immediately. [*E pahū **koke** ana kēnā pāluna.* That balloon (by you) will **quickly** explode.]

kokiʻo native hibiscus with red flowers, state plant. (*kokiʻo keʻokeʻo* = hibiscus with white flowers)

koko blood. [*He pili **koko** ko ʻolua?* Are you two related by **blood**?]

kōkō carrying net, used for hanging calabashes.

kokoke nearby, close, almost. [***Kokoke** e mākaukau nā pāʻū lāʻī no ka hōʻike hula.* The *tī* leaf skirts are **almost** ready for the hula exhibition.]

kokoleka chocolate, cocoa. [*Ma mua o ka hoʻi a hiamoe ʻana, e inu i ke **kokoleka**.* Before going to sleep, drink **cocoa**.]

kōkoʻo partnership, partner; a number added to *kōkoʻo* specifies the number of partners.

Kōko'ohia is used to ask how many partners or companions are involved. [*He **kōko'ohia** o kēia hui kauka? He **kōko'ohiku** kēia.* How many **partners** does this medical association have? This is a **seven-doctor partnership**.] (*kōko'olua* = companion, associate)

kōkua 1. help, assistance. 2. helper. 3. to help, assist. [*Hiki anei paha iā 'olua ke **kōkua** mai iā ia?* Can you two perhaps **help** him?]

kōkua

kolamu (from English) column.

kōlea 1. bird, plover. 2. stepparent [*ko Kaipo makua kāne kōlea*, Kaipo's **stepfather**] 3. Korea. 4. Korean.

kōlea

kolepa (from English) 1. golf. [*Auē ka nui o nā kahua pā'ani **kolepa** ma O'ahu nei!* Gosh, there are lots of **golf** courses here on O'ahu!] 2. to play golf.

koli to whittle, pare, sharpen. [***Koli** mau ka paniolo i ka lā'au.* The cowboy always **whittles** wood.]

kōli'uli'u dim, distant object or sound, obscure.

kolo to creep, crawl. [*He mau 'elelū ko ka hale popopo e **kolo** nei ma ka papahele.* The rotting house has some cockroaches **crawling** on the floor.]

koloa Hawaiian duck.

koloaka (from English) soda.

kolohe 1. rascal, mischief-maker, misbehavior (also means comic, crook, vandal, lecher, many other meanings). [*'O ka hana **kolohe** a kāna*

*kaikamahine ʻohana ke kumu āna e nuku mau ai
iā ia.* His niece's **misbehavior** is the reason why
he would always scold her.] 2. to misbehave,
cheat. 3. mischievous, naughty, unethical, fraudulent. Note: *Kolohe* covers a wide range of behavior from mischievous to criminal.

kolokolo to track down. (*hoʻokolokolo* = trial, to
investigate, try in court)

kolonahe gentle, mild, softly blowing.

kolopua fragrant, filled with the scent of flowers.
[**Kolopua** *ke ea ma ka pō ikīki.* The air is **fragrant with the smell of flowers** on humid nights.]

kolopupū old, infirm. [*E ola a* **kolopupū** *a hauma-
kaʻiole.* Live until **old**, with eyes like a rat's.
(familiar line in chants and prayers requesting
long life)]

kōmike (from English) committee.

komikina (from English) commissioner.

komo 1. to enter, go into, wear, put on. [*E* **komo** *mai.
Nou ka hale.* **Come inside**, the house is yours.
(traditional greeting in a society where hospitality is very important)] 2. to join a class. 3. to feel
emotion. [*Ua* **komo** *ka huhū i loko ona.* She **felt**
anger.] (*hoʻokomo* = to insert, put into, deposit,
to dress someone) [*Ke* **hoʻokomo** *nei ke kuke i ka
haupia i ka pahu hau.* The cook is **putting** the
haupia (coconut pudding) into the icebox (refrigerator).] [**Hoʻokomo** *ke kupuna kāne i kāna
moʻopuna i ka lole.* The grandfather **dresses** his
grandchild.] (*komo lima* = ring)

komohana west (where sun "enters" sea).

komohewa to trespass. (*komo ʻino* = to invade, enter
wrongly; *komo wale* = trespass, intrude)

kona 1. leeward side of each island, less rainy than
koʻolau, or windward side. 2. his, her. (syn.
kāna).

kōnane 1. bright moonlight. [*ka pā* **kōnane** *a ka*

mahina, the moon's **bright moonlight** (common
line in songs)] 2. ancient game like checkers. 3.
to shine (moon).

koneko (from English) doughnut.

koni to throb, tingle, flutter. [***Koni*** *au i ka wai
hu'ihu'i.* My heart **tingles** for the cool waters.
(song, "Koni Au i ka Wai," by Kalākaua)]
(*konikoni* = to beat, throb with passion or pain)

kono 1. invitation. [*Loa'a mai ke* **kono** *mai Keawaiki.*
An **invitation** has been received from Keawaiki.
(song, "Keawaiki," by H. D. Beamer)] 2. to invite.

konohiki overseer, headman of *ahupua'a.*

ko'o brace, support, prop.

ko'oko'o cane, staff, rod, support. [*E ola a kani
ko'oko'o.* Live until the **cane** sounds. (familiar
line in traditional prayers asking for long life)]

ko'oko'olau native shrub used for medicinal tea.

ko'olau windward side of each island, rainy side (*fig.*
difficulties). (ant. *kona*) [*Aia 'o Hilo ma ka 'ao'ao
ko'olau o ka mokupuni nui.* Hilo is on the **windward side** of the Big Island.]

kopa (from English) soap.

kope (from English) 1. coffee, copy, rake. 2. to make
a copy, to rake. (*kopekope* = to rake)

kou 1. your (1), you have. [*Nani* **kou** *mau maka!*
Your eyes are pretty!] [*He mau maka nani* **kou**.
You have pretty eyes.] (syn. *kāu*) 2. old name for
Honolulu area. Note: *O*-class possessive pronouns
are used before nouns referring to things one is
born with, such as chiefs and gods, land, family,
heritage; they can also include buildings or transportation, and clothes.)

ko'u 1. my, mine, I have. [*'O Hāmākua* **ko'u** *moku.*
Hāmākua is **my** land division (where I'm from).]
[*He 'āina* **ko'u**. **I have** land.] (syn. *ka'u*) 2. to con-
ceive; male potency.

kū 1. to stand, stop, appear, arrive. [***Kū*** *a'e 'o Hi'iaka*

ma ka lua pele. Hiʻiaka **appeared** in the crater.]
2. resembling, having the appearance or character of a parent. [**Kū** *ʻo ia i kona makuahine i kona lauoho.* Her hair is just like her mother's. (Her hair closely **resembles** her mother's.)] (*kū ʻole i ke kānāwai* = illegal) (*hoʻokū* = to stop car or machine) (*kū hou* = to rise again, to resurrect) (*kū ʻiʻo* = fact, truth)

Kū 1. name of important god of ancient Hawaiʻi, often associated with war, human sacrifice, but also a god of the forest, canoe building and other activities. 2. name of days of month in Hawaiian moon calendar, days sacred to god Kū.

kua 1. back, burden. (*huli kua* = to turn one's back, thus insulting someone) 2. to chop, cut. 3. tapa anvil.

kuaʻāina 1. country (vs. city). 2. person from country, rustic.

kuaʻana shortened form of *kaikuaʻana*, older sibling, term of address for older sibling.

kuaʻeho tumor.

kuahaua proclamation, declaration.

kuahine (often pronounced with "t" sound, *tuahine*) shortened form of *kaikuahine*, sister of male. [*Ua hele mai au no **tuahine**.* I have come to fetch my **sister**. (traditional song, "ʻŌpae ē")]

kuahiwi mountain. [*ʻO Mauna Kea ke **kuahiwi** lōʻihi loa o ka honua.* Mauna Kea is the tallest **mountain** on earth.]

kuahu altar in *hālau hula* where various plants are placed to honor Laka and other gods. [*ʻO ka ʻieʻie, ka lama a me ka palaʻā nā mea kanu i kau ai ma luna o ke **kuahu**.* *ʻIeʻie, lama* and *palaʻā* are plants placed on the **hula altar**.]

kūʻai to buy, sell. [*Hiki paha ke **kūʻai** ʻia aku kou mau apolima kula, ʻaʻole paha? ʻAʻole hiki!* Can your gold bracelets be **sold** or not? No, they

can't!] (directionals *mai* and *aku* are often added
to clarify meaning) (*kū'ai aku* = to sell) (*kū'ai
mai* = to buy) (*hale kū'ai* = store)

kū'ai emi sale.

kūakā loud sound, boom.

kuakea faded, bleached, pale, unhealthy looking.

kualā dorsal fin. [*He **kualā** ko ka nai'a.* Dolphins
have **dorsal fins.**]

kualono ridge, region near top of mountain.

kuamo'o backbone, spine, road.

kūamuamu to curse, blaspheme.

kuapā wall of fish pond. (*loko kuapā* = fish pond
made by building a wall on a reef)

kuapa'a 1. servant, slave, hard labor. 2. oppressed,
enslaved.

kuapapa 1. heap, pile. 2. peace, quiet, tranquility.

kuapo 1. belt. 2. to put on a belt. 3. to swap,
exchange. (*kuapo 'ili* = seat belt) [*E komo i kou
kuapo 'ili. Put on your **seat belt.**]

kuapu'u hunchback.

kū'au handle, stem, stick. [*ka wai **kū'au** hoe o
Kalalau,* ('ōlelo no'eau) the water that drips
down the shaft of the paddle at Kalalau. (wise
saying celebrating Kalalau Valley on Kaua'i)]

kū'auhau 1. genealogy. 2. to recite genealogy. (syn.
mo'okū'auhau)

kuawa guava.

kū'ē 1. opposition, opposite. 2. to oppose, resist. [*Ua
kū'ē 'o Kauka Aluli a me ka PKO i ka pōkā pahū
'ana i ka mokupuni 'o Kaho'olawe.* Dr. Aluli and
the PKO (Protect Kaho'olawe 'Ohana) **opposed**
the bombing of the island of Kaho'olawe.]

kuehu to shake, stir up dust. [*ka makani **kuehu** lepo
o Ka'ū,* ('ōlelo no'eau) the **dust-stirring** wind of
Ka'ū.]

kueka (from English) sweater.

ku'eku'e elbow, wrist bone, joint, knuckle. (*ku'eku'e*

lima = wrist; *ku'eku'e maka* = eyebrow; *ku'eku'e wāwae* = ankle, heel; *ku'e* = to push with the elbows)

kuene waiter, waitress, flight attendant.

kuewa vagabond, wanderer, friendless one, exile.

kuha 1. saliva, spit. 2. to spit.

kūha'o independent, standing alone (*fig.* extraordinary).

kūhele to get up and go.

kūhewa sudden attack, stroke. (*pilikia kūhewa* = emergency, sudden trouble)

kuhi 1. to point, gesture. 2. to suppose, guess. [**Kuhi ka lima, hele ka maka.** (*'ōlelo no'eau*) Where the hands **point**, the eyes follow. (hula rule)]

kuhihewa to err in judgment, to suppose wrongly, to think mistakenly. [*A he* **kuhihewa** *ko'u lā aia i ka poli.* **I thought (mistakenly)** she was here in my embrace. (traditional song, "He'eia")] (*inā 'a'ole au i kuhihewa* = if I am not mistaken)

kuhikuhi to show, teach, give orders. (*'ōlelo kuhikuhi* = directions, instructions) (*papa kuhikuhi* = index, prescription)

kuhikuhipu'uone seer, expert on location of house, temple, etc.

kuhina cabinet minister, regent, ambassador. (*kuhina nui* = prime minister) (*kuhina waiwai* = minister of finances)

kūhohonu complex, complicated, deep thought.

kui 1. pin, needle, screw, nail. (*kui kaiapa* = diaper pin; *kuikala* = screwdriver; *kui lauoho* = hairpin; *kui 'onou* = thumbtack) 2. to string on a thread or cord such as flowers for *lei*, fish. (*kui*

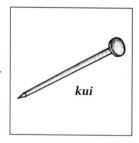

kui

lima = to join hands, go arm in arm) (*kuipapa* = method of *lei* making by sewing flowers onto flat strip of *lauhala* or other material)

ku‘i 1. to pound, punch, strike, join, unite, stitch. (*ku‘i ‘ai* = to pound poi; *ku‘i kā* = to pound smooth; *ho‘oku‘i* = to hit, pound, collide [*fig.* to hurt feelings]) 2. a type of hula. 3. to spread news. [**Ku‘i** ka lono i Pelekane. The news **spread** to England. (chant for Kalākaua, "Kāwika")] 4. artificial. (*niho ku‘i* = false teeth)

kui ‘ai

ku‘ikahi 1. treaty, covenant. [*He mau* **ku‘ikahi** *ko Kauikeaouli me nā ‘āina ‘ē.* Kauikeaouli (Kamehameha III) had **treaties** with foreign countries.] 2. unified, united.

kūikawā temporary, for the time being, special, free and independent, such as independent counsel. [**Kūikawā** *kona ho‘ohana ‘ana i ke ko‘oko‘o kālele.* His using a crutch is **temporary**.]

kū‘ike 1. cash. 2. to know beforehand, in advance. (*uku kū‘ike* = cash payment)

kuiki (from English) 1. quilt (syn. *kapakuiki*). 2. to quilt. [*Nāna, na Meali‘i i* **kuiki** *i kāna* **kapa kuiki**? Was it she, was it Meali‘i who **quilted** his **quilt**?]

ku‘iku‘i 1. boxing. 2. to box.

ku‘ina 1. blow, punch, peal of thunder. 2. joint, joining, seam. [*‘A‘ole hiki ke ‘ike ‘ia ke* **ku‘ina** *ma ke kapa.* **Seams** can't be seen on tapa cloth.]

kuka (from English) coat. (*kuka ua* = raincoat; *kui lā‘ī* = raincoat of old days, made of dried *tī* leaf tied to *olonā* netting))

kūka‘a 1. bolt, roll of cloth or *lauhala*. 2. to roll up as tapa or cloth.

kūkae 1. excrement. 2. to excrete. (*kūkaehao* = rust) (*kūkaelio* = mushroom) (*kūkaeloli* = mildew)

kūkahekahe 1. pleasant conversation. 2. to spend time in pleasant conversation.

kūkā kamaʻilio interview, conference.

kūkākūkā 1. discussion, consultation. [*Na ke kahunapule e alakaʻi ana i ke* **kūkākūkā** *ma ka hālāwai.* It is the minister who will lead the **discussion** at the meeting.] 2. to discuss, consult.

kūkala to proclaim publicly. (*kūkala hewa* = false alarm; *kūkala nūhou* = to broadcast news)

kūkālā 1. auction. 2. to auction. [*E* **kūkālā** *ʻia ana kēlā mau waiwai hoʻoilina.* Those estates will be **auctioned** off.]

kūkapu 1. chastity. 2. chaste.

kuke 1. cook. 2. to cook.

kūkini 1. runner, swift messenger. 2. to run swiftly.

kuko 1. strong desire. 2. to lust. 3. lusty. [**Kuko** *ke kanaka uʻi.* The handsome man is **lusty**. (song, "Ka Pua o ka Makahala," by V.I. Rodrigues and L. Aarona)]

kūkonukonu excessive, deep, profound, complicated. [**Kūkonukonu** *ko kēia moʻolelo ʻaumoana manaʻo.* The meaning of this voyaging story is **profound**.]

kuku to beat, as tapa.

kukū 1. thorn, burr. 2. thorny, prickly. 3. pierced by a thorn.

kuku

kūkū 1. tūtū, grandpa, grandma (from *kupuna*). 2. gourd beat. (*hoʻokūkū* = contest, competition) (*hoʻokūkū hīmeni* = song contest) (*hoʻokūkū hula* = hula competition)

kukuʻe clubfoot; one with a deformed leg or foot.

kukui 1. tree, symbol of Moloka'i. 2. light, torch (*kukui* nuts were lit to provide light at night). (*kukui hele pō* = lantern) (*kukui pa'a lima* = flashlight) (*hale ipu kukui* = lighthouse)

kukui

kuku'i 'ōlelo storyteller.

kūkulu 1. horizon, border. (*kūkulu o Kahiki* = Eastern horizon, portals through which sun rises in direction of ancient Polynesian homeland Kahiki [*lit.* the east, the arrival]) 2. post, pillar. 3. to build a house, set up a tent. [*Pipi'i ke* **kūkulu** *hale 'ana ma Honolulu nei.* **Building a house** here in Honolulu is expensive.] 4. to tie a horse, to park.

kukuna ray of sun, spoke of wheel, spike of sea urchin. [*Ua 'ike mua 'oe i nā* **kukuna** *o ka lā ma ka hikina ma kaiao?* Have you seen the **rays of the sun** in the east at dawn?]

kukupa'u to do with great enthusiasm, with might and main. [**Kukupa'u** *nā 'ōpio i ka wa'u niu.* The young people grate coconut **with great enthusiasm.**]

kula 1. plain, open country, pasture. (*kula iwi* = birth place [*lit.* plain of bones], a place one has close ties to since generations of ancestral bones are buried there). 2. school. (*kula ha'aha'a* = elementary school; *kula ki'eki'e* = high school; *kula nui* = university; *kula pō* = night school; *kula waena* = intermediate school) 3. gold. (*kula pepeiao* = earring) (syn. *mea ho'onani pepeiao*) (*kula waiwai* = source of income, livelihood)

kula'i to push over, knock down, shove to one side, dash to pieces.

kulāiwi native land, homeland.

kulana 1. to tilt, reel. 2. unsteady (*fig.* insecure, hesitant).

kūlana 1. rank, position, reputation. (*kūlana helu 'ekahi* = first place, first prize) [*Ua lilo ke **kūlana helu 'ekolu** i ka hoʻokūkū hula keiki i kā Lahela hālau.* The **third place** in the children's hula contest went to Lahela's *hālau*.] 2. site, place. 3. outstanding, prominent.

kūlanakauhale town, city. [*ʻO Wailuku kekahi **kūlanakauhale** kahiko.* Wailuku is an old **town**.]

Kūlanihākoʻi legendary lake in the sky considered to overflow when it rains, sometimes used symbolically in chants of mourning.

kūlapa 1. to frolic, jump, skip. [***Kūlapa** nā kao keiki.* The baby goats **skip** around.] 2. earth piled at the edge of a taro patch or furrow.

kuleana 1. right, authority, responsibility. [*He **kuleana** ko ka ʻōiwi Hawaiʻi.* The Hawaiian native people have **rights and responsibilities**.] 2. property, title, ownership. 3. cause, justification. 4. small land division.

kuli 1. knee. (*kukuli* = to kneel) 2. deafness, deaf person. 3. deaf. (*kuli ka pepeiao* = deaf the ear [can't hear]) (*kuli hiamoe* = to doze)

kūlia to try, to strive. [*E **kūlia** i ka nuʻu.* **Strive** for the highest. (Kapiʻolani's motto)]

kūlike alike, conforming.

kulikuli 1. noise, din. [***Kulikuli!*** Be quiet (you are making **noise**).] 2. noisy.

kūlina (from English) corn. (*kūlina pohāpohā* = popcorn; *kūlina wali* = cornmeal)

kūloko local, domestic. (*kaua kūloko* = civil war) (*ka nūhou kūloko* = local news)

kūlolo dessert made of baked, grated taro and coconut milk.

kūlou to bow the head, bend down.

kulu 1. drip, leak, flow of tears. [*Ua **kulu** nā waima-*

ka ma ka hoʻolewa. Tears **flowed** at the funeral.]
2. to drip, trickle, leak. (*kulu aumoe* = midnight, late night)

kuluma 1. customary, usual. 2. acquainted with, intimate. (*maʻi kuluma* = chronic illness) (syn. *kaʻa maʻi*)

kūmaka eyewitness (syn. *ʻike maka*).

kūmakahiki annual, yearly.

kumakaia 1. traitor. 2. to betray. 3. traitorous.

kūmakani windbreak.

kūmaumau continuous, regular.

kumu 1. basis, foundation, bottom. [*He **kumu** kahua ko kou hale?* Does your house have a **foundation**?] (*hoʻokumu* = to establish, found, create) [*Ua **hoʻokumu** nā mikionele i ke kula ʻo Lahainaluna.* Missionaries **established** Lahainaluna school.] (*hoʻokumu honua* = creation of the world) (*kumulipo* = origin, source of darkness [name of creation chant]) 2. trunk of tree, handle. (*kumuniu* = coconut tree) 3. pattern, manual. 4. origin, source, beginning, teacher. (Sometimes *kumu aʻo* is used to specify teacher.) (*kumu hula* = hula teacher) 5. reason, cause. [*He aha ke **kumu** no kou uē ʻana, e ka pēpē?* What is the **reason** for your crying, baby?]

kumu aʻo

(*kumuhana* = subject, topic) (*kumu kūʻai* = price, cost) (*kumu manaʻo* = theory) (*kumu hoʻopuka uila* = electrical outlet) (*kumu lāʻau* = tree)

kūmū type of fish, slang for sweetheart.

kumu kānāwai constitution (legal document).

kūmūmū dull, blunt (knife, scissors). [***Kūmūmū** kēnā ʻūpā kahiko, akā ʻo ʻoi nō kēia ʻūpā hou.* That old scissors (by you) is **dull**, but this new scissors is really sharp.]

kūna'au to bear a grudge.

kūna'e to stand firmly against opposition.

kūnāhihi numb, shocked, dazed.

kūnānā puzzled, surprised, bewildered. [*Mai kūnānā me ke kōkua 'ole!* Don't just stand **bewildered** without helping.]

kunāne shortened form of *kaikunāne*, brother of female.

kūnewa to pass, of time, to age.

kuni to burn, blaze, brand.

kūnihi 1. ridge of cliff, feather helmet or hair. 2. steep, precarious. [*Kūnihi ka mauna i ka la'i ē.* The mountain is **steep** in the calmness. (first line of *mele kāhea*, chant requesting permission to enter)]

kunu 1. cough. 2. to cough. [*Ke loa'a 'oe i ke anu, kunu mau 'oe?* When you have a cold, do you always **cough**?]

kūō to cry loudly with joy, pain; howl.

kū'oko'a 1. independence, liberty, freedom. 2. independent, free.

kūola alive and safe (after being in danger).

kū'ono 1. inside corner of a house. 2. bay, gulf.

kū'ono'ono well off, comfortably situated. [*Kū'ono'ono ka nohona o nā kānaka waiwai.* The life-style of the wealthy is **comfortable**.]

kupa citizen, native, well acquainted. [*Ua noho au a kupa i kou alo.* I have become **well acquainted** with you. (song, "Ua Noho Au a Kupa," by J. Almeida)] (*nā kupa o ka 'āina* = the natives of the land)

kūpa'a 1. loyalty, allegiance. 2. firm, steadfast. 3. firmly. [*kūpa'a ma hope o ka 'āina*, standing **firmly** behind the land (song, "Kaulana Nā Pua," by E. Prendergast)]

kūpaʻakai to eat poi or sweet potato with salt, symbol of Hawaiian ideal of hospitality, always offering whatever food is available. [*Me ia nō e* **kūpaʻakai** *ai.* It is with him (the visitor) that we should **eat**, extending hospitality. (chant, "Mele Hoʻokipa")]

kupaianaha surprising, strange, wonderful. [*ʻO* **Kupaianaha** *ka inoa o ka lua pele hou ma Puna.* **Kupaianaha** is the name of the new crater (vent) in Puna.]

kūpaka to kick, smash, writhe, twist.

kūpaku resuscitation.

kūpale 1. defense. 2. to defend, ward off. [*ʻO ka lua kona* **kūpale**. Her **defense** is Hawaiian martial arts.]

kūpalu to stuff with food.

kūpaoa strong, penetrating fragrance. (syn. *paoa*) [**Kūpaoa** *ke onaona o ka pua-kenikeni.* The scent of the *puakenikeni* flower is **strong**.]

kupapaʻu corpse, dead body. (syn. *kino wailua*)

kūpau entirely finished.

kūpeʻe 1. varicolored shellfish. 2. anklet, bracelet, handcuffs.

kūpinaʻi 1. to echo, reverberate. 2. mourn, lament.

kūpipi crowded, as with people or stars.

kūpono 1. honest, proper, fair, just. [*Ua* **kūpono** *kāna hāʻawi ʻana aku i ka pila kīkoʻo iā Lokalia.* Her giving the check to Lokalia was **fair**.] 2. qualified, suitable, fit. [*He moho* **kūpono** *kāna wahine no ke keʻena o kiaʻāina.* His wife is a **suitable** candidate for the office of governor.]

kūpouli dazed, stricken with emotion.

kupu growth, sprout, upstart. (*ke kau kupulau* = spring semester) (*hoʻokupu* = offering) (*He aha ka mea i kupu aʻe ai?* = What happened?)

kupua supernatural being. [*ʻO Māui ke* **kupua** *kaulana loa o ka Pākīpika.* Māui is the best

known **supernatural being** of the Pacific.]
(*pōhaku kupua* = stones considered to have spiritual force or healing powers)

kupuna grandparent, ancestor (pl. *kūpuna*). (*kupuna kāne* = grandfather; *kupuna wahine* = grandmother; *kupuna kuakahi* = great-grandparent; *mai nā kūpuna mai* = from the ancestors)

kupuna kāne

ku'u 1. to release, let go, abandon. [*Ua **ku'u** aku ke kia manu i ka manu āna e ho'opa'a ana.* The bird catcher **released** the bird he was holding.] (*ho'oku'u* = to discharge, release, liberate) 2. my, mine (possessive). Unlike *ko'u* or *ka'u*, which also mean "my" or "mine," *ku'u* is used to express emotional closeness and implies "my beloved," as in *ku'u home*, "my beloved home," or *ku'u ipo*, "my beloved sweetheart."

kū'ula stone god used to attract fish, altar near sea for worship of the fish god.

ku'una 1. slope of hill. 2. traditional, hereditary. (*ma'i ku'una* = inherited disease) 3. relieved, relaxed.

ku'upau 1. to go to the limit, try one's hardest. 2. to release all restraints, inhibitions.

lā 1. sun, day. [*Wela ka* **lā**. The **sun** is hot.] (*lā hana* = workday) (*lā uku* = payday) (*lā puka* = rising sun) (*lā kau* = setting sun [syn. *lā welo, napo'o ka lā*]) (*i kēia lā* = today) [*I kēia lā, ua 'ike 'o Leilehua i ke kualā mano*. **Today**, Leilehua saw the dorsal fin of a shark.] (*lā 'ae'oia* = good old days, past time of youth, beauty) 2. sail, fin.

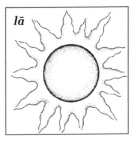

lā

la'a sacred, holy. (*la'a kea* = sacred light, sacred knowledge)

la'amia calabash tree, fruit used to make *'ulī'ulī* (hula implement).

lā'au 1. plant, tree, wood. (*kumulā'au* = tree) (*lā'au 'ala* = fragrant wood, sandalwood [harvest for China trade in early 19th century caused great suffering]) (*lā'au 'ai* = chopsticks) (*lā'au ana* = yardstick, ruler, survey rod) (*lā'au Kalikimaka* = Christmas tree) 2. medicine (herbs were used for medicine). (*lā'au hamo* = salve, ointment) (*lā'au kāhea* = healing through prayer) 3. strength, stiffness. 4. blow of a club. (*lā'au pālau* = war club) 5. medical. (*lā'au hihi* = vine) (*Lā'au Kū*

lā'au 'ai

Kahi/Lā'au Kū Lua = days of the lunar month
sacred to Kū)

lā'au 'ino drugs. [*Kōheoheo kekahi **lā'au 'ino**. Some
drugs are poisonous.]

lā'au lapa'au herbal medicine. [*'O ka **lā'au lapa'au**
kekahi ho'oilina waiwai*. **Herbal medicine** is a
valued heritage.]

lā'au make poison, insecticide. [*E kīkī 'ia ana ka
lā'au make i nā nāhelehele*. **Insecticide** will be
sprayed on the weeds.]

lae 1. forehead. 2. point of land jutting out into
ocean; peninsula. [*'O Kalae ka **lae** nui o Hawai'i
nei*. Kalae is the big **peninsula** here in Hawai'i.]
(*lae o'o* = expert [syn. *lae 'ula, mahao'o*])

laha widespread, widely known, broadcast, spread
out. [*Ua **laha** ka nūhou e pili ana i ka wī ma
Somalia*. The news about the famine in Somalia is
widely known.] (*ho'olaha* = to spread abroad, publish, advertise) (*ho'olaha mana'o* = propaganda)

lā hānau birthday. (*Hau'oli
Lā Hānau* = Happy
Birthday)

laha 'ole rare, unique,
uncommon. [*He mea
laha 'ole 'o Ke Aolama*.
Ke Aolama (Hawaiian
language radio news) is
an **uncommon** thing.]

lā hānau

lahi thin, frail, delicate.

lahilahi delicate, dainty. [*Aloha au iā 'oe lā, kou
pāpālina **lahilahi***. I love you, your **dainty**
cheeks. (song, "Pāpālina Lahilahi," composer
unknown)]

laho scrotum. (*laholena* = lazy, indolent)

laholio 1. rubber, rubber band. 2. elastic, rubbery.

lā ho'omana'o (also *lā piha makahiki*) day of
remembrance, anniversary.

lāhui nationality, race, nation. [*He keu ke akahai o ka* **lāhui** *Hawaiʻi.* The gentle nature of the Hawaiian **race** is outstanding.]

laʻi 1. calmness, stillness, quiet of nature. 2. calm, peaceful, silent. (Pō Laʻi ē = Silent Night)

laiki (from English) rice.

laikini (from English) license. [*Ua hoʻopiha au i ka palapala noi i* **laikini** *kalaiwa kaʻa hou.* I filled out the application for a new driving **license**. (*lai-kini kī pū* = firearms license)

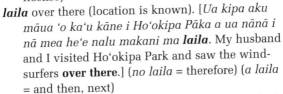

laiki

laila over there (location is known). [*Ua kipa aku māua ʻo kaʻu kāne i Hoʻokipa Pāka a ua nānā i nā mea heʻe nalu makani ma* **laila**. My husband and I visited Hoʻokipa Park and saw the wind-surfers **over there**.] (*no laila* = therefore) (*a laila* = and then, next)

laka 1. (from English) lock. 2. (from English) to lock. [*Ua paʻa ka puka i ka* **laka** *ʻia.* The door was **locked** shut.] 3. tame, domesticated, gentle. [*Ua laka kā Puakea manu aloha.* Puakea's parrot is **tame**.]

Laka 1. name of hula goddess. [*E* **Laka** *ē, e nauē kāua i uka, i ka nahele.* Oh **Laka**, let's move to the uplands, to the forest. (familiar line in hula chants)]

lakeke (from English) jacket.

laki (from English) lucky. (*pakalaki* = bad luck, unlucky)

lako 1. provisions, supplies. 2. well supplied, pros-perous. (*lako keʻena* = office supplies) (syn. *pono keʻena*)

lākou they all (three or more), them.

lala diagonal, slanting, oblique. (syn. *hiō*)

lālā 1. branch, limb. 2. member of a club, group. [*He lālā ʻo Manu o ka hui hīmeni ʻo Hoʻokena.* Manu is a **member** of the singing group Hoʻokena.] (*hoʻolālā* = to plan) [**Hoʻolālā** *ka ʻahahui e hoʻomoana ma Kualoa.* The organization **plans** to camp at Kualoa.]

lālama 1. to pilfer, meddle. 2. daring, fearless. (*lālama ka lima* = don't meddle, don't goof around [*lit.* the hand meddles])

lālani 1. row, rank, line. 2. line of poetry. (syn. *laina*) [*Nāna e oli i ka* **lālani** *mua.* She is the one who should chant the first **line.**] (*hele lālani* = march in line) (*kū laina* = stand in line)

lalau 1. mistake, blunder. 2. to err, wander, go astray. [**Lalau** *wale nā ʻōpio lapuwale.* The young good-for-nothings **go astray.**]

lālau to seize, reach out for, take hold of. [*Ua* **lālau** *ka ʻelemakule i ke apolima kula.* The old man **seized** the gold bracelet.]

lalawe thrilling, overwhelming, overcome with emotion. [*Ke* **lalawe** *nei kuʻu nui kino.* My entire body is **overcome with emotion.** (song, "Ahi Wela," by M. Doirin and L. Beckley)]

lale to hurry, hasten, urge on. (*hoʻolale* = to hurry, hasten, incite)

lalo 1. depth. 2. down, under, low. [*Aia kāu nūpepa ma* **lalo** *o kou noho.* Your newspaper is **under** your chair.] 3. a leeward, southerly direction. [*E holo kai kākou i* **lalo**. Let's sail downwind, **leeward.**]

lama 1. native plant with yellow wood used as symbol of light and knowledge, used in hula altar. 2. symbol of enlightenment. 3. torch, light, lamp. (*lama kuhikuhi* = beacon, signal light)

lamakū large torch.

lamalama 1. torch fishing at night. 2 to go torch

fishing. 3. bright-looking, vivacious, animated.

lana 1. to float. [*Ua lana mālie ka ʻiwa ma ka ʻale.* The frigate bird **floated** calmly on the ocean swell.] 2. floating, buoyant. 3. lowest platform of oracle tower. (*hoʻolana* =

lamalama

to launch a project, canoe [*fig.* to cheer up]) [*Āhea ana e **hoʻolana** ʻia ai ka waʻa kaulua hou?* When will the new double-hulled canoe be **launched**?] (*manaʻolana* = hope, to hope)

lanaau to drift with the current, wander aimlessly.

lānai porch, patio.

Lānaʻi island that is part of Maui County; in ancient days, Lānaʻi was believed to be inhabited by evil spirits who were chased away by Kaululāʻau.

Lānaʻi

lanakila 1. victory, triumph. 2. to win, triumph, overcome. [*ʻO wai ke kime i **lanakila**?* Which team **won**?]

lananuʻumamao oracle tower of *heiau* with three levels or platforms for different purposes. (*lana* = lowest platform; *nuʻu* = middle platform; *mamao* = highest platform, most sacred)

lani 1. sky, heaven. 2. high chief, majesty. 3. heavenly, spiritual. (*ka makua lani* = heavenly father)

lanipō dense, dark (luxuriant growth of vegetation, rain).

lā nui holiday, various types. (Lā Heleuī = Halloween; Lā Hoʻomaikaʻi = Thanksgiving; Lā Kalikimaka = Christmas; Lā Pakoa = Easter)

lapa 1. ridge, steep ravine. 2. overactive, cavorting

like young animal. (*lapa ahi* = blaze, flame)
(*lapalapa* = many ridges, to bubble, boil) (*lapa
kai* = restless sea)

lapa'au medical practice. (*lā'au lapa'au* = herbal
medicine) [*Holomua nā kumu lā'au lapa'au
Hawai'i.* Hawaiian **herbal medicine** teachers are
making progress.]

lapalapa 1. many ridges. 2. to bubble, boil, cavort.

lapauila 1. lightning flash. 2. to flash, as lightning.

lapu 1. ghost, apparition. 2. to haunt. 3. haunted.
(*kiliki o lapu* = trick or treat)

Lāpule Sunday (*lit.* day of prayer).

lapuwale 1. vanity, foolishness. 2. good-for-nothing
person, wastrel, scoundrel. 3. worthless.
[*Lapuwale ka hopohopo.* Worrying is **worthless**.]

latitu (also *lakikū*) latitude (geographic). [*He
'umikūmāiwa kekele ka latitu 'o Hawai'i nei.*
Hawai'i's **latitude** is 19 degrees.]

lau 1. leaf. [*Holunape ka lau o ka niu.* The **leaf** of
the coconut is swaying.] 2. four hundred. 3.
numerous, many.
(Kīlauea = numerous
spoutings up of gases
[place name of volcano
area])

laua'e 1. fern with fragrant
leaf with scent reminis-
cent of *maile*. 2.
beloved.

laua'e

lauahi to destroy by fire,
lava. [*Ua lauahi 'ia ka
hale pule Kalawina ma Kalapana.* The Protestant
church at Kalapana was **destroyed by lava**.]

lau'ai edible leaves, salad, vegetables.

lauākea 1. commoner. 2. common. [*Lauākea ke
kani manu ma nā kumu'ōhi'a.* Bird calls are
common in *'ōhi'a* trees.]

lauhala 1. leaf of *hala* tree 2. baskets, hats, mats or other items woven from this leaf.

lauhalalana vagabond, drifter (*lit.* floating *hala* leaf).

laukanaka 1. to populate. 2. densely populated, many people, crowded (with the public). [**Laukanaka** *mau ʻoe i ka lehulehu.* You are always **crowded** with the public. (song, "Haleʻiwa Pāka," by A. Namakelua)] (*hoʻolaukanaka* = to have many people around, to dispel loneliness with people) [*Loaʻa mai ke kono mai Keawaiki, e kipa, e nanea a e **hoʻolaukanaka**.* An invitation has been received from Keawaiki (Francis Brown's home) to visit, to relax and to **dispel loneliness with people**. (song, "Keawaiki," by Helen Desha Beamer)]

lau kapalili fluttering leaf, part of name of first taro plant, Hāloanakalaukapalili.

laulā broad, wide, general. [*ʻO ke olakino ke kumuhana **laulā**.* The **broad** topic is health.] (*maʻi laulā* = epidemic, contagious disease) (*manaʻo laulā* = broadminded, general theme or idea)

laulau 1. wrapping, wrapped package. 2. a bundle of food wrapped in *tī* leaves and steamed, a favorite dish at parties and *lūʻau*. Usual ingredients in *laulau* are pieces of pork, fish, taro leaves.

lauleʻa 1. peace, happiness, friendship. 2. happy, glad, genial. (*hoʻolauleʻa* = festival, celebration, to hold a celebration, to restore peace, friendship)

lau liʻi a small leaf, a variety of *maile* found especially on Kauaʻi.

laulima cooperation (*lit.* many hands), working together. [*Ua mākaukau koke ka hana haipule i ka **laulima** a ka ʻekalesia.* The church service was quickly prepared due to the **cooperation** of the congregation.]

launa 1. to socialize, have fun. 2. friendly, sociable.
(*launa palapala* = correspondence, to correspond)
(*hoʻolauna* = to introduce people) [*E hoʻolauna
ana koʻu hoaaloha iaʻu me ke Kenekoa.* My friend
will **introduce** me to the Senator.]

launa ʻole beyond compare, unique. [*He leo
nahenahe launa ʻole ko ka puʻukani.* The singer
has an **incomparable** sweetness of voice.]

lau niu coconut leaf.

lauoho hair of head. (*huluhulu* = body hair)

laupapa reef. (syn. *ʻāpapa, pāpapa*)

lauwili circuitous, unstable, fickle, two-faced. [*Hō ke
ʻano lauwili o nā moho koho pāloka!* Darn the
two-faced character of political candidates!]

lawa 1. enough, ample, satisfied. 2. possessed of
enough, therefore, wise, capable.
(*ua lawa* = that's enough [call used sometimes at
end of hula or song])

lawaiʻa 1. fisherman. 2. to fish.

lawakua 1. to bind or tie fast (*fig.* to be a dear
friend). 2. strong back, bulging with muscles.

lāwalu cooking technique, barbecuing fish wrapped
in *tī* leaves on coals).

lawe 1. to take (*lawe aku*). 2. to bring (*lawe mai*).
(*lawe leka* = postman) (*lawe ola* = manslaughter,
to take a life) (*lawe pio* = conquest, to capture,
take prisoner) (*lawe wale* = extortion, to take
without right) (*hoʻolawe* = subtract, deduct) [*Ua
hoʻolawe ʻia aku ʻelua kaukani kālā mai kāu
mau ʻauhau e uku ai.* Two thousand dollars were
deducted from the taxes you have to pay.]

lawea to drift apart, to depart.

lawehala 1. sin, sinner. 2. delinquent, evil. (*lawehala ʻōpiopio* = juvenile delinquent) (*hoʻolawehala* =
accusation, to accuse) [*Hoʻolawehala ka ilāmuku
i ke kālepa lāʻau ʻino.* The sheriff **accuses** the drug
seller.]

lawehana 1. to do labor, work. 2. industrious. [*He po'e **lawehana** nā Pilipino ma Hawai'i.* The Filipinos in Hawai'i are an **industrious** people.]

lawelawe 1. to serve, attend to, wait on tables. (*lawelawe 'ana* = service) [*Maiau ko ke kuene **lawelawe 'ana** mai.* The waitress's **service** is skilled.]

lawelawelima 1. to pitch in, lend a hand. (*lawelawelima 'ana* = pitching in, lending a hand) [*Ho'opau koke ke kūkulu hale ma ka 'āina ho'opulapula i ka **lawelawelima 'ana**.* Housebuilding on Hawaiian Homes lands is quickly finished due to **pitching in**.]

le'a 1. joy, happiness. 2. sexual gratification, orgasm. 3. delightful, happy, completely successful.

le'ale'a fun.

lehe lip. (*lehe luhe* = pouting lip)

lehelehe 1. lips 2. labia of vagina.

lehia 1. expert. [*He **lehia** 'o Pua i ke kuku kapa.* Pua is an **expert** at beating tapa.] 2. skilled. (syn. *loea*)

leho general term for cowry shell, used in octopus lures.

lehu 1. ashes. 2. four hundred thousand. 3. numerous, very many. 4. ash colored.

lehua tree and blossom of the *'ōhi'a lehua*, symbol of Hawai'i island.

lehulehu multitude, crowd, the public. [*Nui a **lehulehu** nā pua mamo i 'ākoakoa mai e ho'olohe i ka pāna puhi 'ohe 'o ka Royal Hawaiian Band.* Numerous indeed were the **multitudes** of Hawaiians who gathered to hear the Royal Hawaiian Band.]

lei

lei 1. garland, necklace. 2.

yoke, wreath. 3. to wear
as *lei* (*fig.* a beloved
child, person). Kinds of
lei include *lei pua*
(flower *lei*), *lei pūpū*
(shell *lei*), *lei 'ano'ano*
(seed *lei*), *lei 'ā'ī* (neck
lei), *lei hulu* (feather *lei*).
Familiar styles of *lei*-
making include *haku*
(several types of
flowers/foliage are braided), *wili* (flowers/foliage
are bound with twine to
tī leaf or other backing),
hili (one type of foliage or
flower is braided), *kui*
(single flowers are strung

lei hulu

lei po'o

on a thread). (*lei po'o* = head *lei*) (*ho'olei* = to
wear as *lei*, to fling, toss, throw and retrieve)
[**Ho'olei** ka paniolo i ke kaula 'ili. The cowboy
throws the lariat.] (*ho'oleilei* = to juggle)

lē'ia abundance. (Mokulē'ia = land district full of
abundance) [*Ka moena pāwehe o* **Mokulē'ia**.
(*'ōlelo no'eau*) The patterned carpet of the **abundant land**.]

leina 1. places on each island where spirits gathered
then leaped together into
the underworld, Milu.
(syn. *leina ka 'uhane*) 2.
leap, bound.

leinakia (from English) rein-
deer.

lei niho palaoa whale tooth,
ivory pendant from
whale's tooth, symbol of
high rank.

*lei
niho
palaoa*

leiomano weapon with single shark's tooth.

leka letter, mail. (*hale leka* = post office; *kāleka* = postcard, card [syn. *pepa poʻoleka, kāleka poʻoleka*]; *lawe leka* = postman; *pahu leka* = mail box; *poʻoleka* = stamp; *wahī leka* = envelope)

lekapī (from English) recipe.

leki (from English) cellophane tape, tape. [*E wahī i ka makana i ka pepa me ka* **leki**. Wrap the present with paper and **tape**.]

lekiō (from English) radio.

lēkō watercress.

lekuke (from English) lettuce.

lele 1. a jump, leap, attack. 2. a hula step. 3. sacrificial altar of *heiau*. 4. to fly, jump, leap. [*E* **lele** *i Kalalau*. (*ʻōlelo noʻeau*) **Fly off** to Kalalau. (equivalent in meaning to "Go jump in a lake.")] Note: *Lele* has many other meanings. (*lele kawa* = to leap into the ocean feet first without splashing, a game in ancient days) (*lele koali* = to jump rope, swing) (*lele koke* = to leap suddenly [*fig.* short-tempered]) (*lele lupe* = to rise and fall like a canoe in rough seas [*fig.* rise and fall of emotions]) (*lelepau* = to trust completely) (*lele wai* = to cleanse, purify with water, to purge) (*lele wale* = phrase at end of ancient prayer, to speed prayer on) (*hoʻolele* = to fly plane, kite) [*Ua* **hoʻolele** *ko kākou mau kūpuna i nā lupe ʻano poepoe*. Our ancestors **flew** kites that were sort of round.] (*hoʻolele lupe* = to fly a kite)

leleʻē to jump to conclusions, speak prematurely.

lelele to jump about, hop around, to beat swiftly (heart).

leleponi to die suddenly, as in accident, by stroke.

lelepono to jump carefully (*fig.* to live a happy life, to rise rapidly to success, to do business justly).

lemi (from English) lemon, lime.

leo voice, tone, command, advice. (*leo mana* = voice

of authority) (*leo mele* = tune of song, notes of scale) (*leo nui* = loud voice, to speak loudly) (*leo ʻole* = agreeable, uncomplaining) (*leo paʻa* = deaf mute, unable to speak)

lepa flag, tapa cloth on stick used to mark boundaries, as of *kapu* areas.

lepahū to lose courage, give up. [*Mai* **lepahū** *a lilo i hōhē!* Don't **give up** and become a coward!]

lepe 1. hem or fringe of any garment. 2. rooster comb, turkey wattles. [**lepe ʻulaʻula, lepe** *a ka moa*, red **comb** of the rooster (sexual reference). (song, "Lepe ʻUlaʻula," by Kaimanahila)] (*lepelepe o Hina* = monarch or Kamehameha butterfly) (*lepe lua* = turncoat)

lepo 1. dirt, earth, filth. 2. excrement, used as euphemism for *kūkae*. 3. dirty, soiled. [*Ma hope of ka holoi ʻana, maʻemaʻe paha kou mau lole* **lepo** *loa?* After washing, will your very **dirty** clothes be clean?] (*moe lepo* = bum, shiftless person)

lewa 1. sky, atmosphere, upper heavens. The ancient Hawaiians had separate names for different biogeographic zones of the Earth. They also named different sections of the sky and sea. *Lewa lani* refers to the highest section of the sky, while *lewa nuʻu* is the section just below that. [*E nā akua o ka* **lewa lani**, *o ka* **lewa nuʻu**, Oh gods of the **highest stratum**, of the **upper heavens** (familiar line in ancient chants and prayers)] 2. to float, dangle, swing. (*lewa hoʻomakua* = space just above Earth's surface, lower atmosphere) (*lewa lilo loa* = outer space) (*hoʻolewa* = funeral, to

lewa

lift up and carry) [*Aia ka* **ho'olewa** *ma ka Lāpule.* The **funeral** is on Sunday.]

lī 1. chill. (*lī lua* = extremely chilly) 2. shoelace. 3. to have chills, feel horrified. 4. hang, gird.

lewalewa dangling.

li'a 1. strong desire, yearning. 2. to yearn for. [*'O 'oe ka'u mea e* **li'a** *mau ai.* You are the one I always **yearn for**. (a common line in love songs)]

līhau 1. gentle rain. 2. moist, fresh.

lihi 1. edge, border, boundary. (*ka lihikai* = the edge of the sea) 2. rain. 3. small quantity or amount. [*He 'ike* **lihi** *ko kēlā haumāna.* That student has a **small amount** of knowledge.]

lihilihi 1. eyelashes. [*Lō'ihi ko kē keiki kāne mau* **lihilihi** *maka.* That (by you) boy's **eyelashes** are long.] 2. flower petal. 3. lace. 4. crochet.

liholiho very hot, glowing, fiery.

li'ili'i small, little. (*ka wā li'ili'i* = childhood)

like like, alike, similar, equal. [*Ua* **like** *nō a like au me ku'u one hānau.* I am just **like** my birthplace. (song, "Moloka'i Nui a Hina," by M. Kāne)]

like 'ole various, different. (*nā 'ano 'oihana like 'ole* = various kinds of careers, businesses) (*nā 'ano nananana like 'ole* = all different kinds of spiders)

likiki ticket, receipt. (syn. *kikiki*) [*Ua nalowale ka'u* **likiki** *mai ka panakō mai!* My **receipt** from the bank disappeared!]

liko 1. leaf bud (*fig.* a child or youth). 2. to bud, put forth leaves. (*liko lehua* = bud of *lehua*, new leaf buds of *lehua*, used in Hawaiian herbal medicine) (*likoliko* = fresh, young, oily)

lili 1. jealousy. 2. highly sensitive to criticism. (*ho'olili* = to provoke jealousy, jealous)

līlia (from English) lily. [*'A'ala ku'u pua* **līlia**. My **lily** flower is fragrant. (song, "Pua Līlia," by A. Alohikea)] (*līlia lana wai* = water lily) *liliha* nauseating, nauseated, of fatty, rich foods (*fig.* revolted, heartsick).

liliko'i passion flower and fruit.

lilinoe fine mist.

Lilinoe goddess of the mists.

lili'u scorching, smarting, burning (of eyes). Note: Lili'uokalani was given her royal name because of the burning, painful eyes suffered by the Kuhina Nui (regent) Kīna'u, a maternal relative, at the time of her birth. Although Lili'uokalani was her royal name, the queen is reported to have preferred her childhood name, Lydia.)

lilo 1. to be lost, gone. [*Ua* **lilo** *ka hale leka i ka makani pāhili.* The post office was **lost** in the hurricane.] 2. to become, turn into. [*E* **lilo** *ana kā ke kumu kaikamahine i luna awa.* The teacher's daughter will **become** a harbor master.] 3. to be engrossed, absorbed in an activity. [*Lilo 'o Mikala i ka pā'ani hei.* Mikala's **absorbed** in playing string figures.] (*lilo loa* = permanently lost, completely engrossed) 4. far, distant. (*ma uka lilo* = far upland) (*ho'olilo kālā* = spendthrift, to spend money)

lima 1. arm, hand, sleeve, finger. 2. five. (*kanalima* = fifty) (*lima 'ākau* = right hand) (*lima hema* = left hand) (*lima ikaika* = to handle roughly, a strong arm or hand, power) (*lima koko* = assassin, murderer, shedder of blood) (*lima kuhi* = index finger) (*lima kuhikuhi* = hands of clock) (*lima ulu* = green thumb)

limahana laborer, employee, labor.

limalima to pilfer, to hire. (*ho'olimalima* = lease, rental, to lease, rent) (*hale ho'olima-lima* = rental house) (*ka'a ho'olimalima* = taxi, rental car)

limu general name for seaweed, an item in traditional diet.

linohau dressed to perfection, beautifully decorated.

[***Linohau*** *wāhine holo lio i ka pā'ū.* The women *pā'ū* riders are **dressed to perfection**.]

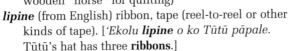

linohau

lio 1. horse. [*Kīau nā* **lio** *ma ke kahua hānai pipi.* **Horses** gallop at the ranch.] 2. tight, taut. (*lio lā'au* = merry-go-round, wooden "horse" for quilting)

lipine (from English) ribbon, tape (reel-to-reel or other kinds of tape). [*'Ekolu* **lipine** *o ko Tūtū pāpale.* Tūtū's hat has three **ribbons**.]

lipo 1. dark blue-black. [*'O ka* **lipo** *o ka lā, 'o ka* **lipo** *o ka pō,* **Dark blue-black** of the day, **dark blue-black** of the night (line from *Kumulipo*, creation chant)] 2. dim, distant.

liu 1. bilge. 2. to leak.

li'u slow, tardy, taking a long time.

li'ulā twilight, mirage.

liuliu prepared.

li'uli'u to spend much time (*'a'ole i li'uli'u* = not long afterward)

loa 1. distance, length, height. [*'Ehia mau mile ka* **loa** *o ka heihei paikikala?* How many miles is the **distance** of the bike race?] 2. very, very much, most, excessive.

loa'a 1. to find, get, obtain, receive. [**Loa'a** *kāna kālā i kā kēia luahine mo'opuna kāne?* Does this old lady's grandson **get** her money?] (*loa'a ke ahipele?* = got a match?) 2. wealth, property, earnings. Note: *Loa'a* has many other meanings.

loea 1. skill, ingenuity, cleverness. 2. expert, skillful, clever. [*'O Kau'i Zuttermeister ka* **loea** *hula hope loa.* Kau'i Zuttermeister was the last of four master hula teachers honored with the title of "*loea*."]

lohe 1. to hear, mind, obey. 2. obedient. (*lohe pepeiao*

= hearsay) (*lohe pono* = listen carefully, attentive)
(*hoʻolohe* = to listen) [*E nānā aku i ke kumu, e
hoʻolohe mai.* Look to the teacher and **listen.**
(song, "Alu Like," by H. Apoliona)]

lohelohe to eavesdrop, listen carefully.

lohi slow, late, mentally retarded. [*Komo **lohi** ka
haumāna i kāna papa.* The student comes to
class **late.**] (*ʻūlōlohi* = late; *lohiʻau* = retarded,
backward, slow; *hoʻolohi* = to delay; *lohina* = a
delay)

loi to look over critically, to criticize.

loʻi irrigated terrace for growing taro, later used for
rice. [*He papa **loʻi** a he
mau ʻauwai ko ke kula
nui.* The university has a
field of **taro patches** and
water ditches.]

loʻi

lōʻihi 1. length, height. 2. tall,
long (time or physical
dimension). [***Lōʻihi** loa nā
hōkele hou.* The new
hotels are really **tall.**]

loiloi to evaluate, judge. (*luna loiloi* = judge in
speech, hula, or song contest) [*He **luna loiloi** ʻo
ʻAnakē Pat ma ka Merrie Monarch.* Aunty Pat is
a **judge** at Merrie Monarch.]

loina custom, tradition. (syn. *kuluma*) [*He **loina** ka
ʻaha waimaka ma ko lākou ʻohana.* The gather-
ing one year after a death is a **tradition** in their
family.]

loio (from English) lawyer. [*Makemake nō ʻo Mike
Hawaiʻi e lilo i **loio**.* Miss Hawaiʻi really wants to
become a **lawyer**.]

lōkahi unity, agreement, accord, harmony. [*Inā
lōkahi ka ʻohana, ʻaʻohe mea e ālai aʻe ai.* If the
family is united in **harmony**, there is nothing to
create obstacles.] (*manaʻo lōkahi* = unanimous)

loke (from English) 1. rose. 2. rosy.

lokelani pink rose, symbol of Maui island.

lokelau green rose. [*no ka pua* **lokelau** *ke aloha,* love for the **green rose** (song, "Green Rose Hula," by J. Almeida)]

loko 1. interior, pond, lake, character, entrails. [*Nani 'o* **loko** *o ka hale pule pena 'ia.* The **interior** of the painted church is beautiful.] 2. internal. 3. inside. [*Aia kā Kawelu kāwele i* **loko** *o ko Wailani kalaka.* Kawelu's towel is **inside** Wailani's truck.] (*loko i'a* = fishpond; syn. *loko kuapā* [fishpond with walls built on top of a reef]) (*loko wai* = freshwater lake, fountain)

loko 'ino 1. unkindness. 2. evil, merciless, heartless. [*E pale aku i ka* **loko 'ino**. Defend against **unkindness**. (prayer for protection)]

lokomaika'i generosity, kindness, goodwill. [*Nui ko Nākila* **lokomaika'i** *i kona kāko'o iā "Ka Leo Hawai'i."* Nākila is very **generous** in his support of "Ka Leo Hawai'i" (Hawaiian language radio program).]

loku downpour of rain, blowing of wind (*fig.* deep sorrow, pain, emotion, to cry). [*ka ua* **loku** *a 'o Hanalei,* (*'ōlelo no'eau*) the **pouring rain** of Hanalei (Reverence for nature and delight in names are combined in poetic descriptions of places, often including the names of the winds and rain of that place, such as the heavy rains of Hanalei, Kaua'i.)]

lola 1. rolling pin, cassette tape. [*Ua loa'a iā ia ka* **lola** *hou a kākou e ho'olohe ai?* Does he have the new **cassette** that we're supposed to listen to?] 2. to roll. 3. droopy, sluggish.

lole 1. cloth, clothes, dress. 2. to reverse, unfold, handle, turn over. (*lole 'au'au* = swimming clothes) (*lole holoi* = dirty laundry; syn. *lole lepo*) (*lole wāwae* = pants, shorts) (*ho'ololi lole* = to change

clothes) [*E* **ho'ololi lole** *'oukou, e nā keiki.*
Change clothes, children.]

lolelua variable, two-faced, fickle. [*He* **lolelua** *ke 'ano o ka meia.* The mayor's character is **two-faced**.]

loli 1. to change, alert. [*Ua* **loli** *ka waiho'olu'u o ka pua hau.* The color of the *hau* flower **changed**.] 2. sea slug. 3. speckled, dotted, changed. (*ho'ololi* = to change, take a new form)

lōli'i relaxed, at ease, carefree.

lolo brains, bone marrow. (*lolo ka'a* = dizziness)

lōlō paralyzed, numb (*fig.* stupid, dumb). (*pakalōlō* = marijuana [*lit.* cigarette that makes you paralyzed and stupid])

loloa 1. length. 2. long.

lolouila computer (*lit.* electric brain). (syn. *kamepiula*) [*Lohi kā ka mea kū'ai hale* **lolouila**. The realtor's **computer** is slow.]

lolokū midday.

lomi to rub, press, squeeze.

lomilomi 1. masseuse, masseur, one who massages. 2. to massage.

lono news report, remembrance. (*lono papa* = news spread far and wide) (*ho'olono* = to listen, hear, obey)

Lono one of the four main gods of ancient days. Lono i ka makahiki presided over the harvest season, when war was forbidden.

lōpā 1. peasant, farmer. 2. shiftless.

lopi (from English) thread.

lou 1. hook, long pole for picking fruit. 2. to hook, fasten with a hook. [*Ke* **lou** *nei ka mahi'ai i ka pea a me ka hē'ī.* The farmer is **hooking** avocados and papayas.]

loulu native fan palm used to weave mats, hats.

lū to scatter, sow seed, spend recklessly.

lua 1. hole, pit, grave, toilet, outhouse. (*lua pele* = volcanic crater) (*lua 'uhane* = tear duct, where

soul exits and reenters
body during sleep)
2. ancient martial arts.
3. two, twice, double.

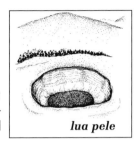

lua pele

luaahi victim. [*Na wai e kākoʻo i ka luaahi ma ka hana ʻino?* Who will support the **victim** of abuse?]

luahine old woman.

luaʻi to vomit, throw up. [*Poluea ʻoe i ke holokai? Mai luaʻi!* Are you nauseated from sailing? Don't **throw up!**] (*luaʻi kū* = disgusting; *luaʻi pō* = outcasts)

luaiele to lead dissipated life, not taking care of health. [*Inā luaiele ka ʻōpio, pilikia auaneʻi.* If the youth **doesn't take care of his health**, he will have trouble later on.]

luakini a large kind of *heiau* (temple, church.) Note: Perhaps because *luakini* were large *heiau*, the term is often used to indicate any place of worship, including churches and temples of various religions, and no longer refers exclusively to the human sacrifice *heiau* that was introduced into ancient society by Pāʻao in about 1200.

luana to enjoy yourself, relax, socialize.

lua ʻole incomparable, unequaled, unmatch-ed. [*He nani lua ʻole ko ke mele Hawaiʻi.* Hawaiian poetry has **incomparable** beauty.]

lua puhi blow hole.

lūʻau young taro leaves, used in many food items at a *pāʻina* or party, therefore, by extension, party with traditional Hawaiian food.

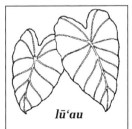

lūʻau

luhe to droop, hang down.

lūheʻe 1. fishing lure for octopus with cowry shell and stone for weight. 2. to fish with this type of lure.

lūheʻe

luhi weary, tired. (*luhi hewa* = tired from activity that ends without results) (*hoʻoluhi* = to bother, disturb, burden)

luku 1. destruction. 2. to destroy. [*Ma Wailuku i lanakila ai ko ka naʻi aupuni mau koa.* It was at Wailuku (*lit.* waters of **destruction**) that the conqueror's soldiers were victorious.]

luli 1. to shake head, to wag tail. 2. to totter, sway to and fro, pitch about, as a ship.

luliluli shaky, unsteady. [***Luliluli** ke keiki ma ka noho lio.* The child is **unsteady** in the saddle.]

lulu 1. calm, peace, shelter. [***Lulu** ke awa kū moku ʻo Māmala.* Honolulu harbor (Māmala) is **calm**.] 2. to lie at anchor in calm water. (Honolulu = calm bay)

lūlū 1. to shake, scatter, sow seeds. 2. to make donation. (*lūlū hua* = sower, to sow seeds) (*lūlū lima* = to shake hands) [*E **lūlū lima**, e kuʻu wahi ʻīlio!* **Shake hands**, my sweet doggie!]

lumaʻi to capsize (*fig.* to destroy).

lumi (from English) room. (*lumi ʻauʻau* = bathroom [*syn. lumi hoʻopau pilikia*]; *lumi hoʻokipa* = living room; *lumi kuke* = kitchen; *lumi moe* = bedroom)

luna 1. above, on top of, high up. [*Aia ka manu i **luna** o ke kumukōpiko.* The bird is **on top of** the kōpiko tree.] 2. foreman, boss, overseer, manager. [*He **luna** kona kupuna kāne ma ka mahikō.* His grandfather was an **overseer** on the sugar plantation.] (*luna ʻauhau* = tax collector; *luna aupuni* = government official; *luna awa* = harbor master;

luna helu kālā = bank teller; *luna hoʻoponopono*
= editor; *luna ʻike hala* = conscience [syn.
lunawae-manaʻo]; *luna kānāwai* = law judge;
luna makaʻāinana = representative in legislature)

lupe kite. (*hoʻolele lupe* = to
fly a kite) [*Ma Kapiʻolani
Pāka e **hoʻolele lupe** ai
ka lehulehu.* It's at
Kapiʻolani Park that the
public **flies kites**.]

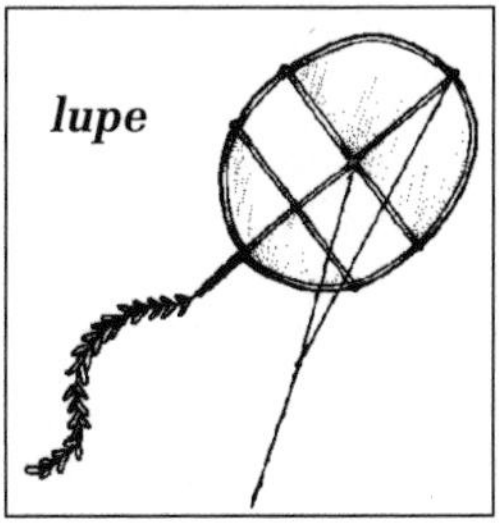

lupe

luʻu to dive, plunge into
water. (*hoʻoluʻu* = to dip,
immerse, dye cloth)

luʻuluʻu burdened with
weight, trouble, grief; painful, sorrowful. [*Ua
luʻuluʻu ke kāne wahine make i ke kaumaha.*
The widower was **burdened with grief**.]

ma in, on, at, by, to. [*Aia kā Leilani mau pā lolouila* **ma** *luna o ka lolouila.* Leilani's computer diskettes are **on** top of the computer.] (*ma ka Pō'akolu* = on Wednesday)

mā 1. to fade away. (*mā wale* = to fade quickly) 2. faded, wilted, stained, discolored. 3. used after person or place name to indicate several people, places. [*Waipahe 'o Ku'ulei* **mā**. Ku'ulei folks (Ku'ulei **and at least one other person**) are courteous.] [*Wela 'o Makena* **mā**. Makena **and those places** are hot.]

ma'a used to, accustomed to, experienced, familiar. [**Ma'a** *'o Mahina mā i ka hīmeni 'ana ma mua o ke anaina.* Mahina folks are **used to** singing in front of an audience.] (*ho'oma'ama'a* = to practice, become used to)

ma'alahi 1. simplicity, contentment. 2. easy, simple. [*'A'ole* **ma'alahi** *ka hō'ike waena-kau.* The midterm exam wasn't **easy**.]

ma'alea 1. craftiness, cunning, deceit. 2. crafty, cunning. [*He hana ma'alea kā ka mea pā'ani pepa.* The card player did a **cunning** thing.]

ma'alili 1. cooled down (food). [*E 'ai kāua o* **ma'alili** *ka 'i'o.* Let's eat or else the meat will be **cooled down**.] 2. abated, cooled down passion.

mā'alo to pass along, pass by. [*Ke kipa aku 'o 'Anakē iā Lilia,* **mā'alo** *'o ia i ka mākeke i'a 'o Tamashiro.* Whenever Aunty visits Lilia, she **passes by** Tamashiro fish market.] (syn. *kā'alo*)

ma'amau usual, customary, common. [*'O ka poi a*

me ka poke kāna mea 'ai **ma'amau**. Poi and poke are her **usual** food.]

ma'awe thread, wisp, faint footprint. (*ma'awe ala* = faint path (*fig.* departure of soul after death)

mae 1. to fade (clothes), to wilt (flowers), wither. 2. to waste away in illness.

mā'e'ele numb, horrified. [*He hu'i* **mā'e'ele** *ko'u nui kino.* My entire body is **numb** (with shock). (song, "Lā 'Elima," by the family of Diana Aki)]

ma'ema'e clean, pure, chaste, attractive. [*He po'e* **ma'ema'e** *ka lāhui Hawai'i.* The Hawaiian people are a **clean** people (personal cleanliness is important).] [**Ma'ema'e** *kou mau lima?* Are your hands **clean**?]

māewa swinging, fluttering, unstable.

ma'ewa reproachful, scornful. (*ho'oma'ewa* = to reproach, sneer at, mimic, ridicule) [*Mai* **ho'oma'ewa** *iā ha'i!* Don't **ridicule** others!] Note: *Ha'i* can be used as a noun meaning "someone else, other people."

maha 1. temple, forehead. 2. to rest, repose, vacation. [*Ke pi'i mākou i Lē'ahi,* **maha** *iki mākou ma ka 'ānu'u hope loa.* Whenever we (us three, not you) climb Lē'ahi (Diamond Head), we **rest** a little on the last step. (*ho'omaha* = to vacation, take a rest) (*ho'omaha loa* = to retire, retirement)

mahalo 1. gratitude, thanks. 2. respect, admiration, praise. [*Nui ko'u* **mahalo** *i nā ali'i wahine o Hawai'i kahiko.* I have a great **respect** for the chiefly women of ancient Hawai'i.]

mahamaha 1. fish gills. 2. to show love, affection. (*ka pili mahamaha* = affectionate relationship)

mahana warmth. (syn. *mehana*)

maha 'oi bold, overly aggressive (an offensive trait to Hawaiians).

māhele 1. portion, part, share, division. (*māhele kālā* = dividend) (*māhele kino* = body organ, body

part) (*ho'omāhele* = to divide up, distribute)
[*E **ho'omāhele** i nā manakō a 'oukou i 'ako ai.*
Divide up the mangoes that you folks picked.] 2.
to translate, interpret.

mahi 1. plantation, farm. 2. to cultivate, farm. [***Mahi**
kona kupuna wahine i kona māla 'ai.* Her grandmother **cultivates** her vegetable garden.] (*mahikō*
= sugar plantation) (*mahi
pua* = horticulture)

mahi'ai 1. farmer, farm. [*He
mahi'ai lēkō ko Sumida
mā.* Sumida folks have a
watercress **farm**.] 2. to
farm.

mahi'ai

māhiehie 1. delightful,
charming, pleasant. 2.
delightfully. [*Ulu
māhiehie nā pua ma ka māla.* Flowers grow
delightfully in the garden.]

mahiki 1. a seesaw, to seesaw. 2. to peel, pry off. 3.
to jump, leap, move up and down. 4. to exorcise
spirits.

mahikina lā crack of dawn.

mahikō sugar plantation.

mahina moon, moonlit, month. [*He **mahina** wela 'o
'Aukake.* August is a hot
month.] (*mahina hapalua
mua* = waxing moon;
mahina hapalua hope =
waning moon; *mahina
hou* = new moon; *mahina
piha* = full moon [syn.
Māhealani, night of full
moon in Hawaiian moon
calendar])

mahina

mahiole feather helmet. [*He **mahiole** a he 'ahu'ula
ka lole o ke ali'i.* A **feather helmet** and a feather

cape were the clothes of
the chief.]

māhoe twins. (*Māhoe Hope* =
month of Hawaiian calen-
dar, approximately mid-
September to mid-
October) (*Māhoe Mua* =
month of Hawaiian calen-
dar, approximately mid-
August to mid-September)

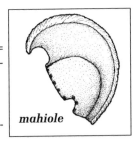

mahiole

mahole to bruise, skin, scrape, hurt feelings.

māhu 1. steam, vapor. 2. to steam, exude vapor. [*I ka
māhu 'ia 'ana o ka laulau, ua mo'a ka 'i'o pua'a.*
When the *laulau* was **steamed**, the pork was
cooked.]

mahū 1. weak, flat, as stale beer. 2. insipid.

māhū 1. homosexual of either sex. (syn. *ho'okāmaka,
aikāne* [male homosexuality])

māhua to increase, grow. [*Ke **māhua** nei nā 'ōpio e
hiki ke 'ōlelo Hawai'i.* The number of youths who
can speak Hawaiian is **increasing**.] (*ho'omāhua* =
to increase, multiply, grow).

mahu'i to guess, suppose, expect, imagine. (*'ike
mahu'i* = to catch a glimpse of) (*lohe mahu'i* = to
hear a hint of, without detail)

mahuka to flee, escape, elope. [*E **mahuka** aku ana
nā pio kaua.* The war prisoners will **escape**.]

mai 1. particle indicating movement or action in
direction of the person speaking. [*E hele **mai**.*
Come **here**.] 2. command "don't" when followed
immediately by a verb. [***Mai** hana pēlā!* **Don't** do
that!] 3. from (*mai* <u>place</u> *mai/aku*). [*Ua heihei nā
wa'a pe'a **mai** O'ahu **aku** a hiki i Kaua'i.* The
sailing canoes raced **from** O'ahu to Kaua'i.] Note:
Either *mai* or *aku* is used after the place of origin. If *mai* is used, it indicates that the travel was
from the place of origin toward the place where

the speaker is. If *aku* is used, it indicates that the travel was from the place of origin away from the place where the speaker is. Both *mai* before place of origin and *mai/aku* after it are necessary to translate as "from."

ma'i 1. illness, disease. [*Ho'omanawanui ka mea **ma'i**. The patient endures **illness**. 2. genitals. 3. menstrual period. 4. ill, sick. (*ma'i 'a'ai* = cancer; *ma'i ahulau* = epidemic; *ma'i hana ei* = AIDS, sexually transmitted diseases; *ma'i huki* = convulsion; *ma'i kau* = chronic disease; *ma'i koko pi'i* = high blood pressure; *ma'i lele* = contagious disease; *ma'i mimikō* = diabetes; *ma'i pu'uwai* = heart disease; *ma'i wahine* = female illness, menstrual period; *mea ma'i* = sick person, patient; *mele ma'i* = chant/hula celebrating reproductive ability of chiefs, symbolic of giving life to the Hawaiian nation)

maiā from (refers to a person; used before a name or pronoun; *maiā* <u>person</u> *mai/aku*) [*Ua loa'a iā māua kekahi leka **maiā** Lahela mai. **Maiā** wai mai kāu leka?* We (us two, not you) received a letter **from** Lahela. Who is your letter **from**?]

mai'a

mai'a general term for banana.

maiau 1. neat and careful in work, correct and careful in speech. 2. carefully, skilled, expertly, ingenious. [*Kālai **maiau** 'o Kana'e i ka pahu niu.* Kana'e **expertly** carves the coconut drum.]

māihi to peel, strip bark. (*māihi ola* = to escape by the skin of your teeth, barely escape)

ma'ihi dwarf.

maika ancient game similar to bowling.

maika'i 1. good, fine, well. [***Maika'i** kā kēia mau haumāna mau kumu.* These students' teachers are **fine**.] 2. good-looking, beautiful. [*He kāne **maika'i** 'o ia ala ke nānā aku.* He (over there) is a **good-looking** man.] (*ho'omaika'i* = congratulations, to congratulate)

mā'ila 1. light-brown skin, as some part-Hawaiians have. 2. clear (as the sea on sunny days, as when the depths are visible).

maile native shrub whose leaves are stripped for fragrant *lei*.

māino 1. cruelty, misery, harm. 2. cruel, miserable, hurt. (*ho'omāino* = to treat cruelly, abuse, persecute) (*hana māinoino i nā holoholona* = cruelty to animals)

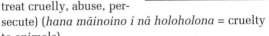
maile

mā'ino'ino 1. graffiti. [*E holoi i kāu hana **mā'ino'ino** ma ka paia!* Wash your **graffiti** off the wall!] 2. to deface, mar, spoil, ruin. (*ho'omā'ino'ino* = to defame, slander)

maka 1. eye, face, sight, view, mesh of net, beloved person. [*He 'upena **maka** nui kēnā.* That (by you) is a big-**meshed** net.] (*maka'ā* = wide, staring eyes) (*maka 'ē* = to look askance) (*makaaniani* = eyeglasses; *makaaniani pale lā* = sunglasses) [*Ma mua o ko 'oukou hehi 'ana i ke one, e komo i ka **makaaniani pale lā** a me ka 'aila hamo pale lā!* Before you all step onto the sand, put on **sunglasses** and sunscreen!] 2. raw, ripe,

makaaniani

fresh. (*ka iʻa maka* = raw fish) (*maka mua* = first time, beginning, commencement) [*ʻO ka **maka mua** kēia o kou hula ʻana?* Is this the very **first time** you've danced the hula?] (*maka hilahila* = bashful, shy) (*maka hiamoe* = sleepy, drowsy) (*hoʻomaka* = to start) [*Ma ka hola ʻehia e **hoʻomaka** ai ka hālāwai?* What time does the meeting **start**?]

māka (from English) 1. mark, target, grade. 2. to mark.

makaʻāinana commoner, citizen. (*luna makaʻāinana* = legislative representative)

makaʻala alert, vigilant, watchful, careful. [*E **makaʻala**! **Look out**!* (syn. *E akahele!*)]

makaʻalā blind but with eyes that look normal.

mākaha fierce, savage, ferocious.

mākāhā sluice gate of fishpond. [*I mea aha ka **mākāhā**? I mea e komo ai ka iʻa i loko o ka loko iʻa.* What's a **sluice gate** for? It's to let fish enter the fishpond.]

makahehi admiration, desire for. 2. to admire. [*E **makahehi** ʻia ana nā ʻōiwi ʻōlelo Hawaiʻi.* The native people who speak Hawaiian will be **admired**.]

makahiki 1. year, ancient festival lasting several months during rainy season, when war was forbidden. 2. annually. (*makahiki hou* = new year) (*makahiki lā keu* = leap year) (*i kēia makahiki aʻe* = next year) (*i kēlā*

makahiki

makahiki aku nei = last year) [*I kēlā **makahiki aku nei**, ua kūʻai aku māua ʻo Pahikaua i ko māua kahua hānai pipi ma Kohala.* **Last year**, Pahikaua and I sold our (two) ranch in Kohala.]

ma kai toward the sea, downhill direction.

ma kai

māka'i police officer, guard. [*He **māka'i** maka'ala ko kēia kahu ma'i kupuna wahine.* This nurse's grandmother is a watchful **police officer**.]

mākaia traitor, treachery, revenge, vengeance. [*He **mākaia** ke kumuhana o nā ki'i 'oni'oni Samurai.* **Vengeance** is a theme of Samurai movies.]

māka'ika'i 1. tourist. 2. to visit, sightsee, stroll around. [*Nui ka po'e **māka'ika'i** Kepanī ma Honolulu.* There are lots of Japanese **tourists** in Honolulu.]

maka 'ike to see clearly, more than most, especially supernatural things, to have gift of second sight.

māka'ikiu detective.

makakēhau heart's desire (*lit.* dewy-eyed)

makakilo 1. to watch with great attention. 2. observant, watchful eyes.

makalapua 1. many blossoms. 2. to blossom forth. 3. handsome, beautiful. [*'o **makalapua** ulu māhiehie,* **many blossoms** growing delightfully (song, "Makalapua," by Konia/E. Holt)]

maka launa friendly.

maka lena unfriendly.

makali'i tiny, very small.

Makali'i 1. name of month in Hawaiian calendar. 2. Pleiades. [*i ke au o **Makali'i** ka pō,* at the time when the **Pleiades** appear in the night sky (line from *Kumulipo,* creation chant)]

makalike uniform. [*He **makalike** kaila ko ke kuene.* The waiter has a stylish **uniform**.]

makaloa sedge from which fine mats were woven, especially on Ni'ihau.

makamae priceless, of great value. [*'O ko kākou ho'oilina hīmeni he mea **makamae***. Our heritage of song is a **precious** treasure.]

makamaka intimate friend, host (*fig.* anything very helpful). [*Ho'okahi nō **makamaka**, 'o ke aloha*. There is only one **helpful** thing, that is love. (line from "E Nihi Ka Hele," by D. Kalākaua)]

makana gift, present, scholarship, prize. (*makana kūlana 'ekahi* = first prize)

makani wind, breeze, ghost, spirit. (*makani pāhili* = hurricane) [*He **makani pāhili** 'ino nō 'o 'Iniki*. 'Iniki was a very bad **hurricane**.]

makapehu suffering from hunger, hungry person, swollen (*lit.* swollen eyes). [***Makapehu** nā keiki ma Somalia*. Children in Somalia **suffer from hunger**.]

makapō blindness, blind person. (*maka pa'a* = person blind in one eye)

makau fishhook. [*'O Mānaiakalani ka **makau** mana a Māui*. Mānaiakalani is Māui's powerful **fishhook**.]

makau

maka'u 1. fear, risk, danger. 2. frightened, dangerous. (*maka'u wale* = coward, cowardice; *syn. hōhē*) (*ho'omaka'u* = to frighten) [*Mai **ho'omaka'u** i kāu keiki!* Don't **frighten** your child!]

mākaukau 1. proficiency, competence, preparation. 2. able, competent, capable, qualified. (*ho'omākaukau* = to prepare, get ready)

mākaukau 'ole incompetent, unskilled, unprepared.

makauli'i thrifty, economical, miserly, avaricious.

makawalu numerous, much, many (*lit.* eight eyes). [***Makawalu** nā hōkū lele ma ka mahina 'o*

'Aukake. There are **numerous** shooting stars in the month of August.]

makawela hatred, anger.

make 1. death, peril, misfortune. 2. to die, to faint. (*ho'omake* = to put to death, kill) 3. killed, defeated, dead. (*make loa* = extinct) ['*Ane'ane* **make loa** *ka 'alalā.* The *'alalā* (Hawaiian crow) is almost **extinct**.] (*make pōloli* = to starve to death) (*make 'ole* = immortal)

makehewa 1. vain attempt. 2. in vain, useless. [**Makehewa** *kā Mikana ho'ā'o.* Mikana's experiment was **useless**.]

mākeke outdoor market. [*Pa'apū* **nā mākeke** *mahi'ai.* The farmers' **markets** are crowded.]

makemake to desire, want, wish. [*He aha kou* **makemake**? What do you **want**?] Note: often shortened to *mamake* in colloquial speech.

makemakika (from English) math.

mākēneki (from English) magnet.

makepono profitable. [*He 'oihana* **makepono** *ka halihali 'ana i nā pono hale.* Transport-ing furniture is a **profitable** business.]

makewai 1. thirst. 2. thirsty. [*I ko Mika lāua 'o Leinani holopeki 'ana ma ka pāka,* **makewai**, *akā ke inu wai lāua, ua kena.* When Mika and Leinani jog at the park, they are **thirsty**, but when they drink water, (their thirst is) quenched.]

mākia 1. motto, purpose, aim. ['*O* "'*Onipa'a*" *ko Lili'uokalani* **mākia**. Lili'uokalani's **motto** was "Steadfast."] 2. pin, nail, spike. 3. to strive for, concentrate on, to nail, bolt.

makika (from English) mosquito.

makoa fearless, courageous. (*ho'omakoa* = to act bravely)

mākoi fishing pole. [*Mai 'a'e i ka* **mākoi**. Don't step over the **fishing pole**.] 2. to fish with a pole.

mākole red-eyed, inflamed. [**Mākole** *ko ka lawai'a*

maka i ka lā. The fisherman's eye is **inflamed** due to the sun.]

mākonā hard-hearted, mean, nasty. [*Mākonā kā kaʻu kāne luna.* My husband's supervisor is **hard-hearted**.]

mākou us, we (not including the person being spoken to). [*Ke holoi nei mākou i ko ka lehulehu mau kaʻa i mea e ʻimi kālā ai no ke kalapu.* **We** are washing the public's cars as a thing that would raise money for the club.]

makua parent, relative of parents' generation. (pl. *mākua*) (*mākuakua* = aged, old) (*makua kōlea* = stepparent) (*makua papekema* = godparents [*lit.* baptism parents]) (*hoʻomakua* = to grow into maturity)

makuahine mother, aunt. (*makuahine kōlea* = step-mother)

makuahūnōaikāne father-in law. (*hūnōnakāne* = son-in-law)

makuahūnōaiwahine mother-in-law. (*hūnōnawahine* = daughter-in-law)

makua kāne father, uncle. (*makua kāne kōlea* = stepfather)

makua kāne

māla garden, cultivated field. (*māla ʻai* = vegetable garden) (*māla aʻo* = kindergarten) (*māla pua* = flower garden)

mālaʻe cloudless. [*Mālaʻe ka lewa i ke kauwela.* The sky is **cloudless** in summer.]

Malaki (from English) March.

malama month, light, moon. (syn. *mahina*)

mālama 1. care, preservation, loyalty, custodian, caretaker. 2. to care for, preserve, take care of. [*E mālama i ka honua!* **Take care of** the earth!]

(*mālama ola* = to support financially, means of livelihood, social security; *helu mālama ola* = social security number)

mālamalama clarity of thinking or explanation, shining, clear. (*hoʻomālamalama* = to cause light, to enlighten, inform) [*E* **hoʻomālamalama** *i ka malama,* **to cause light** to shine in the moon (line from the beginning of the *Kumulipo,* best known of the Hawaiian creation chants)]

mālānai undisturbed, serene. [**Mālānai** *ka hoʻomoana ma ke kahakai ʻo Kīholo.* Camping at the beach at Kīholo is **serene.**]

male (from English) 1. marriage, wedding. 2. to marry. [*Ua* **male** *ʻia lāua ma waho.* They were **married** outdoors.] (*paʻa male* = married couple) (*ʻoki male* = divorce)

paʻa male

mali to flatter, soothe, persuade, cajole. (*hoʻomalimali* = to flatter, soothe, quiet)

mālie 1. calmness, quietness. 2. calm, quiet, still, gentle. [*He nohona* **mālie** *ko ke kuaʻāina.* The country person has a **calm** lifestyle.]

malihini 1. stranger, newcomer, guest, foreigner. 2. unfamiliar, strange, foreign. [*Hoʻokipa mau nā hālau hula o kēia pae ʻāina i nā hula hālau* **malihini** *mai nā ʻāina ʻē mai.* The hula schools of this island chain always welcome guest hula schools from **foreign** lands.]

malino calm, quiet (sea), peaceful (spirit), smooth, unwrinkled. [*ke kai* **malino** *aʻo Kona,* (*ʻōlelo noʻeau*) the **calm** sea of Kona. Specific natural phenomena, such as wind, rain, and clouds, were often noted in poetic references to a place; here

the calmness of the ocean at Kona, which was a
favorite residence of chiefs, may also represent
the calm weather and abundance of the land.]

maliu to heed, give attention to. [*Eia ala e **maliu**
mai.* **Pay attention.** (song, "Ku'u Ipo i ka He'e
Pu'e One," by Likelike)]

malo male loincloth. (*hume i ka malo* = to put on
loincloth)

mālo'elo'e tired, stiff. [*E **mālo'elo'e** ana ko Keali'i mau
po'ohiwi ma hope o kona huki 'ana i ka lū'au kalo
ma ka lo'i.* Keali'i's shoulders will be **stiff** after he
pulls the taro leaves in the taro patch.]

malohi drowsy.

mālolo general name for flying fish.

malo'o dry, dried up, evaporated. [*He 'āina **malo'o** 'o
Makena.* Makena is **dry** land.] (*hīmeni malo'o* = a
capella singing, without accompaniment) (*kai
malo'o* = low tide)

malu 1. shade, shelter, protection, government, control, strength. [*Ma lalo o ka **malu** o ke aupuni, he
mau pono kīwila ko ke kanaka.* Under the protection of the **government**, citizens have civil
rights.] 2. shaded, peaceful, quiet. (*ho'omalu* =
probation, to protect, restrict, quarantine, govern)

malū secretly, clandestinely, illegally. [*Ua hui **malū**
nā kipi.* The rebels met **secretly**.] (*ho'opae malū*
= to smuggle)

Māluaki'iwai sea breeze with showers, famous in
hula.

mālualua 1. rough terrain. 2. bumpy, pitted road.

maluhia 1. peace, quiet, security, safety. [*E **maluhia**
ka honua!* Let there be **peace** on earth!] 2. peaceful, restful, solemnity, awe during ceremony.

māluhiluhi tired.

māmā fast, quick, lightweight. [***Māmā** ko ka pōpoki
po'i 'ana ma luna o ka manu.* The cat's pouncing
on the bird is **quick**.]

māmaki native tree used for tapa, medicine.

māmala fragment, splinter, chip, stroke of war club. (Māmalahoe = law of splintered paddle [proclaimed by Kamehameha I to guarantee safety of all travelers])

māmala ʻōlelo sentence (*lit.* speech fragment). (syn. *hopuna ʻōlelo*)

māmalu 1. protection, defense. 2. umbrella. [*Auē nō hoʻi ē! ʻAʻohe āu* **māmalu** *a pulu hoʻi i ka ua Tuahine!* Oh wow! You didn't have an **umbrella** and got soaked in the Tuahine rain (of Mānoa)!]

mamao far, distant, remote. (*kū mamao* = aloof)

mamo bird, black Hawaiian honeycreeper, now extinct, whose yellow feathers were prized for cloaks and *lei*. 2. descendant, posterity. [*He* **mamo** *Hawaiʻi au na koʻu mau kūpuna.* I am a Hawaiian **descendant** of my ancestors.]

mana 1. spiritual power, divine power, authority. [*He* **mana** *ko ke kiaʻāina.* The governor has **authority**.] (*mana hoʻokolokolo* = jurisdiction, power of passing judgment) (*mana makua* = parental authority) 2. branch, limb, variations, versions of story. [*Nui nā* **mana** *o nā kaʻao manō.* There are lots of **versions** of shark tales.] (*hoʻomana* = religious sect, to worship [pre-missionary], empower, authorize)

māna food chewed by adult for child, trait acquired from those who raise child.

mānā desert.

mānai 1. *lei* needle. 2. to string *lei*.

manakā boring, dull, monotonous, uninteresting.

manakō (from English) mango.

manakuke (from English) mongoose.

mānaleo native speaker.

mānalo 1. drinkable, as water. (*waimānalo* = drinkable water) 2. to appease. [**Mānalo** *ka ʻohana i ke kupuna kāne kuakahi pōniuniu.* The family

> **appeases** the confused great-grandfather.] 3. safe
> from harm, danger.

manamana lima finger. (*manamana lima komo* =
ring finger; *manamana lima kuhi* = index finger;
manamana lima nui = thumb; *manamana wāwae*
= toe)

manaʻo 1. thought, idea, belief, meaning, theory. [*He
aha ka* **manaʻo** *o "piʻo"?* What's the **meaning** of
"*piʻo*"?] (*manaʻo hāiki* = narrow mind, intolerant;
manaʻo hoʻomanamana = superstition; *manaʻo
ikaika* = zeal; *manaʻo kuhihewa* = delusion;
manaʻo laulā = tolerant, broad-minded, general
idea; *manaʻo nui* = important idea or meaning;
manaʻo paʻa = conviction, determination, firm
intention; *manaʻo ulu wale* = whim, fancy,
impulse, imagination) (*hoʻomanaʻo* = to remember,
recall, remind) (*kia hoʻomanaʻo* = monument,
statue, memorial) 2. to think. (syn. *noʻonoʻo*)
(*manaʻo wale* = to suppose, presume)

manaʻoʻiʻo faith, confidence, to have faith, confidence.

manaʻolana 1. hope, expectation. [*Ka manaʻoʻiʻo, ka
mana ʻolana, a me ke aloha.* Faith, **Hope** and
Charity.] 2. to hope. [**Manaʻolana** *nā mākua e
hoʻokumu i mau kula kaiapuni hou ma nā wahi
like ʻole o nā mokupuni.* Parents **hope** to establish
several new immersion schools at various sites on
the islands.]

manawa time, turn, season, date. (*holo ka manawa* =
time passes by) (*i kekahi manawa* = sometimes)
(*manawa kaʻawale* = free time) (*manawa kūpono*
= appropriate time, opportunity) (*no ka manawa* =
temporary; syn. *kūikawā*) (*ʻo kou manawa kēia* =
it's your turn)

manawaleʻa 1. charity, donation. 2. to give freely. 3.
benevolent. [**Manawaleʻa** *ko ke kauka maka
kōkua ʻana aku i ka poʻe ʻilihune.* The eye doctor's helping poor people is a **benevolent** act.]

manawanui 1. patience, fortitude. 2. to have patience, fortitude. (*e ho'omanawanui* = be patient, put up with the situation)

manene shuddery sensation of fear, revulsion. [*'Oiai ko'u kaikunāne e lele kawa ana, pi'i ko'u* **manene**. While my brother was playing *lele kawa*, I felt that **shuddery feeling**. (*Lele kawa* was a sport of ancient days in which contestants jumped into the ocean from a cliff, feet first. The one who created the smallest splash won.)]

mane'o 1. itch. 2. itchy, sexually stimulated, "horny." [*Hiki paha iā 'oe ke wa'u i ko'u kua? Ua* **mane'o**! Can you perhaps scratch my back? It's **itchy**! (*ho'omane'o* = to tickle)

māneoneo barren.

mānewanewa 1. grief, sorrow, mourning, exaggerated expression of grief, such as tattooing tongue, knocking out teeth (sometimes done in old Hawai'i upon the death of a high chief). 2. unkind, to treat unkindly.

manini 1. small reef fish with stripes. 2. stingy. (syn. *pī*) [**Manini** *ko kēlā luna ho'oponopono 'ano*. That editor has a **stingy** personality.]

mano 1. four thousand. 2. thick, many, numerous. (*ho'omano* = to increase, do repeatedly, persistently)

manō shark. [*pau Pele, pau* **manō**, (*'ōlelo no'eau*) oath "to do or die" (*lit.* destroyed by lava, destroyed by shark)]

manō

manoa numerous, many.

mānoa thick, solid, great depth. Mānoa valley on O'ahu is known for the large number of people who lived there in ancient days.

mānoanoa 1. depth, thickness. 2. thick, solid, vast.
   3. coarse, dull-witted, stupid.

mānowai dam, stream (*fig.* heart and circulatory system).

manu bird (*fig.* person).
   (*manu hulu* = wealthy
   person, *lit.* feathered
   bird) [*He mau* **manu**
   hulu *nā kahu waiwai o*
   ka panakō. The bank
   trustees are **wealthy peo-**
   ple.] (*manu aloha* = parrot; *manu kū* = dove;
   manu mele = canary)

manu

manuahi free, no charge. [**Manuahi** *ka likiki*
   mokulele. The airplane ticket is **free.**] (*kāne man-*
   uahi = common-law husband) (*wahine manuahi*
   = common-law wife)

manuea 1. type of seaweed. 2. careless, blundering,
   slipshod.

mao clear (sky after rain). [*Ma uka nei o Honouliuli,*
   helele'i ka ua ma ka pō akā **mao** *ke kaiao.* Here
   in the uplands of Honouliuli, rain falls at night
   but dawn is **clear.**]

ma'o 1. native cotton. 2. green.

mā'oki'oki streaked, cut into pieces. [*Ke kai*
   mā'oki'oki *a'o Kona,* (*'ōlelo no'eau*) the **streaked**
   ocean of Kona]

maoli native, indigenous, true, real. [*'O ka 'apapane*
   a me ka 'ōma'o kekahi mau manu **maoli.** The
   'apapane and the *'ōma'o* are some of the **indige-**
   nous birds.] (*ke kanaka maoli* = native Hawaiian)

mā'ona (often pronounced *mā'ana*) satisfied after
   eating, full stomach. [*'Ai a* **mā'ona,** *inu a kena.*
   (*'ōlelo no'eau*) Eat until **full,** drink until (your
   thirst is) quenched.]

maopopo to understand, recognize clearly, know.

('*a'ole maopopo ia'u* = I don't know, I don't understand) [*Maopopo kēia mo'olelo iā ia? E kala mai! 'A'ole maopopo iā ia.* Does she/he **understand** this story? I'm sorry! **She doesn't understand.**] (*ho'omaopopo* = to make clear, tell clearly) (*maopopo 'ole* = unintelligible)

māpele a type of *heiau* for worship of Lono. Note: Unlike at *luakini heiau*, no human sacrifices were made at *māpele*.

māpu 1. windborne fragrance, bubbling, wafted. (syn. *māpuana*) 2. surging, as emotions.

māpuna bubbling spring, froth of rough sea (*fig.* surging emotions). (*māpuna hoe* = dip of paddle) [*E komo 'oe i kāu* **māpuna hoe**. ('*ōlelo no'eau*) Pitch in and help (*lit.* put in your **dip of the paddle**).] (*māpuna leo* = whispered words of love)

mau 1. to continue, persevere. 2. always, unceasing, perpetual. [*Mau nō ke aloha.* Love is **unceasing**.] (*a mau loa aku* = forever) 3. pluralizer. [*He* **mau** *lei pua onaona kā lāua.* They (two) have **some** sweet-smelling flower leis (they made).] (*ho'omau* = to keep on, persist, continue) [*E* **ho'omau** *i ka 'imi na'auao.* **Keep on** seeking knowledge/wisdom.]

ma'ū damp, moist, wet, cool, refreshing. [*He mau'u* **ma'ū** *ko ka pā hale i kēia kakahiaka.* The yard has **wet** grass this morning.] [*He* **ma'ū**, **ma'ū**, **ma'ū** *i ka pu'u ke moni.* It's **moist, cool, refreshing** in the throat when you swallow. (song, "Niu Haohao," by B. Mossman)]

māua we (2, not including person spoken to).['*Elima a* **māua** *mo'opuna.* **We** (she/he and I) have five grandchildren.]

mau'a'e to intrude, transgress, interrupt. [*Mau'a'e nā kānaka kū'ē i kā ka moho ha'i 'ōlelo.* The people opposing her **interrupt** the candidate's speech.]

mauhala 1. grudge, resentment. 2. unforgiving.

Maui second-largest island in the archipelago; Maui County includes the islands of Maui, Lānaʻi, Molokaʻi and Kahoʻolawe.

Māui trickster hero of Polynesia. [*ʻO **Māui** ke kupuʻeu kaulana o ka Pākīpika.* **Māui** is the famous hero of the Pacific.]

ma uka toward the mountains, uphill direction, inland (if one is on the ocean, *ma uka* means on shore).

maʻule 1. to faint. 2. fainthearted, dispirited.

mauleho callused. (*hoʻomauleho* = to cause calluses, to overwork, oppress)

mauli life, heart, spirit, ghost. (*mauli ola* = breath of life) (*kihe a mauli ola* = "sneeze and live," a blessing said after someone sneezes; often shortened to *ola*)

maumau frequent.

mauna mountain, mountainous region. (syn. *kuahiwi*)

māuna waste, mistreatment.

māunauna extravagant, wasteful. [*ʻAʻole ka nohona **māunauna** he hana mālama i ko kākou ʻāina.* A **wasteful** lifestyle is not something that protects our land.]

maunu bait.

mauʻu grass. (*hoʻomauʻu* = to give nothing of value)

māwae 1. cleft, fissure in rocks. 2. to separate, sort, select, to cleanse from defilement.

me with. [*Hana ʻo Mokihana* **me** *ia a* **me** *aʻu.* Mokihana works **with** him and **with** me.]

mea general word for thing or person. (*mea ʻai* = food; *mea ʻai māmā* = snack; *mea inu* = beverage, drink; *mea ʻono* = dessert, cake, pastries) (*mea halihali ʻōpala* = garbage man; *mea hali ukana* = porter; *mea hana noʻeau* = craftsman; *mea hoʻokani pila* = musician; *mea hoʻokipa* = receptionist; *mea kaha kiʻi* = artist; *mea ʻohi kālā* = cashier; *mea pāʻani* = player) (*mea hao* = hardware, metal; *mea hoʻohana* = tool, implement; *mea hoʻolohe* = hearing aid) (*mea hou* = news, new) [*He aha ka* **mea hou**? What's **new**?] (*mea kanu* = plant) (*mea kaua* = weapon) (*mea kolo* = insect) (*mea makamae* = treasure) (*mea nui* = important thing, person) (*mea oli* = chanter) (*he mea iki* = "you're welcome" [response to *mahalo, lit.* it's a small thing]) (*hoʻomeamea* = to pretend, disguise) [**Hoʻomeamea** *wale ka ʻōpio ē he laikini kalaiwa kaʻa kāna.* The young person just **pretends** that he has a driver's license.]

mea oli

mea ʻole inconsequential, insignificant. [**Mea ʻole** *ka luli i ka lana mālie.* Swaying is **nothing** to disturb our calm enjoyment. (song, "Holo Waʻapā, by L. Machado)]

meʻe hero, heroine. (syn. *kupuʻeu*) [*ʻO koʻu hulu kupuna wahine kuʻu* **meʻe**. My honored grandmother is my beloved **heroine**.]

mehameha 1. loneliness, solitariness. 2. silent, lonely.

mehana 1. warmth. 2. warm. (*aloha pumehana* = warm greetings)

meheu track, footprint. (*ho'omeheu* = to trace, track down) [*'O ka* **ho'omeheu** *i ko 'oukou mau kūpuna kā 'oukou hana?* Is **tracing** your ancestors what you all are doing?]

Mei (from English) May.

meia (from English) mayor.

mekala (from English) medal, metal.

mekanika (from English) mechanic.

mele music, song, chant. (*mele aupuni* = national anthem) (*mele ho'onānā keiki* = lullaby; syn. *mele ho'ohiamoe keiki*) (*mele inoa* = name chant) (*mele kāhea* = chant calling out to request permission to enter house, *hālau* [hula school])

melemele yellow. (*lenalena* = orange-yellow)

meli (from English) bee, honey.

melia plumeria.

melu decomposed.

menehune legendary small people, possibly an early migratory group.

mihi 1. repentance. 2. to repent, apologize, confess. [*Ke* **mihi** *ala ka 'aihue i kona mau mākua.* The thief is **apologizing** to her parents.]

mika (from English) Mister.

mike (from English) Mrs., Miss.

miki quick, active, nimble, prompt.

miki'ala alert, prompt.

miki'ao 1. fingernail, toenail. 2. claw.

mīkini (from English) machine. [*He* **mīkini** *miki ka lolouila.* The computer is a quick **machine**.]

mikioi dainty and neat in doing everything, made with skill.

mikionele missionary.

miko salted, seasoned with salt. [**Miko** *ka pipi kaula me ka he'e kaula'i.* The beef jerky and dried octopus are **salted**.]

mīkole to eat in small bits, persevere.

mile (from English) mileage, mile.

mili 1. to handle, fondle, caress, beloved. 2. slow, inefficient at work. (*mili ka'a* = to do repeatedly, caress over and over)

mili'apa slow, slowpoke.

mililani to praise, exalt, to treat as a favorite.

milimili toy, plaything, favorite, beloved, darling. [*A he* **milimili** *'oe, a he hiwahiwa na'u a he lei 'oe no ko'u kino.* You are a favorite for me and you are a garland for my body. (song, "Ka Makani Kā'ili Aloha," by M. Kāne)]

milo 1. tree used for medicine and dyes. 2. curl. 3. abortion. 4. to curl, twist.

milu 1. underworld which spirits jump into after death.

Milu ruler of the underworld.

mimi 1. urine. 2. to urinate. [*Pono 'oe e* **mimi**, *e ka pēpē?* Do you have to **urinate**, baby? (*mimikō* = diabetes)

minamina 1. to regret, be sorry, deplore. [**Minamina** *nā Hawai'i i ka 'ike kahiko i lilo loa.* Hawaiians **regret** that ancient knowledge has been swept away.] 2. to prize greatly. 3. thrifty, economical, covetous.

mino 1. dimple, depression. 2. dimpled, creased.

mino'aka smile.

minomino wrinkle, as with age.

minuke (from English) minute (time). [*'Ehia* **minuke** *i koe a mo'a ka mea 'ono?* How many **minutes** left until the dessert is cooked?]

miomio 1. precise, neat, clear-cut. 2. to dive into water without splashing.

moa 1. chicken. 2. primitive plant with medicinal uses.

mo'a cooked, done. [*Ua* **mo'a** *ka 'i'o moa.* The chicken is **cooked**.] (*mo'a kolekole* = rare cooked [meat])

Moaʻe trade wind. [*Pā mai ka makani* **Moaʻe** *i ka hapanui o ka makahiki.* The **trade winds** blow most of the year.]

mōakāka clear, plain, intelligible. [*Mōakāka ko ke alakaʻi wehewehe ʻana.* The leader's explanation was **clear**.]

moana ocean, open sea. (*hoʻomoana* = to camp) [*Ma ke kauwela,* **hoʻomoana** *kona ʻohana ma kahakai.* In the summer, his family **camps** at the beach.]

moani 1. light breeze with fragrance, wafted fragrance. 2. to blow perfume. [*ke ʻala e* **moani** *nei,* the gentle **fragrance** that wafts sweetly on the breeze. (song, "Moanikeʻala," by Nawahi/Beamer)]

moe 1. bed, dream. 2. to lie down, sleep. [*E* **moe** *iho ana kāu ʻīlio ma luna o ka moe.* Your dog is going to **lie down** on the bed.] 3. horizontal, prone. (*moe hewa* = nightmare, to have nightmare, sleep restlessly) (*moe like* = parallel) (*moe luliluli* = cradle) (*moe ʻuhane* = dream, to dream)

moena couch, bed, mat. (*moena pāwehe* = fine mat woven in patterns, especially from Kauaʻi and Niʻihau, sometimes with *makaloa* sedge)

moena

mōhai sacrifice.

mōhala 1. to blossom, develop (open flower or youth). [*Ke* **mōhala** *nei ka pua.* The flower is **opening** now (the child is developing).] 2. evolved, developed. (*hoʻomōhala* = to develop, evolve, development) [*He mau hana* **hoʻomōhala** *haʻawina kā nā kumu kula.* The school teachers have some curriculum **development** activities.]

moho candidate, representative. [*He* **moho** *'o Kaleleonālani no ka mō'ī Hawai'i.* Kaleleonālani was a **candidate** for sovereign of Hawai'i.]

mō'ī monarch, sovereign. (*mō'ī kāne* = king) (*mō'ī wahine* = queen) (*aupuni mō'ī* = monarchy, kingdom)

mō'ī

mō'ike 1. dream interpreter. 2. to interpret dreams.

mōkākī 1. mess, chaos, disorder. 2. littered, disordered. (*ho'omōkākī* = to litter, cause disorder) [*Mai ho'omōkākī i nā kahakai!* Don't **litter** the beaches!]

mokihana tree found only on Kaua'i, a symbol of that island; It bears fragrant berries. A *mokihana lei* is much prized for its rarity and its lasting fragrance.]

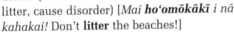

mokihana

mokokaikala (from English) motorcycle.

mokomoko 1. hand-to-hand combat of any kind. 2. to box, fight.

moku 1. island, district. [*aloha ku'u* **moku** *'o Kaho'olawe,* love for my **island** Kaho'olawe (song, "Mele No Kaho'olawe," by H. Mitchell)] 2. fragment, cut. 3. to be cut, severed, amputated.

mokuahi

mokuahi steamship, cruise ship. (*mokukolu* = tugboat) (*moku pe'a* = sailboat)

moku ʻāina state. [*ʻEhia mokupuni o kēia* **moku ʻāina**? How many islands does this **state** have?]

mokulele airplane.

mokuluʻu submarine.

mokupuni island.

mole 1. taproot, main root. 2. smooth, round, bald.

mōlehulehu twilight, dusk. [*Ua ʻike ʻia ka hōkū welowelo ma ka* **mōlehulehu**. The comet was seen at **dusk**.]

moloā lazy, indolent. [*ʻAʻole* **moloā** *nā moʻohelu ma ka panakō. Paʻahana lākou.* The tellers at the bank aren't **lazy**. They're busy.]

Molokaʻi island between Oʻahu and Maui.

momi pearl. [*Waiwai loa ko kona makuahine lei* **momi**. His mother's **pearl** necklace is very valuable.]

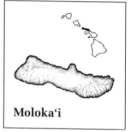

Molokaʻi

momona 1. fertile, rich (soil), fruitful, fat. 2. sweet-tasting, rich-tasting. [**Momona** *ka ʻiʻo puaʻa ma ka lūʻau.* The pork at the *lūʻau* is **rich-tasting**.]

momona

moni to swallow, gulp down, absorb. (*moni ka hāʻae* = swallow spittle, salivate at sight of food, attractive person)

moʻo 1. lizard, reptile, gecko. 2. succession, series. (*moʻo aliʻi* = genealogy of chiefs) (*moʻo lono* = priests of lineage of Lono)

moʻohelu budget, counting, list of expenditures, teller.

moʻokūʻauhau genealogy.

mo'olelo story, history, tradition (*lit.* succession of talk).

mo'opuna grandchild. (*mo'opuna kuakahi* = great-grandchild)

mo'opuna kāne grandson.

mo'opuna wahine granddaughter.

mū 1. insects. 2. legendary people. 3. silent.

mua 1. man's eating house. 2. before, ahead, forward. (*i mua* = go forward) [*I mua a loa'a ka lei o ka lanakila.* **Go forward** until the *lei* of victory is attained. (chant, "Ke au Hawai'i")] (*kā i mua* = initiation ceremony for young boy to men's eating house).

mu'emu'e bitter, sour taste, bitter tasting. (syn. *'awa'awa*) [*Mu'emu'e ka lā'au lapa'au i ka noni.* Herbal medicine made with *noni* is **bitter tasting**.)

muku 1. cut short, amputated, at an end. 2. measurement from fingertip of one hand to elbow of other hand when both arms are extended to the side.

muli 1. after, afterward, behind, following behind. (*muli loa* = youngest born in family) [*'O Nā'ala kā kēia kauka wahine muli loa?* Is Nā'ala this woman doctor's **youngest child**?] (*ma muli o* = through, by means of) [*Ma muli o ko kāna hui 'oihana kāko'o, ua holopono ka 'aha mele 'imi kālā.* **Through** the support of her business, the money-raising concert was a success.]

muliwai mouth of river, estuary. [*Aia i ka muliwai ku'u home nani.* There at the **mouth of the river** is my beautiful home. (song, "Ka Muliwai," by D. Pokipala)]

mūmū 1. to rinse out mouth with water. 2. dull, blunt. [*'Oiai e huki 'ia ana kou niho na'auao, mai poina e mūmū i ka wai pa'akai.* Since your wisdom tooth will be pulled out, don't forget to **rinse your mouth** with salt water.]

mumuhu buzzing, humming sound of insects, flies.
mumule speechless, silent, sullen.
mumulu to swarm, as bees, mosquitoes, flies.
mu'o 1. leaf bud. 2. to bud like a tree or bush. [*Ua
    mu'o a lau a ulu.* (The plant) **budded** and leafed
    and grew. (common line
    in creation chants)]

mu'umu'u 1. loose gown.
    [*'Ane'ane e 'ōkupe 'o
    Nāpua i kona **mu'umu'u**
    lō'ihi.* Nāpua almost
    tripped on her long, **loose
    gown**.] 2. amputee. 3. cut
    off, amputated.

mu'umu'u

na 1. for, by, belong to. [***Na** kēlā makuahine kēiā pēpē uē.* This crying baby **belongs to** that mother.] [*He makana kēia **na** ko kāna ipo hoaaloha.* This is a present **for** her sweetheart's friend.]

nā 1. calm, pacified, assuaged. [*Ua **nā** ka pēpē uē.* The crying baby was **pacified**.] (*ho'onā* = to relieve pain, soothe, quiet) [*Hiki ke **ho'onā** 'ia ko'u po'o 'eha, e ke kahu ma'i?* Can my headache pain be **relieved**, nurse?] 2. plural for "the." (*ka hua moa* = the egg; *nā hua moa* = the eggs)

na'au 1. intestines, bowels. 2. mind, center of emotions, or "heart." [*'Eha kou **na'au** i ka 'eha a ke aloha, 'a'ole anei?* Your **heart** is sore due to the pain of love, isn't that so?] (*na'au 'ino* = malicious, malevolent; syn. *loko 'ino*) (*na'au kūhili* = blundering, careless, thoughtless)

na'auao learned, educated, enlightened. (*ho'ona'auao* = to educate, instruct)

na'au'auā 1. intense grief, great anguish. 2. to mourn. 3. grieving. [*Lohe 'o Ka'iulani i nā leo **na'au'auā** o ko Hawai'i.* Ka'iulani heard the **grieving** voices of Hawai'i's people.]

na'aukake sausage.

na'aupō ignorant, unenlightened, uneducated.

nae 1. shortness of breath. 2. fine mesh (of fishing net). [*He 'upena **nae**, 'a'ohe i'a hei 'ole.* (*'ōlelo no'eau*) It's a **fine mesh** net, there is no fish that isn't caught (*fig.* a good-looking person attractive to everyone).] 3. fragrant.

na'e 1. easterly, eastern, windward. [*'Aia 'o Hālawa ma **na'e** o Moloka'i.* Hālawa is on the **eastern**

side of Molokaʻi.] 2. but, furthermore, yet, however (often used in phrase *akā nō naʻe*).
[*Nāwaliwali kona kino; **akā nō naʻe**, ikaika kona manaʻo.* His body is weak; **however**, his mind is strong.]

naele 1. rock, crevice. 2. full of holes, crevices. 3. stretched out of shape.

nahā 1. cracked, broken. 2. loss of virginity. (*hoʻonahā* = to smash, crack, split)

nahae 1. to tear. 2. torn, rent (*fig.* torn with emotion).

nahele forest, grove, wilderness. [*Me ka ua hāliʻi i ka **nahele**. And the rain spread through the **forest**. (song, "Wehiwehi ʻOe," by S. Kalama)]

nāhelehele weeds, undergrowth.

nahenahe soft, sweet voice or music. [***Nahenahe** ko Kaʻahuanu Lake mā hīmeni ʻana.* Kaʻahuanu Lake folks' singing is **soft and sweet**.]

Nāhiku Big Dipper constellation (*lit.* the seven).

nāhili blundering, confused, perplexed. (*hoʻonāhili* = to cause to blunder, procrastinate, waste time through blundering)

nahoa 1. bold, defiant, daring. 2. intense headache. (*poʻo nahoa* = fractured skull)

nahu 1. to bite, to sting like driving rain. 2. pain of childbirth. [***Nahu** anei kēia ʻano naonao?* Does this type of ant **bite**?]

naʻi 1. to conquer, strive, obtain. (*ka naʻi aupuni* = the conqueror) 2. to endeavor to understand.

naiʻa porpoise, dolphin.

naio a native tree scented like sandalwood, called false sandalwood.

naiʻa

naka to quiver, shake like Jell-o, with fear or cold, crack open (earth)

nakeke rattling, rustling.

nāki'i to tie.

nākolo rumbling, roaring (of surf or thunder), reverberating.

naku'e 1. elbowing, up and down motion. 2. to elbow.

nāku'i 1. to rumble, roar. 2. thrilled.

nakulu 1. echo, clatter. 2. to circulate (gossip, rumor). 3. dripping (liquid), rumbling of stomach.

nalala dinosaur.

nalo 1. housefly. [*Hili 'o Lei i ka **nalo** i loko o ka lumi kuke. Lei hits **flies** in the kitchen. (song, "Nalo," by J. Lum Ho)] 2. lost, vanished, forgotten, concealed.

nalo

nalomeli honeybee.

nalowale 1. to disappear. [*Ua **nalowale** kā ka mea 'ohi kālā 'eke kālā.* The cashier's wallet **disappeared**.] 2. lost, gone. Note: One doesn't "lose" an item in Hawaiian; it simply "disappears" without reference to who lost it.

nalu 1. wave, surf. [*Po'i koke ka **nalu** ma Pōka'ī.* The **waves** break fast at Pōka'ī.] (*nalu miki* = receding wave) 2. to ponder, mull over, speculate. [***Nalu** ke akeakamai e pili ana no ka UFO.* The scientist **speculates** about UFOs.] (*'ale* = ocean swell which, unlike waves, doesn't break)

nalu

nalukai 1. weather-worn. 2. old person who has weathered the storms of life.

nalunalu rough seas with high waves.

namu 1. gibberish, unintelligible mumbling. 2. to speak any foreign language, especially English. [*Mai* **namu** *haole!* Don't **speak English!**]

namunamu to grumble, complain. [***Namunamu*** *mai nā limahana āu.* Your employees **complain.**]

nana to come to life, spread.

Nana name of month in Hawaiian calendar during season of new growth, approximately mid-March to mid-April.

nāna It is she/he who, She/he is the one who... [***Nāna*** *e hōlua, na kāna wahine e he'e nalu.* **He is the one who** goes sledding, his wife is the one who goes surfing.]

nānā to look at, watch, observe, see, care for, inspect. (*nānā pono* = to note carefully, pay particular attention to)

nānahu charcoal.

nanahuki 1. to pull away from. 2. contrary, disdainful.

nānākuli to look at, but not respond when spoken to. (*lit.* deaf looking).

nānā maka to look without helping.

nananana spider. (syn. *lanalana*) [*Nahu nā* ***nananana*** *ma nā naupaka i nā mū.* The **spiders** on the *naupaka* plants bite insects.]

nānā 'ole to disregard, pay no attention to.

nanau 1. to pay no attention to, as former friends. 2. unfriendly, estranged.

nane 1. riddle, puzzle, parable. [*Nanea nā 'ōlelo* ***nane.*** **Riddles** are fascinating.] 2. to riddle.

nanea enjoyable, fascinating, relaxed, at leisure. [*he* ***nanea*** *mai ho'i kau* (idiomatic phrase adding emphasis), so **relaxed** (song, "Holoholo Ka'a," by C. Kinney)]

nani 1. beauty, glory, splendor. 2. beautiful, glorious, splendid, plentiful. [***Nani*** *ka hana no'eau o ke au kahiko.* The crafts of the old time were **splendid.**] [*ka* ***nani*** *a'o Waiakea,* the **beauty** of

Waiakea (song, "Hilo Ē" by M. Heanu)] (*hoʻonani* = to glorify, praise, to beautify) [***Hoʻonani** ka makua mau.* **Glorify** the everlasting father. (opening phrase of the Hawaiian doxology)]

nao 1. ripple, grain, groove. 2. to thrust hands into opening, as in fishing. 3. rippled, grooved.

naonao ants. [*Na nā **naonao** e hāpai aʻe nei i nā huna laiki.* It is the **ants** that are carrying the pieces of rice.]

napa 1. delay, procrastination. 2. uneven, crooked. 3. springy, elastic.

nape 1. to rise and fall as the chest does in breathing. [***Nape** nā nalu kai.* The ocean waves **rise and fall**.] 2. bending and swaying, as coconut fronds do.

napele 1. soft, overripe like fruit. 2. bruised, wounded in spirit.

napoʻo 1. cavity, hollow, depression. 2. to sink down, set of sun. (*ka napoʻo ʻana o ka lā* = sunset) [*Ma Ala Moana mākou i nānā ai i **ka napoʻo ʻana o ka lā**.* It was at Ala Moana that we watched the **sunset**.]

naonao

napoʻo

nau to chew, munch. (***naunau*** = to munch one's words, speak indistinctly)

nāu yours, belonging to you. [***Nāu** kēia lāpaki?* Is this rabbit **yours**?] [***Nāu** e hele, naʻu e noho.* (ʻōlelo noʻeau) **You are the one who** will go, I am the one who will stay.]

na'u mine, belonging to me. [***Na'u** kēnā pepa.* That paper next to you is **mine.**]

naue to move, shake, tremble. [*E **naue** kākou!* Let's **move** it! Let's go.] [*Ku'i ka hekili,* **naue** *ka honua.* Lightning flashes, the earth **shakes.** (common line in chants, sometimes used to symbolize birth pains)]

nāukiuki impatient, irritable, cross. (*ho'onāukiuki* = to cause irritation, provoke, annoy) [*Inā* **ho'onāukiuki** *'oe i kou kaikua'ana, e 'ike ana 'oe i ka hopena.* If you **provoke** your older brother (sister) you will see what happens.]

nāulu 1. sudden shower of rain. 2. to rain suddenly, as a rain squall. 3. showery, irritated by being teased or nagged. [***Nāulu** 'o ia i kona kaikaina.* He is **irritated** at his younger brother's nagging.] (*he ua nāulu* = sudden rain shower)

naunau to munch one's words, speak indistinctly.

naupaka native plant found at the beach, in the mountains.

nāwaliwali 1. weakness, feebleness. 2. weak, feeble, infirm.

nē to fret, nag for something. [*'A'ohe mea **nē** 'ole.* (*'ōlelo no'eau*) There is nothing that isn't **fretted about** (a cranky child or old person).]

ne'e to move a little, step along, squirm. (*ne'e i hope* = to move back, retreat; *ne'e i mua* = to advance, go forward, progress) (*ne'ene'e* = to snuggle) (*ho'one'e* = to move goods, household furniture) [*Pono ko'u hoahānau e **ho'one'e** hale ma ka hopenapule.* My cousin has to **move house** on the weekend.]

ne'epapa to move as a whole, work in unison. [***Ne'epapa** nā helu ma luna o ka 'āina.* The rays (of the sun) are **moving** over the land. (chant, "Mele Noi Na'auao")]

nehe to rustle, as pebbles in sea. [*me ke kai **nehe** i*

ka ‘ili‘ili, with the sea **rustling** the pebbles (song,
"Ku‘u ipo I Ka He‘e Pu‘e One," probably by
Likelike)]

nehinei yesterday. [*‘O **nehinei** ka lā āna i kelepona
aku ai i ka ipo hou āna.* **Yesterday** was the day
he phoned his new sweetheart.]

nei 1. indistinct sound. 2. to rumble, like the movement of the earth in an earthquake. 3. here. [*Ua
nei ka honua.* The earth **moved, rumbled.**]
(Hawai‘i *nei* = here in Hawai‘i)

nele lacking, destitute, needy, poor. [***Nele** ka po‘e
‘ilihune i ke kāko‘o a me ka ho‘ona‘auao.* **Poor**
people lack support and education.]

nema criticizing, critical.

nemanema to belittle, criticize. [***Nemanema** ke ‘ano
o kekahi kanaka.* Some people's nature is to be
critical.]

nemonemo smooth, smoothly polished.

nēnē 1. Hawaiian goose.
[*‘Ano laka nā **nēnē** i
ho‘oku‘u ‘ia.* The
Hawaiian geese that have
been released are sort of
tame.] 2. to chirp, croak,
whimper (like a sleeping
baby). 3. to cherish.

nēnē

neo 1. empty, bare, desolat-
ed. 2. nothing. (*ho‘oneo* =
devastate)

nepunepu plump, full and
round in flesh, bulging.
[***Nepunepu** ko ka wahine
hāpai ‘ōpū.* The pregnant
lady's stomach is **bulging.**]

newa war club, cudgel, stone
inserted in end of war
club.

newa

newe plump, as a pregnant woman; billowy, as a cloud.

nia 1. smooth, round, bald. (*po'o nia* = bald head) 2. calm sea.

ni'a 1. malicious gossip or accusation. 2. slanderous.

niau to move smoothly, swiftly, silently. [*Holo* **niau** *nā wa'a pe'a*. Sailing canoes **move swiftly**.]

nī'au coconut leaf midrib. (*pūlumi nī'au* = broom made of coconut midrib) [*Na ke kahu hale e pūlumi nei i ke kū'ono i ka* **pūlumi nī'au**. It is the caretaker who is sweeping the corner with the **coconut midrib broom**.]

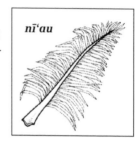

nī'au

nī'aupi'o highest *ali'i* rank, such as that of Nāhi'ena'ena and her brother Kauikeaouli (Kamehameha III); these chiefs were considered to be living gods.

nīele too inquisitive, nosy.

nihi 1. edge, brink, rim, border. 2. stealthily, quietly. 3. to creep silently, stealthily. [*Kaulana wale ka ua a'o Hanalei, ke* **nihi** *a'e nei i nā pali*. The rain of Hanalei is very well known, it's **creeping** along the cliffs. (song, "Ka Ua Loku," by A. Alohikea)]

nihinihi fastidious, overly dainty, strict.

niho tooth, teeth. (*niho 'elepani* = ivory, elephant tooth; *niho hu'i* = toothache; *niho ku'i* = false teeth; *niho 'ole* = toothless; *niho palaoa* = whale tooth, whale tooth pendant, symbol of royalty; *niho peku* = new tooth; *niho pu'u* = buck teeth)

Nihoa 1. island between Kaua'i and Midway. 2. toothed, notched, jagged. 3. firmly embedded, as stones in a fence.

nihoniho serrated, jagged.

ni'i salt-encrusted.

Ni'ihau privately owned
island to the southwest of
Kaua'i where Hawaiian is
the primary language.

nīnau 1. question. 2. to question, interrogate. (*noi* = to
ask a favor)

ninini to pour liquid.

niniu 1. dizziness. 2. dizzy.

nīoi pepper. (*kai nīoi* = chili pepper water)

niolopua handsome. (*niolo* = upright, stately)

Niolopua god of sleep.

nipo 1. to yearn for, be in love with. 2. drowsy, sleepy.

niu 1. coconut. [*i ka 'olu o ka
niu, i ka poli o ke
onaona,* cool **coconut**
grove and in its meat
only sweetness. (song,
"Old Plantation," by
Montano/Nape)] 2. spin-
ning, dizzy.

niuhi man-eating shark.

no for, of, from. [*He inoa no
ka lani Liholiho.* This is a
name chant **for** the chief Liholiho.]

nō an intensifying particle, with various English
translations, including very, indeed, truly, really,
and so on. [*Pōloli nō nā pōpoki keiki.* The kittens
are **very** hungry.]

noa freed from *kapu.* (*'āmama ua noa!* = it's **free**, the
prayer flies off! [ending of traditional prayers])
[*Ua kapu kēlā wahi akā i kēia manawa ua noa.*
That place was forbidden but now it's **free from
restriction**.]

noe 1. mist, spray of rain, fog. 2. misty. (syn. *uhiwai*).

no'eau skilled, clever, skilled with the hands. (*'ōlelo
no'eau* = wise saying of traditional wisdom)

noenoe 1. foggy, misty. 2. foggy feeling due to drinking too much. [*Ke* **noenoe** *mai nei.* It's getting **misty** (that drunken feeling is coming on). (line in songs)]

nohea 1. fine appearance. 2. handsome, good looking. [**Nohea** *kaʻu kāne!* My husband is **handsome!**]

noho 1. seat, chair, bench. 2. to stay or live someplace. [*Aia i hea ʻoe e* **noho** *nei? Ke* **noho** *nei au i Hakipuʻu.* Where are you **living**? I'm **living** in Hakipuʻu (*ahupuaʻa* near Kualoa, Oʻahu).] (*noho aliʻi* = throne, reign) [*I ka* **noho** *aliʻi o Liholiho, ua ʻaʻe ʻia ka ʻaikapu.* In the **reign** of Liholiho, the eating *kapu* was broken.] (*noho huila* = wheelchair) (*noho lio* = saddle) (*noho loa* = to remain long, permanently) (*noho pono* = behaving well) (*hoʻonohonoho* = to edit, file, classify) (*hoʻono-*

noho

noho lio

honoho helu = calculate) [*Hiki paha iā ʻolua ke* **hoʻonohonoho helu** *i ka heluna o ka uku no ke kālai ʻana i ka noho paipai koa?* Can you two perhaps **calculate** the total of the cost for carving (making) the *koa* rocking chair?]

nohona dwelling, residence, life-style. [*Nui nā kapu o ka* **nohona** *kahiko.* The ancient **life-style** had lots of rules (taboos).]

noi 1. favor, request. [*He* **noi** *kaʻu iā ʻoe.* I have a **favor** to ask of you.] 2. to ask favor, request. [*Ke*

noi *nei ka 'ōpio i kona mau mākua e 'ae mai iā ia e kalaiwa i ke ka'a.* The young person is **asking** his parents to allow him to drive the car.]

noi'i to seek knowledge, research, investigate. [*Noi'i mau 'o Ka'imiloa i ka 'ike no ka ho'oulu pōhue.* Ka'imiloa is always **investigating** how to grow gourds.]

noio Hawaiian sea bird, tern.

no ka mea because. [*No ke aha 'oukou i ho'ohenehene ai i kā 'oukou pōki'i? No ka mea, ua nuku mai 'o ia ala iā mākou.* Why did you all tease your baby sister? **Because** she (over there) scolded us.]

noke to persist, continue, persevere, push forward. [*Hoaka e ka lani, noke noke, e Pele e Pele ē.* The sky is shining, Pele (fire goddess) is **pushing forward**. (song, "Aia Lā 'o Pele," traditional chant, Loebenstein)]

no ke aha (phrase) why. [*No ke aha i ha'i mai ai 'o Pi'ilani i kēlā?* **Why** did Pi'ilani tell me that?]

nokule numb. [*Nokule ko Meleana lima 'ākau i ke kikokiko 'ana ma ka lolouila.* Meleana's right arm is **numb** due to typing on the computer.] (syn. *ma'e'ele*)

no laila therefore, so. [*A no laila, e Kahulumealani, he aha ka hopena o kāu noi i ka ho'opi'i 'ana i ka uku?* And **so**, Kahulumealani, what was the result of your request for a raise?] [*He piwa ko kāna hiapo, no laila, ua ho'i lākou.* His (her) eldest child has a fever; **therefore**, they (three or more) went home.]

nolupē graceful, bending, swaying, drenched. [*nolupē i ka ua,* **drenched** in rain]

nome to munch, nibble continuously, as a horse grazes. [*Nome a'ela 'o Pele iā Puna.* Pele then **munches** on Puna (covering the land with lava). (song, "Aia Lā 'o Pele," by traditional chant,

Loebenstein)] (*nomenome* = to mouth words
without speaking)

nona his, hers, indicating object possessed belongs to
him or her. [*'O wai ke kanaka* **nona** *kēia pālule
aloha?* Who is the person this aloha shirt **belongs
to?**] [*No wai kēia hale?* **Nona** *ka hale.* Whose
house is this? The house is **hers/his.**]

noni important medicinal plant.

nonō 1. snore. 2. to snore. [*Inā* **nonō** *kāu kāne, e
ho'āla 'oe iā ia.* If your husband **snores**, wake
him up.] (syn. *nonolo*)

no'ono'o 1. thought, reflection, meditation. 2. to
think, reflect. [*Ke* **no'ono'o** *iho au i ku'u wā
kamali'i, kupu a'ela nā haili aloha i o nā hulu
kūpuna.* Whenever I **think** about my childhood,
beloved memories spring up of the precious
grandparents.] (syn. *mana'o*) (*no'ono'o 'ole* =
thoughtless, without thinking) (*no'ono'o ulu wale*
= imagination)

nou 1. to throw, hurl, pitch. 2. you (1), yours, for
you, belonging to you. [**Nou** *ka lei onaona.* The
sweet-smelling *lei* is for **you.**]

no'u 1. to eat greedily. 2. short, plump. 3. mine, for
me, for you, belonging to you.

nowelo 1. seeking knowledge, searching. 2. to delve,
seek for knowledge.

Nowemapa (from English) November.

nōweo bright, shiny.

nū 1. to cough, roar, groan. 2. mentally agitated,
grieving. (*ho'onū* = to moan, hum)

nu'a 1. thick, piled up, as ocean swells or multitudes
of people. 2. thickly. [**Nu'a** *ka lehua 'au i ke kai.*
The people swimming in the sea **pile up** thickly.
(song, "Kaleleonālani," by Nu'uanu)] (*nu'anu'a* =
soft and fleshy)

nuha sulky. [**Nuha** *kāna keiki kāne i ka nuku 'ia.* His
son is **sulky** because of being scolded.]

nūhou 1. news. [*Ua lohe anei ʻoukou i ka **nūhou**?* Did you all hear the **news**? Note: *Anei* in a question demands a yes or no answer.] 2. new. [*He aha ka **nūhou**?* What's **new**?]

nui 1. quantity, size. [*Pehea ka **nui** o kou lakeke? He waena anei?* What's the **size** of your jacket? Is it a medium?] 2. big, large, great, important. [*He kanaka **nui** ʻo Jesse Kuhaulua.* Jesse Kuhaulua is a **big** man.]

nuku 1. beak, snout, tip. 2. to scold, grumble.

nukuwai mouth of stream. (syn. *muliwai*)

nūnē to speculate, wonder. [***Nūnē** pinepine kākou e pili ana i ke ea.* We all frequently **speculate** about sovereignty.]

nūnū 1. pigeon. 2. cooing.

nunulu to snarl like a dog or warble like a bird; reverberate.

nuʻu 1. height, high place. (Nuʻuanu = cool heights) (Nuʻuhiwa = Marquesas) 2. second platform of oracle tower.

o 1. of, belonging to. [*ʻO kēia kāne ke kupuna **o** kāna kaikoʻeke wahine.* This man is the grandfather **of** his sister-in-law.] 2. or, lest. [*Mai mumule **o** nuku mai ʻo ʻAnakē.* Don't be sullen **or** Aunty will scold you.]

ʻo [particle marking subject, identification sentence pattern] [*Nani **ʻo** Nālei.* Nālei is beautiful.] [***ʻO** wai kou inoa?* What's your name?]

ʻō 1. fork, spear, pin, anything used to pierce. 2. to spear, pierce, vaccinate. [*ʻO ke **ʻō** ʻana i ka iʻa ka mea hoʻomakaʻu i nā keiki āna.* **Spearing** fish is what makes his children scared.]

ʻō

ʻōʻā mixed (nationality, colors in *lei*). [*He koko **ʻōʻā** ko ka hapanui o ko Hawaiʻi poʻe.* The majority of Hawaiʻi's people are of **mixed** blood.]

ʻōahi 1. rocket. [*E pahū ana paha kēlā **ʻōahi**?* Will that **rocket** possibly explode?] 2. clump of burning lava.

Oʻahu

Oʻahu most populated island, located between Kauaʻi and Molokaʻi (*lit.* the gathering place).

ʻoama fish, young stage of *weke*.

oe 1. buzzing, rustling, murmuring sounds of nature, insects. [*ka pūpū kani oe,* the shell that **sounds** (Hawaiian tree snail, which was believed to sing)] 2. a prolonged sound, as chanting. 3. to buzz, rustle, murmur.

'oe you (1). [*Ma'i anei 'oe, e ka haku?* Are **you** sick, boss?]

'o'e 1. to prod, jab, gore. [*'O'e ke kukū o ka wana i ka wāwae o ke kama'āina.* The local person's foot was **jabbed** by the sea urchin's spine.] 2. jagged, spiked.

'oeha'a 1. to waddle, walk awkwardly. [*'Oeha'a ko ka 'elemakule hele wāwae 'ana.* The old man **walks awkwardly**.] 2. crooked, distorted, deformed.

oeoe 1. whistle, siren. 2. prolonged (sound) or elongated (object). (*ho'ōeoe* = to prolong sound, toll bell, yodel high) [*Ua* **ho'ōeoe** *'ia ka pele hale pule ma ka lā nui.* The church bell was **tolled** on the holiday.]

oha 1. spreading vines. 2. greeting. 3. to grow with affection, love, to greet. (*ohaoha/'oha'oha* = affection, greeting)

'ohā taro offshoot growing from root.

'ohāhā flourishing, fully developed, healthy.

'ōhai monkeypod tree.

'ohana family, relatives. (*hui 'ohana* = family reunion) [*E pa'i ki'i ana mākou i kā mākou* **'ohana** *ma ka hui* **'ohana**. We (not including person being spoken to) will take pictures of our **family** at the **family reunion**.]

'ohana

ohaoha (also *'oha'oha*) affection, greeting (from

oha, delight). [*He* **ohaoha** *kūpono ke oli kāhea.* A calling chant is an appropriate **greeting**.]

'ohe all kinds of bamboo. (*'ohe hano ihu* = nose flute) (*'ohe kāpala* = carved bamboo piece used for printing *kapa*, to print *kapa*) (*'ohe nānā* = spyglass, telescope) (*'ohe ho'onui 'ike* = microscope)

'ohe kāpala

'ōhea drowsy after big meal (*fig.* weak, ineffective).

'ōhelo native shrub with reddish berries, a symbol of Pele. (*'ōhelo papa* = strawberry)

'ōhelo

'ohi to collect money, to gather harvest. [*Aia 'o Wini e* **'ohi** *limu nei ma Kuli'ou'ou.* Wini is **gathering** seaweed at Kuli'ou'ou.] (syn. *hō'ili*)

'ōhi'a lehua native tree common in mountain areas, with red blossom, symbol of Pele and island of Hawai'i. (*'ōhi'a mamo* = same tree with yellow blossoms, symbol for native Hawaiians [*'ōhi'a* blossoms range from white to orange]) (*'ōhi'a 'ai* = mountain apple) (*'ōhi'a lomi* = tomato)

'ōhi'a lehua

'ōhiki 1. sand crab. 2. to probe, pry, pick out, pick teeth, nose. [**'Ōhiki** *nā kauka niho i ko lākou mau niho pono'ī.* The dentists **pick** their own teeth.]

'ōhinu 1. roast, grease. 2. shiny, greasy. [**'*Ōhinu** ka
'i'o pua'a. Pork is **greasy**.]

oho 1. hair of head, leaves of plant. 2. to call out, cry
out. (*ho'ōho* = to cheer)

ohohia 1. enthusiasm. 2. enthusiastic, delighted.
[**Ohohia** *nā alaka'i hula.* The hula leaders are
enthusiastic.]

'ohu 1. mist, fog, vapor. 2. adorned with mist or *lei*
(often reduplicated). [**'Ohu'ohu** *'o Haleakalā.*
Haleakalā is adorned with **mist**.]

'ōhua 1. retainers, servants, passenger. 2. young fish
such as *hīnālea, manini.* (*ka'a 'ōhua* = bus)

'ōhule 1. bald person, bald. 2. defeated without getting any score.

'ōhumu 1. plot, conspiracy. 2. to grumble, complain,
conspire. [*Ua* **'ōhumu** *pū nā pūkaua e ho'ouka iā
Kīwala'ō.* The war leaders **plotted** to attack
Kīwala'ō.]

oi to move, turn away in contempt.

'oi 1. sharpness. 2. sharp, pointed, superior, best.
[*Maui nō ka* **'oi**. Maui indeed is the **best**.] [*Ke
aloha kai* **'oi** *a'e.* Love is the **best** of all the rest.
(song, "'Ekolu Mea Nui," by R. Nāwāhine)] (*'oi
aku* = greater than [used for comparison]) [**'Oi
aku** *ka uluwehi o Waimanu ma mua o Kalihi.*
The verdant beauty of Waimanu is **greater than**
Kalihi's.]

'o ia she, he. [*'Ano ma'i kāu kāne a 'a'aka* **'o ia**.
Your husband is kind of sick and **he**'s grouchy.]
Note: *Ia* is the correct form for the objective case.
[*Kōkua ke kelamoku iā* **ia**. The sailor helps **her**.]
Ia is also used for "it" or "that." [*He mea hūnā
ia. It*'s a secret.]

'oiai 1. while. [**'Oiai** *'o ia e ho'oikaika kino ana, ua
pōā 'ia kona ka'a.* **While** he was exercising, his
car was burglarized.] 2. although. 3. meanwhile,
during.

'oia'i'o 1. truth. 2. truly, firmly. (*hō'oia'i'o* = to verify, confirm; syn. *hō'oia*) [*Inā 'imi 'o Nani i kona laikini kalaiwa mokukaikala, pono 'o ia e hō'oia'i'o i kona lā hānau.* If Nani is seeking her motorcycle operator's license, she has to **verify** her birthdate.]

'o ia mau nō (idiomatic phrase) same as always (response to *Pehea 'oe?* How are you?).

'oihana occupation, trade, profession, job, business, career. (*'oihana ho'ona'auao* = educational system, education department) (*'oihana kālā* = finance) (*'oihana kiu* = secret service) (*ka hui 'oihana* = business, corporation)

'ō'ili 1. emotions, heart. 2. to appear, come into view. (*'ō'ili lua* = prominent, conspicuous) (*'ō'ili wale* = to appear for no reason)

'oio (also *hō'oio*) 1. to show off. 2. conceited.

'oi'oi 1. a superior person. 2. full of sharp points, thorns. 3. superior.

'ōiwi native person. (syn. *kanaka maoli, kupa*)

oka 1. dregs, crumbs, sediment, small bits. 2. (from English) to order goods from catalog or food, etc.

'ōka'a 1. to revolve, spin, to roll as mat, top. [*'Ōka'a ka honua a puni ka lā.* The earth **revolves** around the sun.] 2. syn. for *pōka'a*, rolled bundle, as in *'ōka'a lauhala*, roll of pandanus leaves.

'ōkaikai rough (like the ocean), angry, bad tempered.

'Okakopa (from English) October.

'ōkalakala 1. goose bumps, chicken skin, creepy sensation. 2. coarse, rough (texture like sandpaper or rude behavior).

oki to stop, finish. [*Uoki!* **Stop** that!]

'oki to cut, sever, separate. (*'oki 'ino* = to mutilate; *'oki male* = divorce, to divorce; *'oki mau'u* = to cut grass; *'oki'oki* = to cut into pieces; *'oki poepoe* = to circumcise, circumcision; *'oki pu'u* = forest clearing) 'okika (from English) orchid.

'oko'a 1. different, entire. ['**Oko'a** ka 'ōlelo a nā kānaka Ni'ihau. The speech of Ni'ihau people is **different**.] 2. wholly. (kū'oko'a = independence, freedom, liberty, independent, free) (kula kū'oko'a = private school) (holo'oko'a = entire) [E hana ana ko'u makua kāne ma ka hopenapule **holo'oko'a**. My father will work the **entire** weekend.] (hō'oko'a = to separate, distinguish)

'ōkole anus, buttocks. Note: 'Ēlemu is the more polite term for rear end, buttocks.

'ōkolehao liquor from tī plant root.

'ōkoleoioi to turn your back on someone who has angered you, to scorn.

'ōku'eku'e knuckles.

'ōkuma rough, coarse, pimply. ['**Ōkuma** kona maka i ka huehue. His face is **rough** due to pimples.]

'ōkupe to stumble, go astray morally. ['A'ole e '**ōkupe** ana ka po'e 'onipa'a. Steadfast people will not **go astray**.]

'ōku'u 1. to crouch down, squat down. 2. Hawaiian slang, equivalent to "kick back," or relax. [Ma ka wā ho'omaha 'o ia e '**ōku'u** wale ai ma ka hale. It is during vacation that she/he should really "kick back" at home.] 3. to settle, as a mist.

ola 1. life, health, well being, livelihood, salvation. 2. alive, living, healthy, cured (of illness). [He pēpē **ola** kā kēlā makuahine. That mother has a **healthy** baby.] [Ua **ola** ko 'Enoka kunu. 'Enoka's cough was **cured**.] 3. to live, thrive, heal. (ola honua = earthly life) (ola hou = to revive, resuscitate, resurrected) (ola kino = health) (ola mau = immortal) (ho'ōla = salvation, to save, heal, cure, spare, give life to) [E **ho'ōla** lāhui. **Give life to** the Hawaiian race. (Kalākaua's motto)]

ōla'i 1. earthquake. ['**Ōlapa** ka uila, ku'i ka hekili, nei ke **ōla'i**. Lightning flashes, thunder roars, the earthquake rumbles. (common lines in birth and name chants)] 2. to rumble or quake, as in an earthquake.

ʻōlala to bask in the sun. [**ʻŌlala** *kēlā wahi pōpoki keiki āu i ka lā.* That dear little kitten of yours **basks in the sun.**]

ʻōlapa 1. dancer. 2. native tree. 3. to flash (lightning). 4. to dance hula.

ʻole 1. zero, nothing. (*mea ʻole* = nothing) [*He* **mea ʻole** *kēia.* It's **nothing** (you're welcome).] 2. without, lacking, not. (*niho ʻole* = without teeth) (*ʻole wale* = not at all; *ʻole loa* = not at all, not in the least) [*He mea hoihoi* **ʻole loa** *ke kolepa iaʻu.* Golf is **not in the least** interesting to me.] (*hōʻole* = refusal, denial, negative, to deny, contradict, refuse) [**Hōʻole** *nā mākua i kā lākou mau keiki e pāʻani i nā kahua pāʻani i ka pō.* Parents **forbid** their children to play in the playgrounds after dark.]

ʻOle nights of Hawaiian month, considered unlucky or unproductive.

ʻōlelo 1. language, speech, word. 2. to speak, say, tell. (*ʻōlelo aʻo* = counsel, advice, instruction) (*ʻōlelo haole* = English; syn. *ʻōlelo Pelekane*) (*ʻōlelo Hawaiʻi* = Hawaiian language) (*ʻōlelo hōʻike* = affidavit, testimony) (*ʻōlelo hōʻino* = curse, defamation, to curse, defame) (*ʻōlelo hoʻohiki* = oath, vow, promise; syn. *ʻōlelo paʻa*) (*ʻōlelo hoʻoholo* = jury verdict, judgment, decision) (*ʻōlelo hoʻomākeʻaka* = joke) (*ʻōlelo hoʻoweliweli* = threat, to threaten) (*ʻōlelo hou* = say it again) (*ʻōlelo kuhikuhi* = instructions, directions) (*ʻōlelo makuahine* = mother tongue) [*ʻO ka* **ʻōlelo makuahine** *ka* **ʻōlelo** *e mālama ai.* Our **mother tongue** is the **language** we have to preserve.] (*ʻōlelo nane* = riddle, parable) (*ʻōlelo noʻeau* = wise saying, proverb) (*ʻōlelo paʻi ʻai* = pidgin English, *lit.* hard taro speech)

'ōlena turmeric, plant used for dye, medicine.

'ōlepe 1. a shell used for hat *lei*. 2. to open and shut, like window blinds. 3. to upset, overturn. 4. to peel off, like shingles in a gale.

oli 1. chant. 2. to chant. [*Oli mau kēia mau 'ōlapa i ke oli komo.* These dancers always **chant** the entrance **chant**.]

'oli 1. joy, happiness. 2. happy, joyful. 3. to rejoice. [**'Oli ē! 'Oli ē! Rejoice! Rejoice!** (song, "Hawai'i Aloha," by L. Lyons)]

'ōlinolino 1. brightness. 2. bright, sparkling. Many other words, including *'ālohilohi* and *mālamalama*, have similar meanings.

olo 1. to rub back and forth, saw. 2. to resound, long sound. 3. to grate. (*pahiolo* = saw) (*pahiolo uila* = electric saw)

'olo 1. gourd used for water or *'awa*. 2. double chin, sagging chin. 3. to sag, hang down. 4. pendulous, hanging down.

'olohaka 1. emptiness, desolation. [*Kani ka ipu i ka 'olohaka o loko.* (*'ōlelo no'eau*) The gourd sounds due to the **emptiness** within (an empty-headed person).] 2. empty, hollow.

'olohani 1. to strike, mutiny, riot. 2. to cause a strike or mutiny. (*hō'olohani* = to cause a strike)

'ōlohe 1. bare, naked, bald. 2. destitute, needy. [**'Ōlohe** *nā 'ohana pōloli.* The hungry families are **destitute**.] 3. skilled, especially in *lua* fighting.

'olohewa demented, deranged, delirious.

'ololā broad (used in refrain in *Kumulipo* creation chant to refer to female fertility).

'ololī narrow (used in refrain in *Kumulipo* creation chant to refer to male fertility).

olonā 1. shrub from which strong cordage was made. 2. linen. 3. muscle, ligament. [*'Eha wale kona mau olonā 'ā'ī ma muli o ka ulia ka'a.* Her neck **muscles** were painful due to the car accident.]

'olopū 1. blister. [*Nui kona mau* **'olopū** *a me pohole i nā kāma'a puti hou.* She has lots of **blisters** and bruises due to her new boots.] 2. inflated, puffed out, as a sail.

'olu cool, refreshing, soft, supple.

'olua you two. [*'Ono* **'olua** *i ka i'a maka, e ka wahine a me ke kāne?* Are **you two** craving raw fish, lady and gentleman?]

'oluea ease, mental relaxation.

'olu'olu 1. good natured, kind. 2. comfortable, pleasant. 3. "please." [*E* **'olu'olu***, e kelepona i ke kauka holoholona no ka mea, ma'i ka'u pua'a.* **Please** phone the vet because my pig is sick.]

'oma stove, oven, baking pan. (*'oma wiki* = microwave)

'ōma'ima'i chronic illness.

'ōmalumalu cloudy, overcast. [*'**Ōmalumalu** kēia lā.* Today is **cloudy**.]

'ōma'oma'o green color, green plants.

'ōmilo to twist, turn, drill, curl.

'oma

omo 1. to suck. 2. sucking. (*mea omo* = drinking straw) [*Pa'a ka* **mea omo** *i kēnā mau poke hau i kāu kī'aha.* The **straw** is stuck in those (by you) ice cubes in your glass.]

'ōmole 1. bottle. [*Ke omo nei kā Mehana pēpē i kāna* **'ōmole** *wai hua 'ai.* Mehana's baby is sucking his juice **bottle**.] 2. bare, smooth, hairless.

'ōmou to fasten, pin on (corsage, jewelry).

ona 1. infatuated, attracted. 2. his/her, of him, of her.

'ōmole

[*'Ōmou ke kamali'i wahine i nā mekala i ka lole makalike o ka me'e **ona**.* The princess pinned the medals on the uniform of the **infatuated** hero./**her** hero.]

'ona 1. (from English) owner. (*'ona miliona* = millionaire) [*He **'ona miliona** ka ho'okele 'oihana o ka panakō?* Is the bank CEO a **millionaire**?] 2. drunk, intoxicated. [*Pākea ka maka o ke kelamoku **'ona**.* The **intoxicated** sailor's face is ashen.]

onaona softly fragrant, alluring, attractive, lovely.

'ona'ona intoxicated, dizzy.

one 1. sand. 2. sandy. [*He papahele **one** ko ka hale i kūkulu 'ia ma ka 'ae kai.* The house that was built on the sea shore has a **sandy** floor.] (*one hānau* = *lit.* birth sands, a poetic name for birthplace) [*'O Kaupō ko Tūtū Lani **one hānau**.* Kaupō is Tūtū Lani's **birthplace**.]

'oni 1. movement, motion. 2. to move, stir, shift, fidget. [*E **'oni** kou kino.* **Move** your body.]

'ōni'o spotted, streaked with colors. [***'Ōni'o** ke kapa hou.* The new tapa is **streaked with color**.]

'onipa'a steadfast, resolute.

'ono 1. flavor, deliciousness. 2. to crave food, taste. [***'Ono** kou mau hoahānau i ka poke a me ke pola poi.* Your cousins **crave** poke (cubed raw fish mixed with seaweed, onions, and other condiments) and a bowl of poi.] [*Pehea ka **'ono** o ka i'a?* What does the fish **taste** like?] 3. delicious, tasty.

'ōnohi eyeball, center. (*ka **'ōnohi** o ka lā* = the **eyeball** [center] of the sun [*fig.* a favorite person])

o'o mature (fruit, person). [*He kanaka **o'o** ko ke kaikamahine kaikua'ana.* The girl's older sister is a **mature** person.] (*o'o 'ole* = immature)

'o'ō to crow (rooster). [***'O'ō** ka moa kuakahi a holo nā menehune 'ekolu.* The first cock **crowed** and the three *menehune* ran away. (traditional song, "Nā Menehune 'Ekolu")]

'**ō'ō** 1. digging stick. 2. native bird, recently extinct.
   3. to pierce, poke, insert. 4. to abort.

'**o'ole'a** 1. hardness, strength (*fig.* strenuous, rigid,
   severe, obstinate). 2. rigid, stiff, strong, tough.
   ['***O'ole'a*** *ke kino ona.* Her body is **tough.**]

'**o'olokū** 1. fury, rage. 2. boisterous, stormy.

'**o'opa** 1. to limp. 2. lame, crippled.

'**o'opu** goby, general name for a type of native fish
   found in streams, considered to be a delicacy and
   known for its ability to
   climb rocks using a sucker
   on its belly; includes
   '*o'opu nākea,* known for
   its delicious taste.

'*o'opu*

'**ōpae** general name for
   shrimp. ('*ōpae 'ula* = red
   shrimp found in anchia-
   line ponds such as those
   on the Kona coast, used
   for bait or food)

'**ōpaha** dented, flattened on
   one side.

'**ōpaka** prism, to cut as a
   prism, often with eight
   sides.

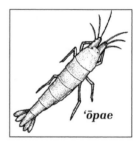

'*ōpae*

'**ōpakapaka** fish prized for
   delicious taste, blue
   snapper.

'**ōpala** trash, garbage, litter.
   (*kalaka halihali 'ōpala* =
   garbage truck) (*kini
   'ōpala* = garbage can)
   (*ho'ōpala* = to litter,
   make garbage)

'**ope** 1. bundle, package. 2. to
   tie in bundle. ('*ope'ope* =
   bundles, to fold [clothes])

'*ōpala*

'ōpe'ape'a Hawaiian bat.

'ōpe'ape'a

'ope'ope 1. bundles. 2. to fold (clothes).

'opi 1. to fold. 2. creased, wrinkled. [*'Opi paha nā pālule i ka paiki?* Are the shirts in the satchel **wrinkled**?]

'opihi limpet, shellfish considered a great delicacy. (*ku'i 'opihi* = to pick *'opihi*)

'ōpikipiki anxiety, mental disturbance.

'ōpio youth, juvenile. [*E hau'oli e nā 'ōpio o Hawai'i nei.* Be happy, **youth** of Hawai'i. (song, "Hawai'i Aloha," by L. Lyons)]

'ōpiopio young, immature, unripe. [*'Ano 'ōpiopio nā ho'okele hou.* The new navigators are a little **immature**.]

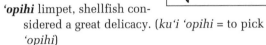

'ōpiopio

ōpū 1. clump of fruit, sugarcane, grass. [*'O ko'u ōpū weuweu lā, nou ia.* My little **clump of grass** (grass house), it is yours. (common line in welcoming chants)] 2. to open, grow.

'ōpū 1. stomach, bladder. 2. disposition.

'ōpua puffy clouds on horizon, a bank of clouds (often used symbolically). [*Kona kai 'ōpua,* (*'ōlelo no'eau*) Kona of the billowy clouds]

'ōpulepule moronic, somewhat crazy.

'ōpu'u a bud, child. [*Ua kupu a lau a mu'o a 'ōpu'u.* (It, plant) sprouted and leafed and formed **buds**. (line frequently used in creation, name chants)]

ou your, belonging to you. (both *ke ola ou* and *kou ola* = your life)

o'u mine, belonging to me. (both *ka 'āina 'ōiwi o'u*
and *ko'u 'āina 'ōiwi* = my native land)

'ō'ū 1. endangered native bird of the honeycreeper
family. 2. to pinch off, as a bud.

'ōuli sign, omen, symptom. [*'O ke ao pouli ka* **'ōuli**
kūpono. The dark clouds are the appropriate
omen.]

'ōwili 1. roll of paper, cloth, skein, coil. 2. to roll up,
coil, to fold arms. [*Ua* **'ōwili** *'ia nā lauhala i
pōka'a.* The *hala* leaves were **rolled up** into a
bundle.]

pā 1. fence, wall, enclosure, house lot. (*pā hale* = house lot, yard) (*pā kaula hao* = chain-link fence) 2. dish, plate. (*pā holoi* = dishpan or basin) (*pā halihali* = tray) (*pā pepa* = paper plate) (*pā mea ‘ai* = plate lunch) 3. to shine (sun), to blow (wind). [*E ka makani e, e* ***pā*** *mai me ke aheahe.* Oh wind, **blow** gently. (song, "Moloka‘i Nui a Hina," by M. Kāne)] 4. prefix to number.

pā mea ‘ai

(*pākahi* = by ones, individually) (*pākolu* = by threes) [*E kama‘ilio* ***pahā*** *ana ‘oukou i kēia pō‘alima a‘e.* You all will converse **by fours** (in groups of four) next Friday.] (*ho‘opā* = to touch, influence)

pa‘a 1. firm, solid, completed, permanent, stuck. [***Pa‘a*** *ka hale holoi lole.* The Laundromat is **completed** (finished being built).] 2. pair. (*pa‘a male* = married couple) 3. memorized, learned in subject. (*pa‘a mo‘olelo* = versed in lore, legends, history) (*pa‘a iwi* = skeleton) (*pa‘a poepoe* = globe, sphere; syn. *poepoe honua*) (*pa‘a lole* = suit of clothes) Note: *Pa‘a* has many other meanings. (*ho‘opa‘a* = hula drummer and chanter, to make fast, firm, to learn, study, hold) [*Le‘a ka hula i ka* ***ho‘opa‘a****.* (*‘ōlelo no‘eau*) The hula is fun due to the **chanter** (*fig.* all details are important).] [*E* ***ho‘opa‘a*** *i ko kou kaikaina lima, e ke* *kaikamahine.* **Hold** your younger sister's hand, girl.] (*ho'opa'a ha'awina* = to do homework) (*ho'opa'a hau* = to freeze) (*ho'opa'a leo* = to record voice) (*ho'opa'a na'au* = to memorize) (*ho'opa'a wikiō* = to make a video)

pa'ahana busy, industrious, hard working. [**Pa'ahana** *kāua i kēia hopenapule a'e?* Are we (you and I) **busy** next weekend?] (*mea pa'ahana* = tool) [*He mea pa'ahana waiwai ke kui kala.* The screwdriver is a valuable **tool**.]

pa'ahao 1. prisoner, convict. 2. to be imprisoned. [*Ko'u noho mihi 'ana a* **pa'ahao** *'ia.* I live in sorrow **imprisoned**. (hymn, "Queen's Prayer," by Lili'uokalani)] (*hale pa'ahao* = jail, prison) (*ho'opa'ahao* = to take prisoner)

pa'a'ili solid. (*pa'a'iliono* = cube)

pa'akai salt. (*pela pa'akai* = salt bed, still used on Kaua'i for collecting sea salt)

pela pa'akai

pa'akikī hard, tough, inflexible.

pa'akūkū to clot, jell.

pā'ani 1. game, sport, amusement. 2. to play game, sport. [**Pā'ani** *ke kime pōhīna'i i 'elima* **pā'ani** *o ka pule.* The basketball team **plays** five **games** a week.]

pa'apa'a dispute, argument. (*ho'opa'apa'a* = to argue, dispute) [**Ho'opa'apa'a** *mau ke keiki maha'oi.* The overly aggressive child always **argues**.]

pa'apa'a'ina to snap, crackle. [**Pa'apa'a'ina** *ka pele 'a'ā hou ke puapua'i 'ia.* New *'a'ā* lava **crackles** when it is spewed out.]

pa'apa'anā to ease pain, to soothe. [**Pa'apa'anā** *'o 'Anakē i ko kāna kāne kua 'eha i ka lomilomi.*

Aunty **soothes** her husband's sore back with
lomilomi.]

pa'apū crowded, congested with people, stuffy,
dense with clouds. (syn. *piha ku'i*) [**Pa'apū** *ke
kikowaena kū'ai 'o Ala Moana me ka po'e
māka'ika'i Kepanī*. Ala Moana Shopping Center
is **crowded** with Japanese tourists.]

pae 1. cluster, row, group. (*pae 'āina* = archipelago)
(*pae niho* = row of teeth) (*ho'opae* = to build an
embankment, row; to land, come ashore) 2. to
catch a wave, to disembark. [*'A'ole i* **pae** *ka wa'a
i ka nalu*. The canoe didn't **catch the wave.**]

pā'ē'ē here and there, everywhere but right place.
(*kuhi pā'ē'ē* = to misdirect, mislead, give inaccu-
rate information)

pā'ele 1. African American, Negro. [*I kēlā kenekulia
aku nei, ua kapa 'ia* **nā Pā'ele** *mua i Hawai'i he
"haole."* In the last century, the first **African
Americans** in Hawai'i were called "haole" (foreigner).] 2. black, dark.

paepae 1. pavement, house platform, prop, support.
(*paepae puka* = threshold) (*paepae pukaaniani* =
window sill) 2. to hold up, support. 3. rows,
aligned in a row. [*He* **paepae** *moku, he lalani
moku*. A **row** of islands, a line of islands (familiar line in voyaging chants)]

pa'ewa misshapen, crooked, imperfect, incorrect.

pā'ewa'ewa biased, partial, unfair.

pāha'oha'o mysterious, incomprehensible.

pahe'e 1. to slip, slide. 2. slippery, smooth. [*He pakika, he* **pahe'e** *ke momoni aku*. It's **smooth** when
you swallow. (song, "Niu Haohao," by B.
Mossman)]

pahi knife, flint. (*pahi kaua* = sword) (*pahi-olo* = saw)

pāhili to blow strongly (wind), to lash (storm).
(*makani pāhili* = hurricane) [*He* **makani pāhili**
'ino 'o 'Iniki. 'Iniki was a bad **hurricane.**]

pahiolo saw. (*pahiolo uila* = electric saw)

pāhoa short dagger, sign of *kapu.*

pāhoehoe 1. smooth, unbroken type of lava (contrast to *ʻaʻā*). 2. satin. [*He mau uhi pela* **pāhoehoe** *kā ka wahine nona kēia hōkele.* The woman who owns this hotel has **satin** sheets.]

pahu 1. box, drum, trunk, barrel, stake, pole. [*Hinuhinu wale ka* **pahu** *kamani.* The *kamani* wood **box** is shiny.] (*pahu heiau* = temple drum) (*pahu hula* = hula drum) (*pahuhope* = goal, goal post) (*pahu kupapaʻu* = coffin) (*pahu leka* = mailbox) (*pahu paʻi kiʻi* = camera) (*pahu ʻume* = dresser drawer, buffet) 2. to push, shove (*fig.* to hurt feelings of others). (*pahu kuʻi* = hypodermic injection, to be injected)

pahū to explode, burst. (*kūlina pahūpahū* = popcorn)

pahu hau ice box (refrigerator).

pahulu 1. nightmare, ghost. 2. worn-out soil. [*Hiki ke mahi ʻia ka ʻuala i ka lepo* **pahulu**. Sweet potatoes can be farmed on the **worn-out soil**.] 3. haunted, unlucky.

pai 1. to encourage, urge, stir up. [*Pono kākou e* **pai** *kekahi i kekahi e ʻōlelo Hawaiʻi.* We have to **urge** each other to speak Hawaiian.] 2. to praise, lift up.

paʻi 1. to slap, clap, print, stamp. [*Na ke aupuni Hawaiʻi i* **paʻi** *i ke kālā a me ke poʻoleka.* The Hawaiian kingdom was the one that **printed** money and stamps.] (*paʻi hewa* = typo, misprint) (*paʻi kiʻi* = to snap pictures with camera, take photograph) [*Ke* **paʻi kiʻi** *ʻia nei koʻu hoaaloha no kāna kāleka kākī.* My friend is being **photographed** now for her charge card.] (*paʻi puke* = to print book, publish) (*paʻi umauma* = to slap chest, in expressing grief or dancing) 2. tie, equal score. (*paʻi a paʻi* = tied score in game, sports, contest) *paia* wall, side of house.

pa'ihi clear (weather), cloudless, neat, well dressed. [*Pa'ihi kona 'ohana ma ka hale pule.* His family is **well dressed** at church.]

paikau to march, drill, parade.

paiki suitcase, satchel, bag. [*paiki, pū'olo pa'a i ka lima,* suitcase, bag held firmly in the hand (song, "Lā 'Elima," composed by the family of Diane 'Aki to commemorate a destructive tidal wave at Miloli'i, a fishing village near South Point, Hawai'i island)]

paiki

paikikala (from English) bicycle.

pā ilina cemetery.

paila (from English) 1. pile, heap. 2. to pile up, heap up. (*kū ka paila!* = What a lot! [*lit.* the pile stands])

pailaka (from English) pilot. [*Ma Līhu'e i pae ai ka pailaka hou.* The new **pilot** landed at Līhu'e.]

pailani 1. to spoil. 2. spoiled. [*'O kā kēlā makua kāne keiki kāne ke keu o nā keiki pailani!* That father's son is the worst of the **spoiled** boys!]

pailua 1. to cause nausea, vomiting. 2. nauseating, abominable. (*ho'opailua* = gross, disgusting) [*Auē ka ho'opailua o ka wai haumia o ke Ala Wai!* Gosh how **gross** the polluted water of the Ala Wai is!]

pa'imalau Portuguese man-of-war. [*E hamohamo i ke one ma kahi 'eha i ka pa'imalau.* Rub sand on the spot that's sore due to the **Portuguese man-of-war**.]

pā'ina 1. meal, dinner, party. [*Aia kō lāua pā'ina piha 'umi makahiki o ka male 'ana ma ka hale* '*aina o Teshima ma Kona.* Their tenth wedding anniversary **party** is at Teshima's restaurant in Kona.] 2. to eat a meal, to have a party. [*Ua* **pā'ina** *'oe i kēia lā?* Have you **eaten** today?] (*pā'ina lā hānau* = birthday party) (*pā'ina male* = wedding feast)

paio to quarrel, argue, fight. (*hoa paio* = opponent, enemy)

paipai 1. to encourage, urge on. 2. to lobby. 3. to rock. (*ho'opaipai* = promotion, agitator, to promote, lobby) (*noho paipai* = rocking chair)

pa'ipa'i 1. applause. 2. to applaud, clap. [*E* **pa'ipa'i** *lima!* **Clap** your hands!]

Paipala (from English) Bible. [*'O ke Kauoha Hou ka māhele o ka* **Paipala** *a ke kahu e heluhelu nei.* The New Testament is the section of the **Bible** that the minister is reading now.]

paipu (from English) pipe, faucet. [*Nui ke kūkaehao ma nā* **paipu** *o ka hale.* There's lots of rust in the **pipes** of the house.]

paka 1. raindrops. (syn. *pakapaka ua*) 2. to strain out dregs. 3. to criticize constructively, teach. [*E* **paka** *ana ke kumu i kā kāna mau haumāna mau ha'i 'ōlelo.* The teacher will **constructively criticize** his student's speeches.] 4. tobacco, cigarette. (*puhi paka* = to smoke a cigarette)

pāka (from English) park. [*'A'ole hiki iā ia ke puhi paka me ka holo pū i ka* **pāka**. He can't smoke a cigarette and run in the **park** at the same time.]

pākaha 1. robbery, raid. 2. to cheat, plunder, rob.

pakalaki 1. (from English) bad luck. 2. to dole out little by little.

pakalana fragrant *lei* flower, one of many scented flowers brought to Hawai'i by Chinese immigrants.

pākali (from English) battery.

pakapaka many, numerous. [***Pakapaka** nā pinao na*

ka loko wai. There are **many** dragonflies at the pond.]

pākaukau table, desk, counter, booth. [*E hāli‘i ‘ia ana ka hāli‘i pākaukau ma luna o ka **pākaukau**. The tablecloth will be spread out on top of the **table**.]

Pākē 1. China. 2. Chinese. [*‘Ono loa nā ‘ano mea ‘ai **Pākē** like ‘ole.* All kinds of **Chinese** food are really delicious.]

pākeke (from English) bucket, pocket.

pakele to escape. [*Na wai nō ‘oe e **pakele** aku?* Who can **escape** you? (line in songs describing an attractive person)] (*ho‘opakele* = to rescue, save) [*Ua **ho‘opakele** ‘ia nā kānaka i hā‘ule i loko o ka lua pele.* The people who fell into the crater were **rescued**.]

pakeneka (from English) percent.

pakī to splash, spatter, squirt. (*ka ‘auwai pakī* = water ditch that barely runs)

pāki‘i flattened.

pākīkē rude, sarcastic.

pākōlī musical scale (transliteration of do re mi).

pakū to burst out.

pākū 1. curtain, screen, veil. [*E huki i ka **pākū** ‘au‘au a pa‘a ke ‘au‘au ‘oe.* Pull the shower **curtain** closed when you take a shower. 2. shield, defense.

pāku‘i 1. to add on, splice, join. [*Ma ka ‘uapo ‘o ia e **pāku‘i** ai i ke kaula i ka ‘upena.* It is on the wharf that she should **splice** the rope to the net.] 2. prefix, suffix, affix.

pala 1. smear, daub of excrement used in insults such as *pala naio*, *pala kūkae*. (*palahe‘a* = stained, smeared) 2. a native fern. 3. ripe, mellow. (*palahū* = overripe, rotten; *palakū* = ripe to perfection)

pala‘ai pumpkin, squash. (syn. *pū* = general term for pumpkin)

pālaha wide, broad, spread out. (*pālahalaha* = widespread, flat, epidemic) (*hina pālaha* = to fall sprawling)

palahē 1. fragile, easily torn. 2. overcooked to point of falling apart.

palahū rotten, overripe.

palai 1. native fern, used as offering to Laka, the hula goddess; also general name for ferns. (syn *palapalai*) 2. to turn face away in embarrassment or confusion. [*Iā ia e komo ai i ke keʻena,* **palai** *ke kākau ʻōlelo.* When he enters the office, the secretary **turns away in confusion.**]

palaʻie children's game with loop and ball made from coconut midribs and tapa.

palaka (from English) 1. block print cotton cloth originally worn on sugar plantations. 2. block. [*Aia ka hale kūʻai hou ma kēia* **palaka** *aʻe.* The new store is in this next **block.**]

palaki (from English) 1. brush. 2. to brush. [*Mai poina e* **palaki** *i kou mau niho ma hope o ka ʻai ʻana.* Don't forget to **brush** your teeth after eating.] (*palaki lauoho* = hairbrush) (*palaki niho* = toothbrush)

palalē to speak indistinctly or with an accent.

pālama sacred enclosure especially for royal women.

Palani (from English) 1. Frank, Francis. 2. French. (*ʻāina Palani* = France)

palaoa 1. sperm whale, ivory. (*lei niho palaoa* = whale tooth pendant braided with human hair, worn by high chiefs) 2. flour, bread, wheat. [*Maloʻo ka pāpaʻa* **palaoa** *ma ke kanuwika āu?* Is the slice of **bread** in your sandwich stale?]

palapala document of any kind, writing of any kind, deed, manuscript, policy, etc. (*palapala ʻaelike* = written contract) (*palapala ʻāina* = map) (*palapala hānau* = birth certificate) (*palapala hoʻāpono* =

passport) (*palapala ho'oilina* = will, testament;
syn. *palapala kauoha*) (*palapala ho'okuleana* =
copyright, patent) (*palapala 'inikua* = insurance
policy) (*palapala kū'ai* = deed or bill of sale)
(*palapala male* = marriage license) (*palapala noi* =
application form, petition)

palapalai fern used by hula dancers; also a general
name for ferns.

palapū wound, flesh injury.

palau 1. engaged, betrothed. [*E lilo ana lāua i pa'a
palau ma ka Lā Aloha.* They two will become an
engaged couple on Valentine's Day.] 2. plow.

pālau 1. to exaggerate, tell tales. 2. war club.

palaualelo lazy, idle person who talks a lot. [*Auē nā
palaualelo ma ke kīwī.* Gosh, the **lazy windbags**
on TV.]

pale 1. to ward off, thrust aside, fend off. (*pale ka'a*
= car bumper) (*pale makani* = windshield)
(*ho'opale* = to defend; syn. *kūpale*) [*'O Nahoa
kae ho'opale aku.i ke kauka i ka 'aha
ho'okolokolo.* Nahoa is the one who may **defend**
the doctor in court.] 2. to ignore a law or command. [*Pale aku 'o Mehana i ka pāpā 'ana i ka
puhi paka.* Mehana **ignores** the smoking prohibition.] (*pale ma'i* = underpants) (*pale waiū* = bra)

palekana 1. safety, security. [*Pono ka 'ohana e
no'ono'o i ka palekana.* The family should think
about **safety**.] 2. safe, rescued, convalescent.

paleki (from English) brake. (syn. *peleki*)

palena boundary, limit, border, margin. [*'O
Waimea ka palena o ka moku 'o Ko'olauloa.*
Waimea is the **boundary** of the Ko'olauloa land
division.] (*kau palena* = to place a limit, set a
deadline, limitation, deadline) [*'O ka lā hope o
ka mahina ke kau palena no nā palapala noi
'oihana.* The last day of the month is the **deadline** for the job applications.]

palena ʻole without limits, without boundaries. [*ʻO ke aloha* **palena ʻole** *ke aloha ʻohana.* Family love is unconditional love, love **without limit**.]

pāleuleu old, worn out (refers to material, clothing, mats). [***Pāleuleu*** *ka lole o kēnā kanaka ʻilihune.* That poor person's clothes are **worn out**.]

pali cliff, precipice, steep hill (*fig.* difficulty, obstacle). [*Pehea oe? Maikaʻi wau i ke alo* **pali**. How are you? I'm fine in spite of **difficulties**. (Aunty Malia Craver)] (*pali kū* = 1. vertical cliff. 2. beginning of a genealogical line [Malo])

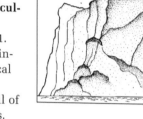

pali

palipali precipitous, full of cliffs and small hills.

pāloka (from English) ballot. (*koho pāloka* = election, to vote) [*Mai poina e* **koho pāloka** *no ke keʻena o kiaʻāina.* Don't forget to **vote** for the office of governor.]

palolo glib gossiping.

pālolo clay, mortar.

palu 1. to lick, lap. 2. relish made from fish head, stomach.

pālua 1. dual. 2. by twos. (*makani pālua* = wind blowing in several directions at once)

pālule (from English) shirt. (*pālule aloha* = aloha shirt) [*Waiwai nā* **pālule** **aloha** *kahiko.* Old **aloha shirts** are valuable.]

pālule aloha

pālulu shield, screen, protection from elements of any kind.

pāluna (from English) balloon.

palupalu soft, fragile, limber, flexible. [*He mau wāwae* **palupalu** *ko ka paniolo.* The cowboy has **flexible** legs.]

pāmalō 1. dry, rainless. 2. expressionless, dull. [**Pāmalō** *paha ka papa 'epekema, 'a'ole paha?* Is science class **dull** or not?]

pana 1. pulse, heartbeat. 2. beat in music. [*'Āwīwī ka* **pana** *mele o ke mele o ke au hou.* The **beat** of the music of modern times is fast.] Note: *Ka mele* is used to indicate a song, *ke mele* for music in general. 3. bow and arrow. (*pua pana* = arrow)(*wahi pana* = legendary places, celebrated places)

pāna'i reciprocity, reward, revenge.

panakō (from English) bank.

panalā'au colony, dependency. [*He* **panalā'au** *'o Kilipaki ma lalo o Kalākaua.* Kiribati was a **colony** under Kalākaua.]

pānānā compass, pilot.

pana pua archery.

pane 1. answer, reply. 2. to answer, reply, speak. (*pane 'ole* = unresponsive)

pane'e 1. delay, postponement. (*ho'opane'e* = to postpone) [*Pono kāua e* **ho'opane'e** *i kā kāua hālāwai a hiki i kēia mahina a'e.* We (you and I) have to **postpone** our meeting until next month.] (*uku pane'e* = interest on principal in banking, finance) 2. to push, move along. [*Ke* **pane'e** *aku nei ke kalaiwa ka'a i ke ka'a poloke i ke kapa alanui.* The driver is **pushing** the broken car over to the side of the road.]

pani 1. to close, cut, substitute. (*pani hakahaka* = substitute, replacement, to substitute, fill a vacancy, replace) 2. closure of medical treatment with food offering. 3. lid, cover, stopper, door.

panina end, conclusion.

pānini prickly pear cactus.

paniolo 1. cowboy. 2. Spain, Spaniard. 3. Spanish.
[*ka **paniolo** pipi me ka pipi ʻāhiu,* the **cowboys**
with the wild cattle
(song, "Huʻi ē," by L.
Kekuewa)] Note: This
word is derived from
espaniolo (which means
"Spanish"), for the
Mexican cowboys
brought to Waimea,
Hawaiʻi, to teach
Hawaiians how to handle
wild cattle.

paniolo

pano dark, as clouds (*fig.* unapproachable, outside
the ordinary).

panoa 1. desert. 2. arid, dry. [*He ʻāina **panoa** ko
Kaʻū.* Kaʻū has a **dry** land (desert).] 3. dry coral
bank at low tide.

panopano deep darkness.

paoa 1. strong-smelling, either good or bad smell. 2.
unlucky, bad luck.

paokeʻe to betray, to slander; traitor.

paona (from English) pound, weight, scale. (*hāpai
paona* = lift weights) (*kau paona* = to weigh
something)

papa 1. foundation, stratum, flat surface. (*papahele* =
floor, level) [*Aia nā pono hale ma ka **papahele**
hea?* What **floor** are the
home furnishings on?]
(*papahele ʻekolu* = third
floor) (*papa ʻāiana* =
ironing board) (*papa
ʻeleʻele* = blackboard)
(*papa hana* = work
method, plan, strategy)
(*papa heʻe nalu* = surf-
board) (*papa kuhikuhi* =

*papa
heʻe
nalu*

index, table of contents)
(*papa kuhikuhi mea ʻai* =
menu) (*papa kuʻi ʻai* =
poi- pounding board)
(*papa lāʻau* = board,
plank) (*papa ola* = board
of health) 2. class, rank.

papa kuʻi ʻai

[*E like me kā lākou mau
keiki, he* **papa** *ʻōlelo
Hawaiʻi kā mākua.* Like their children, the parents have a Hawaiian language **class**.] 3. flat, level. 4. in unison, all together. (*neʻepapa* = to move as a whole, in unison)

pāpā to forbid, prohibit. [*Ua* **pāpā** *ʻia ka puhi paka ma ka mokulele.* Smoking is **prohibited** in airplanes.]

pāpaʻa 1. cooked crisp, burned. [*ʻOno ka ʻili puaʻa* **pāpaʻa**! **Burnt** pork skin is delicious!] (*pāpaʻa lā* = sunburned) 2. slice of bread. 3. scab of sore.

pāpaʻaʻina crackle, snap.

pāpaʻi 1. general name for crabs. 2. temporary shelter.

pāpaʻi

pāpale hat. [*ʻO ka* **pāpale** *lauhala ke ʻano o kā Momi* **pāpale** *punahele. lauhala* **hats** are Momi's favorite kind of **hat**.]

pāpālina cheeks.

papau deeply engaged in activity, absorbed, engrossed. [**Papau** *ʻo Palani i ka pāʻani lolouila.* Palani is **absorbed** in the computer game.]

pāpaʻu shallow. [**Pāpaʻu** *ke kai ma ke kāheka.* The ocean water in the tidepool is **shallow**.]

pāpū 1. fort, fortress. 2. plain, clear space. 3. clear, unobstructed, in plain sight.

pau ended, destroyed, finished. [*Ua* **pau** *ko kāna mo'opuna wahine hale i ke kai e'e.* His granddaughter's house was **destroyed** in the tidal wave.] (*pau hana* = end of work) (*pau 'ole* = unceasing, constant, forever) (*ho'opau* = to finish, cancel, waste) [*Aia a* **ho'opau** *'olua i ka ho'oma'ema'e hale, hiki iā 'olua ke puka i waho.* As soon as you two **finish** cleaning house, you can go outside.] (*ho'opau manawa* = waste time) [*Mai* **ho'opau manawa.** Don't **waste time.**] (*nā mea a pau* = everyone, everything) [*Pōmaika'i* **nā mea a pau.** **Everything** is blessed. (hymn, "'Ekolu Mea Nui," by R. Nāwāhine)]

pa'ū damp, moist. (syn. *ma'ū*)

pā'ū 1. woman's skirt, made of tapa cloth in ancient days; these days often refers to a hula skirt (*pā'ū hula*). 2. outer garment worn by female horseback riders to protect fine clothes underneath, first used on Hawai'i island in 1800s.

pau ahi destroyed by fire.

pa'u hana tedious, constant work.

pa'uhia overcome by sleep, overwhelmed by desire, overtaken by evil, calamity.

pauka (from English) powder, paste. (*pauka niho* = toothpaste)

paukū 1. verse of Bible or song, section, piece, paragraph. 2. to make *lei* with sections of different colors.

pauka niho

paulele 1. faith, confidence, trust. [*He* **paulele** *ikaika kona i ko ke kahunapule mana'o.* She/he has strong **confidence** in the minister's opinion.] 2. to lean on, rely on.

paumauno'ono'o keepsake, memento, souvenir.

pā'umi to count by tens.

paupauaho (also *pauaho*) out of breath, breathless (*fig.* discouraged, faint-hearted, exhausted, despairing). [*Ma hope o ka hula 'ana i ka hula kahiko,* **paupauaho** *nā 'ōlapa.* After dancing ancient-style hula, the dancers are **out of breath**.]

pawa darkness just before dawn. [*Moku ka* **pawa** *o ke ao.* The **darkness** has been broken by the dawn. (common line in chants)]

pāwalu to count by eights.

pāwehe 1. generic name for geometric designs found in mats from Ni'ihau and Kaua'i. 2. to make such designs.

pē 1. crushed, flattened, humble. 2. perfumed, drenched. [*pulu* **pē** *i ka ua,* **drenched** in rain (*fig.* sexual reference). (common line in love songs)]

pea (from English) bear, pear (avocado).

pe'a 1. cross. (syn. *ke'a*) 2. sail of canoe. 3. boundary. 4. to menstruate. 5. menstruating. (*hale pe'a* = house where women stayed during menstruation)

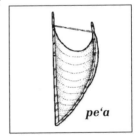

pe'a

pe'ahi 1. fan. 2. to fan, wave. (*pe'ahi lima* = to wave hand, beckon to) [*E* **pe'ahi** *lima aku iā 'Anakala!* **Wave** to Uncle!]

pe'ape'a 1. starfish. 2. entangled, crossing.

pe'e to hide oneself. (*ho'ohūnā* = to hide something)

pehea how, what, how about it? [**Pehea** *ka pa'a 'oki male hou? Hau'oli lāua?* **How** is the newly divorced couple? Are they happy?] (*pehea kou mana'o?* = what's your opinion?) (*pehea lāua?* = how are they [two]?)

pehu 1. to swell (*fig.* conceited). 2. swollen, swelling, distended. (*kai pehu* = swelling sea) (*makapehu* = hungry)

peki (from English) to pace, trudge along, to back up car. (*holopeki* = to trot [horse], jog)

peku 1. kick. 2. to kick. [*Ke* **peku** *'ia nei ka lio e ka mea holo lio.* The horse is being **kicked** by the rider.] (*pōpeku* = football, soccer)

pela (from English) mattress, bale, pail, to spell. (*pela pa'akai* = salt flats, still used on Kaua'i to make salt from sea water)

pēlā like that (what I've just told you). [*Pēlā 'olua e hana ai.* **That**'s how you (two) should do it.] [*Mai hana* **pēlā***!* Don't do **that**!] (*pēlā paha* = maybe) (*a pēlā aku* = etc., and so on)

pelapela filthy, nasty, obscene. (*'ōlelo pelapela* = swearing) [*E kala mai i kā ka'u ipo* **'ōlelo pelapela***.* I apologize for my sweetheart's **swearing**.]

pele 1. lava, volcano, eruption. [*Hū mai ka pele mai ka lua pele 'o 'Ō'ō.* The **lava** erupts from the *'Ō'ō* crater. 2. (from English) bell. [*Kanikani* **pele***, kanikani* **pele***, kani ma 'ō ma 'ane'i.* Jingle **bells**, jingle **bells**, jingle all over the place.]

pele

Pele name of fire goddess.

Pelekane 1. (from English) Britain, England. (*ka 'ōlelo* Pelekane = English; syn. *ka 'ōlelo haole*)

peleki (from English) 1. brake. 2. to apply brakes.

pelekunu bad smelling, musty. [*No ke aha i kapa 'ia ai ke awāwa nani ma Moloka'i 'o* **Pelekunu***?* Why is the beautiful valley on Moloka'i called **Pelekunu**?]

pelu to fold, turn over, bend. (*ho'opelu* = to tuck, hem, fold over)

pena (from English) 1. paint. 2. to paint. (*pena kiʻi* = to paint pictures)

peni (from English) pen, pencil.

penikala (from English) pencil.

pepa (from English) paper, card. (*hainakā pepa* = facial tissue) (*nūpepa* = newspaper) (*pepa hēleu* = toilet paper) (*pepa mānoanoa* = cardboard) (*pepa pipili* = sticker) (*pepa poʻoleka* = post card) (*pepa wahī* = wrapping paper) (*pāʻani pepa* = to play cards)

pēpē 1. baby. 2. flat, squatty.

pepehi to beat, strike, kill. [*Mai **pepehi** i kāu lio!* Don't **beat** your horse!] (*pepehi a make loa* = beaten until dead, beaten to death)

pepeiao 1. ear. 2. to hear. (*lohe pepeiao* = hearsay)

Pepeluali (from English) February.

pewa tail of fish, shrimp, lobster.

pī 1. stingy, frugal. [*ʻO ka ʻawaʻawa ka hopena o ke **pī**.* Bitterness is the consequence of being **stingy**.] 2. to sprinkle on water with the fingers.

pia arrowroot plant, beer.

pī ʻā pā alphabet. (*hua palapala* = letter of alphabet)

piapia white discharge from eyes after sleeping. (*maka piapia* = eye with discharge [insult: one who doesn't see what one should])

piha 1. full, filled (liquid), complete. 2. full-blooded, one hundred percent pure (nationality). [*He Hawaiʻi **piha** ko Kaipo kupuna kāne.* Kaipo's grandfather is a **full-blooded** Hawaiian.] (*piha kuʻi* = jam packed, crowded to limits; syn. *pihaʻū*) (*piha makahiki* = yearly anniversary) (*piha pono* = completely full, complete)

pihapiha 1. gills of fish. 2. full, complete. (*hoʻopihapiha* = to fill out any form) [*E **hoʻopihapiha** i ka palapala noi.* **Fill out** the application form.]

pihe din of voices, shouting, lamentation.

pihi 1. scab, scar. 2. button, badge. [*ʻAkahi nō ʻo ia i *kaomi i ke* **pihi** *i mea e hoʻopio ai i ka mīkini hoʻomaloʻo lole.* He just pressed the **button** to turn off the clothes dryer.]

pīhoihoi excited, worried, disturbed.

piholo to sink, drown, be swamped (canoe filled with ocean water). [*ʻOiai e* **piholo** *ai ka mea heʻe nalu, ʻaʻole makaʻu ke kiaʻi ola.* While the surfer may **sink**, the lifeguard isn't afraid.]

piʻi 1. to climb up, go up, go inland. 2. to rise up (emotions). (*piʻi ka wela* = anger rises up; to get a fever) (*piʻi ke kai* = *lit.* the sea rises, poetic phrase indicating that anger rises up) (*piʻi kuahiwi* = to hike) (*hoʻopiʻi* = lawsuit, court case, to sue) [*E* **hoʻopiʻi** *ana nā ʻōiwi i ke aupuni.* The natives will **sue** the government.]

piʻikoi to claim honors or rank not rightfully yours, to rise above your station. [*Mai* **piʻikoi** *ʻoe i ke akule la.* Don't **try (to rise beyond your station)** for *akule* fish. (song, "He ʻOno," by B. Mossman)]

piʻina climb, ascent. [*Kūnihi ka* **piʻina** *i ka ʻikena i loko o ka lua pele kahiko.* The **climb** up to the view inside the old crater is steep.]

piʻipiʻi 1. curly, wavy. 2. bubbling up. [**Piʻipiʻi** *ko koʻu kupuna wahine lauoho.* My grandmother's hair is **curly**.]

pī kai to sprinkle with salt water in order to purify.

pīkake (from English) jasmine flower, named for Kaʻiulani's peacocks.

Pīkī 1. Fiji. 2. Fijian. 2. PG, Provisional Government.

pikiniki (from English) picnic.

pīkake

piko 1. navel, umbilical cord (*fig.* genitals). 2. crown of head.

pīkoi core of fruit.

pila 1. any musical instrument. [*Kani ka* **pila**! Let **the instrument** sound (play music)!] 2. (from English) bill. [*Inā 'oe i uku i ka* **pila** *uila, inā ua hiki ke nānā i ke kīwī.* If you had paid the electric **bill**, then you could watch TV.] (*pila kīko'o* = bank check)

pilau 1. stench. 2. to stink. 3. rotten, spoiled.

pili 1. to stick, join, be close to. (*pili wale* = to cling for no reason) (*ho'opili* = to mimic, imitate, to bring together, stick) [*E* **ho'opili** *mai ia'u.* **Repeat after** me.] [*Iā ia e* **ho'opili** *ana i ke ki'i i ka pepa, ua pa'a kona manamana lima.* When he was **sticking** the picture to the paper, his finger got stuck.] 2. to be related. [*He* **pili** *'ohana māua 'o Nonohe.* Nonohe and I are **related**.] (*pili mua* = older relative) 3. close relationship. (*pili kāmau* = close friendship)

pilialo beloved wife (*lit.* close to the front of the body).

pilialoha close relationship, beloved companion. (*pili 'ao'ao* = mate, lover)

pilikia 1. trouble of any kind, distress, difficulty, accident. 2. troubled, bothered. [*I ka wā* **pilikia** *me ka wā hau'oli.* In times of **trouble** and in times of happiness.] (*ho'opilikia* = to cause trouble, harm)

pilikino personal, private.

pilikoko blood relationship.

pilikua 1. beloved husband (*lit.* close to the back of the body). 2. giant.

pilina association, union, meeting.

pilipa'a sticking firmly together, associating constantly.

Pilipino 1. Philippines. 2. Filipino.

piliwaiwai 1. bet, wager. 2. to bet. [*Makemake ko'u kaikaina i nā pā'ani* **piliwaiwai**. My younger sister likes **betting** games.]

pilo 1. swampy, polluted. 2. Hawaiian trees of coffee family. 3. foul odor, bad breath.

pinao dragonfly. [*He nani maoli nō ka* **pinao.** **Dragonflies** are truly beautiful.]

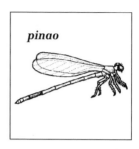

pinao

pine 1. pin, peg, bolt. 2. to pin.

pinepine often, frequent, frequently.

pio 1. captive, prisoner. (*hāʻawi pio* = to give up) 2. to peep, chirp (chicks, birds). Note: In the following example, the reduplication imitates a chirping sound. [**Pio pio** *mau mā pūnua pōloli.* The hungry fledglings **chirp** continuously. 3. extinguished (fire), turned off. (*hoʻopio* = to turn off) [*Hiki paha iā ia ke* **hoʻopio** *i ka lolouila?* Can she perhaps **turn off** the computer?]

piʻo 1. arch, arc, curve. [*He mau* **piʻo** *ko ke kahawai ma ke awāwa ʻo Waipiʻo.* The stream in Waipiʻo valley has **curves.**] 2. an *aliʻi* rank, offspring of brother and sister. 3. to arch, bend. 4. curved, bent, arched.

pipi 1. pearl oyster. [*ʻO ka* **pipi** *ma Puʻuloa ka iʻa hāmau leo.* The **pearl oyster** at Pearl Harbor is the silent-voiced fish (you must not talk when getting it, for if it hears your voice, it will hide).] 2. cattle, beef. (*ʻiʻo pipi* = beef) (*pipi kāne* = bull) (*pipi wahine* = cow)

pīpī 1. sprinkle. [**Pīpī,** *holo kaʻao.* **Sprinkled** about, the story runs on. (traditional ending to stories, giving the idea that a story will live and change in the retelling)] 2. (from English) to urinate (syn. *mimi*). (*pīpīnoke* = to talk incessantly)

pipiʻi expensive. [*He* **pipiʻi** *hoʻi kau nā hale ma Oʻahu.* Houses on Oʻahu are truly **expensive.**]

pipili sticky, tenacious. [**Pipili** *nā po'oleka.* Stamps are **sticky.**]

piwa (from English) fever. [*He* **piwa** *ko ka mea ma'i.* The sick person has a **fever.**]

pō 1. night, darkness, ancient realm from which life originated. 2. weekday. (Pō'akahi = Monday; Pō'alua = Tuesday; Pō'akolu = Wednesday; Pō'ahā = Thursday; Pō'alima = Friday; Pō'aono = Saturday; Lāpule = Sunday) The traditional lunar calendar had names for each night of the lunar month.

pōā 1. robber, thief. [*Ua* **pōā** *ka 'aihue i ka panakō i nehinei.* The **thief** robbed the bank yesterday.] 2. to rob a person or place. (The verb *pōā* implies plundering a place or location, while *'aihue* implies taking away the thing stolen.)

pō'ai 1. circle, circuit, hoop. 2. to go around, make a circuit, coil. 3. surrounded, encircled. (*pō'ai hapalua* = semi-circle) (*pō'ai lani* = horizon) (*pō'ai lō'ihi* = ellipse) (*pō'ai puni* = to circumnavigate, go completely around) (*pō'ai waena honua* = equator)

po'e 1. people, group. 2. pluralizer, used in place of *mau.* [*Nui ka* **po'e** *pōhaku pele ma ko kēlā hale pā.* There are **many** lava rocks in that house's fence.] (*ka po'e kāne* = men) (*ka po'e wahine* = women)

pō'ele'ele 1. darkness. 2. dark.

poepoe 1. globe, sphere. (*ka poepoe honua* = globe of the earth; syn. *pa'a honua*) 2. round, rounded, full (moon). [*He lei* **poepoe** *ka lei kīkā.* The cigar *lei* is a **round** *lei.*]

pohā 1. non-native edible berry. 2. to burst, crack, break forth. 3. bursting, cracking.

pōhāhā breaking forth. (syn. *hua'i*) (*pōhāhāwai* = bubble)

pōhai 1. circle, group, gathering. 2. to encircle, surround, gather in a circle. [**Pōhai** *ke aloha lā i ke* *kino*. Love **encircles** the body. (song, "Pōhai Ke Aloha," by L. Machado and M. Kealakai)]

pōhaku 1. rock, stone, mineral. 2. rocky, stony. (*pōhaku ku'i 'ai* = poi pounder) (*pōhaku lepo* = adobe, brick) (*pōhaku pele* = any lava rock)

pohala 1. to recover consciousness, revive after fainting, recover from illness. [*Ua mā'ule ka mea pena hale wela a ua **pohala** a'ela*. The hot housepainter fainted and then **revived**.] 2. rest, recreation.

pōheoheo knob, any knob-like object, rounded top of poi pounder.

pohihihi obscure, entangled, mysterious, intricate. [***Pohihihi** ka ho'okumu honua*. The creation of the earth is **obscure**.]

poho 1. hollow or palm of hand, foot, depression. [*Ua 'eha kou **poho** wāwae i kou hehi 'ana ma luna o ke kukū kiawe?* Did the **hollow** of your foot hurt when you stepped on the *kiawe* tree thorn?] 2. powder compact, match box. 3. patch on clothes. 4. chalk. (*poho mea kanu* = flower pot)

pohō 1. loss, damage. 2. out of luck, useless. [***Pohō** ka 'imi 'ana i ke kanaka ku'i 'opihi i lilo i ke kai*. (It is) **useless** to search for the *'opihi* picker who was taken by the ocean.]

poholalo underhanded, deceitful, dishonest. [***Poholalo** paha kā Kamehameha hana iā Keouakū'ahu'ula?* Was what Kamehameha did to Keouakū'ahu'ula **deceitful**?]

pohole 1. sore, bruise. 2. bruised, skinned, scraped. [***Pohole** ko ka hope po'o kumu 'ili i ka pūko'a ma ka'e kāheka*. The vice-principal's skin is **bruised** due to the coral head on the edge of the tidepool.]

pohopoho patched. (*kuiki pohopoho* = patchwork quilt)

pōhue general name for gourd plants.

pōhuehue 1. beach morning glory, used to drive fish into nets. 2. to call up surf by a ritual involving striking the sea with *pōhuehue* vine while chanting a prayer of supplication.

pōhūhū dusty, smoky.

poi food made by pounding cooked taro corm (syn. *ka 'ai*, *lit.* the food, indicating the central importance of the *kalo* plant and *poi* to the Hawaiian culture). (*ka 'ai me ka i'a* = fish and poi)

po'i 1. cover, lid, crest of breaking wave. 2. to cover, to break (wave). (*po'ina kai* = place where waves break) 3. to pounce on, catch between the hands. [**Po'i** *ka pōpoki ma luna o ka 'iole.* The cat **pounces on** the mouse.]

poina 1. to forget, forgettable. [*Mai* **poina** *e ho'ouna aku i ka'u mau leka!* Don't **forget** to mail my letters!] 2. forgotten. (*poina wale* = absentminded) (*poina ka no'ono'o* = amnesia, forgetful)

poina 'ole unforgettable. [*He lei* **poina 'ole** *ke keiki.* (*'ōlelo no'eau*) A child is an **unforgettable** *lei.*]

pō'ino 1. misfortune, ill luck, affliction, storm, disaster. 2. unfortunate. (*ho'opō'ino* = to harm, injure, cause damage)

po'ipū 1. attack, onslaught. 2. to cover over entirely with clouds, waves.

pōkā bullet, cannonball, pellet. (*pōkā pahū* = bomb, bombardment, to bomb)

pōka'a 1. ball, coil, spool of string, roll of *lauhala* leaves. 2. to wind, roll, coil.

poke 1. section, slice, piece, cubed raw fish served as appetizer. 2. to cut into cubes, sections. (*poke hau* = ice cube)

poki 1. fine stitches, mesh. 2. (*cap.*) general name for supernatural dogs.

pōki'i younger brother or sister (term of affection). [*Lahela ku'u* **pōki'i**, Lahela, my beloved younger sister (song, "Lahela Ku'u Pōki'i," by L. L. Conn)]

pōkole short. (*pōkole ka naʻau* = quick-tempered)

pola 1. flap of a *malo*, tail of a kite. 2. platform between hulls of a double canoe.

polapola 1. to get well, recover from illness. [*E **polapola** wikiwiki a e hoʻi mai i ka hana!* **Recover** quickly and come back to work!] 2. recovered from illness. (*polapola iki* = a little better) 3. (*cap.*) Tahiti (from Borabora).

poli bosom, breast. [*Ma kuʻu **poli** mai ʻoe e kuʻu ipo aloha.* Here upon my **breast** you are cherished. (song, "Ke Aloha," by L. Collins)]

Poliʻahu goddess of snow on Mauna Kea.

polikua far reaches of ocean or sky that are invisible, beyond the horizon, the "great beyond."

polinahe soft and gentle.

polo thick, plump.

polohina misty, smoky, gray (*fig.* affectionate pity, grief).

polohiwa glistening black.

poloke (from English) broken. [***Poloke** kou mopeka?* Is your moped **broken**?]

pololei correct, right, accurate, straight. [*E kalaiwa **pololei** a hiki i ka huina alanui a e huli hema ma laila.* Drive **straight** ahead up to the intersection and turn left there.] (*hoʻopololei* = to straighten, correct) [*Pono nā haumāna e **hoʻopololei** i nā pepa.* The students have to **correct** the papers.]

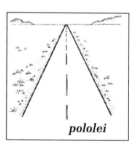

pololei

pōloli 1. hunger. 2. hungry. [***Pōloli** kā koʻu ʻohana mau hānaiāhuhu.* My family's pets are **hungry**.] (*make pōloli* = starved to death)

pololia jellyfish.

pololo talk without tact.

poluea 1. nausea, seasickness, hangover. 2. nauseated, seasick.

pōmaika'i good fortune, blessedness, prosperity. (*ho'omaika'i* = congratulations) (*ho'opōmaika'i* = to bless someone) [*Ua* **ho'opōmaika'i** *'ia ka pēpē e ke kahunapule.* The baby was **blessed** by the minister.]

poni 1. purple. 2. to anoint, consecrate, crown, inaugurate, ordain. [*Ua* **poni** *'o Kalākaua iā ia pono'ī.* Kalākaua **crowned** himself.] (*poni mō'ī* = coronation, carnation)

pōniuniu dizzy. [*Hō ke kūhohonu o ko kēlā mea 'akeakamai mana'o!* **Pōniuniu** *ke po'o!* Goodness how complicated that scientist's ideas are! My head is **dizzy**!]

pono 1. morality, excellence, goodness, duty, true nature. [*E nānā i ka* **pono**. Look to **excellence**.] (*pono 'ole* = dishonest, improper) (*nā pono kiwila* = civil rights) (*pono kope* = copyright) 2. supplies, gear. (*nā pono hale* = furniture) (*nā pono lawai'a* = fishing supplies) 3. should, must, ought to. [*'O ke keiki Kaiapuni Hawai'i, he haumāna e a'o* **pono** *'ia.* A child of the Hawaiian Immersion program **should** be a student who is well taught.] 4. intensifying particle used after word. 5. preceding verb, to do [verb] carelessly, any old way. [*Mai* **pono** *kākau, e kākau* **pono**! Don't write **any old way**, write **properly**!]

pono'ī 1. self, own. (Hawai'i Pono'ī = Hawai'i's own [Hawai'i's people]) 2. directly, exactly.

pono 'ole dishonest, improper.

ponopono 1. mental clearing, restoring balance within individual and/or family. (*ho'oponopono* = to fix [machine], to correct) 2. neat, in order.

po'o 1. head. (*po'o 'eha* = headache) (*po'o kanaka* = skull) (*po'omana'o* = headlines, theme, topic) 2.

summit. 3. director of organization. (*poʻohala* =
to carry on family skills and traditions) (*poʻo
kumu* = school principal) (*poʻo ʻole* = illegiti-
mate) (*poʻoleka* = stamp)

poʻohina gray-haired.

poʻohiwi shoulder.

poʻokela 1. champion, the best. [*He* **poʻokela** *o nā
wāhine heʻe nalu ʻo Rell Sun.* Rell Sun is a **champion** of women surfers.] 2. to excel. 3. superior.

poʻolua of uncertain parentage.

poʻo paʻakikī stubborn (*lit.* hard head). [*ʻO ʻoe ma ka
poʻo paʻakikī!* Gee, how **stubborn** can you be!]

pōpilikia misfortune, trouble, calamity, ordeal.

pōpō roundness, ball for sports.

popohe shapely, round. [*Ka pua i* **popohe** *a mōhala i
ke aumoe.* The flower that became **round** and
blossomed at midnight (*fig.* description of beautiful woman).]

pōpoki cat. (*pōpoki peʻelua* = tabby cat)

pōpolo 1. herb used for medicine, ceremonies. 2.
uncomplimentary slang for a black person; *pāʻele*
is the more polite term.

popopo 1. rot (wood), decay (teeth). 2. to rot.
[**Popopo** *koke ka hale lāʻau ma Hawaiʻi nei.*
Wooden houses quickly **rot** here in Hawaiʻi.] 3.
rotten, decayed.

pou post, main post in house, canoe mast.

pouli 1. eclipse, dark night, darkness. 2. dark. (*pouli
lā* = eclipse of sun)

poupou short and husky (*fig.* mainstay of family).

pū 1. conch shell or any wind instrument. [*Ua kani
ʻia ka* **pū** *ma ka hōʻike hula.* The **conch shell** was
blown at the hula show.] 2. gun, pistol. 3. general
name for pumpkin, squash. 4. together. [*E ʻai* **pū**
kākou i kā ko ʻolua māla ʻai mau **pū** *pala.* Let's
all eat your (two) vegetable garden's ripe **squash-
es together**.] Note: *Pū* has many other meanings.

pua 1. flower, blossom. [*ku'u* **pua** *mae 'ole,* my never-fading **flower** (common line in love songs, comparing the beloved to an unfading flower)] 2. child, descendant, fry of fish. [*ku'u* **pua**, *ku'u lei nani mae 'ole, 'eā,* my **child**, my beloved never-fading *lei* (song, "Ku'u Lei Poina 'ole," by E. de Fries)] 3. to flower, blossom. 4. to appear, come forth.

pua'a 1. pig, pork. [*Aia a hu'e 'ia ka imu, a moni ka hā'ae i ke 'ala o ka 'i'o* **pua'a** *kālua.* As soon as the *imu* is uncovered, (we) salivate due to the smell of the baked **pig**.] 2. banks of fog or clouds over mountain, cloud forms of Kamapua'a.

pua'i to flow out, to bubble, gurgle. [*Pua'i aku ka wai mai ka puna wai.* Water **bubbles** out of the spring.] (syn. *hua'i*)

puakea light color. (*'ili puakea* = white person, light-skinned part-Hawaiian)

pū'ali 1. warrior. (*pū'ali koa* = armed forces, troops) 2. to gird tightly around the waist. 3. grooved, notched. [*Pū'ali ka hau nui i ka hau iki.* (*'ōlelo no'eau*) The large *hau* branch is **grooved** by the small *hau* branch (a little person has conquered a big one).] (*pū'ali'ali* = of varying thickness)

puana 1. refrain of song. [*Ha'ina 'ia mai ana ka* **puana**. Tell again the **refrain**. (line beginning last verse of many songs, indicating song's theme or person honored will be mentioned next)] 2. pronunciation, utterance.

pu'e 1. hill, dune. (*pu'e one* = sandbar, sand dune) (*pu'e 'uala* = sweet potato mound [earth was mounded up to plant sweet potatoes]) 2. to hill up. 3. to rape, force, attack.

puehu 1. scattered, dispersed. [*Puehu ka 'ehu kai i ka makani.* The sea foam is **scattered** by the wind.] 2. peeling (sunburn).

pueo Hawaiian owl, well-known family guardian spirit.

pūhā 1. abscess, ulcer. 2. to belch, burp (syn. *kūhā*). [*Mai* **pūhā** *ma ka pā'ina!* Don't **burp** at the party!] 3. to break, burst.

pūhaka loins, waist.

puhi 1. eel. 2. blowhole. 3. to blow, puff. (*puhi paka* = to smoke a cigarette) (*pana puhi 'ohe* = music band) 4. to burn, set on fire. (*puhi ahi* = arson, to burn, set fire to, cremate) (*puhi pau* = completely burned, blown away)

pueo

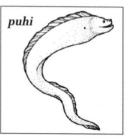

puhi

pūhi'u 1. to break wind. 2. rude, irreverent.

pūhuluhulu hairy, shaggy.

pū'ili bamboo rattles for dancing.

pū'iwa 1. amazement. 2. surprised, astonished. (*ho'opū'iwa* = to startle, astonish)

puka 1. door, opening, hole. (*pukaaniani* = window) (*puka ihu* = nostril) (*pukapuka* = many holes) 2. to emerge, pass through, rise (sun). [*Ua* **puka** *aku kākou i ka wā pōpilikia ma hope o ka makani pāhili.* We all **emerged from** the time of misfortune after the hurricane.] 3. to graduate. [*Ma ke kau kula hea ana 'oukou e* **puka** *ai?* What semester will you all **graduate**?] 4. to say, utter. 5. to gain, win profit. Note: *Puka* has many other meanings.

puka a maka the birth of a child affirms a permanent relationship (*lit.* appears to the eye).

pukaaniani window.

pukana 1. outlet, exit. 2. keepsake, souvenir.

(*pukana aloha* = souvenir of loved one) (*pukana lā* = sunrise)

pukapuka many holes, porous.

puke (from English) book.
(*puke hoʻomanaʻo* = diary, journal) (*puke kuhikuhi* = manual) (*puke wehewehe ʻōlelo* = dictionary)

puke

pūkoʻa coral head.

pūkolu trio, triplet.

pūkuʻi 1. to collect, assemble people or things. [*Na Kawena Pukui i **pūkuʻi** i nā hua ʻōlelo Hawaiʻi.* It was Kawena Pukui who **collected** Hawaiian words.] 2. council of gods, chiefs.

pukupuku 1. wrinkles, frowning. 2. to wrinkle, purse lips. (*pukupuku kūʻē maka* = wrinkled brow)

pula particle, speck.

pulakaumaka obsession (*lit.* particle in eye). [*He **pulakaumaka** ko ke kālai pōhaku.* The rock carver has an **obsession**.]

pūlale to hurry, rush. [*No ke aha lā ʻoe e **pūlale** mai?* Why do you **rush** over here? (song, "Hōkio," by M. Pukui and M. Lam)]

pūlama 1. to cherish, care for. 2. cherished. [*He lei **pūlama** ʻia ke aloha e lei mau ai.* Love is a **cherished** *lei* to wear always.] 3. torch.

pulapula seedling, sprout, descendant. (*hoʻopulapula* = rehabilitation, to rehabilitate, procreate, start seedlings, multiply) (*ʻāina hoʻopulapula* = Hawaiian Homes lands) [*ʻEhia makahiki a kona ʻohana i kali ai a loaʻa ka **ʻāina hoʻopulapula** iā lākou?* How many years did her family wait until they got **Hawaiian Homes land**?]

pule 1. prayer, blessing, church. (*pule hoʻo-pōmaikaʻi* = blessing) 2. week. (*hopenapule* = weekend)

pūlehu to barbeque, cook over coals.

pūlehulehu twilight.

pulelehua butterfly, moth.

pulelo to float, wave, rise (as a flag does). [*E* **pulelo** *ana ka hae Hawai'i.* The Hawaiian flag will **rise** in triumph.]

pūliki to embrace, hug.

pūlima 1. wrist, cuff. 2. signature. 3. to clasp hands. 4. to sign. [*Na ka loio e* **pūlima** *i ka palapala 'oki male.* It is the lawyer who should **sign** the divorce document.]

pūlo'ulo'u crossed sticks topped with a tapa-covered ball, indicating a *kapu* area reserved for *ali'i.*

pulu 1. mulch, coconut husk, tree fern fiber (once used to stuff mattresses, quilts). 2. soaked, moist.

pūlumi broom, to sweep.

pulu pē thoroughly soaked, drenched. [**pulu pē** *i ka ua,* **drenched** in the rain (common line in songs with sexual reference)]

pumehana 1. warmth, affection. 2. warm, warm hearted. [*Me ke aloha* **pumehana**. With **warm** greetings. (common salutation)]

puna 1. spring of water. 2. coral, lime, plaster. 3. (from English) spoon. (*puna kī* = teaspoon) (*puna pākaukau* = tablespoon)

punahele 1. favorite person or thing. [*He* **punahele** *nō 'oe na ka makua.* You are indeed a **favorite** of the parents. (song, "He Punahele Nō 'Oe," by A. Hahale'ā)] [*He aha ke 'ano o kāu mele* **punahele**? What kind of music is your **favorite**?] 2. to treat as a favorite.

punalua shared spouse.

pūnana nest, hive (*fig.* home). (Pūnana Leo = language nest [Hawaiian immersion preschool]) (*pūnana manu* = bird's nest; *pūnua* = fledgling, baby bird) (*pūnana meli* = beehive) *pūnāwai* spring of water.

pūnāwelewele cobweb, spider's web.

pūneʻe couch.

puni 1. to covet, desire. (*puni kālā* = mercenary, greedy; *puni waiwai* = covetous, desirous of others' wealth) 2. surrounded, controlled, overcome with emotion. 3. deceived, deluded. (*puni wale* = gullible, easily swayed) (*hoʻopunipuni* = to lie, tell falsehood)

pūnohu to rise (smoke, mist), to spread out (sail, cloud).

pūnua fledgling, baby bird (*fig.* young child). [*Aia ka* **pūnua** *ma lalo o ko kona makua ʻēheu.* The **fledgling** is under her parent's wing.]

pūʻoʻa tower, steeple, pyramid.

puoho 1. to cry out in shock. 2. startled. 3. to explode, as lava flow.

pūʻolo bundle, bag, container. [*Aia nō a nākiʻi ʻia nā lei i nā* **pūʻolo** *lāʻī, mākaukau ka pāʻina.* As soon as the *lei* are tied in the *tī* leaf **bundles**, the party is ready.]

pūpū 1. general name for shell, beads. 2. snack, relish. 3. bunch, bundle (grass, bouquet).

pupuāhulu 1. to hurry 2. in a hurry. [*Mai hele a* **pupuāhulu**! Don't get **in a hurry**!] 3. to make a careless mistake.

pupuka ugly, unsightly, homely (sometimes used when referring to a beautiful baby, so that jealousy isn't aroused).

pūpūkahi united in cooperation. (syn. *lōkahi*)

pupule crazy, reckless, wild.

pupuʻu to huddle or curl up limbs in a fetal position (*fig.* the womb).

puʻu 1. any kind of bump, protuberance. 2. hill, mound. 3. any protuberance on the body, such as a pimple, Adam's apple, callus, wart, knuckle. (*puʻupuʻu* = kidney, knuckle) 4. heaped, pregnant (*fig.* obstacle, burden, discomfort). (*pu'u kālā* = sum of money) [*'A'ole mākou a'e minamina i ka **pu'u kālā** o ke aupuni.* We place no value on the government's **money**. (protest song, "Kaulana Nā Pua," by E. Prendergast)] (*pu'uaahi* = bonfire) (*pu'upa'a* = virgin) (*pu'u pepa* = deck of playing cards) Note: *Pu'u* has many other meanings.

pu'uhonua place of refuge, asylum.

pu'ukani 1. singer. 2. sweet voiced.

pu'ukū treasurer.

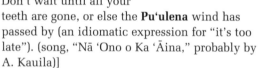

pu'uhonua

Pu'ulena famous cold wind at Kīlauea, Hawai'i. [*Mai kali a pau nā niho, o hala 'ē ka **Pu'ulena**.* Don't wait until all your teeth are gone, or else the **Pu'ulena** wind has passed by (an idiomatic expression for "it's too late"). (song, "Nā 'Ono o Ka 'Āina," probably by A. Kauila)]

pu'ulima fist.

pū'ulu 1. group, crowd. 2. to crowd, assemble.

pu'unaue to divide, share.

pu'upu'u 1. knuckles. 2. full of lumps, piled in heaps. (*pu'upu'u lima* = clenched fist, blow of fist) (*pu'upu'u wāwae* = ankle bones)

pu'uwai heart, lungs. (*haka* = heart-shaped) (*ka pu'uwai hāmana* = open-hearted, generous)

ū 1. breast, udder. [*'Olo'olo ko ka pipi wahine mau ū*. The cow's **udders** are pendulous.] 2. to drip. 3. moist.

'ū 1. grief, sorrow. 2. to moan, groan, sigh, grieve. (syn: *kani'uhū, 'uhū*) (*noho 'ū* = grief-stricken [syn. *lu'ulu'u*])

ua rain. [*noenoe ua kea o Hāna,* white misty **rain** of Hāna (song, "Ua Kea o Hāna," by E. Pu'ukea)] 2. to rain. 3. rainy. 4. verb tense marker for past tense.

'uā to shout, cry out.

'u'a 1. good-for-nothing person. 2. useless, worn out, unattractive. [*'U'a wale nō ka pepehi 'elelū.* Killing cockroaches is **useless**.]

uahi smoke, dust, spray. (*ka uahi a Pele* = a type of taro reserved for ceremonial use [*lit.* Pele's smoke]) (*uauahi* = vog, smog, haze)

uakea white mist of Hāna, Maui.

uaki (from English) watch, clock. (*uaki ho'āla* = alarm clock) [*E ho'opio i kāu uaki ho'āla.* Turn off your **alarm clock**.]

uakoko low-lying rainbow. [*ālai 'ia e ka uakoko,*

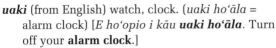

blocked by the **low-lying rainbow** (line from chant)]

'uala sweet potato. [*Poni ka 'uala mai Okinawa mai.* The **sweet potato** from Okinawa is purple.] (*'uala kahiki* = Irish potato [*lit.* foreign potato])

ualo to cry out for help.

'uao 1. peacemaker, arbitrator. [*'O ka mea 'uao ka luna kānāwai hapa Hawai'i.* The part-Hawaiian judge is the **arbitrator**.] 2. to intercede, arbitrate, reconcile.

uapo bridge, pier, wharf. [*ka uapo a'o Māmala, e 'au a'e nei ma hope,* the **pier** of Māmala (Honolulu harbor) that is swimming away behind us (song, "He Aloha Nō 'O Honolulu," by L. Kauwe)]

'ua'u sea bird, dark-rumped petrel.

uaua tough, sinewy (*fig.* hard-headed, willful). [*Uaua kēia 'i'o hipa ma'alili.* This cooled-down mutton is **tough** (to chew).]

uauahi vog, smog, haze. [*'Oiai e hū a'e nei ka pele, uhi 'ia 'o Kona i ka uauahi.* Since lava is bubbling up now, Kona is covered with **vog**.]

uē 1. mourning. (*uē helu* = type of mourning chant recounting experiences shared with deceased). 2. to cry, weep, lament. (*uē 'ino* = tantrum; *uē wale* = to cry for no reason, crybaby)

uea (from English) wire. (*uea makika* = mosquito screen on doors, windows)

'uehe hula step.

'uha 1. waste, extravagance. 2. wasteful, extravagant. [*'O ka uku **'uha** a nā kahu waiwai ka'u mea e ho'o-halahala ai.* The **extravagant** salary of the trustees is the thing I would criticize.] (*'uha 'ai* = to waste food, squander anything)

'ūhā thigh, lap.

'uhaloa weed whose root and leaves are used as medicine for cold, sore throat; a *kinolau* (body form) of Kamapua'a.

'uhane soul, spirit, ghost. (*ka 'uhane hemolele* = the holy ghost) (*lele ka 'uhane* = the soul leaves [death])

'uhene 1. exclamation in songs. 2. to tease, flirt, talk romantically. [***'Uhene** kēnā ipo āu i nā manawa a pau.* That sweetheart of yours **flirts** all the time.]

uhi 1. cover, lid, veil, covering. 2. to cover, spread, conceal, overwhelm (*fig.* to hide truth, deceive). (*uhi moe* = bedspread; *uhi pela* = bedsheet; *uhi pākaukau* = tablecloth [syn. *hāli'i pākaukau*]) 3. solid tattooing.

uhikino body covering, shield.

'ūhini grasshopper. (*'ūhini lele* = cricket)

uhiwai heavy fog, mist.

ūhī'ūhā sounds heard in flowing lava, like huffing and puffing. [***'Ūhī'ūhā** mai ana 'eā, e Pele e Pele ē.* **Huffing and puffing** along, oh Pele. (traditional chant, "Aia Lā 'o Pele," Loebenstein)]

'ūhini

uhu parrot fish.

'uhū to moan, groan, sigh (usually used with *kani*). (syn: *'ū*) [*Kani**'uhū** ka māka'ikiu ma ka 'ao'ao ho'opale.* The detective on the side of the defendant **groaned**.]

ui 1. question, catechism. 2. to ask, question, appeal. [*He* **ui**, *he nīnau aku ana au iā ʻoe, aia i hea ka wai a Kāne?* A query, a **question** I have for you, Where is the water of Kāne? (line from ancient chant, "Ka Wai a Kāne")]

uʻi youthful, handsome, vigorous, beautiful. [*I kona wā* **uʻi**. In his/her **youth** (*lit.* time of physical beauty)]

ʻuī 1. to squeak, squeal. [**ʻUī** *wale ka lekiō i ka uila a me ka hekili.* The radio **squeals** a lot due to the thunder and lightning.] 2. to squeeze, grind.

uiki 1. (from English) wick of kerosene lamp. [*I kekahi manawa, pipī ke kukui i ka* **uiki**. Sometimes the light flickers due to the **wick**.] 2. to glimmer, as a light through a hole or crack.

uila lightning, electricity.

[*ʻōlapa ka* **uila**, *kuʻi ka hekili.* **Lightning** flashes, thunder booms.] [*Ua ʻā anei ka* **uila** *ma ke keʻena hou?* Is the **electricity** on in the new office?] 2. electric. (*lolouila* = computer [*lit.* electric brain]) (syn. *kamepiula*)

uila

uilani restless, irritated by constraint, spirited. [**Uilani** *nā paʻahao i ka laka ʻia i loko.* The prisoners are **irritated** at being locked up inside.]

ʻuʻina 1. crackling sound. 2. to crack, snap, creak. [**ʻUʻina**, *ʻuʻina ē, ʻuʻina nā wai aʻo nā Molokama.* **Crackling** are the waters of Nā Molokama. (song, "Na Wai Aʻo Nā Molokama," by A. Alohikea)]

ʻuʻinakolo 1. roar, rustle. 2. to rustle.

uka inland, up toward mountains. (*hoʻouka* = to load cargo, freight, attack in battle)

ukali 1. follower, attendant. [*ʻO McGuire kekahi o* **nā**

ukali *i ko Kapiʻolani lāua ʻo Liliʻuokalani huakaʻi i ko ko Pelekania mōʻī wahine lā Iubile.* McGuire was one of the **attendants** on Kapiʻolani and Liliʻuokalani's trip to Britain's Queen's Jubilee Day.] 2. to follow, attend, escort.

ukana baggage, luggage, freight, cargo. [*He mau* **ukana** *kaumaha kā nā poʻe waiwai.* Rich people have heavy **baggage.**]

ukana

ʻūkēkē stringed instrument of ancient days; held to the mouth, it could be used to convey spoken words as "sweet nothings" to a lover.

ʻūkele muddy, oily. (syn. *kele*) [*ʻŪkele nā alahele ma ka ʻaoʻao Koʻolau.* The trails on the windward side are **muddy.**]

ukiuki 1. anger, resentment. 2. angry, annoyed, offended. (*hoʻonāukiuki* = to provoke, annoy)

uku 1. pay, wages, reward, price, tax. 2. to pay, compensate. (*lā uku* = pay day) (*uku hana* = salary) (*uku hoʻopaʻi* = fine, forfeit) (*uku kaulele* = overtime pay) (*uku kūmau* = usual fees, dues, taxes) (*uku lawelawe* = tip) (*uku pānaʻi* = refund, ransom, to refund, redeem) (*uku paneʻe* = interest [savings]) [*ʻAʻole nui ka* **uku paneʻe** *ma nā panakō i kēia mau lā.* The **interest** at the banks isn't very high these days.] 3. revenge.

ʻuku louse, flea. (*ʻuku lio* = bedbug; *ʻuku poʻo* = head lice)

ukuhi to dip out liquids, water, to wean child. [*Aia nō a* **ukuhi** *ʻo ʻUlu i ka wai mai ka pūnāwai mai, e inu kāua i ka wai huʻihuʻi.* As soon as ʻUlu **dips out** the water from the spring, let's you and me drink the chilled water.]

'ukulele instrument (*lit.* jumping flea).

ukupau labor paid by job, not by time.

ula Hawaiian lobster.

'ūlāleo 1. voice from spirits. 2. intense appeal to gods.

ulana to weave, knit, braid, plait. [*'O ka* **ulana** *lauhala kā ko'u kupuna wahine hana no'eau.* **Weaving** *lauhala* is my grandmother's craft.]

'ula'ula (*syn.* '*ula*) 1. red color, blood. 2. ghost. 3. sacred. ('*ahu'ula* = feather cloak, symbol of royalty) ('*ili 'ula'ula* = brown Hawaiian skin)

ule penis. (*uhi ule* = condom)

'ūlei native shrub with flexible branches used in making fishtraps; also a medicinal plant.

'ulī to rattle, gurgle. ('*ulī'ulī* = hula rattle)

ulia accident. [*'O ia nei kai 'ike maka i ka* **ulia** *ka'a ma ka huina alanui kahi i hala ai ka luahine.* She/he (this one here) is the one who witnessed the car **accident** at the intersection where the old lady died.] (*ulia pōpilikia* = emergency; *syn. pilikia kūhewa*)

'ūlili 1. tattler bird from Alaska, spends winter in Hawai'i. 2. whistle, to whistle. 3. hula step, also hula implement used to make whirring sound.

uliuli (*syn. uli*) 1. any dark color, green, brown, blue. [*Uliuli ka moana.* The ocean is dark **blue**.] Note: *Polū* (from English) is sometimes used for the color blue; however, many prefer to use *uliuli* for blue. [*e Hawai'i nui kua***uli***,* oh dark-backed big Hawai'i (song, "Ka Na'i Aupuni," composer unknown)] 2. steersman. 3. to steer. (*hoe uli* = steering paddle)

ulu 1. grove, collection, flock. (*ulu lā'au* = forest) 2. to grow, increase. (*ulu a nui* = to grow up) [*Ua* **ulu a nui** *ko mākou mau kūpuna ma ka mahikō.* Our (us, not you) grandparents **grew up** on the sugar plantation.] (*ulu pono* = thriving, successful) (*ulu wale* = to grow easily, overgrown [vegetation] (*ulu hānau* = contemporary, of same age group) [*He mau* **ulu hānau** *'o Ka'ahumanu a me Mānono.* Mānono and Ka'ahumanu were **contemporaries**.] 3. possessed by or inspired by god, spirit. (*ho'oulu* = to grow plants, inspire)

'ulu 1. breadfruit, a staple food. [*'O ka* **'ulu** *ka lau kūpono no kā 'oukou mau kapa kuiki mua loa.* The **breadfruit** is an appropriate design for your (all) very first quilt.] 2. gum used for paste. 3. symbol for growth and being fed, nourished.

ulua fish used in ancient ceremonies as substitute for human sacrifice (*fig.* man, sweetheart).

uluāhewa 1. delusion, craziness, overgrowth. [*He mau* **uluāhewa** *ko ka po'e hehena.* Insane people have **delusions**.] 2. to grow wild (vegetation).

uluaō'a 1. confusion, disturbance, mob. (syn. *haunaele*) 2. jungle.

uluhua frustrated, annoyed.

ulu lā'au forest.

ulumāhiehie 1. to make a fine appearance. 2. festive, attractively adorned. [**Ulumāhiehie** *ke kahua no ka hō'ike lā mua o Mei.* The stage for the May Day pageant is **attractively adorned**.]

'ulu maika ancient sport somewhat like bowling. (*'ulu maika haole* = bowling)

'ulu maika

uluna pillow, cushion.

uluwehi lush and beautiful (of nature), festively adorned.

umauma breast, chest. (*pa'i umauma* = slapping chest, in mourning or in hula dance)

'ume 1. to draw, pull, attract. 2. attractive, alluring. (*pahu* **'ume** = drawer of bureau, desk, etc.) (*'ume makēneki* = pull of magnet)

'umeke bowl, calabash. (*'umeke kā'eo* = full calabash [*fig.* one with deep knowledge]) (*'umeke pala 'ole* = empty calabash [empty mind]) (*'umeke pōhue* = gourd calabash)

'umeke

'umi 1. ten. 2. to strangle, choke, repress desire. (syn. *'u'umi*) [**'U'umi** *i ke aloha me ka waimaka lā.* **Repress** love with tears. (song, "Kaimukī Hula," by A. Richart)] (*'umikūmākahi* = eleven [ten plus one])

'ūmi'i 1. cramp, sharp pain. 2. to clamp, clip, clasp. (*'ūmi'i 'iole* = rat trap, mouse trap) (*'ūmi'i kuapo* = belt buckle) (*mikini 'ūmi'i* = stapler) 3. clutch of car or vehicle. [*Ua poloke ko ko ke kaha ki'i hale ka'a* **'ūmi'i***.* The architect's car's **clutch** was broken.]

'umikūmākahi eleven.

'umi'umi beard, mustache. (*kahi 'umi'umi* = to shave) (*pahi 'umi'umi* = razor)

unahi

unahi 1. fish scale. 2. to scale fish. [*Iā 'olua e* **unahi** *i'a ai, e ho'ohana i ke puna.* When you (two) **scale** fish, use a spoon.]

unauna hermit crab.

une 1. lever. 2. to pry (*fig.* to urge, harass).

unea = nausea. (syn. *poluea*)

'unihipili spirit of dead person, used for sorcery in ancient days.

'ūniki graduation exercises for hula, martial arts.

unu 1. pebble, wedge. 2. to wedge, prop.

'unu to shorten, hoist, jerk upwards.

unuhi 1. translator, interpreter. 2. to take out, with-
draw (money). 3. to translate.

uō to howl, to bellow.

'ūpā 1. scissors, any instrument that opens and shuts
such as tongs, shears. 2. to open and shut, slam,
bang. (*'ūpā makani* = bellows; *'ūpā miki'ao* =
fingernail scissors; *'ūpā 'ūmi'i* = pliers)

'upa'i to flap wings, walk with flapping movement.

'ūpalu gentle, mild, softspoken, fragile.

ūpē crushed, flattened, humble.

'ūpē mucus (*fig.* tears, grief). (syn. *hūpē*)

'upena fishing net, net, web.

> [*He* **'upena** *kiloi ko ka
> lawai'a.* The fisherman
> has a throw **net**.]

'upena

'ūpī 1. sponge, syringe. [*E
ho'oma'ema'e kāua i nā
pākaukau i kēia mau
'ūpī!* Let's (you and me)
clean the tables with
these **sponges**!] 2. to
squirt, squeeze.

'ūpiki 1. trap, snare, treachery. 2. to snap together as
trap. (syn. *'āpiki*) (*'ūpiki lima* = handcuff)

'upu recurring thought, desire, attachment, expectation. [**'Upu** *a'e ka mana'o iā 'oe, e ka ipo.* The
thought of you keeps coming up, sweetheart.] 2.
to desire, long for.

'u'u 1. to strip *maile* (to bring out fragrance). 2. to
hoist sail. 3. to masturbate.

'ū'ū to stutter, stammer.

'u'uku tiny, very small. [**'U'uku** *wale nā pua i'a.* Fish
fry are truly **tiny**.]

wā 1. period of time, epoch, era. [*i ka* **wā** *o Kuali'i*, in the **time** of Kuali'i] (*wā ho'omaha* = vacation) (*wā kamali'i* = childhood) 2. roar, noise. 3. fret of stringed instrument such as *'ukulele*. 4. to make noise, talk a lot. (*'Ikuwā* = month in Hawaiian moon calendar [mid-October] known for stormy weather) (*kai ho'owā* = roaring sea) 5. space between objects or time.

wa'a 1. canoe. (*wa'a 'auhau* = tribute canoe set out to sea during makahiki season) (*wa'a kaulua* = double-hulled canoe such as *Mo'olele*) (*wa'a kaukahi* = single-hulled canoe) 2. trench, furrow.

wa'a kaukahi

wa'apā boat, skiff, rowboat.

wa'awa'a 1. full of gulches. 2. grooved, gullied. 3. muscular. 4. stupid, ignorant.

wae to choose, select, sort. (*wae mana'o* = conscience)

waena 1. middle, center, average. (*waena-konu* = center, middle) (*kikowaena* = center of circle, headquarters) 2. cultivated field, used in place names to indicate an area between mountains and sea. [Kalihi **waena**, **mid**-Kalihi, area near Honolulu Community College]

waha 1. mouth. 2. oral. 3. to talk too much. (*waha he'e* = liar, a lie, to lie, deceitful, lying [syn. *waha wale*]; *waha mana* = voice of authority; *waha nui* = big mouth, to talk too much; *waha 'ōlelo* =

spokesperson; *waha paʻa* = argumentative; *waha pilo* = halitosis, foul mouth; *waha pio* = speechless; *waha puʻu* = protruding lips, unintelligible speech, such as of one who has had a stroke)

wahāwahā to treat with contempt, despise, ridicule. (*hoʻowahāwahā i ka ʻaha* = contempt of court)

wahi place (*ka wahi,* "the place," is often contracted to *kahi*). [*ʻO Liliha **kahi** āna e noho nei.* Liliha is **the place** he is living.] 2. some, a few. 3. to say, according to. [***Wahi** a kaʻu loio,* **according to** my lawyer, my lawyer said] 4. can be used before a noun to indicate one's attitude toward that noun. [*kuʻu **wahi** ʻīlio,* my **sweet little** doggie] [*kēlā **wahi** ʻīlio* = that **darned** dog]

wahī 1. wrapper, envelope. (*wahī leka* = envelope for letter) 2. to wrap, cover, bundle up, roll up. [*Ua **wahī** ʻia ka pēpē i ka lole.* The baby was **wrapped** in the cloth.]

wahie fuel, firewood.

wahī ʻeha bandage.

wahine (pl. *wāhine*) 1. woman, wife, lady. 2. femininity, womanliness. 3. feminine, female. [*He akua **wahine** ʻo Hina.* Hina is a **feminine** goddess.] (*wahine hiʻu iʻa* = mermaid) (*wahine kāne make* = widow) (*hoʻowahine* = to behave like a woman, to grow into womanhood)

wahine

waho outside, beyond, outward. [*Ke waʻu nei lāua i ka ʻiʻo niu ma **waho** o ka hale kaʻa.* They (three or more) are grating the coconut meat **outside** the garage.]

wai 1. water or any liquid other than sea water. (*wai ʻala* = perfume, cologne; *wai ea* = aerated water,

mineral water; *wai hoʻāno* = holy water; *wai
hoʻomaʻemaʻe* = disinfectant, any kind of cleaning
liquid; *wai hua ʻai* = juice; *wai kai* = brackish
water, salty water; *wai meli* = honey; *wai niu* =
coconut milk; *wai puna* = spring water) 2. any liquid discharged from the body. (*hana wai* = menstrual period; syn. *maʻi wahine*) 3. to flow like
water. (*waipahū* = geyser) 4. who, whom. [*ʻO **wai**
kēlā?* Whoʻs that?]

waia 1. dishonor, shame. 2 disgraced. [*Ua **waia** ko
ke keiki lapuwale ʻohana.* The wastrel childʻs
family is **disgraced**.]

wai ʻala perfume, cologne.

wai ʻapo water caught in taro leaf, considered sacred
because it hasnʻt touched the ground (*fig.*
beloved mate).

waiehu file for grinding, polishing.

waiho 1. to deposit, leave something. (*waiho wale* =
to leave without reason, to leave about carelessly)
2. internal organs of the body. 3. funds, treasury.
(*hale waihona puke* = library) 4. to quit, resign,
abandon something.

waihona 1. depository, closet. (*waihona ʻāina* = lay
of land) (*waihona hoʻomanaʻo* = memory) (*waihona kālā* = treasury; syn. *waihona waiwai*) (*waihona meli* = honeycomb) [*Ua kī ʻia ka mahiʻai i
nānao i kona lima i loko o ka pūnana meli e
lālau i ka **waihona meli**.* The farmer who thrust
his arm into the beehive to grab the **honeycomb**
was stung.]

waihoʻoluʻu dye, color. [*He aha nā **waihoʻoluʻu** kapu
i nā aliʻi? ʻO ka ʻulaʻula, ka melemele a me ka
ʻeleʻele.* What were the **colors** sacred to the
chiefs? Red, yellow and black.]

wailana calm, quiet (like a calm sea). [*I ka ʻolu o
Wailana.* In the pleasant **calm** of Wailana. (song,
"Wailana," by M. Kaleikoa)]

wailele waterfall.

waili‘ulā 1. mirage. 2. of changing color, as an opal.

wailua 1. ghost, spirit. 2. corpse (syn. *kupapa‘u*). 3. two waters, a common place name probably used for an area where two freshwater streams mingle.

waimaka tears. [*Kulu ko kona makuahine mau* **waimaka**. His mother's **tears** flow.]

waina 1. place with water. 2. (from English) wine .

waiolina (from English) violin. (*waiolina kū nui* = bass)

wai ‘olu pleasant, attractive, gentle. [*kou piko* **wai ‘olu**, *ua kapu na ka mea waiwai,* your **attractive** center, reserved for the worthy person (song, "Aloha Nō Au I Kou Maka," by Leleiōhoku)

waipahē courteous, gentlemanly, polite, agreeable. [*He mau keonimana* **waipahē** *nā ‘ōlapa ma kāna hālau hula.* The dancers in his hula *hālau* are **courteous** gentlemen.]

waipu‘ilani waterspout.

waiū 1. milk. 2. breast. (*waiū kini* = canned milk) (*waiū paka* = butter) (*waiū paka pa‘a* = cheese)

waiwai 1. property, goods, worth, value. 2. rich, valuable, financial. (*waiwai ho‘oilina* = inherited property, heritage) [*He* **waiwai ho‘oilina** *maka-mae ko nā Hawai‘i.* Hawaiians have a precious **heritage**.] (*waiwai ho‘opuka* = profits) (*waiwai lewa* = liquid assets) (*waiwai pa‘a* = real estate, nonliquid assets) (*ho‘owaiwai* = to enrich)

Wākea legendary ancestor god, sky father whose mating created the islands. [*‘O* **Wākea** *ke kāne, ‘o Papa, ‘o Walinu‘u ka wahine.* **Wākea** was the husband, Papa Walinu‘u was the wife. (birth chant for Kauikeaouli, composer unknown)]

Wakinekona (from English) Washington.

wala to tilt backwards, fall backwards. (*wala kua* = to fall over backwards, rear up, as a horse) [*Ma ke ka‘i huaka‘i i* **wala kua** *ai ko ke Kamali‘i wahine* *o Lāna'i lio.* It was in the parade that the Princess of Lāna'i's horse **reared**.]

wala'au to talk, chatter, converse.

walania 1. anguish, torment, burning pain. 2. agonizing, anguishing.

wale 1. slime, mucus. [*'O ka* **walewale** *ho'okumu honua ia.* It is the **slime** that established the earth. (line from first section of the *Kumulipo* creation chant)] 2. common particle following words, used for emphasis, many possible translations. [*Nani* **wale** *ka 'ikena.* The view is **simply** beautiful.] (*wale nō* = only) [*'O au* **wale nō** *kēia.* It's **only** me.] (*'o ia wale nō* = that's all) (*ho'owalewale* = decoy, temptation, to tempt)

walea to relax. [*E* **walea** *pū 'oe me a'u.* And you are **relaxing** with me. (song, "Green Rose Hula," by J. Almeida)]

walewaha perfect fluency in a language. [***Walewaha*** *ko Ni'ihau i ka 'ōlelo makuahine.* Ni'ihau's people have **perfect fluency** in the mother tongue.]

wali smooth, supple, thin, fine. (*ho'owali* = to mix poi)

waliwali smooth, gentle, easygoing, good-natured. [*Kou ihu* **waliwali** *ka'u i honi.* Your **smooth** nose I have kissed. (song, "Aloha Nō Au I Kou Maka," by Leleiōhoku)]

walu 1. eight. 2. to scratch, rub, claw. 3. (following another word) many. (*makawalu* = many eyes, ubiquitous)

wana sea urchin.

wana'ao dawn. (syn. *kaiao*) [*Ma ka* **wana'ao** *lākou i ha'alele ai.* It was at **dawn** that they (three) left.]

wānana 1. prophecy, prediction. [*Kauka'i nā ali'i i nā* **wānana** *a nā kāula me nā kilo hōkū.* The *ali'i* depended on the **predictions** of the prophet and the stargazers.] 2. to predict, prophesy.

wao 1. biogeographic zone, dividing land into sections

according to usage at different altitudes. (*wao akua* = distant uplands, considered to be inhabited by gods) (*wao kanaka* = lower zone where people could live) 2. *nā wao* were legendary people, said to be ancestors of *nā wā* and *nā mū.*

waokele rain forest. [*E mālama i ka* **waokele!** Protect the **rain forest!**]

wao nahele jungle, rain forest.

wao one desert.

wa'u 1. scraper, such as used to scrape out coconut meat (*mea wa'u niu*). 2. to grate, scratch, claw, to scratch an itch. [*'Oiai mane'o ko'u kua, hiki paha iā 'oe ke* **wa'u** *mai?* Since my back is itchy, can you maybe **scratch** it?]

wauke paper mulberry tree whose bark is used to make tapa.

wawā 1. roar, distant sound. 2. rumored, talked about.

wāwae leg, foot. (*lole wāwae* = pants, shorts) [*Ua pukapuka ko ka lawai'a* **lole wāwae** *pōkole.* The fisherman's **shorts** were full of holes.]

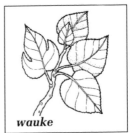

wauke

wāwahi 1. to tear down, break down, demolish. (*wāwahi hale* = burglary, housebreaking) 2. to give change for currency. [*Hiki i ka mea 'ohi kālā ke* **wāwahi** *i kāna kālā iwakālua.* The cashier can **break** his twenty dollar bill.]

we'awe'a 1. pimp, procurer. 2. to help, tempt in love affair.

wehe 1. to open, untie, undo. [*E* **wehe** *i ka pukaaniani! Ua wela kēia lā!* **Open** the window! It's hot today!] 2. to take off clothes. 3. to cleanse, solve problem.

wehewehe to explain. [*E **wehewehe** mai i kou mana'o!* **Explain** your idea to me!] (*puke wehewehe 'ōlelo* = dictionary) (*wehewehe 'ana* = explanation)

wehi 1. decoration. (*wehiwehi* = adorned, festive) 2. a song composed to honor someone. 3. to decorate, adorn. (*ho'owehi* = to beautify, decorate)

wehiwa 1. a choice object. 2. choice, prized.

wehiwehi adorned, festive. [**Wehiwehi** *'oe.* You are beautifully **adorned**. (song, "Wehiwehi 'Oe," by T. Kalama)]

weke 1. fish used as offering. 2. crack, narrow opening. 3. to open a crack, to separate, loosen, free.

wēkiu 1. tip, top, summit. 2. of highest rank or status. [*he pua no ka **wēkiu***, (*'ōlelo no'eau*) a flower from the summit (*fig.* a person of the highest attainment)]

wela 1. heat, temperature (*fig.* lust, passion, anger). [*ahi **wela** mai nei loko i ka hana a ke aloha,* **hot fire** from here within in love-making (song, "Ahi Wela," M. Doirin/L. Beckley)] [*Ke 'ike 'o ia nei i kona kaikunāne, pi'i koke kona **wela**. When this one sees her brother, her **anger** wells up.] 2. hot, burned.

wēlau tip, end, top. [*Ua 'oki 'ia ka **wēlau** o ka lauhala. The **tip** of the hala leaf was cut off.]

Welehu month of Hawaiian calendar (approximately mid-November to mid-December). (*lit.* warm ashes of fire, indicating the weather is cold and rainy)

weleweka (from English) velvet. [*Komo ka wahine male hou i ka holokū **weleweka**. The bride wears a **velvet** holokū (formal fitted mu'u with a long train).]

weli 1. fears, terror. (*ho'oweli* = to frighten, terrify) 2. fearful, afraid.

welina greeting of affection, poetic opening of speech or salutation in letter (used in addressing an audience, formal rather than intimate).

weliweli terrifying, terrible. [**Weliweli** *kau mai* (a well-known phrase in chants for Pele, indicating both dread and reverence at the destructive and creative power of the fire goddess embodied in an active volcano)]

welo 1. to float, flutter (like a flag), to set (sun). [**Welo** *ana e ka hae Hawai'i.* The Hawaiian flag **flutters**. (song, "Kaleleonālani," by Nu'uanu)] 2. family custom or trait.

Welo name of month in Hawaiian calendar, approximately February-March.

welu 1. rag. [*Loa'a ka* **welu**? *Ua hanini ke koloaka.* Got a **rag**? The soda spilled.] 2. ragged.

weluwelu shredded to bits.

wena 1. glow of lava, fire, sunrise. 2. blood relative, close relation.

weuweu 1. grass. 2. bushy, fuzzy. [**Weuweu** *ka'u pōpoki keiki!* My kitten is **fuzzy**.]

wī 1. famine. [*I ka wā* **wī**, *ua 'ai 'ia ka poi 'ulu.* In **famine** times, breadfruit *poi* was eaten.] 2. syn. for *hīhīwai*, freshwater snail. 3. any high, shrill sound. 4. to squeal, tinkle.

wiki 1. to hurry, hasten. 2 quick.

wikiō (from English) video.

wili 1. mill, drill. (*ka hale wili kō* = sugar mill) (*wili kope* = coffee grinder) (*wili makani* = windmill) 2. to twist, turn, drill, mix, dial phone. [*i* **wili** *'ia me maile lauli'i,* **twined** with small-leaf *maile* (common line in songs celebrating love)] (*wili pua'a* = corkscrew)

wilikī (from English) engineer, engineering.

wiliwai whirlpool.

wiliwili 1. to twist, turn, appliqué in quilting. 2. a tree with light wood used for canoe outriggers, fishing floats, and surfboards; its seeds are made into seed *lei*. 3. wind blowing in all directions.

wini 1. sharp, pointed (*fig.* impudent). 2. wind.

wīwī skinny, emaciated. [**Wīwī** *ke kāne i lanakila i ka heihei holo wāwae.* The man who won the foot race is **thin**.]

wiwo fearful, afraid, modest, timid, obedient.

wiwo ʻole fearless, courageous, intrepid.

wohi a chiefly rank.

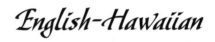

English-Hawaiian

a, an *he.* [*He Hawai'i ha'aheo au.* I am **a** proud Hawaiian.]

abandon *ha'alele* (also means **to quit a bad habit, quit a job** or **leave a place**). [*Ua ha'alele ka wahine i kāna kāne.* The wife **abandoned** her husband.] [*Ua ha'alele 'o Palikū i ka puhi paka.* Palikū **abandoned** (**quit**) smoking.]

able to, can *hiki.* [*Hiki i kona kupuna kāne ke 'ōlelo Pākē.* His grandfather **can** speak Chinese.]

about 1. *no.* [*He mo'olelo kēia no 'Umialīloa.* This is a story **about** 'Umialīloa.] 2. phrase: *e pili ana.* [*Ua no'ono'o au e pili ana i kāna mea i ha'i mai ai.* I thought **about** what he told me.]

above 1. *luna* (also means **top,** or in locative phrase, **on top of**). [*E pena 'oe i ka paia mai luna a i lalo.* Paint the wall from **above** to below (from **top** to bottom).] Note: Locative phrases are frequently used to indicate where something is. [*Aia ko ke kauka ke'ena ma luna o ka pu'u o Mau'umae ma Kaimukī.* The doctor's office is **on top of** Mau'umae Hill in Kaimukī.]

abscess *pūhā.* [*He pūhā ko kona niho hu'i.* Her sore tooth has an **abscess.**]

absent *ma kahi 'ē* (*lit.* someplace else).

absorbed (in an activity) 1. *papau.* 2. *lilo.* [*Lilo ke keiki i ka pā'ani lolouila.* The child is **absorbed** in the computer game.]

abundant *nui* (also means **many, plenty of, lots of**). [*Nui ka ua ma ka 'ao'ao Ko'olau i ka ho'oilo.* There is **abundant** rain on the windward side in the rainy season.]

abuse [n] hana ʻino. [Minamina, ʻaʻole ka **hana ʻino**
he mea laha ʻole ma nā ʻohana. Regretfully,
abuse is not a rare thing in families.] [v] 1.
hoʻomāino. 2. hana ʻino.

accident 1. ulia. [Nui nā **ulia** kaʻa ma kēlā huina
alanui. There are lots of **accidents** at that intersection.] 2. pilikia.

accomplish holo pono (also means **to succeed**).

accustomed to maʻa (also means **used to, skilled at**).
[**Maʻa** kēia mau wāhine no Kona i ka ulana
pāpale lauhala. These women from Kona are
accustomed to weaving lauhala hats.]

acne 1. huehue. 2. puʻu.

acquainted with 1. kamaʻāina. [**Kamaʻāina** kēia hoahana ona i nā lula palekana. This workmate of
his is **acquainted with** the safety rules.]

across ma kēlā ʻaoʻao (lit. on that side).

active 1. ʻeleu. 2. miki. [**ʻEleu** kaʻu ʻīlio. My dog is
active.]

add 1. hoʻokuʻi (add numbers). 2. pākuʻi, hoʻokuʻi
(add on another piece).

administrator 1. kahu. [Ua lilo kāna kaikamahine i
kahu no kā kona makua kāne kālā. His daughter became an **administrator** for her father's
money.] 2. luna hoʻoponopono. (executor =
kahu waiwai)

admirable lehiwa.

admiration makahehi.

admire makahehi. [**Makahehi** nā ʻōpiopio i ka uʻi.
Young people **admire** physical beauty.]

adorn wehi.

adorned wehiwehi.

adornment 1. wehi. [a he **wehi** no koʻu kino, an
adornment for my body (song, "Pua Wehiwa," by
P. Vaughn)] 2. kāhiko.

adult kanaka makua. [Ke piha nā makahiki he
iwakāluakūmākahi iā ʻoe, he **kanaka makua** ʻoe

wahi a ke kānāwai. When you reach 21 years
old, you're an **adult** according to law.]

advertise *ho'olaha.*

advertisement *ho'olaha.* [*Ua 'ike anei 'oukou i ka
ho'olaha a OHA i hō'ike ai ma ke kīwī?* Have
you folks seen the **advertisement** OHA showed
on TV?]

advice *'ōlelo a'o.*

adze *ko'i.* [*Me ke ko'i i kua ai nā kūpuna i nā
kumukoa?* Was it with an **adze** that the ancestors
cut down *koa* trees?]

affection *aloha* (also has many other meanings,
including **sympathy, feeling, greetings**).

affliction *pō'ino.*

afraid 1. *maka'u.* [*Maka'u ka pōpoki i ka uaki
ho'āla.* The cat is **afraid** of the alarm clock.] 2.
wiwo. 3. *weli.*

after *ma hope o* (also means **behind**). [*Holopeki ko'u
hoahana ma hope o ka hana.* My buddy at work
runs **after** work.]

afternoon *'auinalā* (*lit.* descent of sun). [*Auē ua wale
kēia 'auinalā!* Wow, it's so rainy this **afternoon**!]

again *hou* (added after verb). [*E hana hou!* Do it
again!] [*A hui hou kākou!* Until we all meet
again (see you later).]

age [n] *makahiki.* [v] *kūnewa.* [*Ua kūnewa ko Malu
'anakē! He kanawalu ona makahiki.* Malu's auntie has **aged**! She's 80 **years old**.]

aggressive *maha'oi* (also means **aggression, aggressiveness**). [*Auē ka maha'oi o ka malihini!* Gosh,
the **aggressiveness** of the newcomer!]

agitated 1. *pi'oloke.* [*Pi'oloke ka moho ma mua o ka
nīnauele.* The candidate is **agitated** before the
interview.] 2. *luliluli.* 3. *nū.*

agonizing *walania.*

agony *walania.*

agree *'ae.*

agreeable *waipahē*.

agreement 1. *'aelike* (contract). [*Ua pūlima 'o Ipo i ka **'aelike** e unuhi i nā palapala ho'oilina kahiko.* Ipo signed the **contract** to translate old wills.] 2. *lōkahi* (unity).

aid 1. *kāko'o* (also means **support** or **to support**). [*Nui ke **kāko'o** o nā mākuahūnōai i ka makuahine hou.* Plentiful is the **aid** of the parents-in-law for the new mother.] 2. *kōkua* (also means **help**, or **to help**). [***Kōkua** ka hope pelekikena i ke alaka'i 'ana i ka hui 'oihana.* The vice-president **aids** in leading the corporation.]

AIDS *ma'i hana ei* (refers to all sexually transmitted diseases).

aim at *kāki'i*. [***Kāki'i** ka mea pana pua i ke ki'i ma ka mau'u.* The archer **aims at** the picture on the grass.]

air 1. *(ke) ea*. [*Paoa **ke ea** i ka puakenikeni.* The **air** is strong with the scent of *pua-kenikeni* flowers.] Note: *Ea* has many other meanings, including **breath, life force, sovereignty**. 2. *lewa* (also means **sky, to sway**).

air-conditioner *mīkini hō'olu'olu ea*.

airplane *mokulele*.

airport *kahua mokulele*. [*Ma ka hola 'ehia ana e pae ai ka mokulele ma ke **kahua mokulele**?* What time will the plane land at the **airport**?]

airplane

alarm clock *uaki ho'āla*.

alcohol 1. *'alekohola*. 2. *lama*. [*Mai inu i ka **lama** a kalaiwa ma hope!* Don't drink [**alcohol**] and drive later!]

alert *[adj]* 1. *maka'ala*. 2. *miki 'ala*. (Be alert! Watch out! = *E maka'ala!*)

alike 1. *like.* [*E **like** me Likelike,* just **like** Likelike (Kalākaua's sister, mother of Ka'iulani) (song, "Sānoe," by Lili'uokalani)] 2. *kohu.* 3. *kūlike.*

alive *ola.*

all *nā mea a pau* (also means **everyone, everything**). [*Ua ha'alele **nā mea a pau** ma hope o ka 'aha mele.* **Everyone** left after the concert.]

allegiance *kūpa'a.* [***kūpa'a** ma hope o ka 'āina,* **allegiance** to the land (song, "Kaulana Nā Pua," by E. Prendergast)]

allow *'ae* (also means **yes**). [*E **'ae** mai 'oe i kāu kelepona.* **Allow** me to use your phone.]

alluring *'ume.*

almost 1. *'ane'ane.* 2. *kokoke.* (almost finished = *kokoke e pau*)

along *ma.* [*Holo nā keiki **ma** ka'e pā.* The children run **along** the edge of the wall.]

aloud *ma ka leo nui.*

alphabet *pī 'ā pā.* [*He 'umikūmākolu huapalapala o ka **pī 'ā pā** Hawai'i.* The Hawaiian **alphabet** has thirteen letters.]

altar 1. *kuahu* (where offerings are placed in *hula hālau*). 2. *lele* (section of *heiau* where sacrifices were laid).

although *'oiai.* [***'Oiai** hiki ia'u ke hele, pono au e noho.* **Although** I can go, I must stay.]

always 1. *nā manawa a pau.* 2. *mau.* [*Kelepona ko Ha'upu 'anakala iā ia i ka Lāpule a kama'ilio lāua e pili ana i ko lāua mo'okū'auhau i **nā manawa a pau**.* Ha'upu's uncle calls him on Sundays and they (two) **always** talk about their genealogy.]

amazement 1. *pū'iwa.* 2. *kupaianaha.* (Both have other meanings, such as **mysterious, awesome, shocking**.)

amazing *kupaianaha.* [*He hana **kupaianaha** ka hua'i 'ana o ka pele ma ka pō.* The bubbling up of lava at night is an **amazing** thing.]

ambassador *kuhina.* (cabinet minister under monarchy = *kuhina nui*)

ambition *'i'ini.* [*He* **'i'ini** *kona e hoe ma ke kōā 'o Kaiwi.* He has an **ambition** to paddle the Kaiwi Channel.]

ambulance *ka'a lawe ma'i.*

America 1. 'Amelika. 2. 'Amelika Hui Pū 'ia (USA).

amount *heluna* (also means **sum total**). [*'Ehia kālā ka* **heluna** *o ke kālā i uku 'ia mai?* What is the **amount** of the money that was paid?]

amputated 1. *mumuku.* 2. *muku.* 3. *mu'umu'u.*

amputee *mu'umu'u* (also means **long women's dress** adopted under missionary influence).

amuse *ho'ole'ale'a.*

ancestors *kūpuna.* [*Nani ke no'eau o ko kākou mau* **kūpuna** *i ka holo Moana.* The skill of our **ancestors** in ocean voyaging was magnificent.]

anchor 1. *heleuma.* 2. *hekau.*

ancient *kahiko.* [*I ke au* **kahiko**, *nui nā heiau like 'ole.* In **ancient** days there were many different kinds of *heiau.*]

angel *'ānela.* [*He* **'ānela** *kia'i 'o Gabriel.* Gabriel is a guardian **angel.**]

anger 1. *huhū.* 2. *wela.* 3. *inaina.*

angry 1. *huhū.* [*Inā 'oe ho'ohenehene iā ia, hele kāu 'īlio a* **huhū.** If you tease him, your dog gets **angry.**] 2. *wela.* [*Pi'i kona* **wela** *a 'ōlelo pelapela ihola.* His **anger** rises up and then he swears.]

anguish *walania.*

animal *holoholona.* [*'A'ole nui* **nā holoholona** *maoli ma kēia moku 'āina.* There are not many native **animals** in this state.]

animated *'īnana.*

ankle *ku'eku'e wāwae.*

annexation *ho'ohui 'āina.* [*Na wai e 'ole ke ho'āhewa i ka* **ho'ohui 'āina** *o Hawai'i?* Who would not condemn the **annexation** of Hawai'i?]

anniversary 1. *lā ho'omana'o.* 2. *piha makahiki.*
[*Hau'oli lā **piha makahiki!*** Happy **anniversary**!]
announce 1. *hō'ike.* 2. *kūkala.* (to broadcast news =
kūkala nūhou)
announcement 1. *hō'ike.* 2. *kūkala.*
annoy *ho'onāukiuki* (also means **to irritate**). [*Mai
ho'onāukiuki i kou pōki'i!* Don't **annoy** your
younger sibling!]
annoyed 1. *ukiuki.* 2. *uluhua* (also means **frustrated**).
anoint *poni.* (coronation, carnation = *poni mō'ī*)
another *kekahi.* [*Loa'a **kekahi** puke iā kāua?* Do we
(you and I) have **another** book?] *Kekahi* has other
uses, including as a pronoun. [*Aloha **kekahi** i
kekahi.* Love one **another**.]
answer 1. *pane.* 2. *ha'ina. [v]* 1. *pane.* [*Ke kani ke
kelepona, **pane** mau ka pēpē.* Whenever the telephone rings, the baby always **answers**.] 2. *eō*
(respond to name being called).
ant *naonao.* [*Kū ka paila o **nā naonao** e halihali aku
nei i nā huna laiki.* Tons of **ants** are carrying
away the grains of rice.]
Antarctic *'Anealika.*
anthurium *pua haka.* ['*O ka
"obake" kekahi 'ano **pua
haka** nunui hou.* The
"obake" is a new, very
large type of **anthurium**.]
anxiety *hopohopo* (also
means **worry, to worry,
nervous**). [*Pi'i wale a'e
ko'u **hopohopo** ke komo
au i ka haukapila.* My **anxiety** rises when I enter
a hospital.]

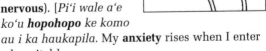

anthurium

any *kekahi.* (*Kekahi* is used before nouns and can
also mean **a, one of the, another.**) [*Loa'a **kekahi**
hua 'ai i ka pahu hau?* Is there **any** fruit in the
icebox?]

apart *ka'awale* (also means **separated, to separate, free,** as in free time = *manawa ka'awale*).

apartment 1. *ke'ena hale.* 2. *hale papa'i.*

apiece *pākahi* (also means **individually**). [*E helu **pākahi** 'olua i nā pila kīko'o a me ke kālā.* You (two) **individually** count the checks and the cash money.]

apologize *mihi.* [*Ke **mihi** a'e nei ke kāne 'ona i ho'oku'i i ko ka hope kia'āina ka'a.* The drunk man who hit the lieutenant governor's car is **apologizing.**]

appeal *[n] noi.* *[v]* 1. *kāhoahoa.* [*No ke aha lā e pono ai nā mākua Hawai'i e **kāhoahoa** mau i ka 'aha 'ōlelo e kāko'o i ka ho'ona'auao 'ana ?* Why should Hawaiian parents always have to **appeal** to the legislature to support education?] 2. *ui* (also means **to question, a query, question**).

appear 1. *puka.* 2. *kū.* [*Ua **kū** a'ela 'o Kamapua'a ma ka pali hāweo.* Kamapua'a then **appeared** on the glowing cliff.]

applaud *pa'ipa'i lima.*

applause *pa'ipa'i lima.*

apple *'āpala.* [*I 'āpana pai **'āpala** nāna, a i 'āpana pai 'ōhelo na'u, ke 'olu 'olu 'oe.* A piece of **apple** pie for her and a piece of 'ōhelo berry pie for me, please.] (mountain apple = *'ōhi'a 'ai*)

appoint *ho'okohu.* [*Na Pelekikena Roosevelt i **ho'okohu** iā Samuel Wilder King e lilo i kia'āina a ma kona poni 'ana i 'ōlelo ai ke kia'āina hou ma ka 'ōlelo 'ōiwi o ka 'āina.* It was President Roosevelt who **appointed** Samuel Wilder King to be governor, and at his swearing-in ceremony, the new governor spoke in the native language of the land.]

appreciate 1. *mahalo.* 2. *ho'omaika'i* (also means **to congratulate**).

appropriate *[adj] kūpono.* [*E ho'opa'a manawa kāua*

*i ka lā **kūpono**. Let's (you and me) make an appointment for the **appropriate** day.]*

approve *'āpono. [Ua '**āpono** 'ia kāu noi.* Your request has been **approved.**]

April *'Apelila* (from English).

apron *'epanelole.*

aquarium *pahu i'a.*

arbitrate *'uao* (also means **to negotiate**). *[Na wai e **'uao** i ka 'aelike hou?* Who should **arbitrate** the new contract?]

arbitrator *'uao.*

arch *pi'o* (also means **arched, curved**). *[**Pi'o** ke ānuenue.* The **rainbow** arches above.]

archer *mea pana pua.*

archery *pana pua.*

archipelago

archipelago *pae 'āina. [Nui wale nō nā mokupuni li'ili'i o ka **pae 'āina**.* There are many small islands in the **archipelago**.]

architect *kaha ki'i hale. ['Imi māua 'o Lahela i ke **kaha ki'i hale** e kaha ki'i hou i ko māua hale mahikō.* Lahela and I are looking for an **architect** to redesign our plantation house.]

Arctic *'Ālika.*

area 1. *kahua* (also means **field**). 2. *nui* (also means **size**). *['Ehia kapu'ai ke ākea o kēia **nui**?* How many feet is the width of this **area**?]

argue 1. *ho'opa'apa'a.* 2. *ho'owahapa'a.*

arise (command) *E ala!* (also means **get up**).

arm *lima* (also means **hand**).

army *pū'ali koa. [Ma hope o kona ho'oku'u 'ia 'ana e ka **pū'ali koa**, e ho'i ana kā lāua kaikamahine i ke kula?* After being released from the **army**, will their (two) daughter go back to school?]

arrest *hopu* (also means **seize**). [*Hopu* nā mākaʻikiu i nā kānaka kūʻai lāʻau ʻino. The detectives **arrest** drug dealers.]

arrive 1. *hōʻea* [*Ua hōʻea aku nā waʻa peʻa i ko Hāna hono.* The sailing canoes **arrived** in Hāna's bay.] 2. *hiki.*

art *hana noʻeau.*

artist *mea kaha kiʻi.*

ashamed *hilahila* (also means **embarrassed**). (bashful, shy = *maka hilahila*)

ashes *lehu.* [*Hū aʻe nā lehu o ka lua i ke kahe ʻana o ka pele?* Do **ashes** of the pit rise up when lava flows?]

Asia 1. ʻĀkia. 2. ʻĀsia.

aside *ma ka ʻaoʻao* (*lit.* on the side).

ask (favor) 1. *noi.* 2. *nonoi.* [*E nonoi i ka Haku e kōkua iā ʻoe.* **Ask** the Lord to help you. (traditional hymn)]

ask (question) *nīnau.* [*He nīnau a he noi kaʻu iā ʻoe.* I have a question and a favor to **ask** of you.]

asleep *hiamoe* (also means **to sleep**). [*Ke hiamoe nei ʻo ia nei.* This one here is **asleep**.]

assign 1. *hāʻawi.* 2. *kauoha.*

astonishing *kupaianaha.*

athlete *ʻālapa.* [*He mau ʻālapa ikaika nā wāhine hoe waʻa.* Women canoe paddlers are strong **athletes**.]

attend *hele.* [*Ua hele ʻoe i ka ʻaha mele?* Did you **attend** the concert?]

attention 1. *nānā.* 2. *maliu.* [*E maliu mai, e kuʻu ipo.* Pay **attention**, sweetheart.]

attractive (person/scene) 1. *māhiehie.* [*Ulu māhiehie ka nani o ka mesia.* The glory of the Messiah grows like an **attractive** garden. (traditional hymn)] 2. *nohea.*

audience *anaina.* [*Hū ka ʻaka o ke anaina.* The **audience**'s laughter burst out.]

August ʻAukake (from English).

aunt *'anakē.*
Australia 'Aukekulia.
average *'awelika.* [*He aha ka **'awelika** o kāu uku hana ma ka mahina?* What's the **average** of your monthly salary?]
awake *ala.* [*Ua **ala** 'oukou?* Are you all **awake**?]
away 1. *aku.* 2. *'ē.* [*E hele ma kahi **'ē**!* Go **away**! (also *Hele pēlā!*)]
awesome *'e'ehia.* [***E'ehia** ka hū 'ana a'e o ka pele a, i kekahi manawa, weliweli nō ho'i.* A volcanic eruption is **awesome** and sometimes also terrible.]
awful *weliweli* (also means **terrible, terrifying**). [*ke kaua **weliweli** ma Europa,* the **terrible** war in Europe (song, "Ke Kaua Weliweli," composer unknown)]
awkward 1. *hemahema.* [***Hemahema** wale nō ko'u hula 'ana.* My hula dancing is totally **awkward**.] 2. *hāwāwā.*
axe *ko'i* (also means **adze**).

baby *pēpē*. [*He **pēpē** hou kā lāua.* They (two) have a new **baby**.]

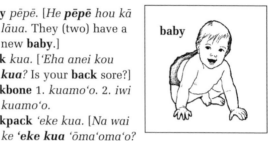

baby

back *kua*. [*'Eha anei kou **kua**?* Is your **back** sore?]

backbone 1. *kuamo'o*. 2. *iwi kuamo'o*.

backpack *'eke kua*. [*Na wai ke **'eke kua** 'ōma'oma'o?* Who does the green **backpack** belong to?]

bad *'ino*. [*Mai mana'o **'ino** mai!* Don't think **bad** things about me!]

bad-smelling 1. *hohono* (body odor). 2. *hauna* (rotting fish). [*Hō ka **hauna** o ka 'ōpala!* Gosh, how **bad-smelling** the garbage is!]

bag 1. *'eke*. 2. *pū'olo*.

bail 1. *kā* (to scoop water out of a canoe). [*E **kā** wa'a!* **Bail** out the canoe!] 2. *[n] pela* (from English; legal term).

bait *maunu*.

baker *mea puhi palaoa*.

bakery *hale puhi palaoa*.

ball *kinipōpō*. [*E hopu i ke **kinipōpō**!* Catch the **ball**!]

balloon *pāluna* (from English). [*E loa'a ana nā pāluna i nā keiki ma ke kaniwala.* The children will get **balloons** at the carnival.]

bamboo 1. *'ohe*. 2. *'ohe kāpala* (carved pieces of bamboo used for printing designs on tapa cloth). [*Me 'elua wale nō **'ohe kāpala** e ho'onani 'ia ai kēia kapa.* It is with only two **bamboo printers** that this tapa cloth should be decorated.]

banana *maiʻa.*

band 1. *pāna.* 2. *pāna puhi ʻohe.* [*Hoʻokani pinepine ka **pāna puhi ʻohe** ʻo Royal Hawaiian i nā mele a nā aliʻi i haku ai.* The Royal Hawaiian **band** often plays songs the royalty composed.]

bandage *wahī ʻeha.* [*E Māmā, loaʻa ka **wahī ʻeha** ma ka wane? Ua moku koʻu wāwae i ka puna.* Mom, got **bandages** in the van? My foot was cut on the coral.]

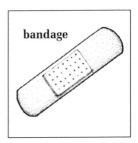

bandage

bang (sound of fireworks or gun) 1. *pohā.* 2. *pahū.*

bank *panakō.* [*Waiho ʻoukou i kā ʻoukou mau pila kīkoʻo uku ma ka **panakō?*** Do you all deposit your pay checks in the **bank?**]

banner 1. *lepa.* [*Ua kau ka **lepa** ma nā kihi o ka pā.* **Banners** were placed in the corners of the lot.] 2. *hae* (also means **flag**). 3. *bana* (from English).

barbeque *pūlehu.* [*Hiki ke **pūlehu** ʻia ka ʻopihi?* Can ʻopihi (shellfish) be **barbequed?**]

bark *[n] ʻili. [v] ʻaoa.* [*ʻAoa nā ʻīlio i ka pōpoki e pāheʻe nei i ka **ʻili** o ke kumulāʻau.* The dogs **bark** at the cat that's slipping on the **bark** of the tree.]

base 1. *kumu* (also means **intellectual or physical foundation, basis**). [*ʻInā maopopo iā ʻoe ka makemakika, he **kumu** maikaʻi ia ʻike no ka hana hoʻokani pila.* If you understand math, that knowledge is a good **foundation** for playing music.] 2. *kahua.*

baseball *pōhili.*

basket 1. *hīnaʻi* (also refers to a kind of **fish trap**). 2. *ʻie.* 3. *ʻeke* (also means **bag**).

basketball *pōhinaʻi.*

bat (animal) *'ōpe'ape'a*. [*'Ano 'ē ka lele 'ana o ka 'ōpe'ape'a*. A **bat**'s flying is odd.]

bat (sports) *lā'au kinipōpō*.

bathe *'au'au* (also means **to swim**).

bathroom 1. *lua*. 2 *lumi ho'opau pilikia*. [*Aia ka* **lumi ho'opau pilikia** *no nā wāhine ma ka 'ao'ao hema o ka hale ki'i 'oni'oni?* Is the ladies' **bathroom** on the left side of the movie theater?]

bathtub *kapu 'au'au* (also means **sink, wash basin**).

battery *pākali*. [*E kū'ai mai i nā* **pākali** *kūpono o ho'ā 'ole ka lekiō*. Buy the appropriate **batteries** or else the radio won't turn on.]

battle *kaua* (also means **war**). (World War II = *Ke Kaua Honua 'Elua*)

beach *kahakai*. [*Ma ke* **kahakai** *'o Keawa'ula e 'ike 'ia ai nā nai'a*. It's at the **beach** called Keawa'ula that dolphins are seen.]

beak (bird, snout of fish, animal) *nuku*.

beard *'umi'umi* (also means **mustache, whiskers**).

beat up *pepehi*.

beautiful 1. *nani*. [*He* **nani** *Ka'ala lae lā lae lae*. Ka'ala (mountain on O'ahu) is **beautiful**. (song, "Nani Ka'ala," composer unknown)] 2. *u'i* (usually refers to humans only).

because *no ka mea*. [*No ke aha e nuku ai ke po'o kumu i ke keiki?* **No ka mea**, *ua 'ōlelo pelapela ke keiki*. Why should the principal scold the boy? **Because** the child swore.]

bed 1. *moe*. 2. *kahi moe*.

bedroom *lumi moe*. [*E ho'i e hiamoe i kou* **lumi moe** *pono'ī, e Nāleipua*. Go to sleep in your own **bedroom**, Nāleipua.]

bee *nalomele*.

beef (meat) *'i'o pipi*.

before, in front of *ma mua o*. [*Ma mua o ka Natatorium kāua e hui ai ma kēia ahiahi*. It's **in**

begin • bird   249

front of the Natatorium that you and I should
meet this evening.]

begin *ho'omaka.* [***Ho'omaka** ka hālāwai ma ka hola
'ehia?* What time does the meeting **begin**?]

behind *hope* (also means **in back of**). [*Aia kāu puke
wehewehe ma **hope** ou.* Your dictionary is
behind you.]

belief *mana'o* (also means **thought, opinion, meaning, to think**).

below *lalo* (also means **under**). [*Aia paha ke 'ō ma
lalo o ke puna?* Is the fork **under** the spoon
maybe?]

belt *kuapo* (also means **to swap, trade**).

bend *pelu* (also means **to fold** [paper]).

bend down *'aui.*

bend over *lo'u.*

berry *hua li'ili'i.*

best *ka 'oi.* [*Maui nō ka 'oi!* Maui indeed is the **best**!]

better *'oi aku ka maika'i.* [***'Oi aku ka maika'i** o kāna
ki'i ma mua o kāu.* Her picture (that she
drew/painted) is **better** than yours.]

beyond *ma 'ō aku o.* [***ma 'ō aku o** ka laupapa,*
beyond the reef]

Bible Paipala. [*E heluhelu i kekahi mau paukū mai
ke Kauoha Hou o ka **Paipala**.* Read some verses
from the New Testament of the **Bible**.]

bicycle *paikikala.* [*Holo **paikikala** kekahi mau kānaka a puni ka mokupuni nui.* Some people ride
bicycles around the Big Island.]

big *nui.*

Big Dipper Nā Hiku (*lit.* "the seven").

bigot *ho'okae 'ili* (also means **racial prejudice**).

bill *pila* (from English). [*Pono ka 'ohana e uku i nā
pila me kēlā mahina kēia mahina.* The family
has to pay the **bills** each and every month.]

bird *manu.* [*Ua loa'a ke ko'e i ka **manu**.* The **bird**
caught the worm.]

birthday card *kāleka lā hānau*. [*Ua hoʻouna mai kou mau hoahānau i nā **kāleka lā hānau**?* Did your cousins send **birthday cards** to you?]

bite *nahu*.

bitter 1. *muʻemuʻe*. [***Muʻmuʻe** paha ka lāʻau Pākē?* Are Chinese herbal medicines **bitter** tasting?] 2. *ʻawaʻawa*.

black *ʻeleʻele*. [***Eleʻele** loa ka pōʻeleʻele o ka pō Muku.* The darkness of the night Muku (the last night of the waning moon) is really **black**.]

blackboard *papa ʻeleʻele*.

blanket *kapa*. (traditional Hawaiian blanket made of five pieces of tapa sewn together, the top layer [*kilohana*] decorated = *kapa moe*)

bleed *kahe koko* (also means **blood flows**). [*Ua moku ko ka malihini wāwae i ka ʻaʻā a ua **kahe koko** nō.* The tourist's foot was cut on the sharp lava and there was lots of **bleeding**.]

bless 1. *hoʻomaikaʻi* (to bless things). 2. *hoʻopōmaikaʻi* (to bless people). [*Ua **hoʻopōmaikaʻi** ke kahunapule i ka pēpē hou.* The minister **blessed** the new baby.]

blind *makapō*. [***Makapō** kēnā luahine?* Is that old lady (near you) **blind**?]

blood *koko*. [*He **koko** Hawaiʻi kona?* Does he have Hawaiian **blood**?]

blooming *mōhala*. (the blooming flower [often refers to young people beginning to grow up] = *ka pua mōhala*)

blow 1. *puhi*. 2. *pā*. [***Pā** mai ka makani Moaʻe.* The trade winds **are blowing**.]

blowhole *puhi* (also means **eel, to be destroyed by burning**).

blue *uliuli* (also means **any dark color**, such as ocean or mountains seen from a distance).

board (transportation) *kau ma luna o*. [*Pono nā ʻōhua e **kau ma luna o** kekahi kaʻa ʻōhua ʻoiai*

ua pōloke ka peleki. The passengers have to
board another bus, since the brakes are broken.]

boat *waʻapā* (small boat such as a whaler). (cruise
ship = *mokuahi*)

body *kino.* [*Maʻemaʻe wale ke **kino** o ka palai.* The
body of the fern is clean and chaste. (song,
"Kaʻililauokekoa," by Henry Waiʻau)]

body surf *kaha nalu.* [***Kaha nalu** ʻnā ʻōpio ma
Makapuʻu.* The young people **body surf** at
Makapuʻu.]

body surfer *mea kaha nalu.*

bold 1. *koa.* 2. *makoa* (also means **brave**).

bone *iwi.* [*ʻAʻohe **iwi** o nā mū.* Bugs don't have **bones**.]

book *puke.* [*He mau **puke** kiʻi kā koʻu hoaaloha no
nā mokupuni like ʻole o ka Pākīpika.* My friend
has picture **books** of the various islands of the
Pacific.]

boots *kāmaʻa puti* (from
English).

border *palena* (also means
limit, boundary). [*Me ke
aloha **palena** ʻole.* With
boundless love. (saluta-
tion)]

boots

bored 1. *pakuā.* 2. *manakā*
(also means **boring**).
[***Manakā** ka hana waele nāhelehele.* Pulling
weeds is a **boring** activity.]

borrow *hōʻaiʻē.* [*Nele māua i ka palaoa no ka
hoʻomākaukau ʻana i pai pika. Hiki iā māua ke
hōʻaiʻē i ʻelua kīʻaha palaoa?* We (two) lack flour
for preparing pizza pie. Can we **borrow** two cups
of flour?]

boss 1. *haku.* 2. *luna* (also means **manager, supervisor**). [*Auē ke ʻano paʻakikī o kaʻu **luna** ma ke
keʻena ʻoihana!* Wow, my **boss** at work has a
stubborn character!]

both *lāua 'elua* (*lit.* they two).

bounce *lelele.*

bowl *pola.* [*Aia ka **pola** poi ma ka pākaukau.* The poi **bowl** is on the table.]

bowl

bowling *ulu maika haole.* [*'Ehia mau kāne ma kā 'olua hui **ulu maika haole**?* How many men are in your (two) **bowling** group?]

box *pahu* (also means **drum, storage chest**). [*He **pahu** pepa mānoanoa ko ka hale leka?* Does the post office have cardboard **boxes**?]

boy *keiki kāne.* [*He **keiki kāne** a i 'ole he kaikamahine kā 'olua pēpē?* Is your (two) baby a **boy** or a girl?]

bra *pale waiū.*

bracelet 1. *apolima.* [*Ua hā'awi 'ia mai ke **apolima** kula Hawai'i mua loa iā Ka'iulani e kona 'anakē 'o Lydia (Lili'uokalani).* The first Hawaiian gold **bracelet** was given to Ka'iulani by her aunt Lydia (Lili'uokalani).] 2. *kūpe'e.*

brag *kaena.* [*Mai **kaena** ma mua o kāu ipo!* Don't **brag** in front of your sweetheart!]

braid 1. *hili* (in *lei* making, braiding one type of plant). [*I ko Kalei **hili** 'ana i ka pala'ā, piha ka lumi i ke 'ala anuhea o ke kuahiwi.* When Kalei **braids** the *pala'ā* fern, the room is filled with cool mountain fragrance.] 2. *haku* (in *lei* making, braiding together several types of plants).

brain *lolo.* [*Ho'iho'i ke a'a koko i ke koko i ka **lolo**.* The veins return blood to the **brain**.]

brake *peleki* (from English). [*Hehi 'o ia i ko kona paikikala **peleki**.* He steps on his bicycle's **brake**.]

branch *lālā* (also means **member of group, club**). [*Ua *hāʻule iho kekahi **lālā** i ka pōʻino.* A **branch** fell down because of the storm.]

bread *palaoa* (also means **flour, dough**). (slice of bread = *pāpaʻa palaoa*)

breadfruit *ʻulu.* [*ʻAʻole ʻo ia ala i ʻai mua i ka **ʻulu**.* That one over there (that person) hasn't eaten **breadfruit** before.]

break 1. *haki* (break something; syn. *haʻi*). [*Ināhea i **haki** ai nā pipi i ka pā lāʻau?* When did the cattle **break** the wooden fence?] 2. *nahā.* 3. *wāwahi.* 4. *ʻaʻe* (to break a *kapu*). 5. *poʻi* (waves).

breakfast *ʻaina kakahiaka.* [*ʻO ka hēʻī me ka maiʻa kāna **ʻaina kakahiaka**.* Papaya and banana are his **breakfast**.]

breakwater *pale kai.*

breast 1. *waiū.* 2. *ū.*

breath 1. *hanu.* 2. *ea.* 3. *aho.*

breathe 1. *hanu.* [***Hanu** ka iʻa i kona pihapiha.* Fish **breathe** through their gills.] 2. *aho.* 3. *hā.*

breeze 1. *makani* (also means **wind**). 2. *ahe-ahe.*

bright (shiny) 1. *hinuhinu.* [***Hinuhinu** ko kēlā wahine lauoho ʻeleʻele.* That woman's black hair is **shiny**.] 2. *mālamalama.* 3. *ʻōlinolino.* 4. *ʻalohi.*

bring *lawe mai.* [*E **lawe mai** i kā ʻolua palapala male, ke ʻoluʻolu.* **Bring** your (two) marriage license, please.]

broad 1. *ākea.* 2. *laulā.* (Both *ākea* and *laulā* also mean **breadth, width, wide.**)

broadcast (news) 1. *kūkala.* [***Kūkala** nūhou lākou ma ka hola ʻeono.* They **broadcast** the news at 6 o'clock.] 2. *hoʻolono.*

broil *pūlehu.*

broken 1. *poloke* (from English). 2. *nahā.* 3. *haki.* [*Iā Pānānā i hāʻule ai, ua **haki** ʻia kona kuʻekuʻe wāwae.* When Pānānā fell, her ankle was **broken**.]

broom *pūlumi* (also means **to sweep up**). (broom

made of coconut midribs tied together = *pūlumi nī‘au*)

brother *kaikunāne* (refers to brother of a woman. A man has *kaikua‘ana* [older brother] and *kaikaina* [younger brother] while a woman uses these same terms to refer to her older and younger sisters.).

brown *palaunu* (from English).

brown skin *‘ili ‘ula*.

bruise *pohole*.

bruised *pohole*. [***Pohole** ko ka mea he‘e nalu wāwae i ka nalu i po‘i ma luna ona.* The surfer's leg is **bruised** due to the wave that broke on top of him.]

brush *palaki* (from English). [*Ke **palaki** nei ‘oe i kou mau niho?* Are you **brushing** your teeth?]

bubble [n] *hu‘ahu‘a*. [v] 1. *pua‘i*. [*Nui nā **hu‘ahu‘a** e **pua‘i** ana i ka wai puna.* There are lots of **bubbles** that **bubble** up in spring water.] 2. *hua‘i*.

bucket *pākeke* (also means **pocket**). [*Piha ka **pākeke** a ka lawai‘a i nā ‘opihi.* The fisherman's **bucket** is full of ‘opihi.]

bud *‘ōpu‘u* (used as a symbol of new growth, a young person about to "blossom").

bug 1. *mū*. 2. *iniseka* (from English).

build *kūkulu* (also means **to set up tent**).

building *hale* (also means **house**). [*He **hale** hāiki a lō‘ihi nō ‘o Aloha Tower nani.* Beautiful Aloha Tower is a narrow and tall **building**.]

bump *pu‘u* (also means **hill, pimple**, many other meanings).

bunch *pū‘ā* (also means **bundle, clump, flock**). [*He **pū‘ā** hulu manu ko ka mea hana lei hulu.* The feather *lei* maker has a **bunch** of bird feathers.]

burn 1. *ho‘ā* (also means **to light a fire, turn on electrical appliance**). 2. *‘ā*.

burned *pāpa‘a*. [*Ua **pāpa‘a** kona manamana lima i ke ahi.* His finger was **burned** in the fire.]

bury *kanu* (also means **to plant**). [*Mai **kanu** i nā pūpū o nalowale.* Don't **bury** the shells or else they will be lost.]

bus *ka'a 'ōhua.* [*Ke kau nei nā 'ōhua ma luna o ke **ka'a 'ōhua**.* The passengers are boarding the **bus**.]

bush *lā'au* (also means **medicine**). (Hawaiian herbal medicine = *lā'au lapa'au*) (vine = *lā'auhihi*)

business *'oihana.* [*He ho'okele **'oihana** kēlā wahine.* That woman is a **business** leader.]

but *akā.* [*'A'aka ka wiliki **akā** akamai 'o ia.* The engineer is grouchy, **but** she is smart.]

butter *waiū paka.*

butterfly *pulelehua* (also means **moth**).

butterfly

buttocks *'ēlemu.* [*'Eha ko ka haumāna **'ēlemu** i ka noho 'ana ma mua o ka lolouila.* The student's **buttocks** are sore due to sitting in front of the computer.]

button *(ke) pihi.* [*Mai kaomi i ke **pihi**!* Don't push the **button**!]

buy *kū'ai mai.* (to shop around = *kū'ai hele*) [*Ke **kū'ai hele** nei ka makuahine a me kāna kaikamahine e **kū'ai mai** i lole pipi'i no ka hulahula 'ana ma ka Prom.* The mother and her daughter are **shopping around** to **buy** an expensive dress for dancing at the Prom.]

cage 1. *pahu holoholona* (*lit.* animal box). 2. *pahu manu* (*lit.* bird box).

cake *mea ʻono* (also means **dessert, any sweet or pastry**).

calabash 1. *ʻumeke.* [*I ke au kahiko, ua hoʻolewalewa ʻia ka **ʻumeke** i ke kōkō ma ka ʻauamo.* In the old days, a **calabash** was made to sway in a net of the carrying pole.] 2. *ipu.*

calculate *hoʻonohonoho helu.* [**Hoʻonohonoho helu** *wikiwiki nā ʻuao i nā helu ʻai ma ka pāʻani pōhinaʻi.* Referees quickly **calculate** the scores in basketball games.]

calendar *ʻalemanaka.* [*Helu ka **ʻalemenaka** kahiko i nā pō mahina.* The ancient **calendar** counts the nights of the moon.]

April						
SUN	MON	TUE	WED	THU	FRI	SAT
	1	2	3	4	5	6
	8	9	10	11	12	13
14	15	16	17	18	19	20
21	22	23	24	25	26	27
28	29	30				

calendar

calico *kalakoa.* [*ʻO ke **kalakoa** kekahi ʻano lole a kekahi ʻano pōpoki nō hoʻi.* **Calico** is a kind of cloth and a kind of cat, too.]

call (phone) *kelepona* (from English).

call out *kāhea.*

calm *mālie.* [**Mālie** *wale ka wanaʻao.* Dawn is very **calm** (implies peaceful).]

calmness *laʻi* (also means **quiet**).

camera *pahu paʻi kiʻi.* [*Hiki anei iā ʻoe ke paʻi kiʻi iā māua i kā māua **pahu paʻi kiʻi** hou?* Can you take our (two, not you) picture with our new **camera**?]

camp *ho'omoana.*

campground *kahua ho'omoana.* [*Ua ho'okapu 'o 'Anakala i ke **kahua ho'omoana** ma Mokulē'ia no kēia hopenapule a'e.* Uncle reserved the **campground** at Mokulē'ia for next weekend.]

can [v] *hiki.* [***Hiki** iā 'oukou ke kōkua mai ia'u?* **Can** you all help me?]

canal 1. *alawai.* 2. *'auwai.*

cancel 1. *kāpae* (skip over, delete). [*E **kāpae** i ka ho'okapu noho ma ka hana keaka, ke 'olu 'olu.* **Cancel** the reservations at the theater, please.] 2. *ho'opau* (put an end to, finish).

cancer *ma'i 'a'ai.* [*Aia ka **ma'i 'a'ai** ma kona 'ake māmā.* The **cancer** is in her lung].

candidate *moho.* [*E lilo paha ana ko ke kamanā kaikuahine i **moho** no ka Papa Alaka'i Ho'ona'auao.* The carpenter's sister may become a **candidate** for the Board of Education.]

candle *ihoiho.*

candy *kanakē.* [*'A'ole paha 'ono ke **kanakē** kōpa'a 'ole.* Sugarless **candy** may not be delicious.]

cane *ko'oko'o.* [*He **ko'oko'o** ko ke kāne 'o'opa.* The lame man has a **cane**.]

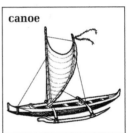

canoe

canoe 1. *wa'a.* 2. *wa'a kaukahi* (single hulled). 3. *wa'a kaulua* (double hulled).

canoe club *hui wa'a.*

cape 1. *lae* (peninsula or point). 2. *'ahu'ula* (feather cloak or cape, symbol of high nobility).

capitol *kapikala* (from English). [*Kohu like ke **kapikala** moku 'āina me ka lua pele ke nānā aku.* The state **capitol** looks like a volcano.]

captain *kāpena.* [*He **kāpena** moku māka'ika'i 'o*

Kanalunui. Kanalunui is a **captain** of a sightsee-
ing boat.]

captive *pio.*

capture 1. *hopu* (also means **to catch, grab**). 2. *lawe*
pio (*lit.* take prisoner).

car *ka'a.* [*'Ehia* **ka'a** *o kou*
'ohana? How many **cars**
does your family have?]

car

card *kāleka.* [*E ho'ouna aku*
ana 'oukou i nā **kāleka**
Kalikimaka ma kēia
makahiki a'e? Will you
all send out Christmas
cards next year?]

career *'oihana* (also means **business, profession**).

careful *akahele.* [*E* **akahele***!* Be **careful***!*]

carpenter *kamanā.* [*He aha kāu 'oihana? He*
kamanā *kūkulu hale au.* What is your career?
I'm a house-building **carpenter**.]

carpet *moena* (also means
mat, bed).

carrot

carrot *kāloke.* [*'Ono ka lio i*
ke **kāloke***.* Horses crave
carrots.]

carry, transport *halihali.*

carton *pahu.*

carve *kālai.* (to carve a canoe
= *kālai wa'a* [also means
canoe builder]) (to carve
an image = *kālai ki'i* [also means image carver])

cashier *kanaka 'ohi kālā.* [*He hana kā ka'u keiki ma*
ke 'ano he **kanaka 'ohi kālā** *ma ka hale kū'ai*
puke. My son has a job as a **cashier** at the book-
store.]

cassette tape *lola.*

cat *pōpoki.*

catch 1. *hopu.* [*Mai ho'ā'o e* **hopu** *i nā pipi 'āhiu o* *pilikia auane'i 'oe.* Don't try to **catch** wild cattle or you'll have trouble sooner or later.] 2. *'apo.* (catch fish = *lawai'a*)

category 1. *māhele* (also means **part, section, to divide, share**). [*Nui nā **māhele** hana i ka hana hulu.* There are lots of **categories** of work in featherwork.] 2. *'ano* (also means **type, brand**).

cattle *pipi.*

cave *ana.* [*Ua komo nā po'e kahiko i ke **ana** kahakai e noho i laila i ka wā kaua.* The ancestors entered the sea **cave** to live there in times of war.]

cavity 1. *puka niho* (tooth cavity). 2. *po'o* (also means **head, whole note**).

ceiling *kaupoku.*

celebrate *ho'olaule'a* (also means **festival, celebration**). [*E **ho'olaule'a** kākou ma kou lā hope ma ka hana.* Let's all **celebrate** on your last day at work.]

cement *kimeki.*

cemetery *pā ilina.* [*Aia ka ho'olewa ma ka **pā ilina** ma ka Pō'aono.* The funeral is at the **cemetery** on Saturday.]

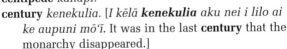

cemetery

cent *keneka.*

center *kikowaena.*

centipede *kanapī.*

century *kenekulia.* [*I kēlā **kenekulia** aku nei i lilo ai ke aupuni mō'ī.* It was in the last **century** that the monarchy disappeared.]

ceramics *ka hana pālolo.*

cereal *sereala* (from English).

chain *kaula.* (chain-link fence = *pā kaula hao*) (chain of islands = *pae 'āina*)

chair *noho.*

chalk *poho.*

change *[n]* 1. *kenikeni* (loose coins). 2. *koena* (change from purchase). [*Eia kou **koena**, e ke kaikamahine.* Here's your **change**, girl.] *[v]* 3. *ho'ololi.* [*E **ho'ololi** lole a e komo i ka lole 'au'au.* **Change** clothes and put on your swimsuit.] 2. *loli.* [*Hō ua **loli** kona mana'o e pili ana i ka huaka'i i Aotearoa!* Gosh, he **changed** his mind about the trip to New Zealand!]

channel *kōā* (ocean or TV channel or space between objects).

chant *oli.* [*Kaulana ke **oli** 'o "'Au'a 'Ia."* "'Au'a 'Ia" is a well-known **chant**.]

chanter *mea oli.*

chase 1. *alualu.* 2. *hāhai* (also means **to follow**).

chase off *kipaku* (also means **to kick out**).

cheap *emi.* [*'A'ole **emi** ke kakalina.* Gasoline isn't **cheap**.]

cheat 1. *kikiki* (from English). 2. *'āpuka* (implies fraud, deceit, much more serious harm than *kikiki*).

check (bank) *pila kīko'o.* [*Hiki anei ia'u ke uku i ka **pila kīko'o**?* Can I pay with a **check**?]

cherish 1. *pūlama.* [***Pūlama** 'ia nō 'oe me ke aloha.* You are **cherished** with love. (song, "He Punahele Nō 'Oe," by A. Nāhale'ā)] 2. *ho'oheno.*

check

chest 1. *houpo.* 2. *poli.* 3. *umauma.*

chicken *moa.* [*Hānai **moa** kāne ko'u hoahānau no nā hakakā moa.* My cousin raises roosters for **chicken** fights.]

chief 1. *ali'i* (also means **nobility, royalty, noble/royal**). 2. *lani.*

child *keiki.* [*He lei poina 'ole ke **keiki**.* ('ōlelo no'eau)

A **child** is a *lei* that cannot be forgotten.] (*pl.* **children** = *nā keiki;* my children = *kā'u mau keiki*)

chilly *hu'ihu'i* (also means **chilled**). [*He kuahiwi* **hu'ihu'i** *'o Mauna Kea.* Mauna Kea is a **chilly** mountain.]

chime *kani.*

chin *'auwae.* [*I ke kahi 'ana ona i kona 'umi'umi, ua kalakala ko kona* **'auwae** *'ili.* When he shaved his beard, the skin on his **chin** was rough.]

China *Kina.*

Chinese *Pākē.* [*He hapa* **Pākē** *paha 'olua?* Are you two part-**Chinese** maybe?]

chocolate *kokoleka.* [*Inu kā'u mau keiki i ke* **kokoleka** *ma ka pō.* My children drink **chocolate** at night.]

choke 1. *'umi* (to choke someone). 2. *kalea* (choke or cough). 3. *ha'u* (choke with sobs).

choose *koho* (also means **choice**). [*'O kēia pālule aloha ka i* **koho** *'ia? He nani ia!* Is this aloha shirt the one that was **chosen**? It's pretty!]

choppy (seas) 1. *hānupanupa.* [**Hānupanupa** *ke kai ma Hāna.* The sea is **choppy** at Hāna.] 2. *'ōkaikai.*

Christmas *Kalikimaka.* (Christmas Day = *ka lā Kalikimaka*)

church *hale pule.* (church congregation = *'ekalesia*) [*Ua kipa aku mākou i ka* **hale pule** *'o Kaumakapili a ua ho'okipa mai ka* **'ekalesia**. We visited Kaumakapili **church** and the **congregation** welcomed us.]

church

circle 1. *pō'ai.* 2. *pōhai.* [**pōhai** *ke aloha,* encircling love (song, "Pōhai Ke Aloha," by L. Machado/M. Kealakai)] 3. *lina poepoe.*

circumference *anapuni.* [*'Ehia kapua'i ke **anapuni** o kēia pō'ai?* How many feet is the **circumference** of this circle?]

circus *hō'ike'ike.*

citizen *maka'āinana* (also means **commoner, a person not of chiefly rank**). (representative = *luna maka'āinana*) [*'O Kūhiō ka **luna maka'āinana** i aloha nui 'ia.* Kūhiō (Kalaniana'ole) was a **representative** of the people who was greatly loved.]

city *kūlanakauhale.* [*He **kūlanakauhale** 'o Kahului ma Maui.* Kahului is a **city** on Maui.]

civil rights *pono kiwila.* [*Ua 'a'e 'ia nā **pono kiwila** o nā Hawai'i i ka hō'ole i ka hapanui o lākou e koho pāloka.* The **civil rights** of Hawaiians were violated by denying the majority of them the right to vote.]

clap *[v] pa'ipa'i lima* (clap hands, applaud).

class *papa* (also means **wood, any flat surface, stratum,** many other meanings). [*Aia i hea kā ke kumu kula **papa** ma kēia lā?* Where is the schoolteacher's **class** today?]

claw 1. *miki'ao* (also means **fingernail**). 2. *māi'u'u* (bird; also means **fingernail, toenail, hoof**).

clay *pālolo.*

clean *ma'ema'e.* *[v] ho'oma'ema'e.* [*Ho'oma'ema'e pinepine ke kāne iā loko o kona kalaka.* The man often **cleans** the inside of his truck.]

clear 1. *ahuwale* (clear view). 2. *mao* (clear weather after rain). 3. *mōakāka* (easily understood). [*Mōakāka ko ke kauka niho wehewehe 'ana pehea e palaki niho ai.* The dentist's explanation on how to brush your teeth is **clear**.]

cliff *pali.* [*Pulu pinepine nā **pali** Ko'olau i ka ua.* The Ko'olau **cliffs** are often soaked wet with rain.]

climb 1. *pi'i.* 2. *pinana.* [*Mai **pinana** i ka pā kaula hao!* Don't **climb** the chain link fence!]

clock *uaki* (also means **watch**). [*Kani ka **uaki** nui ma*

*waho o ka hale pule ma
ka hapahā hola.* The
large **clock** outside the
church chimes on the
quarter hour.]

clock

close *[v]* pani. [*E **pani** i ka
pukaaniani o anuanu 'oe
ma hope.* **Close** the window or you'll be cold
later.]

close (proximity) *kokoke.* [*Aia ka hale leka **kokoke** i
ka Hale Ali'i 'o 'Iolani.* The post office is **close** to
'Iolani Palace.]

close (relationship) *pili.* [*E ho'i mai kāua lā e **pili**.*
Let's come back together and be **close**. (common
line in love songs)]

closed *pa'a* (also means **firm, completed,** many other
meanings). [*Auē! **Pa'a** ka panakō!* Oh, dear! The
bank is **closed!**]

clothes *lole.* [*Pipi'i ko ka pu'ukani **lole**?* Are the
singer's **clothes** expensive?] (clothes washer =
mīkini holoi lole)

cloud *ao* (also means **light,
enlightenment, daytime,**
many other meanings).

cloud

cloudy *'ōmalumalu.*
clown *kalauna* (from
English).
club 1. *hui.* 2. *kalapu* (from
English).
clumsy 1. *hemahema.* 2.
hāwāwā.

coast *kapakai.* [*Eia mākou, kou **kapakai**.* Here we
are, your **coast.** (song, "Queen's Jubilee,"
Lili'uokalani)]

coat *kuka.* (raincoat = *kuka ua*)

coconut *niu.*

coconut husk *pulu* (used to make *'aha*, sennit rope).

coconut leaf *lau niu*.

coconut milk *wai niu*.

coconut tree *kumuniu*.

coffee *kope* (also means **copy**). [*Ke hana **kope** ke kākau 'ōlelo, inu 'o ia i ke **kope**.* When the secretary makes **copies**, he drinks **coffee**.]

coffee

coin 1. *kenikeni* (pocket change). 2. *kālā pa'a*.

cold 1. *anuanu*. 2. *anu*. [*Hō ke **anu** o ka uka 'iu'iu!* Goodness, the high uplands are **cold**!]

collect 1. *hō'ili'ili*. [*Laha 'ole a pipi'i nā po'oleka Hawai'i i **hō'ili'ili** 'ia e ia.* The Hawaiian stamps which were **collected** by her are rare and expensive.] 2. *'ohi*. 3. *hō'ahu*.

collection 1. *hō'ili'ili*. 2. *hō'ahu*.

color *[n]* 1. *waiho'olu'u*. 2. *kala* (from English; also means to color). [*He aha kāu **waiho'olu'u** punahele no ke **kala** ki'i 'ana?* What is your favorite **color** for **coloring** pictures?]

comb *[n]* *kahi* (also means **the place**, many other meanings).[*'O ka 'āina ho'opulapula i kapa 'ia 'o Ho'olehua **kahi** āna i hanai 'ia ai.* The Hawaiian Homes land named Ho'olehua is **the place** she was raised.] *[v]* *kahi* (also means **to shave, scrape down poi bowl**). [*E **kahi** i kou lauoho ma mua o ka ha'alele 'ana i ka hale.* **Comb** your hair before leaving the house.]

combine *ho'ohui*. [*E **ho'ohui** i ke kōpa'a, ka wai niu a me ka palaoa.* **Combine** the sugar, coconut milk and flour.]

come *hele mai*.

come back *ho'i mai*. [*E **ho'i mai**, e ku'u ipo.* **Come**

back to me, my sweetheart. (song, "Poli'ahu," by F. Hewett)]

comfortable *'olu'olu* (also means **kind, nice**). [***'Olu'olu*** *ko ko 'olua mau mākua hale kahiko?* Is your (two) parents' old house **comfortable**?]

command *kauoha.* [***Kauoha*** *ko lākou alaka'i i nā koa.* Their leader **commands** the soldiers.]

common *laha.* (*ant.* rare = *laha 'ole*) [***Laha*** *ka ma'i koko pi'i.* High blood pressure is a **common** ailment.]

community *kaiaulu.*

community college *kula nui kaiaulu.*

compact disc (CD) *sēdē, cēdē.*

compare *ho'ohālike.* [*Inā* ***ho'ohālike*** *'oe i nā pūpū, hiki ke 'ike i ka 'oko'a ma waena o ka pūpū laiki a me ka pūpū Kahelelani.* If you **compare** shells, you can recognize the difference between a "rice" shell and a Kahelelani shell.]

complain 1. *namunamu.* [*'A'ole hiki iā 'oe ke kūnānā wale a* ***namunamu*** *mai.* You can't just stand there undecided and **complain** to me.] 2. *'ōhumu.*

complete *pa'a* (has many other meanings). [*Ua* ***pa'a*** *ka palapala kauoha.* The will is **completed**.]

compose (words/music) *haku.* [*Na Kalākaua i* ***haku*** *iā "Hawai'i Pono'ī."* It was Kalākaua who **composed** "Hawai'i Pono'ī."] (poet, composer = *haku mele*) (author = *haku puke*)

compost *pulu.*

computer 1. *lolouila* (*lit.* electric brain). 2. *kamepiula* (from English).

computer

concept *mana'o* (also means **thought, idea, meaning, opinion, to think, consider**).

concern *kuleana* (also means **rights, responsibility**).

concert *'aha mele*. [*'Ehia mele Hawai'i i hīmeni 'ia ma ka **'aha mele** 'o Kanikapila?* How many Hawaiian songs were sung at the Kanikapila **concert**?]

conclusion *hopena* (also means **result, consequence**). [*E hana pono o 'ike ana 'oe i ka **hopena**.* Work properly or you will suffer the **consequences**.]

condom *uhi ule*.

confirm *hō'oia*. (syn. *hō'oia'i'o*)

confused 1. *huikau*. 2. *pohihihi*. [*'A'ole mōakāka ko ka haku puke mana'o a **pohihihi** ka mea heluhelu puke.* The author's thought isn't clear and the reader is **confused**.]

confusion 1. *huikau*. 2. *pohihihi*.

congratulate *ho'omaika'i*.

congratulations *ho'omaika'i*. [***Ho'omaika'i** iā 'olua i ko 'olua piha makahiki!* **Congratulations** on your (two) anniversary!]

Congress *'Aha'ōlelo Pekelala*. (syn. *'Aha'ōlelo lāhui*)

connect 1. *ho'ohui*. 2. *ho'oku'i*.

conquer *na'i*.

conscience *lunawaemana'o*. (syn. *luna'ikehala*)

consciousness *'ike ho'omaopopo*. (lose consciousness = *pau ka 'ike, kauhola*; regain consciousness = *pohala, ao*)

consent *'ae* (also means **to agree, allow, say yes to**). [*Ua **'ae** ka pa'a male i ka 'aelike male.* The married couple **consented** to the marriage contract.]

consider 1. *mana'o*. 2. *no'ono'o*.

considerate *no'ono'o*.

constant *mau* (also means **enduring, ongoing**, many other meanings). [***Mau** nō ke aloha o ka makua i kāna keiki.* The love of a parent for his child is **constant**.]

constellation 1. *huihui*. [*'O Nāhiku ka **huihui** e kuhi ana i ka Hōkū Pa'a.* The Big Dipper is the constellation that points to the North Star.] 2. *ulu hōkū.*

constitution (legal document) *kumu kānāwai.*

construct *kūkulu.*

construction worker *lima hana.*

contact lenses *pilimaka.*

container 1. *ipu.* 2. *pū'olo.*

contest *ho'okūkū* (also means **competition**). [*'O ka Merrie Monarch ka* **ho'okūkū** *hula kaulana loa o Hawai'i nei.* The Merrie Monarch is the most famous hula **contest** here in Hawai'i]. (spelling bee = *ho'okūkū hua 'ōlelo*)

continent *'āina puni 'ole.*

continue *ho'omau.*

conversation *kama'ilio.*

converse *[v]* 1. *kama'ilio.* 2. *wala'au* (informally).

cook 1. *kuke.* 2. *kālua* (in an *imu*).

cooked (food) *mo'a* (also means **done**). [*Ua* **mo'a** *ka 'i'o moa.* The chicken is **done.**]

cool *hu'ihu'i* (also means **chilly**).

cooled down *ma'alili* (refers to cooked food that has cooled, also to cooled passion).

copy *[n]* *kope* (from English). *[v]* *hana kope* (also means **to photocopy**). [*Hiki ke* **hana kope** *'ia kēia 'ao'ao.* This page can be **copied.**]

coral 1. *puna.* 2. *'āko'ako'a.* (coral head = *pūkoa*) Note: There are many names for individual corals.

cord 1. *kaula* (also means **rope**). 2. *'aha* (coconut fiber). 3. *aho.* 4. *piko* (umbilical).

corner 1. *kihi* (outside). 2. *kū'ono* (inside). [*mai luna a lalo, mai kekahi* **kihi** *a i kekahi* **kihi**, from top to bottom, from one

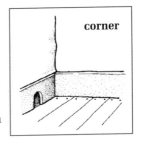

corner

corner (of house) to another (common line in house-blessing chants)]

correct *pololei*. [***Pololei** ka māka'i, ua hewa kou kalaiwa 'ana me ka inu pia pū.* The policeman is **correct**, your driving and drinking beer too is wrong.]

cost *kumu kū'ai* (also means **price**).

cotton 1. *pulu.* 2. *ma'o.* [*Komo ko'u makuahine i nā lole **ma'o** wale nō ma ke kauwela.* My mother wears only **cotton** clothes in the summer.]

cough *kunu.* [*He anu ko kāna pēpē a **kunu** mau ka pēpē.* His baby has a cold and the baby constantly **coughs**.]

count *helu.* [*E **helu** i kāu mau puke ma mua o ka ho'okomo 'ana i loko o nā pahu.* **Count** your books before inserting them in the boxes.]

country *'āina.* [*'O Keālia kou **'āina?** Is Keālia your **country** (the place where you are from)?]

country person *kua'āina.*

county *kalana.* [*Aia ma lalo o ke **kalana** 'o Maui nā mokupuni 'o Lāna'i, Kaho'olawe, Maui a me Moloka'i.* Under the **county** of Maui are the islands of Lāna'i, Kaho'olawe, Maui and Moloka'i.]

courageous *koa* (also means **long-lived, soldier**).

court 1. *aloali'i* (royal). [*Kā'alo ke **aloali'i** o ka ho'olaule'a ma ka lā mua o Mei i ke anaina.* The **royal court** of the May Day festival goes past the audience.] 2. *'aha ho'okolokolo* (trial court).

cousin *hoahānau.*

cove *kū'ono* (also means **bay**).

cover [*n*] 1. *po'i* (lid). [*Aia i hea ke **po'i** o kēia 'umeke?* Where is the **cover** of this calabash?] 2. *uhi* (veil, spread, film). [*v*] *uhi.*

cow *pipi wahine.*

cowboy *paniolo.* [*Holo lio nā **paniolo** ma ke kahua hānai pipi.* **Cowboys** ride horses on the ranch.]

crab *pāpa'i.*

crack *[n] māwae* (opening in rocks). *[v] naka* (also means **to split open, break**).

cracked *nahā*.

cracker *palena* (also means **border, boundary**). [*Ho'olu'u 'o Pāpā i ka palena i kāna kope.* Dad dips the **cracker** in his coffee.]

cracking noise *'u'ina* (*'u'i* means **to roar, rumble**). [*'U'i, 'u'i 'u'ina lā ka wai a'o Nā Molokama.* The waters of Nā Molokama (mountains at Hanalei, Kaua'i) **rumble and roar**. (song, "Nā Molokama," by A. Alohikea)]

craft *hana no'eau* (also means **art, artwork**). [*Nani maoli nō nā hana no'eau of Hawai'i kahiko, e like me ke kuku kapa a me ka hana hulu manu.* The **crafts** of old Hawai'i, like tapa beating and featherwork, were truly beautiful.]

craftsman *mea hana no'eau*.

cramp *huki* (also means **convulsion, stroke**). [*Ua loa'a ka 'elemakule i ka huki i kona wāwae.* The old man had a **cramp** in his leg.]

crash *ho'oku'i*. [*E ho'oku'i 'ia ana ka pukaaniani e ka lā'au ke hao mai ka makani?* Will the window be **crashed** into by the board when the wind blasts?]

crater *lua pele*. [*Noho 'o Pele ma ka lua pele 'o Halema'uma'u.* Pele lives in the Halema'uma'u **crater**.]

crawl *kolo*. [*Ke ho'omaka nei kāu pēpē e kolo. E nānā!* Your baby is starting to **crawl** now. Look!]

crayons

crayon *kala*. [*'Elima wale nō āna kala e kaha ki'i ai.* She has only five **crayons** to draw with.]

crazy 1. *pupule*. 2. *hehena*.

cream *kalima* (from English).

create 1. *hoʻokumu* (also means **to establish, found**). [*Na nā mikionele i **hoʻokumu** i ke kula mua o Hawaiʻi, ʻo Lahainaluna.* It was the missionaries who **founded** the first school of Hawaiʻi, Lahainaluna.] 2. *hana* (also means **to work, make, do an activity, job,** many other meanings).

creep along *nihi.* [*E **nihi** ka hele, mai hoʻopā.* **Creep along** carefully, don't touch. (song "E Nihi ka Hele," written by Kalākaua warning his wife Kapiʻolani to be diplomatic in her travels, not to offend)]

crew *poʻe hoʻokele moku* (*lit.* people who navigate a ship).

crime *kalaima* (from English).

crooked *kapakahi* (also means **off center**). [*ke alanui **kapakahi** e,* the **crooked** street (song, "Tūtū Ē," composer unknown)]

crowd *lehulehu* (also means **public, multitudes**).

crowded 1. *piha kuʻi.* 2. *paʻapū.*

crown *kalaunu* (from English). [*He kalo ko ko Kalākaua **kalaunu.*** Kalākaua's **crown** has a taro plant.]

crutches *koʻokoʻo.* [*Ma muli o ka haki ʻia ʻana o ko ke kahunapule kuʻekuʻe wāwae, ʻaʻole hiki iā ia ke hele wāwae, koe wale me ke **koʻokoʻo.*** Due to the minister's ankle being broken, she can't walk, except with **crutches**.]

cry *uē.* [*Nui ko ka pepe **uē** ʻana ke pulu kona kaiapa.* The baby **cries** a lot whenever his diaper is wet.]

cube *poke.* [*He mau **poke** hau ko ka pahu hau?* Does the icebox (refrigerator) have ice **cubes**?]

cultivate *mahi* (see farm, farmer).

culture *moʻomeheu.* [*Nui nā loina o ka **moʻomeheu** kahiko.* There are many traditions in the ancient **culture**.]

cup *kīʻaha* (also means **drinking glass**). [*Aia iā wai kāu **kīʻaha?*** Who has your **cup**?]

cure *hoʻōla* (also means **heal**). [*Hiki paha ke **hoʻōla**
ʻia ko nā mākua mau puʻu ʻeha?* Can the parents'
sore throats perhaps be **healed**?]

curiosity *nīele*. [*Nui ko ka ʻelepaio **nīele**. ʻElepaio*
birds have lots of **curiosity**.]

curious *nīele*.

curly (hair) 1. *milo*. 2. *piʻipiʻi*.

custom *loina*. [*He mau **loina** ko ke kālai waʻa*. Canoe
carving has **customs**.]

cut *ʻoki*. (divorce, to divorce = *ʻoki male*)

dagger *pāhoa.*

dainty 1. *ʻauliʻi* (also means **neat, cute**). 2. *mikioi* (also means **fine work, excellently made**).

damp *maʻū.* [***Maʻū** ka mauʻu i ke kēhau.* The grass is **damp** with dew.]

dampness *maʻū.*

dance 1. *hula* (Hawaiian dance). 2. *hulahula* (ballet, disco, non-Hawaiian dance).

dangerous *makaʻu* (also means **afraid, frightening**). [***Makaʻu** ka piʻi kuahiwi ma ka pō.* Hiking at night is **dangerous**.]

dark *pōʻeleʻele.* [***Pōʻeleʻele** ke kakahiaka nui.* The early morning is **dark**.]

darling 1. *eia nei* (this phrase is used to call politely to someone whose name you don't know and can be translated in a variety of ways such as, "hello there," "hey," "you there," "dear one"). [***Eia nei**, aia i hea ka hale leka?* **Hello there**, where is the post office?] 2. *makamae* (also means **precious, treasured**).

daughter *kaikamahine* (also means **girl**). (*pl. kaikamāhine*) [*ʻO kēnā **kaikamahine** noʻeau kā ʻolua **kaikamahine**?* Is that skilled **girl** (by you) your folks' **daughter**?]

daughter

dawn 1. *wanaʻao.* [*Ua ao ka **wanaʻao**.* Day has **dawned**.] 2. *kaiao.* (all night = *a ao ka pō*) [*Hana* *'o ia **a ao ka pō**. She works **all night** (*lit*. until light the dark).]

day *ao* (also means **daytime, daylight**). (all day = *a pō ke ao*)

daylight 1. *ao* (also means **light, wisdom**, many other meanings). [*Ikaika ke **ao** ma Hawai'i nei.* **Daylight** is strong here in Hawai'i.] 2. *lā*.

dead 1. *make* (also means **to pass away, die**). 2. *hala* (also means **to pass away, die, pass by**). [*Ua pau, ua **hala** lākou, a koe nō nā pua.* They are finished, they have **passed away**, and their descendants remain. (song, "Nā Ali'i," by S. Kuahiwi)]

deaf *kuli*. [***Kuli** kona pepeiao.* Her ear is **deaf**.] (be quiet [you're making noise] = *kulikuli*)

dear 1. *aloha* (greeting in letter). 2. *auē* (exclamation "Oh, dear!"). [*E ke Kenekoa, **Aloha** kāua.* **Dear** Senator, hello to you and me.]

death *make*.

debt *'ai'ē*. [*Pōpilikia maoli nō ka 'āina i nā **'ai'ē** o nā ali'i i nā malihini.* The country was greatly troubled due to the **debts** of the chiefs to the newcomers.] (to pay off debt = *ho'oka'a*)

deceive 1. *ho'opunipuni*. 2. *'āpiki*.

December Kēkēmapa (from English).

decide *ho'oholo*. [*Ināhea 'oukou i **ho'oholo** ai e 'ai i ka 'ai Wai'anae?* When did you all **decide** to eat the Wai'anae diet?]

decimal *kekimala* (from English).

declare 1. *ha'i* (also means **to tell**). 2. *hō'ike* (also means **to reveal, to demonstrate**). 3. *'ōlelo* (also means t**o speak, speech, language**).

decline *hō'ole* (to say no to).

decorated 1. *kāhiko*. [*Ua **kāhiko** 'ia ka Hale Ali'i no ka poni 'ana o ke kia'āina.* The Palace was **decorated** for the governor's inauguration.] 2. *ho'onani*.

dedicate *ho'ola'a*.

deep *hohonu* (means both deep water and complex thought, meaning). [*Hohonu ka manaʻo o nā mele kahiko.* The meanings of ancient poetry are **deep.**]

defecate 1. *kiʻo.* 2. *hana lepo* (euphemism).

defend 1. *pale.* 2. *kūpale.*

defiled *haumia* (also means **unclean, vile, polluted**).

degree *kekele* (means both educational degree and temperature). [*Ke ʻimi nei kou hoa-hānau i kāna kekele loea?* Is your cousin seeking her M.A. **degree?**]

delicate 1. *lahilahi* (also means **thin, frail**). 2. *ʻauliʻi.*

delicious *ʻono.* [*ʻOno nō ka poke i ka inamona.* The raw fish is **delicious** due to the *kukui* nut condiment.] (Used as a verb, *ʻono* means to crave a specific food.) [*ʻOno nā keiki i ka haukōhi.* Kids **crave** shave ice.]

delighted, pleased *ohohia* (also means **enthusiastic**). [*Ohohia nā keiki ma ke kula Hawaiʻi hou.* The children at the new Hawaiian school are **delighted.**]

deliver 1. *hāʻawi* (also means **to give**). 2. *lawe* (also means **to bring, to take**).

delusion *manaʻo kuhihewa.*

demonstrate *hōʻike.* [*Ke hōʻike aku nei ʻo Maluʻihi i kāna hana ulana pāpale lauhala.* Maluʻihi is **demonstrating** her *lauhala* hat weaving now.]

demonstration *hōʻike* (also means **show**). [*Ma ka pāka e nānā ana nā mākaʻikaʻi i ka hōʻike hula.* It's at the park that the tourists will watch the hula **show.**]

dented *ʻōpaha.* [*ʻŌpaha ke kini.* The tin can is **dented.**]

dentist *kauka niho.*

depend on *kaukaʻi.* [*Hiki ke kaukaʻi i kā kāu kaikamahine kāne?* Can you **depend on** your daughter's husband?]

deposit *waiho.*

depository *waihona.* (treasury = *waihona kālā*)
(archives = *waihona palapala kahiko*)

depth *hohonu.* [*'Elua kapua'i ka **hohonu** o ke kai ma
ka laupapa ma ke kai piha.* Two feet is the **depth**
of the sea on the reef at high tide.]

deranged 1. *hehena.* 2. *kūpikipiki'ō.*

descend *iho.* [*E nauē kākou a **iho** ma uka a ke kai.*
Let's all get a move on and **descend** from the
mountains to the sea.]

descendant *mamo.* [*Nā **mamo** a Hāloa.* The **descendants** of Hāloa (first human, younger brother of
the first taro of same name, according to ancient
legend).]

describe *huliko'a.*

description *huliko'a.* [*'Auli'i kāna **huliko'a** i ko ka
'aihue helehelena.* His **description** of the thief's
facial features is precise and clear.]

desert *'āina pānoa.* [*He **'āina pānoa** ko Ka'ū.* Ka'ū
has a **desert**.]

desk *pākaukau.*

dessert *mea 'ono.* [*'Ono
māua i ka **mea 'ono**
kokoleka a me ka hau-
pia, e ke kuene.* We're
craving a chocolate
dessert and *haupia*
(coconut pudding), wait-
ress.]

dessert

destroy *luku.* [*Ma 'Iao i **luku**
'ia ai ko Maui koa e ka na'i aupuni.* It was at 'Iao
that Maui's soldiers were **destroyed** by the conqueror.]

detective *māka'ikiu.*

detergent *wai ho'oma'ema'e.* [*'O ka **wai
ho'oma'ema'e** hea ka mea e wehe ana i ka lepo?*
Which **detergent** is the one that will remove dirt?]

detest *ho'okae.* [*Minamina, **ho'okae** 'o ia i kona*

hoanoho. It's too bad he **detests** his roommate.]
(racial prejudice = *ho'okae 'ili*)

develop *ho'omōhala* (*lit.* to cause to bloom).
[**Ho'omōhala** *ha'awina nā kumu ma ka hālāwai*.
Teachers **develop** curriculum at the meeting.]

devil *kepalō* (from English).

devotion *aloha*.

diabetes *mimikō*.

diameter *anawaena*. [*'A'ohe **anawaena** o ka
huinakolu. Loa'a ke anawaena i ka pō'ai.*
Triangles don't have **diameters**. Circles do.]

Diamond Head 1. Kaimana Hila (from English). 2.
Lē'ahi.

diaper *kaiapa* (from English).

die 1. *hala* (also means **to pass by**). 2. *hā'ule* (also
means **to fall down**). 3. *make*.

diet *ho'ēmi kino* (also means **to lose weight**). [*Inā 'oe
i ho'oikaika kino, inā ua **ho'ēmi kino** pū*. If you
had exercised, you would have **lost weight** as
well.]

difficult *pa'akikī* (also means **hard**). [*'A'ole **pa'akikī**
ka hāpai paona*. Lifting weights is not **difficult**.]

dig *'eli*. [*Makemake ka 'īlio e **'eli** i ke one*. Dogs like
to **dig** in sand.]

dinner *'aina ahiahi*.

direction 1. *'ōlelo kuhikuhi* (instructions). [*Ke kūkulu 'oe i ka mea pā'ani hou, e heluhelu mua i nā
'ōlelo kuhikuhi.* Whenever you put together a
new toy, first read the **directions**.] 2. *'ao'ao* (compass direction).

dirt *lepo*.

dirty *lepo*. [*E waiho i ko kāua mau lole **lepo** i ka
mīkini holoi*. Leave our (your and my) **dirty**
clothes in the washing machine.]

disaster *pōpilikia*. [*He **pōpilikia** maoli ka makani
pāhili*. A hurricane is a real **disaster**.]

discard *kiloi* (also means **to throw away**). [*Mai **kiloi**

aku i nā palapala kahiko! Don't **discard** the old
documents.]

discipline *aʻo ikaika.*

discover *ʻimi a loaʻa.* [*Ua **ʻimi a loaʻa** ʻo ia i kekahi
lāʻau hou.* He **discovered** a new medicine.]

discuss *kūkākūkā.*

disease *maʻi.* [*He maʻi ahulau pōpilikia ka **maʻi** hana
ei.* Sexually transmitted **diseases** are a disastrous
epidemic.]

dish *pā.* [*Aia nā **pā** ma ka hakakau.* The dishes are
on the shelf.] (plate lunch = *pā mea ʻai*)

dishwasher *mīkini holoi pā.*

disinfectant *wai hoʻomaʻemaʻe.*

disk *pā.* [*Loaʻa ka polokalamu lolouila hou ma ka **pā**
hea?* Which **disk** has the new computer program
on it?] (CD = *sēdē, cēdē*)

dismiss *hoʻokuʻu* (also means **to release, let go**). [*E
hoʻokuʻu hikiwawe i kāu papa i kēia ʻauinalā.*
Dismiss your class early this afternoon.]

display *hōʻike.*

distance *mamao.* [*ʻEhia mile ka **mamao** mai kou
hale aku i kou keʻena hana?* How many miles is
the **distance** from your house to your office?]

distant *mamao.*

distinguished *hanohano.* [***Hanohano** wale ʻoe, e
Haleʻiwa Pāka.* You are so **distinguished**,
Haleʻiwa Park. (song, "Haleʻiwa Pāka," by A.
Nāmakelua)]

distribute *hoʻomāhelehele* (also means **to divide up**).

district 1. *moku.* [*Nui nā pali kai i ka **moku** o
Hāmākua ma Hawaiʻi.* There are many ocean
cliffs in the **district** of Hāmākua on Hawaiʻi.] 2.
ʻāpana.

distrust *kānalua* (also means **doubt**).

distrustful *kānalua.* [***Kānalua** ka mea maʻi i ko ke
kauka manaʻo.* The patient is **distrustful** of the
doctor's opinion.]

ditch *'auwai* (also means **canal, sewer**). Note: *'Auwai* were man-made ditches used to divert water from streams into taro patches.

divide 1. *māhele* (share things). 2. *ho'onaue* (math).

divorce *'oki male*. [*'A'ole i 'oki male pinepine ko ko'u mau mākua hānauna.* My parents' generation didn't often get **divorced**.]

dizzy *pōniuniu*.

doctor *kauka*. [*Lō'ihi ke kali 'ana i ko ke kauka ke'ena.* The wait in the **doctor**'s office is long.]

dog *'īlio*. [*He aha ke 'ano o kāna 'īlio? He* "poi dog" *kāna.* What kind of **dog** does he have? He has a "poi dog" (mixed breed.)]

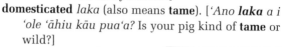

dog

doll *ki'i pēpē*. [*'O wai kāu ki'i pēpē Pā'ele?* What's the name of your African-American **doll**?]

dolphin *nai'a*. [*Holo anei nā nai'a me nā koholā i ka ho'oilo?* Do **dolphins** swim with humpback whales in the rainy season?]

domesticated *laka* (also means **tame**). [*'Ano laka a i 'ole 'āhiu kāu pua'a?* Is your pig kind of **tame** or wild?]

donkey *'ēkake*. [*'Āhiu nā 'ēkake ma Kona.* The **donkeys** in Kona are wild.]

donkey

don't *mai* before verb. [*Mai hana pēlā!* **Don't** do that!]

door *puka*. [*E pani i ka puka, ke 'olu'olu.* Close the **door**, please.]

dormitory *hale noho haumāna*.

dorsal fin *kualā.* [*Kainō 'o ka nai'a ka i holo i ko'u 'ike 'ana i ke* **kualā.** I thought (but I was mistaken) that a dolphin was the thing that was swimming by when I saw the **dorsal fin.**]

down *iho* after verb. [*Ua noho* **iho** *ke kupuna.* The grandparent sat **down.**]

downtown *kaona* (from English).

drag *kaualakō.* [**Kaualakō** *ka mea ulana lauhala i nā lau i piha i ke kōkala.* The *lauhala* weaver **drags** the leaves full of thorns.]

dragon *mo'o.*

dragonfly *pinao* (also means **damselfly**). [*Nui nā 'ano* **pinao** *me nā waiho'olu'u nani ma Hawai'i.* There are many kinds of **dragonflies** with lovely colors in Hawai'i.]

draw picture *kaha ki'i.*

dream *moe 'uhane.* [*He hō'ailona ka* **moe 'uhane** *i nā Hawai'i.* **Dreams** have symbolic meaning for Hawaiians.]

drenched *pulu* (also means **soaked with rain**). [*Pulu nō nā keiki i ka ua Kanilehua o Hilo.* The children are really **drenched** due to Hilo's Kanilehua rain.]

dress *lole* (also means **cloth, clothes**). [*He lole 'olu'olu ka* **lole** *palaka.* Palaka **clothes** are comfortable **clothes.**] (*Palaka* is a checkered cotton cloth previously used for work clothes on sugar plantations.)

drink *[n] mea inu. [v] inu.* [*Ke loa'a 'oe i ka pu'u 'eha, e* **inu** *i ka* **mea inu** *wela me ka meli.* If you get a sore throat, **drink** a hot **drink** with honey.]

drinking glass *kī'aha* (also means **measuring cup**).

drip *kulu.* [**Kulu** *ka pakapaka ua mai ka 'ōhi'a.* Raindrops **drip** from the 'ōhi'a tree.] (tears fall = *kulu waimaka*)

drive *kalaiwa.* [*'Oiai 'o ia e* **kalaiwa** *ana, ua kulu kona waimaka.* While she was **driving,** her tears fell.]

droop *luhe.* [**Luhe** *i lalo ke poʻo o ke kanaka maka hiamoe.* The head of the sleepy person **droops** down.]

drop of rain *paka ua.* [*Liʻiliʻi nā* **paka ua** *o ka ua Kilihune.* The **raindrops** of the Kilihune rain are small.]

drown *piholo* (also means **to sink down**). [*Ua* **piholo** *ʻo Halaʻea i kona ʻānunu.* Halaʻea **drowned** because of greediness. (traditional story of greedy *aliʻi* whose people heaped his canoe with fish until it sank)]

drowsy *maka hiamoe.* [*Ua* **maka hiamoe** *ka ʻōpio i holo wāwae i ka heihei.* The young person who ran in the race was **drowsy**.]

drug *lāʻau ʻino.*

drum [n] *pahu.* [*Hoʻopaʻa ke kumu hula i ka* **pahu.** The hula teacher beats the **drum**.] (to drum = 1. *hoʻopaʻa* 2. *hoʻokani pahu*)

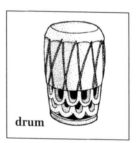

drum

drunk *ʻona* (also means **"high" on drugs**). [*E nānā! Kūlanalana ke kanaka* **ʻona.** Look! The **drunk** person is staggering.]

dry [v] *hoʻomaloʻo.* [*E* **hoʻomaloʻo** *i nā kāwele i ka mīkini hoʻomaloʻo.* **Dry** the towels in the dryer.] [adj] *maloʻo.* [*Ulu ke kiawe ma ka ʻāina* **maloʻo.** Kiawe trees grow on **dry** land.] (to dry in the sun, e.g. fish salted and dried in the sun to preserve them = *kaulaʻi*)

dryer *mīkini hoʻomaloʻo.*

dual *pālua.*

duet *leokū pālua.* [*Hīmeni* **leokū pālua** *nā ipo.* The sweethearts sing a **duet** together.]

dull (not interesting) 1. *manakā.* 2. *pāmalō.* 3. *pākūā.*

dull (not sharp) *kūmūmū.* [*E hoʻokala i ka pahi
    kūmūmū ma mua o ka ʻokiʻoki ʻana aku i nā lau
    ʻai.* Sharpen the **dull** knives before chopping up
    the vegetables.]

dumb 1. *leo paʻa* (mute). 2. *mū* (mute). 3. *hūpō* (stu-
    pid).

dump [n] *kahua waiho ʻōpala.* [*Nāu e halihali i nā
    lau popopo i ke **kahua waiho ʻōpala.*** You are
    the one to haul the rotten leaves to the **dump.**]

dust *ʻehu lepo.* (sea foam = *ʻehu kai*). [*Nui ka **ʻehu
    lepo** ma ke alanui mahikō.* There's lots of **dust**
    on the plantation road.] (syn. *ehu*)

dusty *ʻehu* (also means **pollen, dark red Hawaiian
    hair, spray, foam**).

duty *kuleana* (also means **rights, responsibility**).

dye *waihoʻoluʻu* (also means **color**). [*ʻO ke ʻōlena
    kekahi mea kanu **waihoʻoluʻu.*** The ʻōlena is a
    dye plant.] (Many plants were used to dye or to
    add fragrance to tapa cloth.) (to dye = *hoʻoluʻu*)

ear *pepeiao.*

early *hikiwawe.* [**Hikiwawe** *ka hōʻea ʻana o ka waʻa mua ma ka heihei.* The first canoe in the race arrived **early.**]

early morning *kakahiaka nui.* [*Ala mau ka lawaiʻa i ke* **kakahiaka nui.** The fisherman always gets up in the **early morning.**]

earn *loaʻa.* (Note: *Loaʻa* has many other meanings.)

Earth *honua.* [*E mā-lama i ka* **honua.** Take care of the **Earth.**]

Earth

earthquake *ōlaʻi.* [*Nāueue ka honua i ke* **ōlaʻi.** The earth shakes due to the **earthquake.**]

east *hikina.* [*Puka ka lā ma ka* **hikina.** The sun emerges in the **east.** (chant)]

Easter *Lā Pākoa.* [*Hoʻoluʻu a hoʻonani nā keiki i nā hua moa no ka* **lā Pākoa.** The children dye and decorate eggs for **Easter.**]

easy *maʻalahi.* [**Maʻalahi** *ka unahi a me ka hoʻomaʻemaʻe iʻa.* Scaling and cleaning fish is **easy.**]

eat *ʻai.* [*Pōloli mau ka ʻōpio a* **ʻai** *pinepine ʻo ia.* The young person is always hungry and **eats** often.]

echo 1. *wawā.* 2. *kūpinaʻi* (also means **to mourn**).

edge 1. *kaʻe.* [*Ma* **kaʻe** *kahawai māua i pikiniki ai.* It was at the **edge** of the stream that we picnicked.] 2. *kapa.* [**kapa** *wai lana mālie,* the **edge** of the slow-moving water] 3. *lihi.*

educate *ho'ona'auao.* [*Na wai e **ho'ona'auao** i nā keiki Hawai'i?* Who should **educate** Hawaiian children?]

educated *na'auao* (also means **enlightened, wise**).

education *ho'ona'auao.*

eel *puhi.*

effort *ho'ā'o* (also means **experiment, to try**).

egg 1. *hua* (refers to any offspring or product of animal, plant, human; also means **to reproduce**). 2. *hua moa* (egg of chicken). (fruit = *hua 'ai*)

elbow *ku'e lima.*

elder *kupuna.*

eldest *hiapo.* [*'O kou kaikua'ana ka **hiapo**, e Kawaiola?* Is your older sibling the **eldest**, Kawaiola?]

elect *koho pāloka* (from English "ballot"). [*Mai poina e **koho pāloka** i ka moho e kāko'o 'ana i ka ho'ona'auao.* Don't forget to **elect** the candidate who will support education.]

election *koho pāloka.* (election day = *lā koho pāloka*)

electric *uila.* [*He mīkini **uila** ko Tūtū no ka wa'u 'ana i ka niu.* Grandpa (Grandma) has an **electric** machine for grating coconut.]

electrical outlet *puka uila.* [*Pono e pāpā i nā keiki e ho'opā i ka **puka uila**.* (You) have to forbid children to touch **electrical outlets**.]

electricity *uila.*

elementary school *kula ha'aha'a.*

elephant *'elepani* (from English).

elephant

embarrassed *hilahila* (also means **ashamed**). [***Hilahila** kona mau kūpuna e komo i loko o ke kula ha'aha'a.* His grandparents are **ashamed** to enter the elementary school.]

emergency 1. *ulia pōpilikia*. 2. *pilikia kūhewa*.

employ 1. *hoʻohana* (also means **to use**). 2. *hai* (also means **to hire**; probably from English "hire"; original Hawaiian word means offering, sacrifice, to sacrifice, to follow).

empty *hakahaka* (also means **blank**). [*Hakahaka nā hakakau o ka hale kanaka ʻole*. The shelves of the house without people in it are **empty**.]

enchanted by *hoʻohihi*. [*Hoʻohihi ka manaʻo i ka nani o Nuʻuanu*. My thoughts are **enchanted by** the beauty of Nuʻuanu.]

encourage *hoʻopaipai*. [*Pono kākou e hoʻopaipai kekahi i kekahi e mālama i ke ola kino*. We have to **encourage** each other to take care of our health.]

encouragement *hoʻopaipai*.

end *[n]* 1. *panina*. [*I ka panina o ka hālāwai, pule lākou*. At the **end** of the meeting, they pray.] 2. *pau ʻana*. *[v] hoʻopau* (also means **to finish**). [*Ke hoʻopau ka mekanika i ka hoʻoponopono i ko kāua kaʻa, e uku iā ia*. When the mechanic **finishes** fixing our (your and my) car, pay him.]

endangered *ʻane make loa* (*lit.* almost extinct). [*ʻAne make loa ka hapanui o nā manu ʻōiwi o Hawaiʻi*. Most of the native birds of Hawaiʻi are **endangered**.]

enemy 1. *hoa paio*. 2. *ʻenemi* (from English).

energetic *ʻeleu*.

engineer *wilikī*. [*Kūkulu ka wilikī i ka uapo*. **Engineers** build bridges.]

English (language) 1. *ʻōlelo haole*. 2. *ʻōlelo* Pelekane. [*He ʻōlelo laha ka ʻōlelo Pelekane*. **English** is a common language.]

enjoy 1. *luana* (also means **to relax, socialize**). 2. *hoʻonanea* (also means **enjoyable**).

enlighten *hoʻomālamalama*.

enlightened *naʻauao* (also means **educated, wise, wisdom**).

enough *lawa*. [*Ua kui a **lawa** ko'u lei*. (**Enough** flowers have been strung so that my *lei* is completed. (song, "Wehiwehi 'Oe," by S. Kalama)]

enroll *kākau inoa* (sometimes shortened to *kau inoa*). [*Inā no'ono'o 'oukou e koho pāloka, pono 'oukou e **kākau inoa** ma mua*. If you all are thinking about voting, you have to **enroll** beforehand.]

entangled (in problems) *hihia*.

enter *komo*. [*"E **komo** mai," i heahea aku ka mea ho'okipa*. "**Enter**," the hostess called out.]

entertain *ho'okipa* (also means **to welcome, extend hospitality**). [*E **ho'okipa** ana mākou i nā malihini mai Aotearoa mai*. We (three or more, not you) will welcome and **entertain** the guests from New Zealand.]

enthusiasm *ohohia* (also means **delight**). [*Nui ke **ohohia** o nā kelamoku hou*. New sailors have great **enthusiasm**.]

envelope *wahī leka*. [*Hiki iā ia ke ku'ai mai i **wahī leka** ma ka hale leka?* Can he buy an **envelope** at the post office?]

epidemic *ma'i ahulau*.

equal 1. *like*. 2. *like nō a like*.

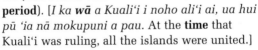

envelope

era *wā* (also means **time period**). [*I ka **wā** a Kuali'i i noho ali'i ai, ua hui pū 'ia nā mokupuni a pau*. At the **time** that Kuali'i was ruling, all the islands were united.]

erase *holoi* (also means **to wash something**).

eraser *mea holoi*.

erect *kū* (also means **upright**). [*Kū kekahi kumuniu, hina kekahi*. Some coconut trees are **erect**, others fall over.]

err *hewa*.

error *hewa* (also means **mistake, guilt, sin, guilty, mistaken**). [*'A'ohe āna **hewa** ma ka hō'ike kalaiwa ka'a.* He had no **errors** on the driver's license exam.]

erupt *hū ka pele.* [*Ua **hū ka pele** ma Kalapana a uhi 'ia 'o Kaimū.* The lava **erupted** at Kalapana until Kaimū beach was covered.]

eruption *ka hū 'ana o ka pele.*

escape *pākele.* [*Ma ka mahina 'o Iune e **pākele** ai nā keiki mai ke kula aku.* It is in the month of June that children **escape** from school.]

establish *ho'okumu.* [*Na kā Pauahi kāne i **ho'okumu** i ka Hale Hō'ike'ike 'o Pīhopa.* It was Pauahi's husband who **established** Bishop Museum.]

estimate *koho* (also means **guess, choice, to choose**).

Europe *'Europa.*

evening *ahiahi.* [*Ke pā'ani pepa nei mākou ma kēia **ahiahi**.* We all (not you) are playing cards this **evening**.]

event *hanana.*

ever *mau.* (forever = *a mau loa aku*)

every *a pau.* [*Mahalo iā 'oukou **a pau**!* Thanks to **every** one of you!]

exactly *pono* (also means **directly**, many other meanings). [*E kuhi **pono** ana māua i ka ha'ina!* We (two, not you) are going to point **exactly** to the answer!] [*'O wai kēnā ma hope **pono** ou?* Who is that **directly** behind you?]

exam *hō'ike.*

example 1. *ho'ohālike.* 2. *la'ana.*

excel *po'okela* (also means **outstanding, champion**).

excellence *maika'i loa.*

excellent 1. *kilohana.* 2. *maika'i loa.*

except *koe wale.* [*Ua piha ko kāu mo'opuna kāne hau'oli i kona pā'ina lā hānau, **koe wale** kēia, 'eha kona pu'u i kona uā mau 'ana.* Your grandson was completely happy at his birthday party,

except for this, his throat was sore due to his constant shouting.]

excessive *pākela.* (gluttony = *pākela ʻai*) (heavy drinker, to drink to excess = *pākela inu*)

excited, exciting 1. *pīhoihoi.* [**Pīhoihoi** *ʻo ia i kāna hana hou.* She's **excited** by her new job.] 2. *ʻeuʻeu.*

excrement 1. *kūkae.* 2. *lepo* (also means **dirt**, used in place of *kūkae* to be more polite).

excuse 1. *kala* (also means **forgive**). [*E kala mai iaʻu!* **Excuse** me, I'm sorry! (Response is *Ua huikala ʻia* or *kala ʻia.* You are forgiven.)] 2. *huikala* (also means **forgive**). 3. *kumu* (also means **reason, basis**).

exercise *hoʻoikaika kino.* [*ʻOiai* **hoʻoikaika kino** *koʻu makuahine a piula, ʻaʻole ʻo ia e hoʻēmi kino nei.* Although my mother **exercises** until she's exhausted, she's not losing weight.]

exhausted 1. *paupauaho* (also means **out of breath**). 2. *piula.*

exhibit *hōʻike.*

exit *[n]* *puka.* *[v]* *puka* (also means **to emerge**). [*Ua* **puka** *aku nā mea hanohano mai ka* **puka** *ma ka ʻaoʻao hema.* The distinguished people **emerged** from the **exit** on the left.]

expel *kipaku.* [*Ma muli o ko ke kanaka waha wale* **kipaku** *ʻia ʻana mai ka hale inu aku, ua kuʻi ʻo ia i ke kiaʻi.* Due to the loudmouth's being **expelled** from the bar, she hit the guard.]

expensive *pipiʻi.* [**Pipiʻi** *ke ʻeke poi ma ka hale kūʻai mea ʻai.* A bag of poi at the grocery store is **expensive**.]

experience *ʻike* (also means **to see, know, feel**).

expensive

$5000.⁰⁰

['*Akahi nō a* **'ike** *'o Makanani i ke anu o ka hau kea ma Mauna Kea*. Makanani finally **experienced** the coldness of snow on Mauna Kea.]

experiment *ho'ā'o* (also means **effort, to try**). [*Ke holopono nei ka* **ho'ā'o**. The **experiment** is succeeding.]

expert 1. *kahuna*. 2. *loea*. [*He* **loea** *hula 'o Lokalia Montgomery*. Lokalia Montgomery was a hula **expert**.] 3. *lehia*.

explain *wehewehe*. [*E* **wehewehe** *mai i ko 'oukou mau mana'o*. **Explain** your (all) opinions to me.]

explode 1. *ho'opahū* (to cause an explosion). [*Na wai i* **ho'opahū** *i nā mea ho'opahū ma Kaho'olawe?* Who **exploded** the bombs on Kaho'olawe?] 2. *pahū*. 3. *pohā*.

explore *'imi loa*.

explosion *halulu* (also means **to roar, rumble**).

extend 1. *ho'oloa* (to prolong, lengthen, stretch). 2. *kīko'o* (to extend hands, draw money from bank, stretch) (to stick out tongue = *kīko'o alelo*)

extinct *make loa*. [*E* **make loa** *ana ka 'alalā a me ke kāhuli?* Will the Hawaiian crow and the Hawaiian tree snail become **extinct**?]

extinguish *ho'opio* (also means **to turn off electrical appliance**). [*Ma hope o kāu pā'ani, e* **ho'opio** *i ka lolouila*. After your game, **turn off** the computer.]

extinguished *pio* (also means **turned off**). [*Ua pio ke ahi ma ka hale*. The fire in the house is **extinguished**.]

extremity 1. *welelau* (tip of leaf). 2. *wēlau*. 3. *wēkiu* (mountain summit).

eye *maka* (also means **face, fresh, raw, beloved**).

eyeball *'ōnohi maka*.

eyebrow *ku'e maka*.

eyelash *lihilihi*.

face *maka* (also means **eye, fresh, raw, beloved**).

face powder *pauka maka.*

faint *ma'ule.* [*Inā* **ma'ule** *ke kanaka ma'i, he aha kā ke kahu ma'i hana?* If the patient **faints**, what does the nurse do?]

fair (just) *kaulike.* [*Pono e ho'oponopono i ka hana a ke ke'ena 'āina ho'opulapula a* **kaulike**. The work of the Hawaiian Homes office has to be fixed until it is **fair**.]

fall *hā'ule.* [*Ma hope o ko ka pēpē* **hā'ule** *'ana iho, ua kū a'e 'o ia.* After the baby **fell** down, she stood up again.]

fallen over *hina.*

false *ho'opunipuni* (also means **to lie**).

fame *kaulana.*

familiar *kama'āina.* [**Kama'āina** *paha 'oe i ke kahua hānai pipi 'o 'Ulupalakua?* Are you perhaps **familiar** with 'Ulupalakua ranch?]

family *'ohana.*

famous *kaulana.* [*Aia nō a* **kaulana** *ko kona makuahine inoa, pau ko māua pili.* As soon as his mother's name becomes **famous**, our (his and my) closeness is over.]

fan

fan *pe'ahi.* (wave hand = pe'ahi lima).

far *mamao.* [**Mamao** *ke kahakai 'o Lumaha'i mai 'Anini aku?* Is Lumaha'i beach **far** from 'Anini?]

farm *mahi'ai* (also means **farmer**).

fast 1. *wikiwiki.* 2. *ʻāwīwī.*

fasten *hoʻopaʻa.* [***Hoʻopaʻa*** *ka paniolo i ke kaula hao ma ka ʻīpuka.* The cowboy **fastened** the chain on the gate.]

fat *[n] aila.* [*He mea ʻai* ***aila*** *iki ko ka hale ʻaina? Does* the restaurant have low-**fat** food?] *[adj] momona* (also means **sweet-** or **rich-tasting, fertile land**). [*Hō ka* ***momona*** *o kēia kūlolo!* Boy, how **sweet-tasting** this *kūlolo* (traditional dessert made with taro, sugar, coconut milk steamed in *imu*) is!]

father *makua kāne.* [*Haʻaheo ka* ***makua kāne*** *i kāna keiki.* The **father** is proud of his son.]

fault *hewa.*

favor 1. *hana lokomaikaʻi* (to do a favor). 2. *makemake* (to prefer).

favorite *punahele.* [*ʻO "Sānoe" kaʻu mele* ***punahele***. "Sānoe" is my **favorite**. (song composed by Liliʻuokalani)]

feather cloak *ʻahuʻula.* [*He hōʻailona ka* ***ʻahuʻula*** *no ke aliʻi.* The **feather cloak** is a symbol of noble rank.]

fear *makaʻu.* [*Mai* ***makaʻu*** *i ka lanalana.* Don't **be afraid of** spiders.]

February *Pepeluali* (from English).

federal *pekelala* (from English).

feed *hānai* (refers to feeding animals or people, also means **to raise a child**, including the traditional Hawaiian "adoption").

feel 1. *hāhā* (an object). [***Hāhā*** *ke kauka i ka puʻu ma ko Kunihi ʻāʻī.* The doctor **feels** the lump on Kunihi's neck.] 2. *ʻike* (an emotion). Note: There are many specific words that deal with feelings, which are often expressed poetically.

fence *pā* (also means **any enclosed area**). (hula mound = *pā hula*) (house lot, yard = *pā hale*)

fern *palapalai* (1. fragrant fern often used by hula

dancers for leis, offerings 2. general name for all ferns).

festival *hoʻolauleʻa.*

few *kakaʻikahi.* [*Kakaʻikahi nā wāhine kuku kapa o ke au nei.* There are **few** women beating tapa (tapa makers) these days.]

field 1. *mahina.* 2. *kīhāpai* (cultivated field). 3. *kahua.* (playing field = *kahua pāʻani*) (school campus = *kahua kula*)

fight *hakakā.* [*E Pāpā, ke **hakakā** nei kou mau kaikaina ma ʻō aku o ka pā!* Daddy, your younger brothers are **fighting** on the other side of the fence!]

fight

Fiji *Pīkī.*

Filipino *Pilipino.*

fill *hoʻopihapiha.* [*E **hoʻopihapiha** i nā hakahaka.* **Fill** in the blanks.]

fin (fish) *pewa.*

final *hope loa.* [*ʻO kāna hoʻāʻo **hope loa** kēia.* This is his **final** try.]

find *loaʻa.* [*Ua kaha ke kuke i ka iʻa a ua **loaʻa** kekahi komo lima kaimana iā ia.* The cook sliced open the fish and **found** a diamond ring.]

fine 1. *hunehune* (minute). [***Hunehune** ka ʻehu o ka wailele.* The waterfall's spray is very **fine**.] 2. *maikaʻi* (well).

finger *manamanalima.*

fingernail *mikiʻao* (also means **claw**). [*Pohole ko ka mea hoʻopaʻahao **mikiʻao** i kona pakele ʻana.* The prisoner's **fingernail** was bruised in her escape.]

finish *hoʻopau* (also means **put an end to, cancel**).

finished *pau* (also means **destroyed**). [*Ua **pau** ka hana ma ka hola ʻehā o ka ʻauinalā.* Work was

finished at four p.m.] Note: idiomatic expressions such as *pau ka hana* (work is finished) and *pau ka papa* (class is finished) are common. [*Ua **pau ka hana** ma ka hola 'ehā o ka 'auinalā.* **Work was finished** at four p.m.] The following example shows the more usual meaning: [*Ua **pau** nā hale i ke ahi.* The houses were **destroyed** in the fire.] *Pau au i ka papa* means "I am destroyed by the class" and not "I have finished the class."

fire *ahi.*

firefighter *kinai ahi.*

fireplace *kapuahi.*

fireworks *kao lele* (also means **rocket**). (syn. *ahikao*)

fire

first *mua* (also means **in front, before**). [*Ua holoi **mua** ke kauka holo-holona i kona mau lima a laila ua hamohamo i ka'u pōpoki.* The vet **first** washed his hands and then he petted my cat.]

first birthday party *pā'ina lā hānau mua.*

first time *makamua.* [*'O ka **makamua** kēlā 'o ko lāua 'ike i ka 'eha o ke aloha.* That was the very **first time** they (two) knew the pain of love.]

fish *[n] i'a.* [*Aloha ka manini me ka pōpolo, he **i'a** noho ia i ka laupapa,* Love for the *manini* and the *pōpolo* **fishes** that live on the reef (song, "Aloha ka Manini," by L. Kauwe)] *[v] lawai'a.*

fisherman *lawai'a.* [*Ua kāmākoi ka **lawai'a** a lawa nā i'a i loa'a iā ia.* The **fisherman** fished with a pole until he had enough fish.]

fishing pole *kāmākoi.*

fix *ho'oponopono.*

flag *hae.* [*Ua welo ka **hae** kalaunu ma luna o ka hale ali'i.* The crown **flag** waved above the palace.]

flashlight *kukui pa'a lima.*

flat *pālahalaha.* [*'A'ole **pālahalaha** kēia kahua kolepa ma uka nei.* This golf course here in the uplands isn't **flat**.]

flea *'uku.* [*Loa'a ka **'uku** i ka moena?* Are there **fleas** in the carpet?]

fledgling *pūnua.* [*He **pūnua** ko ka 'alalā?* Does the *'alalā* have a **fledgling**?]

flight *lele.* [*Mamao ka **lele** o ke kōlea.* The plover's **flight** is a long distance.]

flight attendant *kuene.*

float *lana.* [*nā wa'a kālua **lana** mālie,* the double-hulled canoes **floating** calmly (song, "Song of Hōkūle'a," by K. Tauā and R. Cazimero)]

flood *kai a ka Hinali'i.*

floor *papahele.* [*Aia nā wikiō Hawai'i ma ka **papahele** hea?* Which **floor** are the Hawaiian videos on?] (first floor = *papahele mua*)

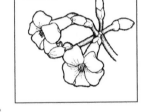

flower

flower *pua* (also means **descendant, child**). [*'A'ala ka hapanui o nā **pua** lei.* Most of the *lei* **flowers** are fragrant.]

flush (toilet) *ho'oholo i ka wai* (also means **to run the water**). [*Mai poina e ho'oholo i ka wai!* Don't forget to **flush the toilet!**]

flute *puhi 'ohe.* (Hawaiian nose flute = *'ohe hano ihu*)

flutter *welo.* [***Welo** ka hae i ka makani.* The flag **flutters** in the wind.]

fly *lele* (also means **to jump**). [***Lele** a'e ka mālolo.* The *mālolo* (flying fish) fish **jumps**.]

fly (something) *ho'olele.* [***Ho'olele** ka pailaka i ka mokulele.* The pilot **flies** the plane.] (fly a kite = *ho'olele lupe*)

foam 1. *'ehu* (also means **spray, mist**). 2. *hu'a* (also means **bubble, froth**).

fold 1. *pelu* (to fold paper). 2. *'ope'ope* (to fold cloth or clothes).

follow *hahai*. [*Mai **hahai** mai ia'u! E **hahai** aku iā ia!* Don't **follow** me! **Follow** her!]

food *mea 'ai*. [*Ke ho'omākaukau mākou i ka lū'au, nui nā 'ano **mea 'ai** Hawai'i like 'ole.* When we (us all, not you) prepare a *lū'au*, there are all different kinds of Hawaiian **food**.]

foolish 1. *hūpō* (also means **stupid**).

foot *wāwae* (also means **leg**).

foot (measurement) *kapua'i*. [*'Ehia **kapua'i** ke ākea o ko 'oukou lumi ho'okipa?* How many **feet** wide is your (all) living room?]

football *pōpeku*. [*'O ke kime hea ke kime i lanakila i ka pā'ani **pōpeku** i ka pō nei?* Which team won the **football** game last night?]

forbid 1. *ho'okapu*. 2. *pāpā*. Note: *Ho'okapu* means to restrict access to a place or object, implying its use is reserved for special people or activities. *Pāpā* means to prohibit an activity, such as smoking or a hula dancer's cutting her hair.

forbidden 1. *kapu* (also means **restricted, reserved**). [*He wahi **kapu** ka heiau.* The religious site is a **restricted** area.] 2. *pāpā 'ia*. [*Ua **pāpā 'ia** ke kuha 'ana i loko.* Spitting indoors is **forbidden**.]

forehead *lae* (also means **peninsula, spit of land surrounded by ocean**). [*Kahe ka hou o ka **lae**.* Sweat pours off the **forehead**.]

foreign *'ē* (also means **strange**). [*nā 'āina **'ē**,* the **foreign** lands, not Hawai'i] 2. *malihini* (used to denote someone or something not from Hawai'i).

foreign lands *nā 'āina 'ē*.

foreigner *malihini* (also means **newcomer, guest**).

forest *ulu lā'au*. [*Laha 'ole ka **ulu lā'au** koa i kēia*

mau lā. Koa **forests** are
rare these days.]

foretell wānana.

forever a mau loa aku.

forget poina. [Ua **poina** 'oe e
ho'opa'a manawa me ke
kauka niho? Did you **forget** to make an appoint-
ment with the dentist?]

forest

forgive 1. kala. [E **kala** mai ia'u! **Forgive** me, I'm
sorry!] 2. huikala.

fork 'ō. [Aia ke **'ō** ma lalo o ke puna? Is the **fork**
under the spoon?]

fort pāpū.

fraction hakina. [He hana pohihihi ka ho'onaue 'ana
i nā **hakina**. Dividing with **fractions** is confusing.]

fracture haki (also means **to break**). [E **haki** 'ia ana
paha ko ka 'ālapa manamana lima i ka pā'ani
pōpa'i lima. The athlete's finger might be **broken**
in the volleyball game.]

fragrant 'a'ala. [Nani pua **'a'ala** onaona i ka ihu e
moani nei. Beautiful is the **sweet-smelling** flower
whose attractive scent is borne to me on the
breeze (song, "Kamalani 'o Keaukaha," by L.
Machado)]

France Palani (also means **French, Frances, Frank**).

free 1. manuahi (no charge). [**Manuahi** nā manakō i
hā'ule i lalo. The mangoes that fell down are
free.] 2. ka'awale (not in use). [He manawa
ka'awale kou ma ka hopenapule? Do you have
free time on the weekend?] 3. noa (free from
kapu, indicating end of imposed period of kapu
restrictions).

freedom kū'oko'a (also means **independence, sovereignty**).

fresh maka (also means **raw**). ['Ai nā Hawai'i i ka i'a

maka *a me ka limu* **maka.** Hawaiians eat **raw** fish and **fresh** seaweed.]

friend *hoaaloha.* [*He* **hoaaloha** *maika'i 'oe na'u.* You are a good **friend** to me.]

friend

frog *poloka.* [*He leo ha'aha'a ko ka* **poloka. Frogs** have low (bass) voices.]

front *mua.* (in front of, before = *ma mua o*) [*E komo kāua i ke kāma'a puti* **ma mua o** *ka pi'i kuahiwi 'ana ma Mauna Loa.* Let's put on boots **before** hiking on Mauna Loa.]

fruit *hua 'ai.*

fruit juice *wai hua 'ai.*

frustrated *uluhua.* [*'A'ole i* **uluhua** *iki kēia kaikamahine i kona a'o 'ana ma ka loloulia.* This girl isn't even a little **frustrated** when she learns on the computer.]

fry *palai* (from English). [*'Ono ka 'ōpelu i* **palai** *'ia.* The *'ōpelu* fish that was **fried** is delicious!]

fulfill (command or desire) *ho'okō.* [*'A'ole na ke aupuni e* **ho'okō** *i ko Hawai'i 'i'ini e mālama i ka 'āina.* It is not the government that will **fulfill** Hawai'i's people's desire to protect the land.]

full 1. *piha.* [**Piha** *ka pahu hau i nā palapalai.* The icebox (refrigerator) is **full** of ferns.] 2. *mā'ona* (refers to someone who has just eaten).

fun *le'ale'a* (refers to all kinds of joyous activities, including sex).

funeral *ho'olewa.*

fur *huluhulu* (also refers to **body hair** as opposed to *lauoho,* hair on head).

furniture *nā pono hale.* [*Pono kāua e ho'one'e i* **nā**

pono hale *ma kēia pule!* We (you and I) have to move the **furniture** this week!]

future *ma kēia mua aku.* [*E hoʻomāhuahua aʻe ana nā kānaka ʻōlelo Hawaiʻi **ma kēia mua aku**.* The number of people who speak Hawaiian will greatly increase in the **future**.]

fuzzy *weuweu.* [*Lōʻihi ko ka pōpoki keiki huluhulu a **weuweu** maoli ia.* The kitten's fur is long and it is truly **fuzzy**.]

gain *[n]* 1. *loaʻa.* [*He **loaʻa** liʻiliʻi ka uku pāneʻe ma ka panakō.* The interest at the bank is a small **gain**.] 2. *puka.*

gallon *kālani* (from English).

gamble *piliwaiwai.* [***Piliwaiwai** nā wāhine Pākē e pāʻani ana i ka Mah-Jongg.* The Chinese women who are playing Mah-Jongg **gamble**.]

game *[n] pāʻani. [v] pāʻani* (to play a game, sport). [***Pāʻani** kāua i ka **pāʻani** kahiko i kapa ʻia ʻo kōnane.* Let's **play** the ancient **game** called *kōnane* (like checkers).]

garage *hale kaʻa.*

garbage *ʻōpala.* [*Pono kākou e ʻohi i ka **ʻōpala** ma kapa alanui.* We must gather up the **garbage** from the side of the road.]

garbage can *kini ʻōpala.*

garbageperson *kanaka halihali ʻōpala.*

garden 1. *māla.* [*kou mau **māla** pua nani ē,* your beautiful flower **gardens** (song, "Hawaiʻi Aloha," by L. Lyons)] 2. *kīhāpai* (cultivated field). 3. *māla pua* (flower). 4. *māla ʻai* (vegetable).

garden

gas *ea* (also means **life force, sovereignty**, many other meanings).

gasoline *kakalina.* [*ʻEhia kālā ke kumu kūʻai o ke **kakalina** ma Kohala?* What is the price of **gasoline** in Kohala?]

gate *'īpuka.*

gather *'ohi.*

gecko *mo'o* (also means any **reptile, succession or lineage**).

gecko

genealogy *mo'okū'auhau.* [*Ma o kona* **mo'okū'auhau** *i hō'ike a'e ai ke ali'i i kona kūlana ali'i.* It was through his **genealogy** that a noble revealed his chiefly status.]

general *laulā* (also means **broad, widespread**). [*He aha ka mana'o* **laulā**? What's the **general** idea?]

generation *hanauna.* (auntie = *makuahine hanauna*) (nephew = *keiki kāne hanauna*)

generous *lokomaika'i.* [*Nui ko ko Nihipali Tutukāne* **lokomaika'i**. Nihipali's grandpa is very **generous**.]

genesis *kinohi* (also means **origin, beginning**). [*Aia ka mo'olelo no Adamu me 'Ewa ma ka puke 'o* **Kinohi** *ma ka Paipala.* The story about Adam and Eve is in the book of **Genesis** in the Bible.]

genitals *ma'i.* [*he mele* **ma'i** *no Kalākaua,* a song praising Kalākaua's **genitals** (*Mele ma'i* are traditional at the end of a hula performance, as a chief gave life to his entire nation)]

gentle *akahai.* [*He po'e* **akahai** *maoli nō nā Hawai'i.* Hawaiians are a truly **gentle** people.]

genuine 1. *maoli.* 2. *maoli nō.* [*He po'oleka aupuni Hawai'i* **maoli** *kāu po'oleka i kū'ai mai ai?* Is the stamp you bought a **genuine** Hawaiian kingdom stamp?]

germ *mū* (also means **insect**).

German *Kelemania.*

Germany *Kelemania.*

gesture *kuhi.* [**Kuhi** *ka lima, hele ka maka.* Where the hands **gesture**, the eyes follow. (*'ōlelo no'eau* stating a rule in hula)]

get *loaʻa* (also means **to find, discover, receive,** many other meanings).

ghost 1. *lapu.* 2. *akua.* 3. *ʻuhane.* [*Ka makua, ke keiki a me ka* **ʻuhane** *hemolele,* Father, Son and Holy **Ghost** (prayer)]

gift *makana.*

gill *pihapiha.*

ginger *ʻawapuhi.*

gird *pūʻali* (also means **grooved, compressed in middle, to compress, warrior**).

girl *kaikamahine.* pl. *kaikamāhine.*

give *hāʻawi.* [*Aia nā makana i* **hāʻawi** *ʻia aku e nā kaikamāhine ma luna o ke pākaukau.* The gifts which were **given** away by the girls are on top of the table.]

give birth *hānau.* [*Āhea ana kou kaikuahine e* **hānau** *ai, e ke kāne?* When will your sister **give birth**, mister?] (to be born = *hānau ʻia*) [*Aia i hea i* **hānau** *ʻia ai kou kupuna kāne?* Where was your grandfather **born**?]

glad *hauʻoli.*

glass 1. *aniani* (material). 2. *kīʻaha* (drinking glass).

glad

glasses (eyeglasses) 1. *makaaniani.* 2. *makaaniani pale lā* (sunglasses).

glide *kīkaha.* [***Kīkaha** ka ʻiwa, he lā mālie.* (*ʻōlelo noʻeau*) The *ʻiwa* bird glides on the wind, it's a calm day.]

gloomy 1. *kaumaha* (also means **depressed**). 2. *pōʻeleʻele* (dark).

glowing 1. *hāweo* (*fig.* distinguished). [***Hāweo** ka wena o ka pele.* The reflection of the lava is **glowing**.] 2. *ʻena* (*fig.* angry).

glue *tuko* (apparently from Duco, a brand name of glue; also means **paste**). [*ʻOki a* **tuko** *nā mākua*

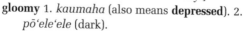

kaiapuni Hawai'i i nā puke hou. The Hawaiian Immersion school parents cut and **glue** new books.]

go 1. *hele.* 2. *hele aku* (move away from speaker). [*E hele aku! E hele pēlā!* **Go away**, get out!]

goal *pahuhopu* (also means **goalpost**).

goat *kao.*

go get (fetch) *ki'i.*

go home *ho'i.* [*E ho'i kāua.* Let's **go home**.]

gold *kula.* [*Nui ko kēlā wahine mau apolima kula.* That lady has many **gold** bracelets.]

golf *kolepa* (from English). [*Nui nō nā kahua kolepa ma O'ahu nei.* There are lots of **golf** courses here on O'ahu.]

good *maika'i* (also means **fine, well**). [*Maika'i wale 'o Kaua'i.* Kaua'i is very **fine**. (traditional chant, "Maika'i Wale 'o Kaua'i," melody by H. Wai'au)]

good-looking *nohea* (also means **handsome**). [*'Ano nohea paha kāu kāne?* Is your husband maybe sort of **handsome**?]

goose *nēnē* (endangered native Hawaiian goose). [*Ua 'ōlelo 'ia, loa'a nā pūnua i nā nēnē i ho'oku'u 'ia ma Nualolo.* It is said that the **nēnē** geese which were released at Nualolo have got fledglings.]

got (in possession of) *loa'a* (also means **get, have**). [*Loa'a ka poi ma ka hale hana poi ma Waiāhole i kēia lā?* Does the poi factory at Waiāhole **have** poi today?]

gourd *ipu.* [*E ho'opa'a i kā 'oukou mau ipu, e nā haumāna hula.* Beat your **gourds**, hula students.]

govern *ho'omalu* (*lit.* to protect). [*Ho'omalu pono ke aupuni?* Does the government **govern** well?]

government *aupuni* (also means **kingdom, country**).

governor *kia'āina.* (lieutenant governor = *hope kia'āina*)

grab *hopu* (also means **to catch, take, arrest**). [*Ua hopu 'ia kā ko'u 'anakala lio e ke kinai ahi.* My uncle's horse was **caught** by the fireman.]

graduate *puka* (also means **to emerge, come out**).
[*Ināhea i **puka** ai kāna kaikamahine 'ohana mai ke kula ki'eki'e mai?* When did her niece **graduate** from high school?]

grain *huna* (small speck of something; also means **secret, hidden, sea spray**). (grain of rice = *huna laiki*)

grand *kilakila* (also means **majestic, royal**). [*he nani kū **kilakila**, 'alo lua i nā pali,* a beauty **grand** in appearance, the two faces of the cliff. ("Moloka'i Waltz," by M. Kane)]

grandchild *mo'opuna.*

granddaughter *mo'opuna wahine.*

grandfather *kupuna kāne.* [*Ha'aheo ke **kupuna kāne** hou.* The new **grandfather** is proud.]

grandmother *kupuna wahine.*

grandmother

grandparent *kupuna* (also means **ancestor**). (*pl. kūpuna; nā kūpuna* = the grandparents, the ancestors; *kou mau kūpuna* = your grandparents) [*Ua ma'a ko kākou mau **kūpuna** i ka holo moana.* Our **ancestors** were familiar with ocean voyaging.]

grandson *mo'opuna kāne.*

grape *hua waina.* (grape juice = *ka wai hua 'ai hua waina*)

grass *mau'u.* [*Mae ka **mau'u** i ka wela o ka lā.* The **grass** wilts in the heat of the sun.]

grate *wa'u* (also means **to scratch, scrape, scraper**). (coconut grater = *wa'u niu*)

gratitude *mahalo* (also means **respect, admiration**). [*Mau nō ka mahalo o nā Hawai'i i nā ali'i o ke au i hala.* The **gratitude** of Hawaiians to the chiefs of times past still continues.]

graveyard *pā ilina.*

greasy *ʻaila.*

great 1. *nui* (also means **large, big**). 2. *piha* (also means **full**). [*Ua **piha** ko ke kāne hauʻoli i kona male ʻana.* The bridegroom's happiness was **great** at his wedding.]

green *ʻōmaʻomaʻo.*

grief 1. *kaumaha.* 2. *kūmākena.* 3. *luʻuluʻu.*

grieve (also means **mourn**) 1. *uē.* 2. *kanikau.*

grieving (also means **mourning**) 1. *kaumaha.* 2. *mākena.* 3. *luʻuluʻu.* 4. *kanikau.* [*Auē ke **kanikau** ma ka hoʻolewa!* Gosh, the **grieving** at the funeral!] Note: *Kanikau* refers to a chant of grief (a dirge or lament) and also means "grieving."

groan 1. *ʻū* (also means **to moan, wail**). 2. *ʻuhū* (also means **to moan, sigh, grunt**).

grocer *kanaka kūʻai mea ʻai.*

gross (slang) *hoʻopailua.* [***Hoʻopailua** maoli kekahi mau mea e ʻike ʻia ma ke kūkala nūhou.* Some things seen on the news are really **gross**.]

grouchy *ʻaʻaka.* [*Ke hele ʻo Māmā a **ʻaʻaka**, e akahele!* Whenever Mom gets **grouchy**, watch out!]

ground *honua* (also means **earth**).

group 1. *pūʻulu.* 2. *hui.*

grow *ulu.* [*he kīhāpai pua **ulu** māhiehie,* the delightfully **growing** flower garden (song, "Kimo Henderson Hula," by H. D. Beamer)]

grumble 1. *namunamu.* 2. *ʻōhumu.* [*Mai **ʻōhumu** aku iā ia!* Don't **grumble** to him.]

guard (protect) *kiaʻi.* [*Nāu e **kiaʻi** a e mālama mai iā mākou.* May you **guard** and take care of us. (a common line in prayers)]

guava *kuawa.*

guess 1. *koho* (also means **to choose**). [*E **koho** ʻoe i ka haʻina!* **Guess** the answer!] 2. *mahuʻi* (also means **to suspect**).

guest 1. *hoakipa*. 2. *malihini*.

guide *alaka'i* (also means **to lead, leader**). [*Ke alaka'i nei ke alaka'i hula i ka papa ho'oma'ama'a.* The hula **guide** is **leading** the practice class.]

guilty *hewa* (also means **wrong, sin**). [*Hewa ke kanaka ma ka hale pa'ahao?* Is the person in jail **guilty**?]

gulch 1. *'oawa*. 2. *awāwa* (also means **valley**).

gum *kēpau* (also means **tar, pitch, resin, lead.** Sap from breadfruit, *pāpala* and other trees was used to catch birds, as glue or caulking, and so forth.) [*Ua ho'ohana nā kāpili manu i ka pāpala kēpau.* Bird catchers used gum (sap) from the *pāpala* tree.]

gum (chewing) *kamu* (from English).

gun *pū*. (to shoot a gun = *kī pū*)

guts *na'au* (considered to be the seat of emotions, the Hawaiian "heart").

habit *hana maʻa.* [*He* **hana maʻa** *hoʻonāukiuki ka nonolo.* Snoring is an irritating **habit**.]

hair 1. *lauoho* (on head). [*Pono ʻoe e kahi mua i kou* **lauoho** *a laila palaki ma hope.* You have to first comb your **hair** and then brush (it) afterwards.] 2. *huluhulu* (body hair; also means **fur**).

hairbrush *palaki lauoho.*

half *hapalua.* [*He* **hapalua** *koko Pilipino ko ko ʻoukou makuahine.* Your (all) mother has half Filipino blood.]

hairbrush

Halloween *Heleuī.* (trick or treat = *kiliki o lapu* [*lit.* treat or be haunted]) (Halloween costume = *ʻaʻahu Heleuī*)

hammer *hāmale.* [*Kuʻi ke kamanā i ke kuʻi i ka* **hāmale**. The carpenter hits the nail with the **hammer**.]

hand *lima* (also means **arm**).

handkerchief *hainakā.* (facial tissue = *hainakā pepa*) [*Ke kulu nei ka hūpē mai ko ka pēpē ihu aku, akā ʻaʻohe* **hainakā pepa** *a kona makua.* Nasal discharge is dripping from the baby's nose, but his parent doesn't have a **tissue**.]

handle *ʻau.* [*E makaʻala! Wela loa ke* **ʻau** *o ka ipuhao!* Watch out! The **handle** of the pot is really hot!]

handy 1. *mākaukau* (ready, prepared). 2. *noʻeau* (clever, skillful).

hang *lī* (also means **shoelace, to lace shoe, gird, furl sail**).

happiness *hau'oli*.

happy *hau'oli*. [***Hau'oli*** *Lā Ho'omaika'i*. **Happy** Thanksgiving.]

harbor *awa kū moku*. [*Kū nā moku kaua ma ke* ***awa kū moku*** *'o Pu'uloa*. Battleships anchor in the **harbor** named Pearl Harbor.]

hard 1. *pa'akikī* (difficult, stubborn). 2. *'o'ole'a* (tough condition, not soft). [*He po'o* ***pa'akikī*** *ko ko Malulani kupuna wahine*. Malulani's grandmother has a **hard** head.]

hardware (metal) *mea hao*.

harm 1. *pōpilikia* (also means **misfortune, emergency**). 2. *hana 'ino*. 3. *ho'opōpilikia*.

hat *pāpale*. (*lauhala* hat = *pāpale lauhala*)

hate *inaina*.

Hawaiian *Hawai'i*. [*He mau kānaka ha'aheo nā* ***Hawai'i***. **Hawaiians** are proud people.] [*He mau hana no'eau* ***Hawai'i*** *ke kuku kapa a me ka ulana lauhala*. Beating tapa and weaving *lauhala* are **Hawaiian** crafts.]

Hawaiian hawk *'io* (endangered native hawk). [*Ke 'ike maka 'oe i ko ka* ***'io*** *lele 'ana, maopopo iā 'oe no ke aha i kapa 'ia ai nā ali'i ma hope o ia manu kelakela.* When you witness the flight of the **Hawaiian hawk**, you understand why the chiefs were named after that majestic bird.]

Hawaiian
hawk

haze (vog) *uauahi*.

hazy *uauahi*. [*Mai puka i waho ke hū ka pele o pilikia kou hanu 'ana i ka lā* ***uauahi***. Don't go outside when lava erupts or you'll have trouble breathing due to the **hazy** day.]

he *'o ia* (also means **she**).

head (Use with *ke.*) *po'o.*

headache *ke po'o 'eha.*

heal *ho'ōla* (also means **salvation**, many other meanings).

health *ola kino.*

healthy *ola* (also means **alive**). [*Ola kā ka makuahine hou pēpē.* The new mother's baby is **healthy**.]

heap 1. *paila* (from English "pile," often used in the idiomatic expression *kū ka paila* as an exclamation of surprise at a large amount). [*Kū ka **paila** o nā niu!* Gosh, what a **heap** of coconuts!] 2. *pu'u.* 3. *ahu.*

hear *lohe.*

hearing aid *mea ho'olohe.*

heart *pu'uwai.*

heart disease *ma'i pu'uwai.*

heart (shape) *haka.* [*E ho'ouna aku ana lāua i **haka** kokoleka kekahi i kekahi ma ka Lā Aloha.* They (two) are going to send each other chocolate **hearts** on Valentine's Day.]

heat *wela.*

heaven 1. *lani.* 2. *lewa.* [*Nā akua o ka **lewalani**, o ka **lewanu'u**.* Gods of the **lower stratum of the sky**, gods of the **upper stratum**. (a common line in ancient prayers)] Both *lani* and *lewa* also mean **sky**. *Lewa* also connotes space, while *lani* can refer to a noble or royal rank or person. Ancient Hawaiians divided the sky into various sections from the horizon to the zenith, each having a name, just as they labeled the diverse biogeographic zones of the islands. *Lewalani* refers to the highest stratum, while *lewanu'u* is lower, where birds fly. See Malo, *Hawaiian Antiquities.*

heavy *kaumaha* (can refer to physical weight or

emotional sadness/depression). [*Kaumaha ka pahu lā'au.* The wooden chest is **heavy**.]

heel *ku'eku'e wāwae* (also means **ankle**).

height *ki'eki'e* (also means **high, tall, altitude, majestic**). [*'Ehia 'īniha ke ki'eki'e o ke ki'i kū?* How many inches is the **height** of the statue?]

heir *ho'oilina* (also means **heritage, inheritance**). [*'O Ka'iulani ka ho'oilina mō'ī hope loa o ke aupuni mō'ī.* Ka'iulani was the last royal **heir** of the Hawaiian kingdom.]

help *kōkua.* [*Mai kōkua mai ia'u! E kōkua aku iā ia!* Don't **help** me! **Help** him!]

hemisphere *'ao'ao.* [*Aia 'o Nuku Hiva i ka 'ao'ao hema.* The Marquesas are in the southern **hemisphere**.]

her (also means **his**) 1. *kona.* 2. *kāna.* (See explanation at entry for **my**. *Kona* is used in the same instances as *ko'u*; *kāna* is used in the same instances as *ka'u*.)

herbs (medicinal) *lā'au lapa'au* (also means **person who practices herbal medicine**).

here 1. *ma 'ane'i* (place). [*Aia nā manakō ma 'ane'i.* The mangoes are **here**.] 2. *eia* (handing something over). [*Eia kāu kī.* **Here**'s your tea.] (here comes someone = *eia a'e*) [*Eia a'e 'o Moke.* **Here comes** Moke.]

heritage *waiwai ho'oilina* (also means **inheritance**). [*He waiwai ho'olina makamae ko kākou.* We have a precious **heritage**.]

hero 1. *me'e.* 2. *kupu'eu.* [*Hō nā hana kupaianaha a nā kupu'eu ma nā ka'ao kahiko.* My goodness, how astonishing are the feats of the **heroes** of ancient stories.] 3. *koa.*

hero

hew *kua* (also means **to chop down**).

hibiscus *puaaloalo.*

hidden *huna* (also means **fine particle, sea spray**).

hide 1. *pe'e* (hide yourself). 2. *ho'ohūnā* (to hide something). [*Ke **pe'e** nei ka 'īlio pēpē ma lalo o ke kalaka a ma laila i **ho'ohūnā** 'ia kāna iwi.* The puppy is **hiding** under the truck and that's where his bone was **hidden**.]

high *ki'eki'e.*

high school *kula ki'eki'e.* [*Āhea ana e puka ai kāu mo'opuna mai ke **kula ki'eki'e**?* When will your grandchild graduate from **high school**?]

high tide *kai piha.*

highway *alaloa.* [*Pa'apū ke **alaloa** i nā kalaka.* The **highway** is crowded with trucks.]

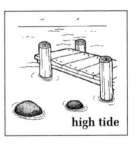

high tide

hike *pi'i kuahiwi.* [***Pi'i kuahiwi** pinepine ka hui a ma'a lākou i ka lepo 'ūkele ma ke alahele.* The club often **hikes** and they all are used to mud on the trail.]

hiking trail *alahele* (also means **trail, pathway**).

hill *pu'u.*

hip *kīkala.* [*'Oni ke **kīkala** o ka 'ōlapa i ka 'ami.* The dancer's **hips** move in the *'ami* (hula step with hip movements).]

his (also means **her**) 1. *kona.* 2. *kāna.* (See explanation at entry for **my**. *Kona* is used in the same instances as *ko'u*; *kāna* is used in the same instances as *ka'u*.)

hiss *hīhī* (also means **to purge**).

history *mo'olelo* (also refers to a story believed to be true, as opposed to *ka'ao,* fictional stories). [*Pono nā Hawai'i e no'ono'o hou no ko ko kākou lāhui*

mo'olelo. Hawaiians have to rethink our nationality's **history**.]

hit 1. *ku'i* (punch, crash). 2. *pa'i* (slap).

hobby *hana ho'ohau'oli*. [*He aha kāna **hana
ho'ohau'oli**? 'O ke kuiki kapa Hawai'i kāna **hana
ho'ohau'oli**.* What's her **hobby**? Hawaiian quilting is her **hobby**.]

hoe *[n]* hō. *[v]* 1. hō. 2. *kālai* (also means **to carve**).
(slang used on sugar plantation for hoeing rows
of sugarcane = *hō hana*)

hold *ho'opa'a*. [**Ho'opa'a** *ke kaikamahine i ka
ho'okupu lā'ī.* The girl **holds** the *tī* leaf offering.]

hole 1. *lua* (in ground; also means **toilet, grave, two**).
2. *puka* (hole through something; also means
door, to emerge).

holiday *lā nui*. [*He **lā nui** ka lā 'apōpō?* Is tomorrow
a **holiday**?]

holy *hemolele* (also means **pure, pristine, perfect**).
[*ka 'uhane **hemolele**,* the **holy** ghost]

home *home* (from English). Note: Ancient houses con-
sisted of several separate buildings called *kauhale*.
Pūnana (*lit.* bird's nest) or "nest" conveys the idea
of emotional attachment to a house, although
"*home*" is undoubtedly used more often today.

homeland 1. *one hānau*. 2. *'āina hānau*. [*Aia i hea
kou **'āina hānau**?* Where is your **birthplace**?]

honest *kūpono*. [*He pu'ukū **kūpono** 'o ia ala ma ke
kalapu.* That one (over there) is an **honest** treasurer in the club.]

honey *meli*.

honeybee *nalo meli*. [*Mumulu nā **nalo meli** i nā pua
mōhala.* **Bees** swarm around the blooming flowers.]

honor (someone) 1. *ho'ohanohano*. [*Ma kēia mahina
a'e e **ho'ohanohano** 'ia ana nā haku mele
Hawai'i.* It is next month that Hawaiian composers will be **honored**. 2. *ho'ohiwahiwa*.

hoof *māiʻuʻu* (also means **claw**). [*Pehu ko ka pipi wahine **māiʻuʻu**. The cow's **hoof** is swollen.*]

hook *[n] lou* (also means **picking pole**). *[v] lou* (also means **to pick with a picking pole**). [*E **lou** i ka manakō i ka **lou**. **Pick** the mango with the **picking pole**.*]

hope *manaʻolana*. [***Manaʻolana** au e kipa aku i ka ʻāina o nā Maori ma Aotearoa. I **hope** to visit the land of the Maori in New Zealand.*]

horizon 1. *hālāwai.* 2. *kūkulu.* 3. *ʻalihi lani.* [*Nānā pinepine ka hoʻokele i ka **ʻalihi lani**. The navigator often looks at the **horizon**.*]

horn 1. *kiwi* (animal horn). 2. *pū* (musical instrument, also conch shell).

horrible *weliweli* (also means **horrified, terrible, terrifying**).

horrified *māʻeʻele* (also means **numb**). [*ʻAia nō a ʻike mākou i ke ōlaʻi ma ke kīwī, ua hele mākou a **māʻeʻele**. As soon as we saw the earthquake on TV, we became **horrified**.*]

horse

horse *lio.* [*Kīau ka **lio** ma ke kahua mauʻu. The **horse** gallops on the grassy field.*]

hospital 1. *haukapila.* 2. *hale maʻi.* Some Hawaiian speakers object to the literal meaning of *hale maʻi* (sick house), since calling a place "sick" is counter to Hawaiian thinking about health. However, this is a commonly used term. Perhaps *hale hoʻōla* (house of healing) would be more appropriate.

hospitality *hoʻokipa* (also means **to welcome, entertain**).

hostile *kūʻē* (also means **to oppose, opposite**). [*He *aha ka hua ʻōlelo **kūʻē** iā "pōkole"?* What word is the **opposite** of "short"?]

hot 1. *wela.* 2. *ikīki* (hot and humid). [*Ikīki loa ka mahina ʻo Kepakemapa.* September is a very **hot and humid** month.]

hotel *hōkele* (from English).

hour *hola* (from English). [*Hoʻomaka ka hālāwai ma ka **hola** ʻehia?* What **time** does the meeting start?]

hotel

house *hale* (also means **building**). [*He **hale** kahiko a kaulana ʻo Washington Place.* Washington Place is an old and well-known **house**.]

house

howl *uō.* [*ʻAoa nā ʻīlio a **uō** nā kānaka ma ka pō Māhealani.* Dogs bark and people **howl** on the night of the full moon.]

hug 1. *ʻapo.* 2. *pūliki.* [*Mai poina e **pūliki** kekahi i kekahi.* Don't forget to **hug** one another.]

hula *hula.* (non-Hawaiian dance, including ballet = *hulahula*)

hula dancer *ʻōlapa* (after tree of same name whose leaves shake in the wind; also means **to flash**, as lightning).

hula school *hālau hula.*

hula teacher *kumu hula.* [*Hoʻopololei ke **kumu hula** i ko nā ʻōlapa hehi ʻana.* The **hula teacher** corrects the dancers' steps.]

hull *kaʻele* (also means **empty, hollow like a bowl or canoe hull**).

human *kanaka.* pl. *kānaka* (also means **person, people**). [*'A'ole au he 'ānela, he **kanaka** au.* (*'ōlelo no'eau*) I am not an angel, I'm **human** (I'm not perfect).]

humble *ha'aha'a* (also means **low in height, humility**). [*Ha'aha'a ka mea lehia maoli.* A true expert is **humble**.]

humid 1. *ma'ū.* 2. *pa'apū* (also means **crowded**). [*'Oiai ke pā mai nei ka makani Kona, **pa'apū** ka lā.* Since the Kona wind is blowing, the day is **humid**.] 3. *ikīki* (hot and humid).

hundred *haneli.* [*i ho'okahi **haneli** makahiki ma kēia mua aku,* one **hundred** years in the future]

hungry *pōloli.* [*I ko'u wā kamali'i, ke **pōloli** mākou, 'ai mākou i ka 'uala.* In my childhood, when we were **hungry**, we ate sweet potatoes.]

hunt 1. *hahai* (also means **to follow**). 2. *alualu* (also means **to chase**).

hurray [exclamation] *hulō.* [*Hipa, hipa, **hulō** no nā kamali'i wahine pā'ū ma ke ka'i huaka'i!* Hip, hip, **hurray** for the *pā'ū* princesses in the parade!]

hurricane *makani pāhili.* [*'Ehia manawa 'oe i 'ike maka ai i ka **makani pāhili**? Ho'okahi manawa, ua lawa.* How many times have you experienced a **hurricane**? Once is enough.]

hurry *'āwīwī* (also means **quick, fast**).

hurt *'eha* (also means **sore, painful**). [*'Eha kou pu'u, e ke keiki?* Is your throat **sore**, child?]

husband *kāne.* [*'A'ohe **kāne** hānai nalo.* (*'ōlelo no'eau*) There is no **husband** who feeds his wife flies (husbands did the cooking in old Hawai'i).]

hymn *hīmeni* (from English; also means **to sing**).

hypocrite *ho'okamani.* [*Inā 'oe i ho'okō i kāu mea i ho'ohiki ai, 'a'ole 'oe e lilo i **ho'okamani**.* If you had fulfilled the promise you made, you wouldn't have become a **hypocrite**.]

ice *hau.*

icebox (refrigerator) *pahu hau.* (ice cube = *poke hau*)
[*Aia nō a hoʻopio ʻoe i ka* **pahu hau***, heheʻe nā* **poke hau***.* As soon as you turn off the **icebox***,* the **ice cubes** melt.]

ice cream 1. *ʻaikalima.* 2. *haukalima.* (shave ice = *haukōhi, hau momona*)

idea *manaʻo* (also means **thought, opinion, mentality**). [*He* **manaʻo** *maʻalea kēlā.* That's a cunning **idea**.]

identical *kūlike* (also means **alike, resembling**). [***Kūlike** nā makalike o nā koa.* The soldiers' uniforms are **identical**.] (exactly alike = *kūlike loa*; idiomatic phrase *ua like nō a like*, lit. just alike, is more common) [***Ua like nō a like** au me kuʻu one hānau.* I'm **just like** my birthplace. (song, "Molokaʻi Nui a Hina," by M. Kāne)]

identify *hōʻoia* (also means **to verify, prove, confirm**; syn. *hōʻoiaʻiʻo*). [*Ke* **hōʻoia** *nei ʻo Kawelo i ko kona mau mākua male ʻana ma o ka ʻimi ʻana i ka palapala male.* Kawelo is **verifying** his parents' marriage by searching for the marriage certificate.]

ignorance *naʻaupō* (also means **ignorant, uneducated**). [*ʻAʻohe waiwai o ka* **naʻaupō***.* Ignorance has no value.]

ignore *nānā ʻole.*

ill *maʻi.*

illegal *kū ʻole i ke kānāwai.*

ill

[*Kū ‘ole i ke kānāwai ke ‘ano o kāu hana?* Is your activity **illegal**?]

illness 1. *ma‘i* (also means **disease, menstruation**). 2. *ka‘a ma‘i* (chronic illness). 3. *ma‘i ahulau* (chronic illness; also means **epidemic**). 4. *‘ea* (common illness).

image *ki‘i* (also means **picture, idol, memorial, statue**, many other meanings).

imagine *kuhi* (also means **to point, to suppose**). [*E **kuhi** kākou i ka ho‘omaluhia i ka honua holo‘oko‘a.* Let's all **imagine** the creation of peace on the whole earth.]

imitate *ho‘opili* (also means **to repeat after the teacher**). [*E **ho‘opili** mai ia‘u.* **Repeat** after me.]

immediately 1. *koke.* [*Na ke kauka e pane **koke** i ke kelepona pa‘a lima.* The doctor is the one who should **immediately** answer the cellular phone.] 2. *‘ānō.*

impatient *ahonui ‘ole.*

imperfect *kīnā* (also means **blemish, flaw, any physical defect**). (syn. *ke‘e*)

implement *mea ho‘ohana* (also means **tool**). [*He **mea ho‘ohana** nui ke ko‘i i ke au kahiko a ua nui nā ‘ano ko‘i like ‘ole a nā kūpuna i ho‘ohana ai.* The adze was an important **implement** in ancient days and there were many different types of adzes that the ancestors used.]

important *nui.* (VIP = *maka nui* or *mea nui*)

impossible *hiki ‘ole.* [***Hiki ‘ole** kou lilo ‘ana i manu lele.* It's **impossible** for you to turn into a flying bird.]

imprison *ho‘opa‘ahao.* [*I ho‘okahi haneli makahiki aku nei, ua **ho‘opa‘ahao** ‘ia ka mō‘ī wahine ‘o Lili‘uokalani i ka Hale Ali‘i ‘o ‘Iolani.* One hundred years ago, Queen Lili‘uokalani was **imprisoned** in ‘Iolani Palace.]

improper *kūpono ‘ole.*

improve *holomua* (also means **to go forward, make progress**). [*Ke **holomua** nei ke a'o 'ana aku i ka 'ōlelo makuahine ma ke kīwī.* The teaching of the mother tongue on TV is **improving**.]

improvement *holomua* (also means **progress**).

inappropriate *kohu 'ole.*

in between *ma waena* (also means **among**). [*Ma **waena** o nā holokai i kū a'e ai ko'u hoaaloha ma ka hana ho'ohanohano.* It was **in between** the ocean voyagers that my friend stood at the ceremony.]

inch *'īniha.*

incident *hanana.* [*Ua kohu 'ole kā ka 'ōpio 'ōlelo ma ka **hanana** pōpilikia.* The young person's words at the unfortunate **incident** were inappropriate.]

incompetent *mākaukau 'ole* (also means **unprepared, incapable**).

incomplete *hapapū.* [***Hapapū** nō kāna hana.* His work is really **incomplete**.]

increase *ho'onui.* [*E **ho'onui** a'e ana nā keiki hapa Hawai'i.* The number of part-Hawaiian children will **increase**.]

indecent *haumia* (also means **contaminated, defiled, unclean**).

independence 1. *ea* (also means **life force, gas, sovereignty**, many other meanings). 2. *kū'oko'a* (also means **freedom**).

independent *kū'oko'a* (also means **free**). [***Kū'oko'a** ko ko'u hoaaloha mau mana'o.* My friend's opinions are **independent**.] (independent [private] school = *kula kū'oko'a*) (government [public] school = *kula aupuni*)

index *papa kuhikuhi.* [*He **papa kuhikuhi** ko ka puke mea kanu Hawai'i maoli?* Does the Hawaiian native plants book have an **index**?]

indigenous *maoli* (also means **native, real**). [*'A'ole ka uhi he lā'au **maoli**.* The yam is not a **native** plant.]

indulge *pailani* (also means **to spoil someone**). ['*O ke kuleana o nā kūpuna ka **pailani** 'ana i nā mo'opuna?* Is **spoiling** grandchildren the privilege of grandparents?]

inexpensive *emi.* ['*A'ole kēnā 'ano uaki he uaki **emi.** That kind of watch (near you) isn't **inexpensive.**]

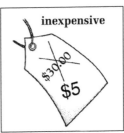

inherit *ho'olina* (also means **heritage, inheritance**). [*He 'āina **ho'oilina** kēia kahua hānai pipi.* This ranch is **inherited** land.]

initiate 1. *ho'okumu* (also means **to establish business, school**, etc.). 2. *ho'omaka* (also means **to start, begin**). [*Na wai i **ho'okumu** i nā kula kaiapuni Hawai'i i **ho'omaka** i 'umi makahiki aku nei?* Who **established** the Hawaiian Immersion schools that **began** 10 years ago?] 3. *ho'olilo i lālā* (also means **to make someone a member of an organization**).

inject 1. *hou* (also means **to shove, stab, pierce**, etc.). 2. *hano.*

injection *hoene* (also means **medicine, enema, abortion, soft sound, rustle**).

injure *hana 'ino* (also means **to abuse, harm**). [*Ke **hana 'ino** 'oe iā ha'i, **hana 'ino** ho'i 'oe iā 'oe iho.* When you **injure** others, you also **injure** yourself.]

injustice *kaulike 'ole.* [*Ua 'ike ka lāhui Hawai'i i ka 'eha o ke **kaulike 'ole.*** The Hawaiian race has known the pain of **injustice.**]

ink *'īnika.* [*Aia nō a mākaukau ka **'īnika,** ho'omaka ke kahunapule Pākē e kākau iho me ke kaha ki'i pū.* As soon as the **ink** is ready, the Chinese priest starts to write and draw at the same time.]

innocent 1. *hewa 'ole.* 2. *hala 'ole.*

insect *mū*. (syn. *iniseka* [from English])

insecticide *lā'au make* (also means **poison, pesticide**). [*I ke aupuni e kīkī ana i ka lā'au make ma kapa alanui, nalowale nā lā'au maoli.* When the government sprays **insecticide** on the roadside, native plants disappear.]

insert *ho'okomo*. [*E ho'okomo 'oe i ka pā lolouila i ka lolouila.* **Insert** the computer diskette into the computer.]

inside *ma loko o*. [*Ikīki ma loko o ke ka'a.* It's hot and stuffy **inside** the car.]

inside

insomnia *hia'ā* (also means **insomniac, unable to sleep**). [*Hia'ā paha 'oe i kēia pō, e Māmā?* Do you have **insomnia** tonight, Mom?]

inspect *nānā*.

inspired *ulu* (also means **to grow**). (to grow a plant, inspire = *ho'oulu*) [*E ho'oulu ana 'o Laka i ke kumu hula.* Laka (goddess of hula) will **inspire** the hula teacher.]

instant *manawa pōkole loa* (*lit.* very short time).

instantly 1. *koke*. 2. *'emo 'ole*.

instead *ma kahi o* (also means **approximately**). [*E hula ana au ma kahi o ko'u kaikaina i ka hō'ike hula.* I will dance **instead** of my younger brother at the hula show.]

instrument *pila ho'okani*. [*Ho'okani kēia kāne i nā pila ho'okani hula kahiko wale nō.* This man plays only ancient hula **instruments**.]

insult 1. *kūamuamu*. [*Kūamuamu ka 'ōpiopio na'aupō i kona kaikua'ana.* The ignorant youth **insults** his older brother.] 2. *hō'ino*.

insurance *'inikua* (from English). [*Ke pi'i a'e nei ka* *'inikua no ke kalaiwa ka'a.* **Insurance** for driving your car is rising in cost.]

intelligence *na'auao* (also means **wisdom, enlightenment**).

intelligent *na'auao* (also means **educated, wise**). [*Na'auao ka 'elemakule e a'o nei i ka lomilomi.* The old man who is teaching Hawaiian massage is **intelligent**.]

interesting *hoihoi.* [*Hoihoi wale nō ka mo'olelo Hawai'i.* Hawaiian history is very **interesting**.]

interfere 1. *'āke'ake'a* (also means **obstruction, to block, hinder**). [*Ua 'āke'ake'a nā kānaka kū'ē i ka hālāwai.* The protestors **interfered** with the meeting.] 2. *hōkake.* (to disturb).

interior *loko* (also means **inside**). [*Hiki ke 'ai 'ia ka na'au o ka manini. Loa'a ka limu ma loko.* The intestines of the *manini* fish can be eaten. There's seaweed **inside**.] [*Aia kāu mau niho hou i loko o kēnā kī'aha?* Are your new teeth **inside** that glass (by you)?]

intermediate school *kula waena.*

international (phrase) *o nā 'āina 'ē.* [*He 'ahahui o nā 'āina 'ē ka UN.* The UN is an **international** organization.]

interpret *unuhi.*

interrupt *kahamaha.* [*Kahamaha ke keiki i kā kona 'anakala kama'ilio 'ana.* The child **interrupts** his uncle's conversation.]

intersection *huina alanui.*

intestines *na'au* (seat of emotions in Hawaiian thinking). [*Mālie ko'u na'au.* My **"heart"** is calm.]

intoxicated *'ona.* [*'Ona anei 'oe i ka lā'au 'ino?* Are you **"high"** on drugs?]

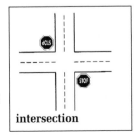

intersection

(Note: *'ona* encompasses both alcoholic intoxication and drug "high.")

introduce *ho'olauna.* [*Makemake au e* **ho'olauna** *iā 'oe me ka haku puke.* I'd like to **introduce** you to the author.]

invade *ho'ouka* (also means **to attack, battle**).

in vain 1. *makehewa* (also means **useless**). 2. *pohō* (also means loss, damage). [**Pohō** *ka 'imi 'ana i ke kanaka ku'i 'opihi o ka nalu i po'i ai.* Looking for the *'opihi* picker that the wave broke over was **in vain.**]

invest *ho'opuka* (also means **make profit**). [*Ua* **ho'opuka** *'olua i ka pili waiwai?* Did you (two) **make a profit** gambling?]

investigate *kolokolo.* [**Kolokolo** *ka māka'ikiu i ko ke kelamoku kū'ai 'ana aku i nā kaimana.* The detective **investigates** the sailor's selling diamonds.]

invitation *kono.* [*Ua hiki mai ke* **kono** *i ka Holokū Ball i kākau 'ia ma ka 'ōlelo makuahine.* The **invitation** to the Holokū Ball which was written in Hawaiian (the mother tongue) has arrived.]

invite *kono.* [*Ua* **kono** *'ia 'oukou i ka 'aha pā'ina?* Were you all **invited** to the banquet?]

inward *i loko.*

Ireland *ka 'āina 'Ailiki.*

Irish *'Ailiki.*

iron 1. *'aiana* (clothes iron). 2. *hao* (metal, also general name for **hardware**).

irrigate *hanawai* (also means **irrigation, urination, menstrual period, to urinate**).

irritable 1. *ho'onāukiuki.* 2. *'a'aka.*

irritate 1. *ho'onāukiuki* (also means **tease**). [*Mai* **ho'onāukiuki** *i kāu hānaiāhuhu o nahu 'ia mai auane'i.* Don't **tease** your pet or else you'll be bitten after a while.] 2. *ho'ouluhua.*

irritated *nāukiuki.*

island *mokupuni.*
island chain *pae 'āina.* [*Nui nā mokupuni li'ili'i ma ka **pae 'āina** 'o Tuamotu.* There are lots of small islands in the Tuamotu **island chain**.]

island

itchy *mane'o* (slang for sexually stimulated, "horny"). [***Mane'o** kona lima i ka 'ōhune.* His skin is **itchy** due to the rash.]

jacket *lakeke.* [*'O ka lakeke mehana ka lole kūpono ma nā wēkiu.* A warm **jacket** is the appropriate clothing on the summits.]

jagged *nihoniho* (also means **serrated, scalloped**). [*Nihoniho ka wēlau o ka pahi.* The tip of the knife is **jagged**.]

jail *hale pa'ahao* (also means **prison**). [*Aia kekahi mau kānaka hewa 'ole ma ka hale pa'ahao.* There are some innocent people in **jail**.]

jam *kele* (also means **jelly**). [*'Ono loa ke kele pōhā.* Pōhā berry **jam** is yummy.]

jail

January *Iānuali* (from English). [*Ho'omaka kāna hana hou ma ka mahina 'o Iānulai.* His new job starts in the month of **January**.]

Japan *Iāpana* (from English). [*Huaka'i pinepine kāna hālau hula i Iāpana.* His hula troupe frequently voyages to **Japan**.]

Japanese *Kepanī.*

jasmine *pīkake* (*lit.* peacock, named for the peacock birds in Ka'iulani's garden at 'Āinahau in Waikīkī, where the first jasmines imported to Hawai'i by her father, Alexander Cleghorn, were planted.)

jaw *ā.* [*Ua ku'i 'ia ko kēia loio ā luna e kekahi hoaloio i kū'ē i kāna e 'ōlelo ana.* This lawyer's upper **jaw** was punched by a fellow lawyer who opposed what she was saying.]

jealousy *lili.*

jellyfish *pololia.* [*Mai hehi i ka **pololia** o 'eha koke kou wāwae.* Don't step on the **jellyfish** or else your foot will be sore immediately.]

jiggle 1. *'oni'oni.* 2. *hō'oni'oni* (to jiggle something). [***Hō'oni'oni** mau ka pēpē i kāna ki'i pēpē.* The baby constantly **jiggles** his doll.]

job 1. *hana* (also means any **activity**). [*He aha kāu **hana** i ka pō nei?* What **(activity)** did you do last night?] 2. *'oihana* (also means **profession, career, business**). [*He aha kāu **'oihana**?* What is your **profession**?]

join 1. *kāpili* (to put together). [*Ua **kāpili** 'ia nā 'āpana o ka nane 'āpana.* The pieces of the jigsaw puzzle were **joined** together.] 2. *pili* (become emotionally close). (my intimate friend = *ko'u hoapili*) 3. *hui* (become a member of a group or club).

joint (of body) 1. *ku'ina.* 2. *ku'eku'e.* [*Mālo'elo'e ko Nohea **ku'eku'e** lima i ka pā'ani kenika.* Nohea's elbow **joint** is stiff due to playing tennis.]

joke *'ōlelo ho'omake'aka.*

journey *huaka'i* (also means **trip, voyage, parade, to travel, take a trip**). [*Ua **huaka'i** 'o Kila i Polapola e ki'i iā La'amaikahiki.* Kila **journeyed** to Tahiti to get La'amaikahiki.]

joy *'oli* (also means **rejoice, joyous, joyful**).

judge *[n] luna kānāwai* (court judge). *[v]* 1. *ho'okolokolo* (in law). 2. *loiloi* (evaluate, judge contest). (judge in contest = *luna loiloi*)

judgment *'ōlelo ho'oholo* (also means **verdict**). [*'Oiai he mea nui ke kuleana i ka wai, na wai e pakele aku i ka **'ōlelo ho'oholo** a ka luna kānāwai e ho'okolokolo ai?* Since water rights are important, who can help but be affected by the **judgment** that the judge will make?]

juggle *ho'oleilei.*

juice *wai hua 'ai.* [*Inu mau kāu pēpē i ka **wai hua 'ai** kuawa?* Does your baby always drink guava **juice**?]

July *Iulai* (from English).

jump 1. *lele* (also means **to fly**). 2. *lelele* (jump continuously).

June *Iune* (from English). [*E male ana māua 'o ka'u ipo ma kēia **Iune** a'e.* My sweetheart and I will marry next **June**.]

jump

jungle *wao nahele* (also means **rain forest**). [*Laha 'ole nā mū a me nā mea kanu ma ka **wao nahele** Hawai'i.* The insects and plants in the Hawaiian **jungle** are rare.]

just (fair) *kaulike.* [***Kaulike** ka 'ōlelo ho'oholo a ke kiule.* The verdict of the jury is **just**.]

justice *kaulike.* [*E loa'a ana ke **kaulike** ma lalo o ka malu o ke aupuni hou.* There will be **justice** under the protection of the new government.]

juvenile *keiki.* [*He mau **keiki** lāua, 'a'ole he mau kānaka makua.* They (two) are **juveniles**, not adults.]

kayak *kaiaka.*

keel *kuamoʻo* (also means **spine, backbone, genealogy**). [*ʻAno like ke **kuamoʻo** o ke kino a me ka waʻa.* The **"backbone"** of the body and of the canoe are sort of similar.]

keep *mālama* (also means **to protect, take care of**). [*E **mālama** i nā wao kele.* **Protect** the rain forests.]

keeper *kahu* (also means **caretaker**). [*He **kahu** ko ka pā ilina o nā aliʻi.* The royal cemetery has a **caretaker**.]

key *kī* (also means **tea, tī leaf plant**). [*Aia iā wai ke **kī**?* Who has the **key**?]

key

kick *peku*. [*E **peku** i ke kinipōpō.* **Kick** the ball.]

kidney *puʻupaʻa* (also means **virgin**).

kill 1. *hoʻomake*. 2. *pepehi* (also means **to beat up**).

kind *[n] ʻano* (type). [*He aha ke **ʻano** o kēia kī aʻu e inu nei?* What **kind** of tea am I drinking?] *[adj] ʻoluʻolu* (good natured).

kindergarten *māla aʻo*. [*He kumu **māla aʻo** ʻo Moana.* Moana is a **kindergarten** teacher.]

king *mōʻī* (also means **sovereign**).

kingdom *aupuni mōʻī* (also means **monarchy**). [*Ua lilo ke **aupuni mōʻī** i lepupalika.* The **kingdom** became a republic.]

kiss *honi* (also means **to smell**). [*E **honi** kāua wikiwiki.* Let's **kiss** quickly).

kitchen *lumi kuke*. [*He **lumi kuke** nui ko koʻu mau

hoahānau hale kahiko. My cousins' old house has a big **kitchen.**]

kite *lupe.* [*Nui nā **lupe** e ho'olele 'ia ai ma ka pāka 'o Kapi'olani.* There are lots of **kites** flown at Kapi'olani Park.]

knee *kuli.*

kneel *kukuli.* [*Ke pule 'oe, **kukuli** 'oe i lalo?* When you pray, do you **kneel?**]

knife *pahi.*

knock *kīkēkē.* [*Ua lohe 'ia **ke kīkēkē** 'ana ma ke kulu aumoe a pi'i a'ela ko'u manene.* **Knocking** was heard at midnight, and I got that creepy feeling.]

knot *hīpu'upu'u.*

knowledge *'ike.* [*He **'ike** ko Tui e pili ana i ka hei Hawai'i?* Does Tui have **knowledge** about Hawaiian string figures?]

knuckle *pu'upu'u* (also means **lumps, lumpy**). [*Moku kou **pu'upu'u** i ka lau kō.* Your **knuckle** is cut by the sugarcane leaf.]

Korea *Kōlea.*

Korean *Kōlea.* [*Nani nō nā lole o nā wāhine **Kōlea.*** The clothes of **Korean** women are beautiful.]

labor *hana.*

laborer *limahana* (also means **employee**). [*Lawakua ka limahana.* The **laborer's** back bulges with muscles.]

lack *nele* (also means **need**). Note: There is no word in Hawaiian for "need." *Nele* is used by some native speakers, since by implication lacking something indicates a need. *Makemake* can also be used. [*Nele au i kou kōkua no ka mea, nele kaʻu keiki i ka lāʻau.* I **need** your help because my child **lacks** medicine.]

lacking *nele* (also means **deficient, destitute, needy**).

ladder *alapiʻi* (also means **staircase**). [*He alapiʻi hāiki ko ke kalaka kinai ahi.* Fire trucks have narrow **ladders**.]

lagoon *kuaʻau.*

lake *loko wai* (also means **pond**). [*Kiaʻi ʻia kēia loko wai e ka moʻo wahine?* Is this **pond** guarded by a "lizard woman" (traditional guardian of freshwater ponds)?]

lame *ʻoʻopa.* [*ʻAno ʻoʻopa ʻo Lanikeha i nā ʻoʻopū.* Lanikeha is sort of **lame** due to blisters.]

lament *uē* (also means **to mourn, cry**). [*Oli ke kāne wahine make i ka uē helu me ka uē pū.* The widower chants his **lament, crying** as he does so.]

lamp

lamp *kukui* (also means **light fixture**).

land *[n]* ‘āina. [*He ali‘i ka **‘āina**, he kauā ke kanaka.* (‘ōlelo no‘eau) The **land** is a chief, man is its servant.]. *[v]* pae. [*Ke **pae** mai nei ka mokulele.* The plane is **landing** now.]

landlord 1. haku ‘āina. 2. haku hale. [*Pena kāu **haku hale** iā loko o ka hale?* Does your **landlord** paint the inside of the house?]

language ‘ōlelo. (Hawaiian language = ‘ōlelo Hawai‘i) (English language = ‘ōlelo Haole or ‘ōlelo Pelekane) (Japanese language = ‘ōlelo Kepanī)

lantern kukui helepō.

lap ‘ūhā (also means **thigh**). [*E noho ‘oe ma ko Kūkū **‘ūhā**.* Sit on Grandma's lap.]

lantern

last hope (also means **behind, in back of, after, later on**). [*‘O ‘oe ka mea **hope** ma ka heihei holo wāwae!* You're the **last** one in the footrace!]

last century i kēlā kenekulia aku nei.

last month i kēlā mahina aku nei. [*Ināhea ‘olua i male ai? **I kēlā mahina aku nei** māua i male ai.* When did you (two) get married? (It was) **last month** that we (two) got married.]

last week i kēlā pule aku nei.

last year i kēlā makahiki aku nei.

late 1. lohi. 2. ‘ūlōlohi. [***‘Ūlōlohi** mau ko‘u hoahana i ke kakahiaka.* My buddy at work is always **late** in the morning.]

laugh ‘aka‘aka.

laughter ‘aka. [*Hū ka **‘aka** o ke anaina e ho‘olohe nei iā Frank DeLima.*

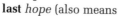

laughter

Laughter bursts out from the audience listening to Frank DeLima.]

laundry *lole lepo* (*lit.* dirty clothes).

lava 1. *pele*. 2. *pāhoehoe* (smooth type). 3. *'a'ā* (rough type). [*Moku nā wāwae i ka hehi 'ana a'e i ka **pele 'a'ā**.* Feet are cut when stepping on **'a'ā-type lava**.]

law *kānāwai*.

lawyer *loio*. [*Ma hope o ka ho'opa'i 'ia 'ana ona, ua pi'i ko ka **loio** wela.* After he was fined, the **lawyer** got angry.]

layer *papa* (also means **list, stratum**, many other meanings). (floor = *papahele*) [*Aia nā mīkini holoi lole ma ka **papahele** hea?* Which **floor** are the washing machines on?]

lazy *moloā*. [*'A'ole 'eu ke kāne **moloā** e alaka'i ana i nā māka'ika'i.* The **lazy** man leading the tourists isn't lively.]

lead *alaka'i* (also means **to guide**).

leader *alaka'i* (also means **guide**). [*Ma'a ke **alaka'i** ma ka papa lu'u kai i nā 'ano i'a like 'ole.* The **leader** of the diving class is used to all kinds of fish.]

leaf *lau* (also used to indicate great numbers as in *laukanaka* = crowded with people). [*He **lau** ākea ko ka 'ulu.* The breadfruit has a wide **leaf**.]

leap *lele* (also means **to jump, fly**).

learn *a'o mai*. [*He aha kāu i **a'o mai** ai i kēia lā?* What did you **learn** today?]

leave *ha'alele* (also means **to quit**). [*E **ha'alele** kākou i ka hapahā hola 'elua o ke kakahiaka nui.* Let's (all) **leave** at 2:30 a.m.]

ledge *kaulu*.

leeward *lalo* (downwind). [*E hoe i **lalo**.* Paddle **downwind**.]

left 1. *hema* (directional; also means **south**). 2. *koe* (remaining).

leftovers *koena* (also means **change from purchase**). [*Ma hope o ka Lā Hoʻomaikaʻi, e ʻai ana koʻu ʻohana i ke koena no hoʻokahi paha pule.* After Thanksgiving, my family will eat **leftovers** for perhaps one week.]

leg *wāwae* (also means **foot**). [*ʻEhia wāwae o kēnā mū?* How many **legs** does that insect (by you) have?]

legends 1. *moʻolelo* (considered to be true stories; also means **history**). 2. *kaʻao.*

legions *lehulehu* (also means **public, multitude**).

legislator *kau kānāwai* (also means **to enact laws, legal**).

lend *hōʻaiʻē.* [*E ʻoluʻolu, hōʻaiʻē mai i ʻelua hapahā kālā.* Please **lend** me two quarters.]

less 1. *hapa iki.* 2. *hapa ʻuʻuku.*

let (allow) *ʻae.*

letter *leka* (also means **to write letter**).

lettuce *lekuke.*

liberty *kūʻokoʻa* (also means **freedom, independence, free**). [*ʻAʻole noho kūʻokoʻa ka hapanui o nā lāhui a puni ka honua.* Most of the peoples around the world do not live in **liberty**.]

library *hale waihona puke.*

lice *ʻuku* (also means **flea**). (jumping flea = *ʻukulele*)

lie *hoʻopunipuni.* [*I ke kuene e hoʻopunipuni ana, ua piʻi ko ke kuke huhū.* While the waiter was **lying**, the cook's anger rose up.]

lie down *moe.*

letter

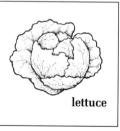

lettuce

life *ola* (also means **live, alive, healthy, cured of disease, salvation**, many other meanings). [*He aha ka manaʻo o ke* **ola**? What is the meaning of **life**?]

lifeguard *kiaʻi ola.*

life style *nohona.* [*He* **nohona** *pipiʻi ko ka wahine kāne make waiwai.* The rich widow has an expensive **life style**.]

lift up *hāpai* (also means **to carry, be pregnant**). [*Ke* **hāpai** *nei ka makua kāne hauʻoli i kāna hiapo ma kona kua.* The happy father is **lifting up** his eldest child onto his back.]

light *[n] ao* (also means **daylight, consciousness, enlightenment**, many other meanings). *[adj] māmā* (weight). [**Māmā** *hoʻi kēia pahu pepa mānoanoa!* This cardboard box is **light**, too!]

lighthouse

light fixture *kukui.*

lighthouse *hale ipu kukui.*

lightning *uila* (also means **electricity**). [*ʻŌlapa ka* **uila**, *kuʻi ka hekili.* **Lightning** flashes, thunder booms. (common imagery in chants)]

like *makemake.* [**Makemake** *au i ka muʻumuʻu lōʻihi.* I **like** a long *muʻumuʻu.*]

limit *[n] palena.* [*ʻO hoʻokahi kaukani kālā ka* **palena** *o ke kīkoʻo ʻana ma kāna kāleka kākī.* One thousand dollars is the **limit** of the credit on her charge card.] *[v] kau palena.*

limpet

limp 1. *ʻoʻopa* (lame). 2. *malule* (weak; also means **soft, fragile, flexible**).

limpet *ʻopihi.*

line (fishing) *aho*. [*Ho'ohana ka lawai'a i ke **aho**, akā ho'ohana ke kālai wa'a i ka 'aha*. The fisherman uses a fishing **line**, but a canoe maker uses sennit (coconut rope).]

lip 1. *lehe*. 2. *lehelehe*. [*E komo i ka 'aila hamohamo ma luna o kou mau **lehe** i 'ole e malo'o i ka makani e pā mai nei*. Put ointment on your **lips** so they won't be dry due to the wind that's blowing now.]

liquid *wai*.

list *papa helu* (also means **scoreboard**).

listen *ho'olohe*. [*E **ho'olohe** pono i nā 'ōkuhi*. **Listen** carefully to the directions.]

litter *'ōpala* (also means **garbage**). [*E 'ohi i ka **'ōpala**. Pick up **litter**.]

little *li'ili'i*.

live *ola* (also means **life, alive, healthy, cured of disease, salvation**, many other meanings). [*E **ola** mau loa, e ku'u lei*. **Live** forever, my beloved *lei* (child). (song, "Ku'u Lei Poina 'ole," by E. Defries)]

live (someplace) *noho*. [*Aia i hea 'oe e **noho** nei?* Where are you **living**?]

lively *'eleu*.

liver *ake*.

living room *lumi ho'okipa*.

lobster *ula*.

local person *kama'āina* (also means **native born, to be familiar with**). [*He **kama'āina** 'o Kindy Sproat no Kohala a kama'āina 'o ia i nā mele paniolo o kona 'āina*. Kindy Sproat is a **local person** from Kohala and he is familiar with the cowboy songs of his land.]

location 1. *kahua* (also means **field, grounds, foundation**). [*Aia ke **kahua** hale hou ma ke kualono*. The new house **location** is on the mountain ridge.] 2. *wahi*. 3. *kahi* (also means **the place**).

lock *laka* (from English).

locked *laka ʻia*. [*Paʻa ka puka i ka **laka ʻia**. The door was closed and **locked**. (song, "Kauoha Mai," by L. Machado)]

loincloth *malo*. [*Eia ka **malo** a Līloa, e hume ʻoe.* Here's Līloa's **malo**, gird it around you (famous line from directions given to ʻUmi when he starts his search for his father Līloa).]

lonely *mehameha*. [*Iaʻu e nānā ana i ke kiʻiʻoniʻoni Maori ʻo Utu, ua hū aʻe koʻu aloha no ia koa **mehameha**.* While I was watching the Maori movie Utu, my empathy for that **lonely** soldier rose up.]

long 1. *loloa*. 2. *lōʻihi*.

look *nānā* (also means **to watch, observe**).

loose 1. *hemo*. 2. *ʻaluʻalu*. [***ʻAluʻalu** kona ʻili i ka hoʻēmi kino.* His skin is **loose** due to losing weight.]

lose 1. *eo* (to be defeated; depending on the sentence structure, *eo* can also mean to win). [*Ua **eo** ʻo Kekuaokalani a me Mānono iā Kalanimoku ma Kuamoʻo.* Kekuaokalani and Mānono **lost** to Kalanimoku at the battle of Kuamoʻo.] 2. *nalowale* (to lose something). [*E akahele o **nalowale** kou apolima.* Watch out or you'll **lose** your bracelet.]

lost 1. *nalowale*. 2. *lilo* (also means **swept away**, many other meanings). [*Ua kokoke e **lilo** nā hale kahakai i ke kai eʻe.* The beach houses were almost **lost** in the tidal wave.] [*Ua **nalowale** kaʻu kī no ke keʻena.* The key to my office is **lost**.]

lotion (skin) *lāʻau hoʻopulupulu ʻili*. [*Ma hope o ka ʻōlala ʻana, e hoʻohana i ka **lāʻau hoʻopulupulu ʻili**.* After sunbathing, use **skin lotion**.]

loud 1. *halulu* (loud noise; also means **roar, explosion**). [*Ua lohe ʻia ka **halulu** ma ka pō mua o ka makahiki e ʻoukou a pau?* Was the **loud noise**

on New Year's Eve heard by all of you?] 2. *leo nui* (loud voice).

loud voice 1. *leo nui.* 2. *'ikuwā* (also name of month in traditional Hawaiian calendar (October-November), a time of storms and lightning at the beginning of the rainy season).

love [n] *aloha.* [*lei* **aloha** *na'u, lei makamae,* a *lei* of **love** for me, a precious *lei* (song, "Lei Aloha, Lei Makamae," by C. King)] [v] 1. *aloha.* 2. *ho'oipoipo* (make love). [*E* **ho'oipoipo** *kāua.* Let's **make love.**]

love of land *aloha 'āina* (also means **patriotism**).

lover *ipo.*

low *ha'aha'a* (also means **humility, humble**).

loyal *kūpa'a.*

loyalty *kūpa'a.* [*Ho'omau ke* **kūpa'a** *o ko Hawai'i po'e i nā ali'i 'ai moku.* The **loyalty** of Hawaiian people to the high chiefs continues.]

luck 1. *ho'omaika'i* (also means **congratulations**). 2. *laki.* [*He mea* **laki** *a i 'ole pakalaki ka pi'o 'ana o ke ānuenue?* Is the arching (appearance) of a rainbow good **luck** or bad?]

lucky *laki* (from English).

luggage *ukana.* [*Kaumaha kāna* **ukana** *i nā puke.* Her **baggage** is heavy with books.]

lullaby 1. *mele ho'ohiamoe keiki.* 2. *mele ho'onānā keiki.*

lunch *'aina awakea.* [*'O kēnā kini kupa wale nō kāu* **'aina awakea**? Is just that can of soup your **lunch**?]

lungs *akemāmā.*

lure (attract) *'ume.* [**'Ume** *mau ke 'ala o ka pua pakalana.* The scent of the *pakalana* flower always **attracts**.]

machine *mīkini.*

mad 1. *huhū* (angry). [*Ua hele ʻo Tūtū a **huhū** i kāna mau moʻopuna i hoʻohenehene mai iaʻu.* Tūtū became **angry** at her grandchildren who teased me.] 2. *pupule* (crazy). 3. *hehena* (crazy).

made *hana ʻia.* [*Ua **hana ʻia** ka lei hua kukui ma Molokaʻi.* The *kukui* nut *lei* was **made** on Molokaʻi.]

magic *hoʻokalakupua.*

magician *hoʻokalakupua.* [*He **hoʻokalakupua** ko ka hōʻikeʻike.* The circus has a **magician**.]

magnet *mākēneki.* [*Aia paha he **mākēneki** e hoʻopili ai i ka pānānā i ke kalaka?* Is there maybe a **magnet** that would stick the compass to the truck?]

maidenhair fern *ʻiwa ʻiwa.*

mail [n] *leka* (letters).

mailbox *pahu leka.*

mail carrier *lawe leka.* [*E lawe mai ana paha ka **lawe leka** i kekahi leka iā ʻoe i kēia lā?* Will the **mail carrier** perhaps bring a letter to you today?]

mailbox

mainland 1. *ʻāina nui.* 2. *loko.* [*Ma **loko** e hana nei kekahi mau poʻe Hawaiʻi.* Some Hawaiians are working on the **mainland**.]

majestic 1. *kilakila.* [***Kilakila** nā Koʻolau.* The Koʻolau mountains are **majestic**.] 2. *kelakela.* 3. *ʻihiʻihi.*

majority *hapanui.* [*ʻAʻole ʻōlelo Hawaiʻi ka **hapanui***

o nā Hawai'i. The **majority** of Hawaiians don't speak Hawaiian.]

make (a thing) *hana* (also means **to work, any activity, job**). [*Na ka'u kāne i* **hana** *i ko 'olua mau noho paipai koa.* My husband is the one who **makes** your (two) *koa* rocking chairs.] (make a joke = *ho'omāke'aka*) (make a video = *ho'opa'a wikiō*) (make a fine appearance = *ulumāhiehie*) (make a tour around the island = *ka'ahele, ka'apuni*) (make a circuit, go around = *ho'opō'ai*) (make noise = *hanakuli, kani, ho'owā*)

male *kāne.* [*'O kēlā koloa ke kakā* **kāne.** That *koloa* bird is the **male** duck.]

malicious *na'au 'ino.* (malicious gossip or accusation = *ni'a*)

malignant *'a'ai.*

man *kāne* (male). [*He* **kāne** *kāko'o i nā 'ilihune ke kia 'āina hou?* Is the new governor a **man** who supports poor people?]

manager 1. *mea ho'oponopono.* 2. *luna.* [*Alaka'i maika'i ka'u* **luna** *i nā limahana.* My **manager** leads the employees well.]

mange *kāki'o.* [*Auē! Loa'a kēia 'īlio i ke* **kāki'o.** Gosh! This dog has **mange.**]

mango *manakō.*

mango

mangrove *kukuna o ka lā* (*lit.* rays of the sun).

mankind *kanaka.* [*Mai nānā 'ino'ino nā hewa o* **kanaka.** Don't look severely on the sins of **mankind.** (song, "Queen's Prayer," by Lili'uokalani)]

manslaughter *lawe ola.*

manual (book) 1. *puke kuhikuhi.* [*Aia ka wehewehe 'ana i ka ho'ā 'ana i ka mīkini ma ka 'ao'ao hea*

*o ka **puke kuhikuhi**?* On which page of the **manual** do they explain how to turn on the
machine?] 2. *puke kumu.*

manuscript *palapala* (also means **document,
writing**, many other meanings).

many 1. *lau.* 2. *nui.* 3. *lehu.* 4. *kini.* [*E nā **kini** maka
o ka ʻāina.* Oh the **many** friends of the land. (traditional greeting)]

map *palapala ʻāina.* [*Iā ʻoe e hoʻomākaukau ana no
ka piʻi kuahiwi, mai poina i ka **palapala ʻāina.***
When you prepare for the hike, don't forget the
map.]

mar *māʻinoʻino.* [*Mai **māʻinoʻino** i nā palapala
kahiko!* Don't **mar** the old documents!]

marbles *kinikini.*

march 1. *paikau* (often refers to military parade). 2.
kaʻi huakaʻi. 3. *naue.* [*E **naue** i mua, hema,
ʻākau, hema.* **March** forward, left, right, left.]

March Malaki (from English).

marijuana *pakalōlō.* [*Hoʻoulu ʻia ka **pakalōlō** ma nā
mokupuni a pau.* **Marijuana** is grown on all the
islands.]

mark *kaha.*

market *mākeke.* (farmers'
market = *mākeke
mahiʻai*) [*ʻO kaʻu wahi
punahele no ke kūʻai
ʻana mai i nā lau ʻai me
nā hua ʻai, ʻo ia ka
mākeke mahiʻai.* My
favorite place for buying

market

vegetables and fruits is the **farmers' market.**

marlin (fish) *aʻu.*

Marquesas Nuʻu Hiwa. [*Kūnihi nā pali ma **Nuʻu
Hiwa**.* The cliffs of the **Marquesas** are steep.]

marriage *male ʻana* (also means **wedding**). [*Kipa
mai kekahi mau malihini Kepanī no ka **male***

'ana. Some Japanese tourists visit here in order
to have a **wedding**.]

marriage license *palapala male*.

married couple *pa'a male*.

marry 1. *male* (from English). 2. *ho'āo*.

marsh *nenelu* (also means **bog, swamp, swampy,
soft plumpness**).

marshall *ilāmuku*.

martial arts (Hawaiian) *lua*. [*Kohu like anei ka* **lua**
me ke 'ano hula ha'aha'a? Is **Hawaiian martial
arts** like low-style hula?]

mash *[v]* 1. *ho'owali* (also means **to mix poi**). 2. *ku'i*
(also means **to smash, crush**, other meanings).

mask *makaki'i* (mask that covers eyes or face only).
2. *po'oki'i* (mask that fits over head, such as
head of lion in Chinese lion dance). [*Loa'a i ko'u
hoahānau kekahi mau* **po'oki'i** *Pākē no ka
hulahula liona.* My cousin has some Chinese
masks for the lion dance.]

massage *lomilomi*. [*Hiki ke* **lomilomi** *'ia ko'u po'ohiwi
'eha?* Can my sore shoulder be **massaged**?]

mast of ship *kia*. [*kahi moku* **kia** *kahi, loa'a 'o ka
fea wini,* a **single-masted** ship (which) has a fair
wind (song, "Moku Kia Kahi," by L. Bray)]

masturbate *'u'u*.

mat *moena* (also means **carpet, bed**).

match 1. *ho'okūkū* (sports or contest). 2. *ahipele* (for
lighting fire).

matching 1. *like* (also means **alike**). [*Komo ka pa'a
male i ka lole* **like**. The married couple wear
matching clothes.] 2. *kohu*.

mate *[n]* *pili 'ao'ao*. [*'Imi mau ke kanaka i kāna* **pili
'ao'ao**. Humans always seek a **mate**.] *[v]* 1. *male*.
2. *ho'āo*. 3. *ho'omau*.

math *makemakika* (from English). (math terms: add
= *ho'ohui*; subtract = *lawe*; multiply = *ho'onui*;
divide = *pu'unaue*) (to count = *helu*)

mattress *pela.*

mature 1. *kanaka makua.* [*Kohu **kanaka makua** ke 'ano o kēnā makuahine 'ōpiopio.* The character of that young mother (by you) is like that of a **mature** person.] 2. *o'o.*

May Mei (from English).

maybe *paha.* Note: Unlike "maybe" or "perhaps" in English, *paha* cannot be used alone, but must always follow another word. In sentences, *paha* directly follows the verb. The idiomatic phrase *malia paha* can start a sentence and indicates that maybe the action following will happen, as in the example. [***Malia paha** e kelepona mai ana ke kauka i kēia ahiahi.* **Maybe** (perhaps) the doctor will call tonight.] *Paha* is often added to *'ae* or *'a'ole* to convey the ideas of "probably so" and "probably not." [*E ho'oikaika kino ana 'oe i ka lā 'apōpō? **'Ae paha.*** Will you exercise tomorrow? **Probably so** (*lit.,* yes, maybe)]

mayor *meia* (from English).

meal 1. *'aina.* 2. *pā'ina* (also means **party, to eat**).

mean (disposition) *mākonā* (also means **hard-hearted**). [***Mākonā** kekahi mau luna mahikō.* Some sugar plantation supervisors were **mean.**]

meaning *mana'o.* [*He **mana'o** ko nā 'ano ao like 'ole i ke kahuna kilokilo.* All different kinds of clouds have **meaning** to the weather expert.]

measure *ana.*

measurement *ana.* (the immeasurable heaven = Kalaniana'ole, a descendant of royalty and a representative to Congress famed for helping establish Hawaiian Homes lands)

meat *'i'o* (also means **flesh, muscle**, figurative reference to the "heart" or core of the matter). (beef = *'i'o pipi*) (pork = *'i'o pua'a*)

mechanic *mekanika* (from English). [*Ua hiki anei i ka **mekanika** ke ho'oponopono i ko Kanani* *mokokaikala?* Was the **mechanic** able to fix Kanani's motorcycle?]

medal *mekala* (also means **metal**).

medical practice, herbal medicine *lāʻau lapaʻau.*

medicine *lāʻau.*

meditate *noʻonoʻo* (also means **to think**). [*Noho mālie kaʻu kahunapule a **noʻonoʻo** ihola.* My minister sits calmly and then **meditates**.]

meet 1. *hui.* 2. *launa.*

meeting *hālāwai.* [*Ua launa hauʻoli nā lālā o ka hui hoʻoulu ʻokika i ka **hālāwai** mua.* Members of the orchid-growing club happily interacted at the first **meeting**.]

melody *leo* (also means **voice**). [*He nani wale ka **leo** o "Makalapua."* The **melody** of "Makalapua" is just beautiful.]

melt *heheʻe.* [*Ke **heheʻe** nei ka haukalima i waiho ʻia ma ka pākaukau.* The ice cream that was left on the table is **melting**.]

memento *paumaunoʻonoʻo.* [*Kau ʻo Mehana i kona mau lei i ka ʻumeke me he **paumaunoʻonoʻo** lā.* Mehana places her leis in the calabash as a **memento**.]

memorial *kiʻi hoʻomanaʻo.*

memorize *hoʻopaʻanaʻau.* [***Hoʻopaʻanaʻau** ka hoʻopaʻa i ka mele oli āna e oli ai.* The hula drummer **memorizes** the chant he will chant.]

memory *waihona hoʻomanaʻo* (*lit.* depository of memories). [*Miki kou **waihona hoʻomanaʻo**?* Is your **memory** sharp?] Note: *Waihona hoʻomanaʻo* refers to one's collection of memories or memory bank. *Haliʻa, haili,* and *hoʻomanaʻo* refer to a single memory of an event, place, or person.

men's eating house *mua.* Note: Traditionally, men prepared the food and ate separately from women.

menstrual house *hale peʻa.* Note: In ancient Hawaiʻi menstruating women retired to a separate house.

menstruate 1. *peʻa.* 2. *hana wai.*

menstruation 1. *maʻi wahine.* 2. *hanawai.*

menu *papa kuhikuhi mea ʻai.* [*E ke kuene, make-make au e ʻike i ka **papa kuhikuhi mea ʻai.*** Waiter, I'd like to see the **menu**.]

merciless *loko ʻino.*

mercy *aloha.*

merry *leʻaleʻa* (also means **fun, funny, enjoyable,** including **sexual pleasures**).

Merry Christmas Mele Kalikimaka (from English; *mele* means "song" or "poem" in Hawaiian, but in "Merry Christmas" it is used because it is the closest sound in Hawaiian to "merry").

message *manaʻo* (Note: There is no exact equivalent for "message." *Manaʻo* means **thought, idea,** many other meanings.)

messenger *ʻelele* (also means **delegate, representative**). [*Ua hoʻouna ʻia ʻo Konela Iaukea i ʻEnelani ma ke ʻano he **ʻelele** mai ke aupuni o Kalākaua.* Colonel Iaukea was sent to England as a **messenger** of the Kalākaua government.]

messy *kāpulu.* [***Kāpulu** loa ka lumi kuke i ke kuke ʻana ou i ka mea ʻono?* Is the kitchen **messy** due to your cooking dessert?]

metal. 1. *mekala.* 2. *hao* (iron).

method *ʻano hana.* [*He aha ke **ʻano hana** kūpono e aʻo aku i ka heluhelu ʻana?* What is the proper **method** to teach reading?]

meticulous *maiau.* [***Maiau** ka hana a ka lehia.* The expert's work is **meticulous**.]

midday *awakea* (also means **noon**). [*ʻAʻohe ou aka ma ke **awakea**.* You have no shadow at **midday**.] Note: House blessings and other ceremonies are often done during midday, the time of the greatest light.

middle *waena.*

midnight *kulu aumoe.* [*ke ʻala aʻu i honi i ke **kulu aumoe,*** the scent I smelled at **midnight**. (song, "Pua Ala Aumoe," by I. Beniamina)]

mild *ʻūpalu.*

mile *mile* (from English; also means **mileage**). [*ʻEhia **mile** āu e holopeki ai?* How many **miles** should you jog?]

military *pūʻali koa.*

milk 1. *waiū.* 2. *waiū kini* (canned milk). [*ʻO ka **waiū kini** a i ʻole ka wai niu ka mea e hoʻomomona ai i ke kūlolo?* Is it **canned milk** or coconut milk that sweetens *kūlolo* (a dessert made with taro)?]

Milky Way *Iʻa.* [*Ua huli ka **Iʻa**.* The **Milky Way** has turned (it's past midnight).]

mill *wili.* (sugar mill = *hale wili kō*)

mine (belonging to me) 1. *koʻu.* 2. *kaʻu.* 3. *noʻu* 4. *naʻu. Koʻu* and *kaʻu* are possessive pronouns and can be used before nouns (*kaʻu kālā* = my money) or in possessive sentences: (*He manaʻo koʻu.* I have an idea/opinion.) *Noʻu* and *naʻu* are used to indicate ownership and by extension *kuleana,* responsibility for and guardianship of an object, intellectual property, or even a person. (*Noʻu kēia ʻāina* = This land is mine.) (*Na wai ka pēpē e uē nei? Naʻu!* = Who does the baby who is crying belong to? To me!)

mine (pit) *lua ʻeli.* (gold mine = *lua ʻeli kula*)

minister *kahunapule.* [*Kaulana paha ke **kahunapule** i kona akahai.* The **minister** is well known for her gentleness.]

minister

minus *hoʻolawe* (to subtract).

minute *minuke*. [*ʻO ka iwakālua* **minuke** *i hala ka hola ʻehā kēia*. It's twenty **minutes** past four.]

miracle *hana mana*. [*ʻO ke aloha ka* **hana mana** *e kū aʻe mau ana*. Love is an ever-present **miracle**.]

mirage *wailiʻulā*. [*Ma ke one wela nō i ʻike ʻia ai ka* **wailiʻulā** *e ka lawaiʻa*. It was on the very hot sand that the **mirage** was seen by the fisherman.]

mirror *aniani*. [*Loaʻa kekahi* **aniani** *kū koa kahiko i ko Līhau mau mākua*. Līhau's parents have an old *koa* standing **mirror**.] (hand-held mirror = *aniani paʻa lima*)

mischievous *kolohe* (also means **rascal**). [*Inā ʻoe hana* **kolohe**, *ʻaʻole e ʻae ana ʻo Tūtū iā ʻoe e ʻohi limu me ia*. If you are **mischievous**, Tūtū won't let you gather seaweed with her.]

misprint *paʻi hewa*. [*Hō kū ka paila o nā* **paʻi hewa** *ma ka palapala hoʻoilina!* My, there are a great many **misprints** in the will!]

miss (someone) *haʻo*. [**Haʻo** *au iā ia*. **Haʻo** *anei paha ʻo ia ala iaʻu?* I **miss** him! Does he (over there) maybe **miss** me?]

missionary 1. *mikionele*. 2. *mikanele*.

misstep 1. *kāhehi*. 2. *hehi hewa*.

mist 1. *noe*. 2. *uhiwai*. (the misty rain = *ka ua noe*)

mistake 1. *hewa*. [*He* **hewa** *kāna pane*. Her answer is a **mistake**.] 2. *kuhi hewa*. (if I am not mistaken = *inā ʻaʻole au i kuhi hewa*) [*Inā* **ʻaʻole au i kuhi hewa**, *ua lohe mua au i kou inoa*. If I am **not mistaken**, I have heard your name before.] 3. *lalau*.

mistreat 1. *hana ʻino* (abuse). 2. *hoʻomāuna* (waste, injure). [*E akahele kākou i ʻole e* **hoʻomāuna** *i ka ʻāina*. We all should be careful so we don't **mistreat** the land.]

mix 1. *kāwili* (to mix ingredients in food preparation). [*I ke* **kāwili** *'ana ou i ke kōpa'a me ka palaoa, ho'ohana 'oe i ke puna?* When you **mix** the sugar and flour, do you use a spoon?] 2. *ho'owali* (poi). 3. *wili*.

mixed (colors or textures) *kipona*. [*Kui ko Ni'ihau i ke kaila lei pūpū i kapa 'ia ka lei* **kipona**. Ni'ihau's people string the style of shell *lei* called a **mixed** *lei*.]

mixed up (confused) *huikau*.

moan 1. *'uhū*. 2. *kani'uhū*. 3. *'ū*. 4. *kani'ū*.

mob 1. *uluāo'a*. 2. *po'e ho'ohaunaele*.

modest 1. *waipahē* (also means **courteous, gracious**). [*Waipahē kou 'ano, e ka mea ho'okipa*. You have a **modest** personality, host.] 2. *wiwo*.

moist 1. *ma'ū* (damp). [*Ma'ū i ka pu'u ke moni*. It's **moist** when you swallow it. (song, "Niu Haohao," by B. Mossman)] 2. *pulu* (soaked, drenched in moisture). 3. *līhau*.

monarchy *aupuni mō'ī*. [*E kū hou a'e ana ke* **aupuni mō'ī** *ma Hawai'i?* Will there appear a new **monarchy** in Hawai'i?]

Monday *Pō'akahi*. [*Hui kekahi mau papa ho'oikaika kino ma ke ahiahi o ka* **Pō'akahi**. Some exercise classes meet on **Monday** evenings.]

money *kālā*. (one dollar = *ho'okahi kālā*) [*Ho'okahi wale nō āna* **kālā**. *'Ehia āu* **kālā**? He only has **one dollar**. How much **money** do you have?]

mongoose *manakuke*. [*He 'aihue akamai ka* **manakuke**. The **mongoose** is a clever thief.]

monkey *keko*. [*He mau* **keko** *nā keiki e pā'ani nei ma waho*. The children who are playing outside are (acting like) **monkeys**.]

monster 1. *pilikua nui*. 2. *tutua* (idiom).

month 1. *mahina*. [*'Elima Lāpule o kēia* **mahina** *a'e*. Next **month** has five Sundays.] 2. *malama*.

mood *'ano* (also means **personality, type, brand**).

moon *mahina.* (full moon = 1. Māhealani [name of night of full moon in ancient calendar]. 2. *mahina piha*) [*He **mahina piha** ko ka pō Māhealani.* The night **Māhealani** has a **full moon.**] (new moon = 1. *mahina hou.* 2. *hilo* [name of crescent moon, name of first month in ancient calendar].)

moral *pono* (also means **righteous, proper**, many other meanings).

more *hou* (also means **new, again**). [*Hiki iā lākou ke 'ai **hou** i ka haupia?* Can they (three) eat **more** coconut pudding?]

morning 1. *kakahiaka.* 2. *kakahiaka nui* (early morning). [*Holoholo ko'u 'anakala i ke **kakahia-ka nui.*** My uncle goes out in the **early morning.**]

morning glory (plant) 1. *pōhuehue* (beach morning glory). 2. *koali.*

mosquito *makika.*

moth *pulelehua.* [*Ma nā pō ikīki e mumulu ana nā makika a me nā **pulelehua** a ānehe aku ka mo'o.* It is on hot and humid nights that mos-quitoes and **moths** swarm and the gecko sneaks up (on them).]

mother *makuahine.*

mother-in-law *makuahūnōai wahine.*

Mother's Day Lā Makuahine. [*E waiho ana paha 'oe i nā loke ma ka pā ilina ma ka **Lā Makuahine?*** Will you perhaps leave roses at the cemetery on **Mother's Day**?]

motorcycle *mokokaikala.* [*Le'ale'a a maka'u ka holo **mokokaikala.*** Riding **motorcycles** is fun and dangerous.]

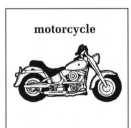

motorcycle

motto *mākia.* [*'O "Ho'oulu Lāhui" ka **mākia**
    kaulana a Kalākaua.* "Increase the nation" was
    Kalākaua's well-known **motto.**]

mountain 1. *kuahiwi* (considered to be older, more
    eroded than *mauna*). 2. *mauna.* [***kuahiwi** kū
    kilakila i ka la'i,* **mountain** that stands majestic
    in the calm (song, "La'i Au Ē," by
    Lili'uokalani)]

mountainside *uka* (also means **uplands, up-slope**).
    [*I **uka** lā, i **uka**, ka ulu lā'au.* There in the
    uplands, in the **uplands** is the forest. (song, "He
    Nani Ke Ao Nei," by M. K. Pukui)]

mourn 1. *makena.* 2. *uē.* 3.
    kanikau.

mouse *'iole* (refers to any
    rodent).

mousetrap *'ūmi'i 'iole.*

mouth *waha.* [*'Oiai he niho
    hu'i ko'u, 'a'ole pehu
    ko'u **waha** holo'oko'a.*
    Although I have a sore
    tooth, my whole **mouth**
    isn't swollen.]

mouse

move 1. *ho'one'e* (furniture, goods). 2. *ne'e* (move
    yourself). 3. *'oni* (wiggle, squirm). (moving
    smoothly, silently = *niau*).

movie *ki'i 'oni'oni.* [*Ma ka hola 'ehia e ho'omaka ai
    ke **ki'i 'oni'oni** a Eddie Kamae mā i ho'opa'a ai?*
    What time does the **movie** that Eddie Kamae
    folks made start?]

much *nui* (also means **big, large size, great impor-
    tance**).

mucus *hūpē.*

mud 1. *kelekele.* 2. *lepo 'ūkele.* 3. *pālolo* (sticky mud
    [such as clay]).

muddy *'ūkele.* [*He alahele **'ūkele** ke alahele ma ka
    naele.* The trail in the swamp is a **muddy** trail.]

mug 1. *pola* (also means **bowl**). [*E ʻoluʻolu e hoʻopiha hou i koʻu **pola** i ke kope*. Please fill my **mug** with coffee once more.] 2. *kīʻaha* (also means **drinking glass**).

mulch *pulu* (also means **soaked with rain, coconut fiber**).

multiply 1. *hoʻonui*. 2. *hoʻomāhua*.

multitude 1. *lehulehu*. 2. *kini*. 3. *makamaka*. [*E nā **kini**, nā **makamaka**, ka **lehulehu***. Oh **multitudes**, **friends**, **public** (common line at beginning of speeches).]

mumble *namunamu* (also means **to complain**). [*Ua hoʻonui ka lehulehu **namu-namu** a lilo i uluaōʻa*. The **complaining** multitudes multiplied until they became a mob.]

munch 1. *nau* (chew). 2. *nome*. [*ʻO Pele ka wahine **nome** honua ma Puna*. Pele is the woman who **munches** the earth at Puna.]

murder *pepehi kanaka*.

murderer *lima koko* (lit. bloody hand).

muscle 1. *ʻiʻo* (also means **meat, flesh**). [*ʻEhia mau **ʻiʻo** o ke kino?* How many **muscles** does the body have?] 2. *olonā* (also refers to a native shrub that yields a very strong fiber used for making cordage).

museum *hale hōʻikeʻike*. [*Aia ke kalaunu Hawaiʻi ma ka **hale hōʻikeʻike** a i ʻole ua hoʻihoʻi ʻia i ka Hale Aliʻi?* Is the Hawaiian crown at the **museum** or was it returned to the Palace?]

mushroom *kūkaelio*.

music *mele* (also means **poetry**).

musician *mea hoʻokani pila*.

muslin *keʻokeʻo* (also means **white**).

must *pono* (also means **have to, should**). [*Pono nā kānaka maoli e mālama i nā loʻi kalo*. The native people **must** take care of the taro patches.]

mustache *ʻumiʻumi*. [*Mai kahi i kou **ʻumiʻumi***. Don't shave your **mustache**.]

musty *pelekunu.*

mute 1. *hāmau.* 2. *mū.* 3. *mumule.*

mutual *like.* [*He kuleana* **like** *ko kāua e hānai pono i kā kāua keiki.* We (you and I) have a **mutual** responsibility for properly raising our child.]

my 1. *koʻu* (used in front of nouns that are things you can't help having, such as family born before you and including your generation, your name, land, friends, chiefs, gods, feelings, illnesses. Also used for anything one can enter into or put on, including any building, mode of transportation, clothes). 2. *kaʻu* (used in front of nouns that are things that can be acquired, including family born after you, your husband or wife, your work or any action, any tool [including computers and televisions], money, anything you make or create, food, drink, books). [*ʻO Maile* **kaʻu** *moʻopuna.* Maile is **my** grandchild.]

mysterious 1. *āiwaiwa* (also means **fantastic, incomprehensible, amazing**). [*Āiwaiwa nā kiʻi pōhaku i kālai ʻia e ko kākou mau kūpuna.* The petroglyphs that were carved by our ancestors are **mysterious**.] 2. *pāhaʻohaʻo.*

myth *kaʻao.*

nail 1. *kui.* [*'O ke* **kui**, *ka hāmale a me ka pahiolo nā mea ho'ohana a ke kamanā.* **Nails**, hammers and saws are the carpenter's tools.] 2. *miki'ao* (fingernail or toenail).

naked 1. *kohana.* 2. *'ōlohelohe.*

name [n] *inoa.* [*He* **inoa** *kaulana anei paha ko kou 'ohana?* Does your family perhaps have a well-known **name**?] [v] *kapa.*

nap *hiamoe iki.*

napkin *kāwele* (also means **towel, to dry**). [*Lawa nā* **kāwele** *i lawe 'ia mai i kahakai?* Are there enough **napkins** that were brought to the beach?]

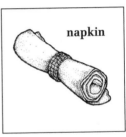

napkin

narrate *ha'i* (also means **to tell, to break**). (show and tell = *hō'ike a ha'i*)

narrow *hāiki.* [**Hāiki** *maoli nō ke alahele ma ka wēkiu.* The trail is really **narrow** at the summit. (fine points, details [or narrow-minded] = *mana'o hāiki*) (main idea, general idea [or broad-minded] = *mana'o laulā*)

nation *aupuni* (also means **kingdom, government, country**).

nationality *lāhui* (also means **ethnic group**).

native [n] 1. *kupa.* 2. *'ōiwi.* 3. *kama'āina.* 4. *kanaka maoli* (*lit.* native person, a recent addition to the language). [adj] *maoli.* [*He holoholona Hawai'i* **maoli** *ka 'ōpe'ape'a.* The Hawaiian bat is a **native** Hawaiian animal.]

native country 1. *'āina hānau*. 2. *one hānau* (also means **birthplace**).

nauseated 1. *poluea* (from motion; seasick). [***Poluea** nā 'ōhua i ka holu 'ana o ka holo mokulele.* The passengers are **nauseated** due to the bumpiness of plane travel.] 2. *liliha* (from eating rich food).

navel *piko* (also means **umbilical cord**, *fig.* fontanel [top of head where *'aumakua* sits], **genitals, summit, center**, many other meanings). [*Ua hamohamo ke kahu ma'i i ka **piko** o ka pēpē hou.* The nurse rubbed the new baby's **navel**.]

navigator *ho'okele* (*fig.* business leader, administrator).

near *kokoke*. [***Kokoke** ko ko'u kaiko'eke wahine hale i ke kikowaena kū'ai.* My sister-in-law's house is **near** the shopping center.]

neat 1. *'auli'i* (also means **cute, dainty**). [***'Auli'i** ko kāna kaikamahine lole.* Her daughter's clothes are **neat**.] 2. *maiau* (also means **meticulous work, speech**).

necessary *pono*.

neck *'ā'ī*. [*'O nā pua melia nā pua ma ko Kana'ina lei **'ā'ī**.* Plumerias are the flowers in Kana'ina's **neck** *lei*.]

need 1. *pono* (also means **necessity**). 2. *nele* (literally means **lacking**; used by some native speakers in place of need). [***Nele** lākou i ke kaula sugi.* They **need** *sugi* fishing line.] Note: *Makemake*, which means "like" or "want," can also be used to convey the idea of needing something. *Makemake au i ke kālā* can mean either "I want," "I like," or "I need money," while *Nele au i ke kālā* means "I lack money" and can be used to imply that since I don't have any I therefore need some.

needle *kui* (also means **nail**). [*He **kui** 'oi kā ka wahine e kuiki nei?* Does the woman who is quilting now have a sharp **needle**?]

negate *hō'ole* (also means to **refuse, protest, contradict**).

[*Mai **hō‘ole** i ke kuluma mai ke au kahiko mai.* Don't **negate** traditions from the old days.]

negative (photographic) *aka ki‘i.* [*Hiki ke pa‘i hou ‘ia ke **aka ki‘i**.* A **negative** can be reprinted.]

neglect *malama ‘ole.* [*Hewa ka luahine i **malama ‘ole** i kāna mau pōpoki.* The old lady who **neglected** her cats was wrong.]

neighbor 1. *hoa noho.* [*‘Olu‘olu ko‘u mau **hoa noho** ma kēia kaiaulu.* My **neighbors** in this community are nice.] 2. *hoalauna.*

nephew 1. *keiki ‘ohana.* 2. *keiki hanauna.*

nerve 1. *a‘a.* 2. *a‘alolo.*

nervous 1. *ha‘alulu.* [*Ma‘a ‘o Kaleo i ke kū ‘ana ma mua o ke anaina a ‘a‘ole ‘o ia **ha‘alulu**.* Kaleo is used to standing before an audience and he isn't **nervous**.]

2. *pīhoihoi* (also means **excited**).

nest *pūnana* (also means **hive, shelter**, *fig.* **home**). [*E komo mai i ko mākou wahi **pūnana**.* Come into our little **nest**.]

net *‘upena* (also means **web**). [*He **‘upena** nae, ‘a‘ohe mea hei ‘ole. (‘ōlelo no‘eau)* It's a fine-meshed **net**, there is nothing that is not caught (refers to a beautiful woman attractive to all).]

new *hou.* [*He aha ka mea **hou**?* What's **new**?]

newcomer *malihini* (also means **stranger, guest**). [*He **malihini** ‘oe i ka ‘ao‘ao Ko‘olau o ka mokupuni nei?* Are you a **newcomer** to the windward side of this island?]

newspaper *nūpepa.* [*Nui nā **nūpepa** ‘ōlelo Hawai‘i i kēlā kenekulia aku nei.* There were lots of Hawaiian language **newspapers** in the last century.]

newspaper

Daily News

New Zealand Aotearoa.

next month *i kēia mahina a'e.*

next week *i kēia pule a'e.*

next year *i kēia makahiki a'e.* [*I kēia makahiki a'e paha ana 'o ia e ho'omaha loa ai.* It is **next year** that he may retire.]

nice 1. *maika'i* (good quality). 2. *'olu'olu* (kind, comfortable).

niece 1. *kaikamahine 'ohana.* (pl. *kaikamāhine 'ohana*) [*E lawe aku ana ko'u 'anakē iā mākou* **kaikamāhine 'ohana** *i ka hale hō'ike'ike.* My auntie will take us **nieces** to the museum.] 2. *kaikamahine hanauna.*

night *pō* (also means **darkness, nighttime**, many other meanings). [*Pō'ele'ele ka* **pō** *Kāne.* The **night** called Kāne (ancient lunar calendar) is dark.]

nimble *'eleu* (also means **lively**).

nine *'eiwa.* [**'Eiwa** *mahina o kā ka'u kaikamahine pēpē.* My daughter's baby is **nine** months old.]

no *'a'ole* (also means **not**). [*Pehea 'olua? Hau'oli paha 'olua?* **'A'ole** *loa. Kaumaha nō māua.* How are you two? Are you folks happy? **Not** at all. We two are very sad.]

noble [n] 1. *ali'i.* 2. *lani.* [adj] *ali'i.*

nobody *'a'ohe mea.* [**'A'ohe mea** *e hō'ole i kāna noi.* **Nobody** can refuse her request.]

nod *kūnou.*

noise 1. *hana kuli.* 2. *kulikuli.* 3. *wawā.*

noisy 1. *kulikuli.* 2. *wawā.* [*I ka pō 'ino, he* **wawā** *nō ke ku'i a ka hekili.* On a stormy night, the thunder is really **noisy**.]

noon *awakea.*

normal *'ano mau.* [*Ulu kēia kalo malo'o ma ke* **'ano mau**? Does this dry land taro grow in the **normal** way?]

north *'ākau* (also means **right** [direction]). [*Aia 'o Kaua'i ma ka* **'ākau** *o Ni'ihau.* Kaua'i is to the **north** of Ni'ihau.]

nose *ihu.*

nose flute *'ohe hano ihu.*

nosy *nīele* (implies asking too many questions, considered rude). [*Mai **nīele** aku i kou 'anakala. Mai poina "Pa'a ka waha, hana ka lima."* Don't ask **nosy** questions of your uncle. Don't forget, "Close your mouth and your hands do the work." (traditional Hawaiian concept of learning)]

nose flute

nothing 1. *[n] mea 'ole.* [*He mea 'ole ia.* It's **nothing.**] 2. *'ole* (when added after a word, means someone has none of that thing: *niho 'ole* = toothless; *wai-wai 'ole* = worthless).

notice *[n] 'ōlelo hō'ike* (notification). 2. *[v] nānā* (to observe something). [*Nānā nā mea kilo hōkū i ka hōkū welowelo ma ka 'ohe nānā.* The astronomers **observe** the comet through the telescope.]

November *Nowemapa* (from English).

now *i kēia manawa.* [*Ke hō'au'au ke kauka holo-holona i kāna mau lio **i kēia manawa.*** The vet is bathing his horses **now.**]

nowadays *i kēia mau lā* (also means **these days**).

numb *mā'e'ele* (can mean numb with shock).

number *helu.*

numerous 1. *nui.* 2. *lau.*

nurse *kahu ma'i.*

nut *hua* (also means **fruit of plant, offspring of animal, human, egg, produce**). [*Hō ka 'ono o ka **hua** "macadamia"!* Wow, how delicious macadamia **nuts** are!]

number

oar *hoe.* [*'Ano kaumaha ka* **hoe** *koa.* A koa **oar** is rather heavy.]

oath *ho'ohiki* (also means **promise, swear an oath**). [*Pono e ho'okō i kāu mea i* **ho'ohiki** *ai.* (You) have to fulfill the thing you **swore an oath** to do.]

obey 1. *ho'olono.* 2. *lohe.*

observatory (astronomical) *hale kilo lani.* [*Ke māhuahua nei nā* **hale kilo lani** *ma luna o Mauna Kea.* The **observatories** on top of Mauna Kea are multiplying.]

observe 1. *nānā.* 2. *hākilo.*

obsession *pulakaumaka.* [*He* **pulakaumaka** *ka hāpai hao i kekahi mau kānaka.* Lifting weights is an **obsession** to some people.]

obstruct *ālai.* [**Ālai** *'ia e Nounou,* **obstructed** by Nounou (mountain on Kaua'i) (line from "Kūnihi ka Mauna," a chant asking permission to enter *hula hālau*)]

obstruction *ālai.*

obtain *loa'a* (also means **to find, catch, receive, have possession of**). [**Loa'a** *anei ke ahipele iā 'oe?* Do you **have** a match?]

occur *kupu.* [*Ua* **kupu** *a'e ka ulia pōpilikia ma ko'u ke'ena i 'elua manawa, a i ka hanana 'elua, ua ālai 'ia ka puka.* Emergencies **occurred** at my office two times, and on the second occurrence, the door was blocked.]

occurrence *hanana.*

ocean *moana* (refers to deep, open ocean, whereas *kai* refers to all seas, channels between islands, etc.).

[*Holo **moana** nā wa'a kaulua.* Double-hulled canoes sail the open **ocean**.]

ocean side *ma kai.*

o'clock *hola* (also means **time**). [*'O ka **hola** 'ehia kēia? 'O ka **hola** 'umikūmākahi o ke aumoe!* What **time** is it? It's eleven **o'clock** at night!]

October *'Okakopa* (from English).

octopus *he'e.* [*'Ono ka **he'e** i ka leho a no laila he pūpū leho ko ka lūhe'e.* **Octopus** crave cowrie and therefore the octopus lure has a cowrie shell.]

odd *'ano 'ē* (idiomatic phrase meaning strange, bizarre, not normal). [*He kani **'ano 'ē** ko ko Wailana ka'a 'enekini.* Wailana's car's engine has an **odd** sound.]

octopus

off *pio* (also means **extinguished**). (to turn off = *ho'opio*) [*E **ho'opio** i ka mīkini.* **Turn off** the machine.]

offend *ho'onāukiuki* (also means **to irritate, provoke**). [*'A'ole 'oe e **ho'onāukiuki** i kāu luna 'oihana o pilikia auane'i.* You shouldn't **offend** your boss at work or there'll be trouble later.]

offering *ho'okupu* (*lit.* to cause to sprout; spiritual offering at sacred site).

office *ke'ena.* [*Aia i hea kou **ke'ena**?* Where's your **office**?]

often *pinepine.* [*Waiho **pinepine** ka lehu-lehu i nā 'ano ho'okupu like 'ole ma Halema'uma'u.* The public **often** leave all sorts of offerings at Halema'uma'u (crater considered to be Pele's dwelling place).]

oil *'aila* (also means **tar, grease, greasy**). [*Kau nā wāhine Polapola i ka **'aila** niu i ko lākou mau* *lauoho a hinuhinu.* The women of Tahiti put coconut **oil** on their hair until it's shiny.]

oily 1. *hinuhinu.* 2. *kelekele.*

ointment *'aila hamo* (also means **massage oil**).

old *kahiko.*

old man *'elemakule.* (*pl. 'elemākule*)

old woman *luahine.* (*pl. luāhine*) [*Na nā **luāhine** e alaka'i i ko lākou mau 'ohana.* The **old women** are the ones who lead their families.]

omen *hō'ailona* (also means **sign, symbol**).

omit *kāpae* (also means **skip, pass**). [*E kāpae i ko'u manawa.* **Omit** my turn.]

one 1. *'ekahi* (used for counting). 2. *ho'okahi* (used to indicate possession of one item). [*No laila, **ho'okahi** ou kaikunāne? Pololei, **ho'okahi** wale nō o'u kaikunāne.* Therefore, you have **one** brother? Correct, I have only **one** brother (woman speaking).]

onion 1. *'aka'akai.* 2. *'aka'akai lau* (green onions).

only *wale nō* (follows word it modifies; an intensifier that can also be translated **just, very**). [*'O nā kumuniu **wale nō** nā kumulā'au e ulu ana ma ke one.* **Only** coconut trees are growing in the sand.]

open *[v]* *wehe* (also means **to remove, take off**). *[adj]* 1. *mōhala* (open blossom). 2. *hāmama* (open door, open-hearted). [*Hāmama nā hale kū'ai ma ke ahiahi pō'alima?* Are the stores **open** on Friday evenings?]

operate 1. *hana* (to operate machinery, do or make something). 2. *kaha* (to cut open, perform surgery).

oppose *kū'ē* (also means **to protest**).

opposite *kū'ē.* [*'O wai ka hua 'ōlelo **kū'ē** iā "waho"? 'O "loko" ka pane pololei.* What is the **opposite** word of "outside"? "Inside" is the right answer.]

or *a i 'ole* (phrase, lit. "and if not"). [*I wai hua 'ai **a i 'ole** i koloaka nāu?* Would you like juice **or** soda?]

orange *'alani* (refers to fruit and color).

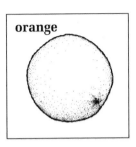

orange

ordeal *pōpilikia* (also means **trouble, problem, misfortune**). [*Inā ua ulu a'e 'oe a he 'elemakule, ua 'ike maka 'oe i nā* **pōpilikia**. If you have lived to be an old man, you have experienced **ordeals**.]

order 1. *ka'ina* (succession, sequence of action, logic). [*He aha ke* **ka'ina** *hana pololei i ka ho'opakele ola?* What is the correct **order** of action in saving a life?] 2. *kauoha* (command, to command).

ordinary 1. *ma'a mau* (also means **usual**). [*He mea* **ma'a mau** *ke kaula'i 'ōpelu ma Kona.* Drying *'ōpelu* fish in the sun is an **ordinary** thing in Kona.]

organ 1. *māhele kino* (body part). 2. *'okana* (from English; musical instrument).

organic *maoli* (also means **native, real**).

organization *'ahahui* (also means **club**). [*Nui nā* **'Ahahui** *Kiwila Hawai'i ma Kaleponi?* Are there lots of Hawaiian Civic **Clubs** in California?]

organize *ho'onohonoho* (also means **to edit, put in order**).

origin 1. *kinohi* (genesis). 2. *kumu* (source, foundation). [*Mai* **kinohi** *mai,* From the beginning]

other 1. *kekahi*. [*E mālama* **kekahi** *i kekahi.* Take care of each **other**.] 2. *'ē a'e*. [*Aia i hea nā ipuhao* **'ē a'e**? Where are the **other** pots and pans?]

our (yours and my): 1. *ko kāua*. 2. *kā kāua*. (hers/his and my): 1. *ko māua*. 2. *kā māua*. (all of us, 3 or more): 1. *ko kākou*. 2. *kā kākou*. (3 or more, not your): 1. *ko mākou*. 2. *kā mākou*. *Ko kāua, ko māua, ko kākou,* and *ko mākou* are used in front of nouns that are things you can't help having, such as family born before you and including your generation, your name, land, friends, chiefs, gods, feelings, illnesses. Also used for anything one can enter into or put on, including any building, mode of transportation, clothes. *Kā kāua, kā māua, kā kākou,* and *kā mākou* are used in front of nouns that are things that can be acquired, including family born after you, your husband or wife, your work or any action, any tool [including computers and televisions], money, anything you make or create, food, drink, books.

outlet (electric) *kumu hoʻopuka uila.*

outrigger boom *ʻiako.*

outrigger float *ama.* [*E hāpai i ka ʻiako a e kau ma luna o ke* **ama***.* Lift the boom and place it on the **outrigger float**.]

outside *waho.* [*Aia nā ʻalani me nā lemi āna i ʻako ai ma* **waho** *o ka pahu hau i mehana lākou ke ʻai ʻia?* Are the oranges and lemons he picked **outside** of the icebox (refrigerator), so that they will be warm when eaten?]

outside

outstanding *poʻokela.* [*He mau mahiʻai* **poʻokela** *kēlā mau kānaka hoʻoulu pua.* Those flower growers are **outstanding** farmers.]

oven 1. *ʻoma* (stove). 2. *imu* (pit lined with hot lava rocks in which food is cooked by steaming).

overbearing *hoʻokelakela.*

overcast *ʻōmalumalu.* [*Ua* **ʻōmalumalu** *ka lewa ma mua o ka hōʻea ʻana o ka makani pāhili.* The sky was **overcast** before the arrival of the hurricane.]

overcome 1. *lanakila* (to win, be victorious). 2. *lo'ohia* (overwhelmed with emotion).

overthrow *ho'okāhuli.* [*He hana 'ino maoli ka* ***ho'okāhuli*** *aupuni i ka lāhui 'ōiwi.* **Overthrowing** the government was a great harm to the native population.]

overwhelm *po'ipū.*

overwhelmed 1. *pa'uhia.* [***Pa'uhia*** *ke kākau 'ōlelo i ka hana.* The secretary is **overwhelmed** with work.] 2. *lo'ohia.*

owe *'ai'ē* (also means **debt**). (to lend = *hō'ai'ē*)

oyster 1. *'ōlepe* (also means any **mussel**, any type of **bivalve**). 2. *pipi* (pearl oyster).

Pacific Pākīpika. [*Holo moana ko kākou mau kūpuna a puni ka* **Pākīpika**. Our ancestors voyaged all around the **Pacific**.]

pack 1. hoʻoukana. [*I loko nō o kona* **hoʻoukana** *ʻauliʻi ʻana i kāna lole i ka paiki, ua mino nā holokū ma hope.* In spite of her carefully **packing** the suitcase, the *holokū* (long formal *muʻumuʻu* with a train) were wrinkled later on.] 2. hoʻokomo.

package pūʻolo (originally a *tī* leaf bundle tied around offerings or leis; also means **bag, bundle, parcel**). [*Na ka hoa noho i waiho i kēia* **pūʻolo** *manakō na kākou.* It was the neighbor who left this **package** of mangoes for us all.]

pad pale (also means **to defend, protect, shield**).

paddle (canoe) hoe waʻa.

paddler mea hoe waʻa.

page ʻaoʻao (also means **side, hemisphere**). [*Aia kekahi mau kiʻi o ke kumu ʻōlapa ma ka* **ʻaoʻao** *kanahā o kēnā puke.* There are some pictures of an *ʻōlapa* tree on **page** forty of that book (by you).]

painful ʻeha (also means **hurt, sore**). [*ʻAʻole* **ʻeha** *ka hoene.* Injections are not **painful**.]

paint pena. [*Aia iā wai ka* **pena** *ʻōmaʻomaʻo?* Who has the green **paint**?]

pair paʻa. (suit of clothes = *paʻa lole*) [*Ma hea ʻoe i hoʻolimalima ai i kou* **paʻa lole** *no ka ʻaha hoʻohanohano?* Where did you rent your **suit of clothes** for the celebration?] (pair of shoes = *paʻa kāmaʻa*) (married couple = *paʻa male*)

palace *hale aliʻi.* [*Aia ka* **Hale Aliʻi** *ʻo Huliheʻe ma kapa kai ma Kailua, Kona.* Huliheʻe **Palace** is at the edge of the sea in Kailua, Kona.]

pale *hākeakea.*

palm 1. *pāma* (from English; plant). 2. *niu* (plant). 3. *poho* (palm of hand).

pants 1. *lole wāwae.* 2. *lole wāwae pōkole* (shorts). [*E komo i kou* **lole wāwae** *ma mua o ka pāʻani pōpeku wāwae.* Put on your **pants** before the soccer game.]

papaya *hēʻī.*

paper 1. *pepa.* 2. *nūpepa* (newspaper).

paper napkin *kāwele pepa.*

paper plate *pā pepa.*

parade 1. *kaʻi huakaʻi.* 2. *paikau* (military parade).

Paradise 1. Paliuli (a legendary "heavenly" place in the uplands of Ōlaʻa on Hawaiʻi island). 2. Pihanakalani (another "heavenly" place in the uplands of Hanalei on Kauaʻi).

paragraph *paukū* (also means **verse, section, stanza**).

parallel 1. *moe like.* [**Moe like** *ke ala holo o nā hōkūhele?* Are the paths of the planets parallel?] 2. *kaulike.*

paralyzed 1. *lōlō.* 2. *mū.* [*He lima* **mū** *ko ke kahu maʻi.* The nurse has a **paralyzed** arm.]

parent *makua.* (pl. *mākua*) [*E Nuʻulani, ʻāpono kou mau* **mākua** *i kou hoʻi ʻana i ka hale i ke kulu ʻaumoe?* Nuʻulani, do your **parents** approve of your returning home at midnight?]

park *pāka.* [*Kaulana ka inoa o Kapiʻolani* **Pāka.** The name of Kapiʻolani **Park** is well known. (song, "Kapiʻolani Park," by J. Almeida)]

party *pāʻina.* [*Ma ka hola ʻehia e hoʻomaka ai ka* **pāʻina** *ma kēia hopenapule aʻe a ia hopenapule* *aku?* What time does the **party** start on the weekend after next?]

pass 1. *hala* (also means **to die, pass away**). [*Hala a'e 'o Māmala e 'au a'e nei ma hope.* Māmala (Honolulu Harbor) was **passed** by, swimming behind them. (song, "He Aloha Nō 'o Honolulu," by L. Keawe)] 2. *kā'alo.* [*Ua nānā pono 'oe i kēlā kāne nohea i kā'alo aku nei?* Did you get a good look at that handsome man who just **passed** by?] 3. *mā'alo.*

passenger *'ōhua.* [*Ke namunamu nei ka 'ōhua i ke kalaiwa ka'a 'ōhua.* The **passenger** is complaining to the bus driver.]

passion *kaunu.*

passionate 1. *konikoni* (love). 2. *ko'iko'i* (also means **urgent, stressed, weighty**). [*He mea ko'iko'i ka ho'ōla hou i ka 'ōlelo makuahine i ka hapanui o ka po'e kupa o ka 'āina.* Reviving the mother tongue is a **passionate** matter to the majority of the natives of the land.]

passport *palapala ho'āpono.* [*Ua nalowale anei kā kāua mau palapala ho'āpono?* Have our (your and my) **passports** disappeared?]

past 1. *ka wā i hala.* [*I ka wā i hala, ua nui 'ino nā māla nani o ke kaona nei.* In the **past**, this town had so many beautiful gardens.] 2. *ke au kahiko.*

paste *[n]* 1. *pauka* (also means **powder**). 2. *pauka niho* (toothpaste). (face powder = *pauka maka*) *[v]* 1. *ho'opili.* 2. *tuko.*

pastry *mea 'ono* (also means **dessert**).

patched *pohopoho.*

patchwork quilt *ke kapa kuiki pohopoho.*

path *alahele* (also means **trail**). [*Nui nā alahele e pi'i a'e ana i nā kuahiwi.*

path

There are lots of **paths** that go up into the mountains.]

patience 1. *ahonui*. 2. *ho'omanawanui*. [*'O ka **ho'omanawanui**, 'o ke akahai, 'o ia ka mea e hiki pono ai*. **Patience** and gentleness are the things that make all go well. (hymn from Ni'ihau, "'O Ka Ho'omanawanui," by the Beazly family)]

pattern *ana* (also means **measurement, survey, cave**, many other meanings). [*Kapa 'ia ke **ana** kapa kuiki Hawai'i he "lau."* A Hawaiian quilt **pattern** is called a "leaf."]

pause *ho'omaha* (also means **to rest**).

paw *wāwae* (also means **leg, foot**).

pay *uku* (also means **salary**). [*E **uku** koke i nā pila mai nā kāleka kākī mai*. Quickly **pay** the bills from charge cards.]

payday *lā uku*. [*'O kēia lā ka **lā uku**?* Is today **payday**?]

peace *maluhia*. [*E **maluhia** ka honua*. May there be **peace** on earth.] (make peace = *ho'omaluhia*)

peaceful *maluhia*.

peacock *pīkake*.

peak *pu'u* (also means **hill, bump**, many other meanings).

pear *pea* (from English; slang for avocado; also means **bear**).

pebble 1. *'ili*. 2. *'ili'ili*. [*nā **'ili'ili** nehe i ke kai*, **pebbles** rustling in the sea (song, "Kawaihae," by B. Lincoln)]

pedal *hehi wāwae*.

peddle *kālewa* (also means **trader, merchant, to sell merchandise**). [*Kālewa* nā kaikamāhine i nā mea 'ono kuki. The girls **peddle** cookies.]

peek 1. *ki'ei*. [*Ke **ki'ei** aku 'oe i ka puka kī, he aha kāu mea e 'ike ai?* When you **peek** into the key hole, what do you see?] 2. *hālō*.

peel *māihi*. [*E **māihi** i ka 'ili o ka 'alani ma mua o ka *'ai 'ana.* **Peel** the skin of the orange before eating it.]

peg *kui lā'au.*

pen 1. *peni* (writing implement). 2. *pā* (enclosure for animals).

pencil *penikala.*

penis *ule.*

people 1. *kānaka.* 2. *po'e.* [*He lehulehu nā **po'e** i 'āko'ako'a i ka ho'olewa.* A multitude of **people** gathered at the funeral.]

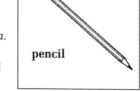

pencil

percent *pakeneka.* [*'Ehia **pakeneka** ka uku pane'e ma kou panakō?* What **percent** is the interest at your bank?]

perch *hakahaka.*

perfect *hemolele* (also means **flawless, holy, many other meanings**). [*'A'ole **hemolele** kā ka'u keiki heluhelu 'ana.* My child's reading isn't **perfect**.]

perform 1. *ho'okō* (also means **to fulfill a command**). 2. *hana* (also means **to work, do something**).

perfume *wai 'ala.* [*Hū ke onaona o kēnā **wai 'ala**!* Wow, how strong your **perfume** is!]

perhaps *paha* (also means **maybe**). Note: Must be used after another word or phrase.

peril *pō'ino* (also means **misfortune, storm**).

period 1. *wā* (also means **era, epoch**). 2. *au* (also means **current**). 3. *ma'i wahine* (*lit.* woman's sickness, menstruation). 4. *kiko pau* (punctuation mark at the end of a sentence).

permanent 1. *pa'a.* 2. *loa.* 3. *mau.* (Each of these words has many other meanings; they can also be combined for added emphasis, such as in the idiomatic expression "*a mau loa aku*," which is one way of expressing the idea of "for-ever and ever.") [*Paʻa kēia pili **a mau loa aku**.* This close relationship is **permanent**.]

permission *ʻae.* [*Ua **ʻae** ke aupuni iā mākou e komo i ke awāwa.* The government gave us (we all, not you) **permission** to enter the valley.]

permit 1. *ʻae* (to allow, agree to). 2. *palapala ʻae* (written permit).

person *kanaka* (also means **human being**). (pl. *kānaka*)

personal 1. *pilikino.* [*He mea **pilikino** ka manaʻolana e loaʻa i ke aloha.* Hoping for love is a **personal** thing.] 2. *ponoʻī.*

perspiration *hou.*

perspire *kahe ka hou.*

pesticide *lāʻau make* (also means **poison**).

pet *[n] hānaiāhuhu.* [*He aha ke ʻano o kāu **hānaiāhuhu**? He lāpaki kāu?* What kind of **pet** do you have? Do you have a rabbit?]. *[v] hamohamo* (also means **to rub**).

petal *lihilihi.*

petition *palapala noi.* [*Nui nā **palapala noi** e loaʻa i ka ʻahaʻōlelo.* There are many **petitions** that the legislature receives.]

petroglyph *kiʻi pōhaku.*

petroglyph

phone *kelepona.* [*Aia a pau kāna hana, e **kelepona** mai ana ʻo Pāpā.* As soon as his work is finished, Daddy will **phone** us.]

photograph *kiʻi* (also means **picture, sculpture, statue, image**). (to take photo = *paʻi kiʻi*)

pick 1. *ʻako* (to pluck, gather). [*ʻAko pinepine kā lākou mau moʻopuna i nā pua melia i ka pā ilina.* Their (three) grandchildren often **pick** plumerias in the graveyard.] 2. *wae* (to cull). 3. *koho* (to choose, select).

picnic *pikiniki.* [*'O Ala Moana kahi a lākou e pikiniki ai.* Ala Moana is the place where they **picnic.**]

picture *ki'i* (also means **photograph, sculpture, image, statue,** etc.). [*He mau ki'i nani nā ki'i a Madge Tennant i pena ai.* The **pictures** that Madge Tennant painted are beautiful **pictures.**]

pie *pai* (from English). [*Ma uka loa i 'ako ai nā keiki i nā hua 'ōhelo no ka pai.* It was far upland that the children gathered *'ōhelo* berries for a **pie.**]

piece *'āpana.* [*I 'āpana pai nāu?* Would you like a **piece** of pie?]

pig *pua'a.* [*Māunauna ka waokele i ka pua'a.* The rain forest is laid to waste by **pigs.**]

pile 1. *ahu.* [*'O ke ahu pōhaku ka hō'ailona o ke ala-hele.* The **pile** of stones is the trail marker.] 2. *pu'u.*

pill *huaale.* [*Mai ale i ka huaale o ma'i 'oe ma hope.* Don't swallow the **pill** or you'll be sick later on.]

pilot *pailaka.* [*'A'ohe mokulele o ka pailaka.* The **pilot** doesn't have a plane.]

pimple 1. *huehue.* 2. *pu'u* (also means **hill, lump,** many other meanings).

pin *kui* (also means **nail, nee-dle, injection**).

pineapple *hala kahiki* (*lit.* foreign *hala* [the fruit of the pineapple and the *hala* plant look alike]).

pineapple

pink *'ākala.* [*'Ākala nō ia hōkele kaulana.* That famous hotel is **pink** indeed.]

pipe *paipu.* [*Ua puhi paipu*

pipe

ku'u Tūtū. My beloved grandparent smoked a
pipe.]

pit 1. *lua* (hole in the ground). 2. *hua* (seed). 3. *'īkoi*
(core of some fruits, such as breadfruit, apple).

pitted *'ālualua* (also means **rough terrain**). [*'Ālualua
ke alanui i kīpapa 'ole 'ia.* The unpaved road is
pitted and rough.]

pizza *pika.* [*Hiki anei ke lawe 'ia mai ka pika i kēia
ahiahi?* Can a **pizza** be delivered this evening?]

place 1. *kau* (to put something some place). 2.
kūlana (rank or position in competition). (first
place = *kūlana 'ekahi*)

plain 1. *maopopo* (clear, easily understood). 2. *kula*
(broad area of land between mountain and sea).

plan *[v] ho'olālā.* [*E ho'olālā kāua i ka 'aha mele
'imi kālā no ke kula 'ōlelo Hawai'i.* Let's (you
and me) **plan** the benefit concert for the
Hawaiian language school.]

plane (airplane) *mokulele.*

planet *hōkū hele.* [*'O 'Iao ka
hōkū hele i kā 'ia e nā
hōkū welowelo.* Jupiter is
the **planet** that was hit by
comets.]

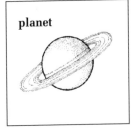

planet

plank *papa lā'au* (*lit.* wood-
en board).

plant *[n] mea kanu. [v] kanu*
(also means **to bury**). [*Ua
kanu ka 'īlio i kāna iwi ma lalo o ka mea kanu.*
The dog **buried** his bone under **the plant.**]

plantation *mahikō* (sugar plantation). [*E mau ana ka
mahikō ma Waialua?* Will the sugar **plantation**
at Waialua continue?]

plastic *'ea.*

plastic bag *ke 'eke 'ea.*

plate *pā.* [*Aia iā 'olua ke pā mea 'ai?* Do you (two)
have the **plate** lunch?]

platform *kahua.*

play 1. *pā'ani* (game, play activity). (play football; football game = *pā'ani pōpeku;* play basketball; basketball game = *pā'ani pōhīna'i;* to play volleyball; volleyball game = *pā'ani pōpa'i lima;* to play golf; golf game = *pā'ani kolepa;* to play baseball; baseball game = *pā'ani pōhili;* to play soccer; soccer game = *pā'ani pōpeku wāwae;* to play instrument = *ho'okani pila*) 2. *hana keaka* (theatrical production). [*Le'ale'a ka* **hana keaka** *hou a ka Hālau Hanakeaka!* The new **play** by the Hawaiian language theater troupe is funny!]

pleasant *'olu'olu.*

please (request) *e 'olu'olu.* [*E* **'olu'olu***, e kōkua mai.* **Please** help me.]

plump *nepunepu.* [*'Ano* **nepunepu** *ka wahine hāpai.* The pregnant lady is sort of **plump**.]

plunge *lu'u* (also means **to dive**). [**Lu'u** *kai ka lawai'a e 'ō i'a.* The fisherman **dives** in the ocean to spear fish.] (to soak, dye = *ho'olu'u*)

plus *a me* (*lit.* and with). [*'Ekolu* **a me** *'umi.* Three **plus** ten.]

pocket *pākeke* (from English; also means **bucket**).

poet *haku mele* (syn. *mea haku mele;* also means **writer, composer**).

poetry 1. *ke mele* (also means **music**). 2. *ka mele* (song, chant).

point 1. *kuhi* (gesture). 2. *lae* (peninsula, land jutting out into sea). 3. *kiko* (dot). 4. *wēlau* (tip).

poison *lā'au make* (also means **insecticide**).

pole *pou.*

police *māka'i.*

police station *hale māka'i.* [*Aia ka* **hale māka'i** *hou ma ke alanui 'o Hale*

police

Māka'i. The new **police station** is on Hale Māka'i
Street.]

polite 1. *waipahē* (also means **courteous, gentle,
modest**). [**Waipahē** *ke keonimana*. The gentleman is **polite**.] 2. *'olu'olu* (also means **kind,
pleasant**).

polluted 1. *haumia*. 2. *pilo*. [*Mai ho'ohaumia i ke kai
a **pilo**! Don't contaminate the ocean until it's **polluted**!]

pond 1. *loko*. 2. *loko wai*. 3. *ki'o wai*.

ponder *no'ono'o*.

pool 1. *loko wai*. 2. *ki'o wai* (also means **puddle,
pond**).

poor *'ilihune*.

popcorn *kūlina pohāpohā*. [*'Ane'ane e mākaukau ke
kūlina pohāpohā. The
popcorn** is almost
ready.]

population 1. *po'e*. 2. *lehulehu*.

porch *lānai*. [*Pale aku ka
lānai nui i ka lā*. A big
porch wards off the sun.]

pork *'i'o pua'a*. [*Inā 'ai
pinepine 'oe i ka **'i'o
pua'a**, pi'i a'e ka 'aila ma loko o kou koko*. If you
often eat **pork**, the fat in your blood increases.]

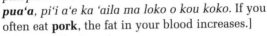
popcorn

porpoise 1. *nai'a*. 2. *nu'ao*.

port *awa kū moku* (*lit.* harbor where boats stop).

porter *mea hali ukana*.

Portuguese *Pukikī*.

position *kūlana* (also means **rank, status**). [*He aha
kona **kūlana** ma ka 'ohana? 'O ka haku 'o ia?*
What is his **position** in the family? Is he the head
of the family?]

possess *loa'a*.

possible *hiki* (also means **to be able to, can**). [**Hiki** *ke* *noho ma ka wao akua?* Is it **possible** to live in the wilderness?]

postal worker *lawe leka.*

post card *kāleka poʻoleka.* [*ʻEhia kenikeni ke poʻoleka no ke **kāleka poʻoleka** i kēia mau lā?* How many cents is the stamp for **post cards** these days?]

poster 1. *pepa hoʻolaha.* 2. *pelaha.* [*Hōʻike ka **pelaha** i nā iʻa maoli.* The **poster** shows native fish.]

post office *hale leka.*

postpone *hoʻopaneʻe.* [*E **hoʻopaneʻe** ʻia ka ʻaha mele ma muli o ka makani pāhili.* The concert should be **postponed** due to the hurricane.]

pot *ipuhao* (also means **pan**). [*Malia paha o hoʻomaʻemaʻe ʻoe i kēnā **ipuhao** lepo i ke one.* Maybe you should clean that dirty **pot** with sand.]

pot

pouch *poho.*

pound *[n] paona* (from English). [*Pipiʻi wale nō ka poi ma ka hale kūʻai: ma kahi o ʻehā kālā no hoʻokahi **paona**.* Poi is really expensive at the store: around four dollars for one **pound**.] *[v] kuʻi* (also means **to smash, crash**). (pound poi, poi pounder = *kuʻi ʻai*)

pour (liquid) *ninini.* [***Ninini** ka makua kāne i ka waiū na kāna kaikamahine.* The father **pours** milk for his daughter.]

pout *nuha* (also means **to sulk, sulky**).

poverty *ʻilihune* (also means **poor, destitute**).

power *mana.* [*He **mana** nō ko ke kiaʻāina.* The governor has real **power**.] Note: *Mana* refers primarily to spiritual power, but is also used for political power, the power to command.

practice *ho'oma'ama'a.* [*E **ho'oma'ama'a** a ma'a.* **Practice** until you get used to it.]

praise 1. *ho'onani.* 2. *ho'omaika'i* (also means **congratulations**). [***Ho'onani** ka makua mau.* **Praise** the eternal father. (Doxology)]

pray *pule.* [*Na wai e alaka'i i ka **pule** wehe?* Who will lead the opening **prayer**?]

precarious *kūnihi* (also means **steep**). [***Kūnihi** ke alahele i uka?* Is the pathway toward the mountains **precarious**?]

precious *makamae.* [*'Oi aku ka **makamae** o ke aloha ma mua o ke kula.* Love is more **precious** than gold.]

precipice *pali.* [*Piha ka 'ao'ao ko'olau o Kaua'i nā **pali** kū.* The windward side of Kaua'i is full of sheer **precipices**.]

precise *miomio.* [***Miomio** wale ka humuhumu 'ana ona.* Her sewing is very **precise**.]

predict *wānana.* [*Na wai e 'ole ke makemake e **wānana** i ka hopena?* Who wouldn't want to **predict** the results?]

prefer *'oi aku ka makemake.* [***'Oi aku ka makemake** o ka hapanui o ka po'e i ka nohona 'ilihune 'ole.* Most people **prefer** not living in poverty.]

prejudice *ho'okae 'ili* (racial prejudice). [*No ke aha i ili mai ai ka **ho'okae 'ili**?* Why did we inherit racial **prejudice**?]

premonition *haili moe.* [*E kupu a'e ana ka **haili moe** i ko'u moe 'uhane?* Will a **premonition** appear in my dreams?]

prepare *ho'omākaukau.*

prepared *mākaukau.* [***Mākaukau** ka imu a wela nā pōhaku.* The *imu* (underground oven) is **prepared** and the rocks are hot.]

prescription *kuhikuhi* (also means **directions**). [*Aia nō a kelepona 'ia mai ke **kuhikuhi**, hiki ia'u ke ho'omākaukau i kāu lā'au.* As soon as the **prescription** is phoned in, I can prepare your medicine.]

presence *alo.* (face to face = *he alo a he alo*)

present *makana* (also means **scholarship, award, prize, gift**). [*'Ehia āu makana ma kou la hānau?* How many **presents** do you have on your birthday?]

president *pelekikena.* [*Kamaehu ka Pelekikena.* The **President** is firm of resolution and purpose.]

president

press *kaomi.* [*Inā kaomi 'ia kēia pihi, ho'ā 'ia ka lolouila.* If this button is **pressed**, the computer is turned on.]

pretend *ho'omeamea.* [*E ho'omeamea kāua, 'o 'oe 'o Hi'iaka a 'o au 'o Lohi'au.* Let's **pretend** you are Hi'iaka and I am Lohi'au.]

pretty 1. *nani.* 2. *u'i* (refers to people).

price *kumu kū'ai.* [*'Ehia kālā ke kumu kū'ai o nā 'ano kanakē like 'ole?* How much is the **price** of the various kinds of candy?]

pride *ha'aheo* (also means **proud**). [*'O ka lā ha'aheo i ka lāhui kēia lā.* Today is the day of **pride** in your ethnic heritage.]

priest *kahunapule* (also means **minister, reverend**).

prince *kamāli'i kāne.*

princess *kamāli'i wahine.*

principal *po'o kumu* (*lit.* head teacher).

print *pa'i.* [*Ua pa'i lima 'ia nā puke mua ma Hawai'i.* The first books in Hawai'i were **printed** by hand.]

prison *hale pa'ahao* (also means **jail**).

prisoner 1. *pio.* 2. *pa'ahao.*

private 1. *pilikino* (personal). [*He leka pilikino kēnā.*

That (by you) is a **personal** letter.] 2. *kū'oko'a* (independent).

prize *makana* (also means **scholarship, award, gift**).

problem *pilikia* (also means **trouble**). [*He **pilikia** ko ko māua ka'a wane, e ka māka'i.* Our (her and my) van has a **problem**, officer.]

proclaim 1. *kūkala* (announce, broadcast). 2. *kuahaua*. [*Ua **kuahaua** 'o Kamehameha i ke Kānāwai Māmalahoe.* Kamehameha **proclaimed** the law of the splintered paddle.]

proclamation 1. *palapala kūkala*. 2. *kuahaua*.

produce *[v]* 1. *hua* (offspring, fruit). [*Ua **hua** ka moku a mu'o a lau a ulu.* The island **produced** life and budded and leafed and grew. (common line in name chants and creation chants)] 2. *ho'ohua*.

profession *'oihana* (also means **career, business**). [*'O ke alaka'i huaka'i kāna **'oihana**.* Her **profession** is tour guide.]

profit 1. *waiwai ho'opuka*. [*Ma hope o ka uku 'ana aku i ka uku pane'e i ka panakō, 'ehia kālā ka **waiwai ho'opuka**?* After paying the interest to the bank, how much is the **profit**?] 2. *loa'a*.

profitable *makepono*. [*He 'oihana **makepono** ka hale 'aina?* Is the restaurant a **profitable** business?]

profound *kūhohonu* (syn. *hohonu*; also means **deep, complex**).

program 1. *polakalamu*. 2. *hō'ike*. 3. *papa hō'ike* (printed).

prohibit *pāpā* (also means **to forbid**). [*Nāna, na ke kumu hula i **pāpā** mai ia'u, 'a'ole au e 'oki i ko'u lauoho.* It was she, it was the hula teacher who **prohibited** me from cutting my hair.]

prominent 1. *ki'eki'e*. 2. *'oi*. [*'Oi kēlā pae pali ma Moloka'i.* That row of cliffs on Moloka'i is **prominent**.]

pronounce *puana* (also refers to **song refrain**).

proof *hōʻoiaʻiʻo* (also means **to prove, verify**; syn. *hōʻoia*).

propaganda *hoʻolaha manaʻo*. [*He manaʻo kūpono a i ʻole he **hoʻolaha manaʻo** kāna e hoʻolohe nei ma ke kīwī?* Is it a proper opinion or is it **propaganda** that he is hearing now on TV?]

property 1. *waiwai* (also means **estate, wealth, value, rich, valuable**). 2. *kuleana* (also means **land division, rights, responsibility**).

prophecy *wānana*.

prophet *kāula*.

protection *malu* (also means **shade, government**). [*Noho mālie ka lehulehu ma lalo o ka **malu** o ke aupuni.* The public lives calmly under the **protection** of the government.]

protest *kūʻē*. [*Na kākou a pau i **kūʻē** i ka ʻaelike o ke aupuni e kākoʻo i ka hana ʻino iā Pele.* It was all of us who **protested** the government's contract to support doing harm to Pele (through geothermal development).]

proud *haʻaheo*.

provisions 1. *pono*. 2. *lako*.

prow *ihu* (also means **nose**).

pry 1. *une* (also means **lever**). 2. *ʻōhiki* (also means **to prod, pick, sand crab**).

public *[n]* *lehulehu*. *[adj]* *ākea*.

publish *paʻi* (also means **to slap, clap, snap**). [*E **paʻi** ʻia ana kāu puke?* Will your book be **published**?]

pudding *pūkini*. [*ʻOno ʻo Anoe i ka **pūkini** tapioca.* Anoe craves tapioca **pudding**.]

pull *huki*. [*E **huki** i ke kaula a paʻa ka peʻa.* **Pull** the rope until the sail's taut.]

punch *kuʻi* (also means **to smash, crash, hit**).

punish *hoʻopaʻi*.

pure 1. *maʻemaʻe*. 2. *hemolele*. [***Maʻemaʻe** wale ke kino o ka palai.* The body of the *palai* fern is **pure**. (song, "Ka ʻIlilauokekoa," by Waiʻau)]

purse *'eke*. (wallet = *'eke kālā*)

pursue *hahai* (also means **to follow**).

push *pahu* (also means **box, drum**). [*Mai **pahu** kekahi i kekahi, e ka lehulehu*. Don't **push** each other, friends.] (push-up = *ko'o lima*)

put *kau*.

put on *komo* (also means **enter**). [*E **komo** i kou pālule hou no ka pā'ina*. **Put on** your new shirt for the party.]

puzzle *nane*. [*Aia iā lāua ka **nane** 'āpana*. They (two) have the jigsaw **puzzle**.]

pyramid *pū'o'a* (also means **tower**).

qualified 1. *mākaukau*. [*'O ia ka moho **mākaukau** no ia 'oihana.* She's the **qualified** candidate for that position.] 2. *kūpono*.

quality 1. *'ano*. 2. *kūlana*. [*He **kūlana** 'ekahi kāna hana?* Is his work top **quality**?]

quantity 1. *nui*. [*He 'ekolu haneli paona ka **nui** o nā lū'au a Keli'i i 'ako ai i nehinei a ia lā aku.* Three hundred pounds is the **quantity** of the taro leaves that Keli'i picked the day before yesterday.]

quarrel 1. *ho'opa'apa'a*. 2. *hukihuki*. [*Auē ka **hukihuki** ma waena o ke kaikua'ana a me ke kaikaina!* Wow, the **quarrel** between the older and younger siblings!]

quart *kuaka* (from English).

quarter (coin) *hapahā kālā*. [*Loa'a ka **hapahā kālā** iā 'oe? Pono au e kelepona aku i ka hale.* Do you have a **quarter**? I have to phone home.]

quarter *[adj]* *hapahā*. [*He **hapahā** Kāmoa kāu kāne?* Is your husband a **quarter** Samoan?]

queen *mō'ī wahine*. [*'O Kaleleonālani ka **mō'ī wahine** i lilo i moho i ke koho pāloka 'ana i mō'ī hou.* Kaleleonālani was the **queen** who became a candidate for the election of the new sovereign.]

queen

quench *ho'okena*.

quenched (thirst) *kena*. [*Ke inu nei 'o ia a **kena** ka makewai.* He is drinking now until his thirst is **quenched**.]

question 1. *nīnau* (also means **to ask question**). 2. *uī*
(also means **query, to question**)

quick *'āwīwī.*

quiet *[n]* *mālie.* *[v]* *ho'onā* (quiet someone; also
means **to soothe, pacify, comfort, relieve pain**).
[adj] *mālie.* [*E ho'onā a e ho'omalimali i nā
māhoe uē a **mālie** lāua.* **Soothe** and fondle the
crying twins until they (two) are quiet.]

quilt *[n]* 1. *kapa kuiki.* 2.
kapa kuiki pohopoho
(patchwork quilt). *[v]*
kuiki.

quit *ha'alele.* [*E **ha'alele** ana
au i ka hana i ka lā
'apōpō.* I will **quit** tomorrow!]

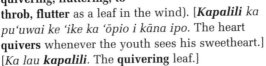
quilt

quiver *kapalili* (also means
**quivering, fluttering, to
throb, flutter** as a leaf in the wind). [***Kapalili** ka
pu'uwai ke 'ike ka 'ōpio i kāna ipo.* The heart
quivers whenever the youth sees his sweetheart.]
[*Ka lau **kapalili**.* The **quivering** leaf.]

quiz *kuisa* (from English).

quote *'ōlelo.* [*He **'ōlelo** kēia maiā Kauikeaouli mai.
"Na wai e 'ole ke akamai i ke alahele i hehi 'ia e
o'u mau kūpuna?"* This is a **quote** from
Kauikeaouli (Kamehameha III). "Who wouldn't
be clever on the path that was treaded by my
ancestors?"]

rabbit *lāpaki.*

race 1. *heihei* (competition). 2. *lāhui* (nationality).

racial prejudice *hoʻokae ʻili.*

radiant 1. *mālamalama.* 2. *ʻālohilohi.*

radio *lekiō.*

raft *huinapapalana.*

rag *welu.* [*E lālau i ka* **welu***! Ua hanini ka waina ma luna o ka mea hāliʻi pākaukau!* Grab the **rag***!* The wine spilled on the tablecloth!]

radio

rage *inaina* (also means **anger, hatred**). [*Piʻi aʻe paha kou* **inaina***?* Is your **rage** rising up?]

raid *pākaha* (also means **to cheat, plunder, rob, robbery**). [*He* **pākaha** *kā ka mākaʻi i nā hale piliwaiwai.* The police have **raids** in gambling houses.]

railroad *kaʻaahi* (also means **train**). [*Mai Kohala a i Hilo i holo ai ke* **kaʻaahi** *ma mua.* It was from Kohala to Hilo that the **train** used to run.]

rain *ua* (usually a specific type and/or name of rain is added). [*ka* **ua** *loku aʻo Hanalei,* the pouring **rain** of Hanalei. (song, "Ka Ua Loku," by A. Alohikea)]

rainbow *ānuenue.* [*Piʻo mai ke* **ānuenue***.* The **rainbow** arches overhead.]

raincoat *kuka ua.* [*ʻO ka ʻahu lāʻī ke* **kuka ua** *o ke au kahiko.* The *tī*-leaf cape was the **raincoat** of ancient days.]

raindrop *pakapaka ua.*

rain forest 1. *wao kele.* 2. *wao nahele.*

rainy *ua.* [*Ua ka wao kele.* The rain forest is **rainy**.]

raise 1. *hoʻoulu* (grow plants; also means **to inspire**).
[*ʻO ka **hoʻoulu** pua haka kā kāna wahine ʻoihana.*
His wife's business is **raising** anthuriums.] 2.
hānai (rear a child; also means **to feed animals or
people, adopt**). 3. *hāpai* (lift up, carry; also means
pregnant). 4. *kāmau* (raise a glass, drink liquor;
also means **to persevere, continue**).

rake *kopekope.*

ranch *kahua hānai pipi.* [*Kokoke ke **kahua hānai
pipi** ʻo Kapāpala i ka lua pele.* Kapāpala **Ranch**
is close to the crater.]

rank (place, position, title) *kūlana.* [*He **kūlana** aliʻi
kiʻekiʻe ko ka naʻi aupuni? ʻAʻole.* Did the conqueror (Kamehameha I) have high chiefly **rank**?
No.]

rape *puʻe* (also means **to attack, force, compel**).

rapture *lilo.*

rare *laha ʻole.* [*Minamina ʻaʻole he mea **laha ʻole** ka
puʻe.* Regrettably, rape is not a **rare** thing.]

rascal *kolohe* (also means **mischievous, naughty**).

rat *ʻiole* (also means **mouse**, any **rodent**).

rattle (sound) 1. *koʻele.* 2. *nakeke.*

raw *maka* (also means **fresh, eye, face, "eye" of net**).
[*ʻO ka poke ka iʻa **maka** i hoʻohui ʻia me ka limu
a me ka paʻakai.* Poke is **raw** fish that has been
mixed with seaweed and
Hawaiian salt.]

ray (sun) *kukuna.*
[*Hoʻomaka nā **kukuna** o
ka lā e neʻe ma luna o ka
ʻāina ma kaiao.* The **rays**
of the sun start to move
over the land at dawn.]

read

read *heluhelu.*

ready *mākaukau*. [*Ua **mākaukau** kākou, e nā hoa? E naue i mua!* Are we all **ready**, friends? Let's move forward!]

real *maoli*.

realize 1. *'ike* (to understand; also means **to see, know, experience**). [*Ua **'ike** ke kanaka pī i kona hewa.* The stingy person **realized** her mistake.] 2. *ho'omaopopo* (to bring to fruition).

reason *kumu*. [*'O ia ke **kumu** a kāna mo'opuna i noho ai i ka haukapila.* That's the **reason** his grandchild stayed in the hospital.]

recede *emi* (also means **inexpensive, reduced, to reduce**). (low tide = *ke kai emi*)

receive 1. *loa'a* (also means **get, catch, find**). [*E **loa'a** ana ka uku lawelawe iā ia ma hope o kona lawe 'ana mai i nā mea inu.* She'll **receive** a tip after she serves the drinks.] 2. *loa'a mai* (also means **get, catch, find**).

recent *hou*.

receptionist *mea ho'okipa* (also means **host, hostess**).

recess *ho'omalolo* (means to adjourn temporarily, not school recess).

recipe 1. *lekapī* (from English). [*Ke huli nei au i ka **lekapī** no ke kele kuawa.* I'm searching for a **recipe** for guava jam.] 2. *'ōlelo kuhikuhi* (also means **directions**).

recite *ha'i*.

recline *kāmoe* (also means **to lie down**).

recognize *'ike* (also means **to see, know, experience**). (it has been recognized, acknowledged [phrase often used at end of chants] = *ua 'ikea* [from *ua 'ike 'ia*])

record *[n] pā leo* (musical album). *[v]* 1. *ho'opa'a* (story or voice). [***Ho'opa'a** wikiō 'o Puhipau i nā kūpuna.* Puhipau **records** videos of the elders.] 2. *ho'opa'a leo* (voice). [*Iā lākou e **ho'opa'a leo** ana i ka pā leo hou, na wai e ho'oholo i ke ka'ina* *hana?* When they are **recording** the new album, who decides the sequence of activities?]

recover *pohala.* [*Ke **pohala** nei ko'u hoaaloha i hō'eha 'ia i ka ulia mokokaikala.* My friend who was hurt in the motorcycle accident is **recovering**.]

rectangle *huinahā loa.*

red *'ula'ula.*

red-eyed *mākole.* [***Mākole** 'o ia nei i ka piwa.* This person is **red-eyed** due to fever.]

reduce *ho'ēmi.* [***Ho'ēmi** ke kauka i kāna mau huaale e ale ai.* The doctor **reduces** the pills that she swallows.] (reduce weight = *ho'ēmi kino*)

reed *'ohe* (also means **bamboo**).

reef 1. *laupapa.* [*'O ka wana a me ka puhi kekahi o nā i'a ma ka **laupapa**.* Sea urchins and eels are some of the sea creatures on the **reef**.] 2. *pāpapa.* 3. *'āpapa.* 4. *hāpapa.*

reflection *aka.*

refrain (song) 1. *puana.*

refrigerator *pahu hau.* [*Mai poina e ho'okomo i kou lei i ka **pahu hau**.* Don't forget to put your *lei* in the **refrigerator**.]

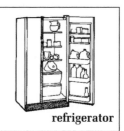

refrigerator

refuge *pu'uhonua.* [*'O Hōnaunau Pāka ma Ke'ei, Kona Hema kahi o ka **pu'uhonua** kaulana loa o Hawai'i nei.* Hōnaunau Park in Ke'ei, South Kona, is the place of the most famous **refuge** here in Hawai'i.]

refuse *[n]* *'ōpala.* *[v]* *hō'ole* (also means **to deny, negate**).

register *kau inoa* (syn. *kākau inoa*, write name).

regret 1. *mihi* (also means **repentance, to apologize**). 2. *minamina* (also means **to value highly**).

reign *noho ali'i.*

rejoice *'oli.*

relationship 1. *pilina*. [*He aha ka* **pilina** *ma waena o kēlā mau wāhine?* What is the **relationship** between those women?] 2. *pilikana.*

relax

relax *nanea* (also means **enjoyable, relaxed, to have fun, fascinating,** many other meanings). [**Nanea** *nā keiki ma ke kauwela.* Children **relax** in the summer.]

release *ho'oku'u* (also means **to dismiss, let go**). [**Ho'oku'u** *ka lawai'a i ka 'upena.* The fisherman **releases** the net.]

religion *ho'omana* (also means **to worship**).

religious site *heiau*. [*'Oiai 'o Pi'ilanihale ka* **heiau** *nui loa o ka pae 'āina, e kipa aku i laila i maopopo iā 'oukou ka ho'omana kahiko.* Since Pi'ilanihale is the largest **religious site** of the island chain, visit there so that you all can understand ancient worship.]

relish *[n] pūpū* (also means **shell, hors d'oeuvre, party snack**). *[v] 'ono* (also means **to savor**).

remain *koe.*

remainder *koena* (also means **leftovers, remnant, change from buying something**). [*Eia kāu* **koena**: *'ekolu kālā me kanahā keneka.* Here's your **change**: three dollars and forty cents.]

remember *ho'omana'o* (also means **to remind**). [**Ho'omana'o** *kākou i ka lā i lilo ai 'o Hawai'i nei i moku 'āina.* We all **remember** the day Hawai'i became a state.]

remote *mamao* (also means **far, distance**).

remove *lawe aku* (also means **to take away**). [*Na ka mea holoi pā e* **lawe aku** *i ke puna lepo.* The dish

washer is the one who should **remove** the dirty
spoon.]

renew *hana hou.*

rent *ho'olimalima.*

repair *ho'oponopono* (also refers to **traditional family counseling/therapy**). [*E **ho'oponopono** 'ia ana
ko ke po'o kumu paikikala i kēia Pō'akolu a'e.*
The principal's bicycle will be **repaired** next
Wednesday.]

repeat *ho'opili* (also means **to imitate**). [*E **ho'opili**
mai ia'u.* **Repeat** after me.]

repent *mihi* (also means **to confess**).

reporter *kākau nūpepa.* [*'O kēlā ka leo mihi o ke
kākau nūpepa i ho'opunipuni i ka luna ho'onohonoho.* That's the confessing voice of the
reporter who lied to the editor.]

repress 1. *'umi (also 'u'umi).* [*'**U'umi** i ke aloha me
ka waimaka lā.* **Repress** love with tears. (song,
"Kaimukī Hula." by A. Richart)] 2. *kāohi.*

reputation *kūlana* (also means **status, rank**).

request 1. *noi.* 2. *nonoi.* [*He **nonoi** kā Kamailelauli'i
iā ia.* Kamailelauli'i has a **request** to ask of him.]

requirement *koi.*

rescue *ho'opakele.* [*I ka manawa a ka pele i hū ai
ma Kalapana, ua ho'omaka nā akeakamai e
ho'opakele i nā holoholona i ho'oku'u 'ia.* At the
time that the lava erupted at Kalapana, the scientists started **rescuing** the animals that had been
abandoned.]

research *noi'i.*

resemble *kohu like.* [***Kohu like** ke kaikunāne i kona
kaikuahine.* The brother **resembles** his sister.]

reserve *ho'okapu.* [*E **ho'okapu** i 'ehā noho ma ka
hale 'aha mele no kēia ahiahi.* **Reserve** four seats
in the concert hall for this evening.]

reserved *kapu* (also means **forbidden**).

residence *hale noho.*

resign *ha'alele* (also means **to leave, to quit**). [*'Akahi nō a* **ha'alele** *ka lawe leka i kana 'oihana a hū a'ela kona inaina.* The mail carrier finally **resigned** his job and then his rage spilled out.]

resist 1. *kū'ē* (also means **to oppose, opposite**). 2. *pale* (also means **to defend, ward off**).

resolute *'onipa'a* (also means **steadfast**; Queen Lili'uokalani's motto).

resources *kumu waiwai*. [*Na wai nō e ho'olilo i nā* **kumu waiwai** *makamae o ka honua nei?* Who is it that would waste the precious **resources** of this earth?]

respect *mahalo* (also means **to admire, be grateful for, thank**).

responsibility *kuleana*. [*'O ko kākou* **kuleana** *ke a'o 'ana aku i ko kākou ho'oilina i ka hanauna hou.* Our **responsibility** is to teach our heritage to the new generation.]

rest *ho'omaha*.

restaurant *hale 'aina*. [*Nui nā 'ano* **hale 'aina** *like 'ole ma ke kaona nei.* There are all kinds of **restaurants** here in town.]

restrain *kāohi* (also means **to control, repress, prevent**). [*Pono ka makua e* **kāohi** *i ka huhū.* A parent must **restrain** his anger.]

restroom 1. *lumi ho'opau pilikia*. 2. *lua*.

retarded *lohi* (also means **late, slow, backward**). [*Nā ko'u kaikua'ana e ho'olālā nei i ka papa a'o i nā haumāna* **lohi**. My older sister (woman speaking) is the one who is planning the class for the **retarded** students.]

retire 1. *hō'olu'olu* (to rest; syn. *ho'omaha*). 2. *ho'omaha loa* (to retire from work).

return 1. *ho'i* (go back; can imply going home). [*E* **ho'i** *kāua.* Let's **go (back)** home.] 2. *ho'iho'i* (return something; also means **restore**). [*Ma mua o kou ho'i 'ana e hiamoe, e* **ho'iho'i** *i nā 'upena i*

loko o ka hale kaʻa. Before you go to sleep,
return the nets inside the garage.]

reveal *hōʻike* (also means **to demonstrate, show**). [*Ke hōʻike mai nei koʻu kupuna wahine i ko mākou moʻokūʻauhau.* My grandmother is **revealing** our genealogy to us.]

revenge *pānaʻi* (also means **substitute, reward, to revenge, pay back**). (syn. *uku*)

reverence *hōʻano* (also means **to revere**).

reverend *kahu* (also means **caretaker**; short for *kahunapule*, which also means **minister, priest**).

reverse 1. *huli* (also means **to turn, to change lifestyle or opinion**). 2. *lole* (also means **cloth, clothes**).

revolve *kaʻapuni*. [*Kaʻapuni nā hōkū hele i ka lā.* The planets **revolve** around the sun.]

reward *makana*.

rhythm 1. *pā* (also means **fence, enclosure, yard**, many other meanings). 2. *pana* (also means **beat in music, heartbeat, to shoot a bow, legendary place**).

rib *iwi ʻaoʻao*. [*ʻOiai ʻo ia i paheʻe ai i ka ʻaila, ua hāʻule iho i lalo a ua pohole nā iwi ʻaoʻao ona.* Since she slid in the oil, she fell down and bruised her **ribs**.]

ribbon *lipine* (also means **tape**). [*He mau lipine nani ko kona lei.* His *lei* has pretty **ribbons**.]

rice *laiki*.

rich *waiwai* (also means **valuable, wealthy**).

riddle *ʻōlelo nane*. [*ʻAʻole hiki ke loaʻa ka pane i ka ʻōlelo nane.* The answer to the **riddle** can't be found.]

ride 1. *holo* (also means **to travel, move**, many other meanings). [*Holo lio nā paniolo.* Cowboys **ride** horses.] 2. *holoholo*.

ridge *kualapa*.

ridicule *hoʻohenehene* (also means **to tease**).

[*Ho'ohenehene nā hoa noho i ka makuahine kāpulu.* The neighbors **ridicule** the slovenly mother.]

right 1. *pono kiwila* (civil). 2. *pololei* (also means **correct, straight**). [*E kalaiwa **pololei** i mua ou no 'elua palaka a laila e huli hema.* Drive **straight** in front of you for two blocks then turn left.] 3. *'ākau* (right side, direction; also means **north**).

righteous *pono* (also means **correct behavior**).

rigid *'o'ole'a* (also means **physically tough, stiff, hard**, many other meanings). [*'**O'ole'a** ko ke koa kino i ka maka'u.* The soldier's body is **rigid** due to fear.]

ring *[n]* *komolima* (*lit.* wear on hand). *[v]* *kani* (also means **to sound, chime**, many other meanings). [***Kani** nā pele o ka uaki kahiko ma ka hale pule.* The bells of the old clock at the church **chime**.]

ring

riot *haunaele.* [*He **haunaele** ko Polapola i ke kū'ē 'ana i ke aupuni Palani.* Tahiti had a **riot** in protest against the French government.]

rip *nāhae* (also means **to tear**).

ripe *pala.* [***Pala** paha nā manakō? A 'o ia!* Are the mangoes perhaps **ripe**? You got it (you're right)!]

rise *ala* (also means **to wake up, awake**). [*E **ala** mai!* **Wake up!**]

risk *maka'u* (also means **risky, danger, dangerous, afraid**). [*Auē! He hana **maka'u** ka ho'oipoipo 'ana i kēia mau lā.* Gosh! Making love is a **risky** business these days.]

ritual *hana ho'ohanohano* (also means **ceremony**).

rival *hoa paio* (also means **opponent in combat**).

river *kahawai*. [*Hālana ke **kahawai** i ka pōʻino*. The **river** floods in a storm.]

road 1. *alanui* (street). 2. *alaloa* (freeway). 3. *alahele* (pathway, trail).

roar 1. *wawā*. [*Ke kuʻi kokoke ka hekeli, nui ka **wawā**.* When thunder claps close by, the **roar** is great.] 2. *uō*. 3. *halulu*. 4. *nākolokolo*.

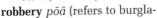

road

roast *ʻoma* (also means **stove, to bake**).

robbery *pōā* (refers to burglary, taking things from inside a location, in contrast to *ʻaihue*, which implies that a particular thing was stolen). [*Ua **pōā** ka panakō a ua **ʻaihue** ʻia ke kula*. The bank was **robbed** and the gold was **stolen**.]

rock *pōhaku* (also means **stone**). [*He pā **pōhaku** ʻalā ko kona hale*. His house has a lava **rock** wall.]

roll 1. *kākaʻa* (means **to turn over**). 2. *pōkaʻa* (bundle of *hala* leaves ready for weaving).

romantic *hoʻoipoipio*. (also means **to make love**). [*ʻAno **hoʻoipoipio** ka mele āna e hīmeni nei?* Is the song he's singing sort of **romantic**?]

roof *kaupoku*. [*Pono e kūkulu hou i ke **kaupoku** o heleleʻi ka ua i loko o ka hale*. The **roof** has to be repaired or else the rain will fall inside the house.]

room *lumi*.

roommate *hoa noho*.

rooster *moa kāne*.

root *mole* (also means **foundation, source, ancestral root**). [*ka **mole** o Lehua,* the foundation **root** of Lehua (a small island off Niʻihau, used as a symbol of the western boundary of Hawaiʻi. Traditional greetings poetically include all islands and all people of Hawai'i, often by mentioning traditional eastern and western boundaries of the archipelago.)]

rope *kaula* (also means **string**). (lasso = *kaula 'ili*) (beef jerky = *pipi kaula*)

rose *loke*.

rotten 1. *palahū* (overripe fruit). [**Palahū** *nā hē'ī a kāua i 'ako ai i kēlā lā aku nei.* The papayas that you and I picked the other day are **rotten**.] 2. *palahē* (fragile, easily torn, as paper). 3. *popopo* (wood, decayed leaves).

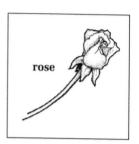

rose

rough 1. *'ōkaikai* (choppy sea). 2. *mālualua* (pitted road, rough terrain). 3. *kalakala* (rough texture). [*Ua 'ānai 'ia ka wa'a i ka lau* **kalakala** *o ka 'ulu a i 'ole i ka pōhaku poepoe i ke au kahiko.* Canoes were rubbed (sanded down) with the **rough-textured** breadfruit leaf or with round stones in olden days.]

round *poepoe*. (the globe = *ka poepoe honua*)

row 1. *lālani*. 2. *pae*.

royal *ali'i* (also means **chief, noble**).

rub 1. *'ānai* (with friction, to sand). [**'Ānai** *ke kālai ki'i i ka lā'au i ka pōhaku hamo.* The image carver **rubs** the wood with the rubbing stone.] 2. *hamo* (with oil, as in massage).

rubber band *lahalio*.

rubbish *'ōpala*. [*Na ke ka'a halihali 'ōpala e lawe aku i ka* **'ōpala**. Garbage trucks are the ones that haul away **rubbish**.]

rubbish can *kini 'ōpala*.

rudder *hoe uli*.

rude 1. *kiko'olā*. [**Kiko'olā** *kā ka mea na'aupō 'ōlelo.*

The ignorant person's speech is **rude**.] 2. *kalakala* (also means **rough texture**).

rule 1. *lula* (from English; regulation). 2. *kānāwai* (law, code, many other meanings). 3. *hoʻomalu* (to govern). 4. *noho aliʻi* (to reign as a noble or king).

rumble, reverberate *nākolo.*

run *holo.* Note: *Holo* is a general term for movement, and its English meanings include to travel, to move, to sail, to swim (fish). *Holo wāwae* specifies running; *holo peki*, jogging; *holoholo*, going around, "cruising."

rural *kuaʻāina.* [*Kamaʻāina ʻo Lilia i nā ahupuaʻa kuaʻāina o Koʻolaupoko.* Lilia is familiar with the **rural** *ahupuaʻa* (land sections from mountain to ocean) of the Koʻolaupoko district.]

rush *pūlale.* [*No ke aha ʻoe e pūlale mai?* Why do you **rush** up to me? (song, "Hōkio," by M. Pukui and M. Lam)]

rust *kūkaehao* (also means **rusty**).

rustle 1. *nehe.* [*ke kai nehe ʻōlelo me ka ʻiliʻili,* the **rustling** sea talking to the pebbles (song, "Kawaihae," by B. Lincoln).] 2. *nākolo.*

rut *napoʻo* (also means **cavity, armpit, to sink down**). (sunset = *napoʻo ka lā*)

sacred 1. *la'a*. [***La'a*** *ka heiau i ho'ola'a 'ia iā Lono*. The *heiau* dedicated to Lono is **sacred**.] 2. *kapu*.

sacrifice *mōhai*. [*'O ka ulua kekahi 'ano **mōhai***. The *ulua* fish is a type of **sacrifice**.]

sad *kaumaha* (also means **depressed, heavy**).

saddle *noho lio*.

safety *palekana*. [*'O ka **palekana** ka mea nui i ka holo 'ana*. **Safety** is the important thing in sailing.]

sail *holo*. (to sail to leeward = *ka'alalo*; to sail to windward = *ka'aluna*)

sailboat *moku pe'a*.

sailor 1. *kelamoku*. 2. *'aukai*. 3. *'aumoana*.

salary *uku hana*.

sale *kū'ai emi*.

sailboat

salesperson *kālepa* (also means **merchant, peddler**). [*'Oiai he kū'ai emi kēia, 'oi aku paha ka li'ili'i o kā ke **kālepa** uku hana?* Since this is a sale, is the **salesperson**'s salary smaller?]

salt *pa'akai*.

salted *miko*. [*Ua **miko** ka 'i'o i ka pa'akai*. The meat was **salted**.]

same *like*. [*'Ano **like** ko ke keiki 'ano me ko kona makua kāne*. The character of the child is the **same** as his father's.]

Samoa *Kāmoa*.

sanctuary *pu'uhonua*. [*'O ke ali'i nō kekahi 'ano **pu'uhonua***. The chiefs themselves were one kind of **sanctuary**.]

sand *one.* [*Ke one wela i ka lā ke hehi a'e.* When you step on it, the **sand** is hot due to the sun. (song, "Ka Uluwehi o Ke Kai," by E. Kanaka'ole)]

sandwich *kanuwika* (from English).

sarcastic *kīko'olā* (also means **rude, impertinent**).

satiated *mā'ona* (means full of food, when one has eaten enough).

satisfy *hō'olu'olu.*

sauce *kai* (also means **gravy, condiment, dressing**). [*Loa'a ke **kai** nīoi?* Got **chili pepper water**?]

sand

sauce

sausage *na'aukake.*

save 1. *ho'opakele* (save a life, rescue). 2. *mālama* (keep, take care of). 3. *ho'āhu* (save up money). [*E **ho'āhu** i kāu kālā a hiki ke kūa'i mai i papa he'e nalu nou iho.* **Save** your money until you can buy a surfboard for yourself.]

saw 1. *pahiolo.* 2. *pahiolo ulia* (electric saw).

say *'ōlelo.* [*Mai **'ōlelo** pēlā!* Don't **say** that!]

scab *pāpa'a* (also means **burned, overdone, slice of bread** [*pāpa'a palaoa*], other meanings).

scale *[n]* 1. *ana paona* (for measuring weight). 2. *unahi* (fish scale). *[v]* *unahi.* [*Me ke puna i **unahi** ai ko Momi kupuna wahine i ka i'a.* It was with the spoon that Momi's grandmother **scaled** the fish.]

scar *'ālina.* [*E Tūtū, e hō'ike mai i kou mau **'ālina** kaua.* Grandpa, show us your battle **scars**.]

scarce *kaka'ikahi* (also means **seldom, infrequently,**

few). [*Kaka'ikahi nā keiki kama'āina 'ole i ka
loloula.* There are **few** children who are not
familiar with the computer.]

scare *ho'omaka'u* (also means **to frighten**).

scatter *ho'opuehu* (also means **to disperse, blow
away, blown away**). [*Ke **ho'opuehu** 'ia nei nā
huna laiki e ka makani.* The grains of rice are
being **scattered** by the wind.]

scenic view point *'ikena* (also means **vista, panora-
ma, view**). [*ka **'ikena** iā Hi'ilawe,* the **view** of
Hi'ilawe falls (song, "Hi'ilawe," by Kuakini/Li'a)]

schedule *papahana.* [*Loa'a ka **papahana** mokulele
iā ia?* Does she have the airplane **schedule**?]

scholarship *makana* (also means **prize, gift**). [*E loa'a
ana ka **makana** 'o "Nā Ho'okama" i kāna
mo'opuna wahine.* His granddaughter will
receive the "Nā Ho'okama" **scholarship**.]

school *kula.* (elementary school = *kula ha'aha'a*;
high school = *kula ki'eki'e*; university = *kula nui*)

school campus *kahua kula.*

schoolhouse *hale kula.*

schoolmate *hoa kula.*

school semester *kau kula.*

science *akeakamai* (also means **philosophy**).

scientist *akeakamai* (also means **philosopher, seeker
of knowledge**). [*Alaka'i nā **akeakamai** kilo hōkū
i ka hana ma nā hale kilo hōkū ma Mauna Kea.*
Astronomers (*lit.* scientists who observe stars)
lead the work at the astronomical observatories
on Mauna Kea.]

scissors *'ūpā.* [*Aia nō a ho'okala 'ia ka **'ūpā**, hiki ke
'oki i ka ana kuiki.* As soon as the **scissors** are
sharpened, the quilt pattern can be cut.]

scold *nuku.* [*Mai **nuku** aku i nā keiki, e ahonui.*
Don't **scold** the children, be patient.]

scrape *kahi.* [*Ke **kahi** nei ka hiapo i ke pola poi.* The
eldest child is **scraping** the poi bowl.]

scratch *wa'u* (also means **to grate**). [*E wa'u mai i ko ka pēpē kua.* **Scratch** the baby's back.]

scream [n] *'alalā* (also means **Hawaiian crow**). [v] 1. *'alalā*. 2. *uā* (also means **to shout, yell out**).

screen *pākū* (also means **curtain, veil, partition**).

screwdriver *kuikala.*

screwdriver

sea 1. *kai*. 2. *moana* (refers to deep ocean far from land).

sea foam 1. *hu'a* (also means **bubble, suds**). 2. *'ehu* (also means **dust**). 3. *huna kai.*

seal 1. *'īlio holo i ka uaua*. 2. *sila* (from English). [*He mea laha 'ole ka 'ikema-ka i ka sila maoli.* Seeing a native Hawaiian monk **seal** is a rare thing.]

seal

seam 1. *ku'ina* (also means **joint, junction**). 2. *humuhumu* (also means **to stitch, sew**).

sear *kuni* (also means **to brand**).

search 1. *'imi*. 2. *huli*. Note: *Huli* refers to searching for something you've misplaced, while *'imi* refers to exploring or seeking something you don't have. [*Iā ia e huli ana i ka huaale, ua hele a pōniuniu.* While he was **searching** for the pill, he became dizzy.]

seashore *'ae kai.*

seasick *poluea* (also means **nausea, nauseated**).

season *kau* (also means **to place something some-where, to board transportation** [*kau ma luna o*]. Note: Ancient Hawaiians noted two seasons in the year: *kau wela, lit.* hot season, or summer, and *kau hoʻoilo*, the rainy season. (for ever and ever [*lit.* from season to season] = *no nā kau a kau*) [*a he lei poina ʻole **no nā kau a kau**,* and a *lei* never forgotten **from one season to the next** (song, "Hawaiian Love Song," by C. King)]

seat *noho* (also means **chair**).

sea urchin 1. *wana*. 2. *ʻina*. 3. *hāʻukeʻuke*.

seaweed *limu*. [*Ke moku kou wāwae i ka pāpapa, e kau i ka **limu** kala.* Whenever your foot is cut on the reef, put *kala* **seaweed** (on it).]

sea urchin

second 1. *kekona* (time). 2. *lua* (sequence). [*ʻO Manuleʻa ka **lua** o kāna mau moʻopuna.* Manuleʻa is the **second** of his grandchildren.] (second floor = *papahele ʻelua*) 3. *kōkua* (second a motion).

secret [*n*] *mea huna*. [*Mai haʻi aku i ka **mea huna**!* Don't tell the **secret**!] [*adj*] *huna*.

secretary *kākau ʻōlelo*. [*ʻOi aku ke akamai o ke **kākau ʻōlelo** ma mua o kāna haku.* The **secretary** is cleverer than his boss.]

secretly *malū* (also means **illegally, stealthily, furtive**). [*Hoʻolālā **malū** nā mea kipi.* The rebels plan **secretly**.]

secretary

section 1. *māhele* (also means **piece**). 2. *paukū* (also means **verse, stanza, paragraph**).

security guard *kiaʻi*. [*E aho nāna e ʻae i ke **kiaʻi** e kelepona aku i ke kaʻa lawe maʻi.* It's better for her to let the **security guard** phone the ambulance.]

see *'ike* (also means **to know, feel**). [*Ua **'ike** mua 'oe iā lāua?* Have you **seen** them (two) before?]

seed *'ano'ano.* [*Nui nā **'ano'ano** li'ili'i o ka hē'ī.* The papaya has lots of little **seeds**.]

seek 1. *'imi* (to look for something you don't have). 2. *huli* (to search for something you've misplaced).

seer *kāula* (also means **prophet, magician**).

seize *hopu* (also means **to grab, catch**). [*E **hopu** 'ia ana nā kānaka ho'opae malū e nā māka'ikiu.* The smugglers will be **seized** by the detectives.]

select 1. *koho* (also means **to guess, to choose**). 2. *wae.*

self *pono'ī* (also means **private, personal, exactly**). [*Nou **pono'ī** kāna mele i oli ai?* Does the chant that he chanted belong to you, your**self**?]

sell 1. *kū'ai aku.* 2. *kālewa.* [***Kālewa** kēia wahine i nā mea ho'onani maka i kona mau hoaaloha.* This woman **sells** cosmetics to her friends.] 2. *kālepa.*

send *ho'ouna.* [*Pipi'i ka **ho'ouna** 'ana i nā pū'olo i nā 'āina 'ē.* **Sending** packages to foreign countries is expensive.]

sensitive *'eha wale* (easily hurt by criticism).

sentence 1. *hopuna 'ōlelo.* 2. *māmala 'ōlelo.*

separate *ka'awale* (also means **separately, apart**). [*Noho **ka'awale** ke kāne a me ka wahine.* The husband and wife live **separate** lives.] *[v]* *ho'oka'awale.*

September Kepakemapa (from English).

sequence *ka'ina.* [*He aha ke **ka'ina** hana pololei ke kūkulu 'oe i ka hale pe'a?* What is the right **sequence** of action when you are setting up a tent?]

serene 1. *mālie.* 2. *la'i.* 3. *maluhia.*

serrated *nihoniho* (also means **toothed, jagged**). [*'O'oi ka 'ao'ao **nihoniho** o ka pahiolo!* The **serrated** side of the saw is sharp!]

servant 1. *ʻōhua* (also means **passenger, member of household**).

serve *lawelawe*.

settle *kau*.

severe 1. *ʻoʻoleʻa*. 2. *koʻikoʻi*.

sew *humuhumu*. [*Pono paha ʻo Nālei e **humuhumu** i ko kona muʻumuʻu pelu.* Maybe Nālei should **sew** up her *muʻumuʻu*'s hem.]

sewer *ʻauwai* (also means **irrigation ditch, taro patch, flume**). Note: *ʻAuwai lawe mea ʻino* specifically refers to "sewer," whereas *ʻauwai* by itself usually refers to the ditch used to divert stream water into taro patches.

shade *malu* (also means **protection, government**). [*Ma luna ou ka **malu** o ka lani.* Above you is the **protection** of heaven. (song, "Queen's Jubilee," Liliʻuokalani)]

shadow *aka*. [*I ka pouli lā, uhi ke **aka** a ka mahina i ka lā a pōʻeleʻele ka lā holoʻokoʻa.* In an eclipse, the **shadow** of the moon covers the sun until the entire sun is dark.]

shake 1. *naue*. 2. *lūlū*. (shake hands = *lūlū lima*)

shallow *pāpaʻu*. [*Pāʻani nā keiki i ke kai **pāpaʻu**.* Children play in the shallow sea water.]

shampoo

shame *hilahila* (also means **embarrassment, ashamed, shy, embarrassed**).

shampoo *[n] kopa lauoho.* *[v] holoi lauoho.*

shape *ʻano*. [*Poepoe ke **ʻano** o ka lei kīkā.* A cigar lei's **shape** is round.]

share *[n]* 1. *māhele*. 2. *kea* (share of stock). [*ʻEhia aʻu **kea** ma ka hui ʻoihana hoʻopuka?* How many **shares** do I have in the profitable business?] *[v]* 1.

māhele. 2. hoʻomāhelehele. (dividend = māhele
kālā)

shark manō. [*Kakaʻikahi nā* **manō** *ʻai kanaka.* Man-
eating **sharks** are rare.]

sharp 1. ʻoi (not dull). 2. ʻoʻoi (prickly). 3. ʻāwini
(bold, forward).

sharpen hoʻokala.

shave kahi (also means **to comb, number one**, many
other meanings).

shave ice 1. haukōhi. 2. hau momona.

shawl kīhei. [*Komo kona makuahine i ke* **kīhei** *ma
ke ahiahi.* His mother puts on a **shawl** in the
evening.]

she ʻo ia (also means **he**).

sheep hipa. [*Hānai* **hipa** *lākou ma Niʻihau.* They
raise **sheep** on Niʻihau.]

sheet 1. uhipela (bed linen). 2. ʻaoʻao (sheet of
paper). 3. lau (surface).

shelf hakakau. [*Aia nā uhipela pāhoehoe ma ka
hakaukau o ka waihona lole.* The satin sheets
are on the **shelf** of the closet.]

shell pūpū. [*Minamina ka nalowale ʻana o nā
waihoʻoluʻu hinuhinu o ka* **pūpū** *i kapa ʻia ke
kāhuli ma nā wao kele.* The disappearance of the
shining colors of the **shell** called the kāhuli
(Hawaiian land snail) in the rain forest is
deplorable.]

shelter wahi lulu.

shepherd kahu hipa. [*Iesu nō ke* **kahu hipa**. Jesus is
indeed the **shepherd**. (traditional hymn)]

shiny 1. hinuhinu. [**Hinuhinu** *ko ke kāne poʻo ʻōhule i
ka hamohamo ʻana i ka ʻaila.* The bald man's
head is **shiny** due to rubbing oil on it.] 2. mālamalama.

ship mokuahi (*lit.* steamship). (sailboat = moku peʻa)

shirt pālule. [*Pipiʻi nā* **pālule** *aloha kahiko i kēia mau
lā.* Old aloha **shirts** are expensive these days.]

shiver *ha'ukeke.* [*Ha'ukeke ka 'īlio maka'u.* The frightened dog **shivers**.]

shock *hikilele* (also means **disturbance**).

shocked 1. *kūnāhihi.* [*Kūnāhihi ka lehulehu i ka 'elepani 'āhiu.* The crowd is **shocked** by the wild elephant.] 2. *mā'e'ele* (also means **numb**).

shoes *kāma'a.* (boots = *kāma'a puti*) (high-heeled shoes = *kāma'a lau li'ili'i*)

shoes

shoot 1. *kī* (also means **to spout up, aim at,** other meanings). [Wai**kīkī** (*lit.* spouting fresh water, named for the many freshwater springs that were part of the extensive wetlands and taro patches there before development)] 2. *kī pū* (shoot a gun). [*Mai 'ae kākou i ke **kī pū**!* Let's not allow **shooting guns**!]

shooting star *hōkūlele.*

shopping center *kikowaena kū'ai.* [*'O ka hale kū'ai hea ka mea hou ma ke **kikowaenakū'ai** 'o Kūhiō?* Which store is the new one at the Kūhiō **shopping center**?]

shore 1. *'ae kai.* 2. *lihikai.* [*He mau pali ko kēia **lihikai**.* This **shore** has cliffs.

short *pōkole.*

shorts *lole wāwae pōkole.*

shoulder *po'ohiwi.*

shout *ho'ōho.* [*Ho'ōho aku ka lehulehu i ka pōpa'ilima.* The public **shouts** at the volleyball game.]

shove 1. *hou.* 2. *pahu.* [*Pahu nā keiki kū laina kekahi i kekahi.* The children standing in line **shove** each other.]

shovel *kopalā* (from English). [*'Eli ka mahi'ai i kona*

kīhāpai i ke **kopalā**. The farmer digs his field
with a **shovel**.]

show *hōʻike*. [*E* **hōʻike** *mai i kou poho.* **Show** me
your palm.]

shower 1. *kiliʻau* (bathing) 2. *nāulu* (sudden rain
squall).

show off *hōʻoio*. [**Hōʻoio** *kā Kamahele kaikamahine i
kona apolima kula hou.* Kamahele's daughter
shows off her new gold bracelet.]

shrewd *maʻalea* (also means **cunning, deceit,
skilled**). [*He ʻōlelo* **maʻalea** *kā ka mea ʻāpuka.*
The deceitful person has **shrewd** speech.]

shrimp *ʻōpae*. [*Aia nā* **ʻōpae** *ʻula i nā loko wai
hapakai.* The red **shrimp** are in the brackish
water pond.]

shut *[v]* *pani*. [*E* **pani** *a e laka ʻia ana ka puka ma ka
hola ʻumi o ke ahiahi.* The door will be **shut** and
locked at 10 in the evening.] *[adj]* *paʻa* (closed).

shy 1. *hilahila* (also means **embarrassed, ashamed**).
2. *ʻāhiu* (also means **unsociable, wild**).

sibling (older) *kaikuaʻana* (of the same sex as the
person who has the sibling). [*He* **kaikuaʻana** *ko
Lāhela.* Lāhela (woman) has an **older sister**.] [*He
kaikuaʻana *ko Palikū.* Palikū (man) has an
older brother.]

sibling (younger) *kaikaina* (of the same sex as the
person who has the sibling). [*He mau* **kaikaina**
ko Lāhela. Lāhela (woman) has several **younger
sisters**.] [*ʻAʻohe* **kaikaina** *o Palikū.* Palikū (man)
has no **younger brothers**.]

sick 1. *maʻi.* 2. *ʻōmaʻimaʻi* (sickly).

side *ʻaoʻao* (also means **page, group, hemisphere**).

sight 1. *ʻike.* 2. *ʻikena* (view).

sign *hōʻailona.*

silent *hāmau*. [*E* **hāmau**! Be **silent**! (stronger than
kulikuli)]

similar *like* (also means **like**). [**Like** *ke kaikaina ou* *me kou kaikua'ana?* Is your younger sister **similar** to your older sister? (a woman is being asked)]

simple *ma'alahi* (also means **easy**).

sin 1. *lawehala*. 2. *hewa* (also means **wrong, guilty**).

since *no ka mea* (because). [*E holoi i ka pahi,* **no ka mea,** *ua lepo.* Wash the knife, **since** it's dirty.]

sing 1. *hīmeni*. 2. *mele*. 3. *kani* (birds).

singer *pu'ukani*. [*Me he leo 'ānela lā ka leo o ka* **pu'ukani** *e hīmeni nei iā "Papakōlea."* The voice of the **singer** who is singing "Papakōlea" seems like the voice of an angel.] 2. *ka mea hīmeni*.

single 1. *kuakahi* (unmarried). 2. *ho'okahi* (one of a thing; one person).

sister (of a female) 1. *kaikua'ana* (older sibling). 2. *kaikaina* (younger sibling). Note: *Kaikua'ana* can refer to either a man's older brother or to a woman's older sister. *Kaikaina* is used to refer to either a man's younger brother or a woman's younger sister.

sister (of a male) *kaikuahine*.

sit *noho* (also means **to live or stay someplace**). [*E* **noho** *i lalo a e 'ai pū kāua.* Let's **sit** down and eat together.]

site 1. *kahua*. 2. *wahi*.

six *'eono*. (syn. *'aono, ono*)

size *nui*. [*Pehea ka* **nui** *o kēnā pālule T? Loa'a anei paha kekahi 'ano "nunui"?* How's the **size** of that T-shirt (by you)? Do you maybe have an extra large?]

skeleton *pa'a iwi*.

skilled *no'eau*. [*He kālena ko Keawe ma nā hana* **no'eau** *Hawai'i.* Keawe is **skilled** in Hawaiian crafts.]

skin *'ili* (also means **bark of tree, surface of sea**).

skip *kāpae*. [*Ke* **kāpae** *kēlā kime i ko lākou manawa, huhū ke alaka'i pā'ani.* Whenever that team

skips their turn, the
leader of the game is
mad.]

hula skirt

skirt *pāʻū.* (hula skirt = *pāʻū
hula*)

skull *iwi poʻo.* [*Pale aku ka
iwi poʻo i ka lolo.* The
skull protects the brain.]

sky 1. *lani.* 2. *lewa* (also
means **space, air, upper heavens**). [*Kau mai ke
ānuenue ma ka **lewa**.* Rainbows appear in the
sky.]

slack *ʻaluʻalu* (also means **loose, baggy**). [*ʻAluʻalu ka
pālule o ka ʻelemakule.* The old man's shirt is
baggy.]

slack key (Hawaiian guitar style) *kī hōʻalu.* [*Hoʻokani
kīkā ʻo George Kuo i ke kaila **kī hōʻalu**.* George
Kuo plays guitar in the **slack key** style.]

slant *hiō* (also means **diagonal, incline, to lean**).

slap *paʻi* (also means **to hit, clap, print, publish**).

slave *kauā* (also means **servant, attendant**).

sled *hōlua* (ancient sport of sledding down hills on
long, narrow sled). [*Holo iho ka meʻe a lele ihola
ma luna o ka **hōlua**.* The hero ran downhill and
then jumped onto the **sled**.]

sleep *hiamoe.*

sleepy *maka hiamoe.* [*E ka **maka hiamoe**, e hoʻi e
hiamoe.* Hey, **sleepy**head, go to sleep.]

slender *wīwī* (also means **slim, thin**).

slice open (fish) *kaha.* [*Unahi mua ka lawaiʻa i nā iʻa
a pau a ma hope **kaha** i ka ʻōpū a wehe i ka
pihapiha a me ka naʻau.* The fisherman first
scales all the fish and later **slices open** the stomach and removes the gills and intestines.]

slime *waliwali.* [*ʻO ka **waliwali** hoʻokumu honua ia.*
It was the **slime** that established the earth. (line
from *Kumulipo* creation chant)]

slip *pahe‘e.*

slippers *kālipa* (from English).

slippery 1. *pahe‘e* (also means **to slide, slip**). [*Pahe‘e ke alahele o uka i ka ua e helele‘i nei.* The mountain pathway is **slippery** due to the rain that is falling.] 2. *pakika* (also means **to slide, slip**).

slippers

slow *lohi* (also means **late, retarded**). [*Lohi ko ke kāne nui holo ‘ana.* The large man's running is **slow**.]

small *li‘ili‘i.*

smart *akamai* (also means **skilled, clever**).

smear *pala* (daub of something, used in insults).

smell *honi* (also means **to kiss**). [*Hiki ke honi ‘ia ke ‘ala o nā pua pīkake e māpu mai nei.* The scent of the *pīkake* flowers being borne on the breeze can be **smelled**.]

smile *mino‘aka.* [*Kū kāna muli loa i kona makua kāne i kona mino‘aka.* Her youngest child's **smile** is like his father's.]

smoke *uahi.*

smoky *uauahi* (also means **voggy**). [*Uauahi ‘o Kona i ka hū ‘ana o ka pele.* Kona is **voggy** due to the eruption of lava.]

smooth *nemonemo* (also means **polished, slick**).

smuggle *ho‘opae malū.*

snack *mea ‘ai māmā.* [*‘O ka hapahā hola ‘elua ka manawa no ka mea ‘ai māmā ma ka Pūnana Leo.* Quarter past two is **snack** time at the Pūnana Leo preschool.]

snail *pūpū* (also means **shell, hors d'oeuvre**).

snake *naheka.* [*‘A‘ohe naheka o Hawai‘i.* Hawai‘i has no **snakes**.]

snatch *kāʻili.*

sneeze *kihe.* [***Kihe** a mauli ola.* **Sneeze** and live. (traditional response when someone sneezes, like "Gesundheit" or "Bless you"; often shortened to "*ola*")]

snout *nuku* (also means **beak, tip, mountain pass, harbor or river entrance**). [*He **nuku** ʻoi nō ko ka lau wiliwili nukunuku ʻoiʻoi.* The *lau wiliwili nukunuku ʻoiʻoi* fish has a truly sharp **snout.**]

snow *hau kea.*

soak *hoʻoluʻu.*

soap *kopa* (from English).

soap

soar *kīkaha.* [***Kīkaha** ka ʻiwa, he lā mālie.* (ʻōlelo noʻeau) The *ʻiwa* bird **soars**, it's a calm day.]

socket *pona.*

soda *koloaka* (from English "soda water").

soda

soft *palupalu* (also means **supple, fragile, tender**). [***Palupalu** ko ka makuahine hou ʻili.* The new mother's skin is **soft.**]

soil *lepo* (also means **dirt, dirty**, euphemism for **excrement**). (to make something dirty = *hoʻolepo*) [*Mai **hoʻolepo** i kou lumi moe.* Don't **dirty up** your bedroom.] (fertile soil = *lepo momona*)

solar *lā.* [*Kaulana ke kula kiʻekiʻe ʻo Konawaena i ke kaʻa **lā**.* Konawaena High School is well known for its **solar** car.]

soldier *koa* (also means **brave, courageous**).

solemn *kūoʻo* (also means **serious, dignified**). [***Kūoʻo***

ka hana hoʻohanohano ma ka hale aliʻi. The ceremony at the palace was **solemn**.]

solid paʻa (also means **stuck, completed,** many other meanings).

solo pākahi (also means **individually, by ones**). (dual, by twos = pālua; by threes = pākolu)

solution haʻina (explanation). [E haʻi mai i ka **haʻina**. Tell me the **solution**.]

someone else haʻi. [E hāʻawi aku i kāu ʻōlelo aʻo iā **haʻi**! Give your advice to **someone else**!] Note: Haʻi has many other meanings, including **sacrifice, to tell, to break**.

something kekahi mea.

sometimes i kekahi manawa. [Luʻu kai ke kamanā **i kekahi manawa**? Does the carpenter go diving **sometimes**?]

son keiki kāne (also means **boy**; keiki can also imply son, boy).

song 1. mele. [ʻO wai ka **mele** a lākou e hoʻokani nei ma ka lekiō? What's the name of the **song** they are playing now on the radio?] 2. hīmeni.

soon koke (also means **immediately**). [E heleleʻi **koke** ana kou lauoho. Your hair will **soon** fall out.] 2. auaneʻi.

soothe hoʻonā. [E **hoʻonā** i kāu keiki i maʻi i ka piwa. **Soothe** your child who is sick with fever.]

sore ʻeha (also means **pain, painful**). (headache = ke poʻo ʻeha)

sorry 1. minamina. 2. mihi. [Ke **mihi** aku nei au i kā kaʻu moʻopuna hana minamina. **E kala mai**. I'm confessing my grandchild's regrettable action. **I'm sorry**.]

sort 1. wae (select). [E **wae** i nā hua kukui a e mālama i nā hua liʻiliʻi. **Sort** the kukui nuts and keep the small ones.] 2. ʻano (kind, type).

soul ʻuhane (also means **ghost, spirit**).

sound kani (also means **to ring, chime**). [**Kani** ka

uaki nui ma ka hapalua hola. The big clock
sounds on the half hour.]

sour *'awa'awa* (also means **bitter**). [*'Awa'awa ka
'awa ke inu iho. 'Awa* is **bitter-tasting** when you
drink it. (*'Awa* is a traditional drink, mildly
intoxicating, used in ceremonies honoring gods
and chiefs; it is also used medicinally.)

source *kumu.*

south *hema* (also means **left**).

South Pacific Pākīpika Hema. [*'A'ole 'o ia i holo ma
ka **Pākīpika Hema**.* She hasn't sailed in the
South Pacific.]

sovereignty *ea* (also means **life force, breath, gas**,
many other meanings).

sow *lūlū* (also means **to shake, donate, donation**).
[***Lūlū** ka mahi'ai i nā 'ano'ano kaloke ma ka
māla 'ai.* The farmer **sows** carrot seeds in the vegetable garden.]

space 1. *wā* (also means **epoch** or **time period, interval**). 2. *kōwā, kōā* (intervening space between
objects, such as channels between islands; also
means **time interval**). 3. *lewa lilo loa* (outer
space). [*Loa'a paha kekahi mea ola ma ka **lewa
lilo loa**?* Is there possibly something alive in
outer space?]

spacious *ākea* (also means **broad, wide**).

sparkling *'ōlinolino* (also means **shining, radiant**).
[***'Ōlinolino** ka wai o kēia kahawai.* The water of
this stream is **sparkling**.] 2. *'ālohilohi.*

speak *'ōlelo.* [***'Ōlelo** pinepine māua 'o ko'u 'anakē i
nā hālāwai o ka Hui Kīwila.* My aunt and I often
speak at the Civic Club meetings.]

spear 1. *'ō* (also means **fork**). (fishing spear = *ke 'ō*).
[*Hopu ko'u kaikunāne i ka he'e i **ke 'ō**.* My
brother catches octopus with a **spear**.] 2. *ihe*
(weapon).

special *kūikawā* (also means **temporary, transitional**).

[*He hana **kūikawā** kā kēia kia'i.* This guard has a **special** job.]

speed 1. *'āwīwī* (also means **fast, quick, quickly**). *2. wikiwiki* (also means **fast, quick, quickly**).

spelling bee *ho'okūkū hua 'ōlelo.*

spider 1. *nananana.* [*Na ka **nananana** i nahu iā Nu'umealani?* Was it the **spider** that bit Nu'umealani?] 2. *lanalana.*

spill *hanini.*

spin *ho'oniniu* (also means **to cause dizziness**). [*E **ho'oniniu** i ka hū.* **Spin** the top (toy).]

spine *kuamo'o* (refers to genealogy, since generations are counted going down the backbone, and ancestors are considered to be a living part of the spine; syn. *iwikuamo'o*).

spiral *pāka'awili.*

spirit 1. *'uhane* (also means **god, ghost**). [*He **'uhane** ko nā mea a pau?* Does everything have a **spirit**?] 2. *akua.*

splash *pakī.* [*Pakī a'e ka 'ehu kai i ko ka mea he'e nalu pae 'ana i ka nalu.* The sea spray **splashes** up when the surfer catches the wave.]

spoil 1. *'ino* (decay). 2. *hōkai* (mar, deface). 3. *pailani* (pamper). [*'O kēlā mau kaikamāhine ko Momi mau kaikua'ana **pailani**.* Those girls are Momi's **spoiled** older sisters.] 4. *palahū* (to become over-ripe, rotten [fruit or food]).

sponge *'ūpī.*

spoon *puna* (use with <u>ke</u>). [*E 'ai 'oe i kēnā pūkini i ke **puna**, 'a'ole i ke 'ō.* Eat that pudding (near you) with the **spoon**, not with the fork.]

spoon

sport *pā'ani* (also means **game, to play game**).

spotted *kikokiko* (also means **freckled, to type**).

spray *[n]* 1. *'ehu kai*. 2. *huna wai*. *[v] kīkī* (also means **to spout or shoot up**).

spread *hāli'i*. [*E **hāli'i** aku i ke kapa ma luna o ka mau'u no ka pikiniki*. **Spread** the blanket on the grass for the picnic.]

spread out *[adj] laha* (also means **common**).

spring (water) *pūnāwai*. [*Hāli'i ka lā'auhihi a puni ka **pūnāwai**. Vines spread out around the **spring**.]

sprinkle 1. *pīpī* (to scatter about, as salt water in house blessings). 2. *kāpī* (to sprinkle fish or meat with salt for flavoring, preservative). A traditional phrase at the end of storytelling is *pīpī holo ka'ao*, lit. sprinkled around, the story travels on; that is, in being retold, a story lives on.

square *huinahālike*.

squeeze *'uī*. [*E **'uī** hou i kāu 'ūpī a e holoi i nā kī'aha*. **Squeeze** out your sponge and wash the glasses.]

squid 1 *he'e* (octopus). 2. *mūhe'e*.

squirm *'oni* (also means **wiggle, move**).

square

stack *pu'u*.

stadium *kahua pā'ani* (also means playing field).

stage *[n] kahua*.

stagger *kunewa*. [***Kunewa** ke kanaka pōniuniu*. The dizzy person **staggers**.]

stair (step) *'ānu'u* .

staircase *alapi'i* (also means **ladder**). [*Hinuhinu ke **alapi'i** koa o ka Hale Ali'i 'o 'Iolani*. The koa **staircase** of 'Iolani Palace is shiny.]

stamp *[n]* 1. *po'oleka* (postage). 2. *'ohe kāpala* (stamp for printing tapa). *[v] hehi*.

stand *kū* (also means **to stop, appear, upright**).

star *hōkū*. [*Kū ka* **hōkū** *ahiahi i ka lewa.* The evening **star** appears in the sky.]

start *hoʻomaka*. [*Ma ka hola ʻehia e* **hoʻomaka** *ai ka hālāwai?* What time does the meeting **start**?]

state *mokuʻāina*. [*He kanalima* **mokuʻāina** *o ʻAmelika Hui Pū ʻia.* The U.S.A. has fifty **states**.]

statue 1. *kiʻi* (also means **picture, image**). 2. *kiʻi kū*. [*He* **kiʻi** *kū o ka naʻi aupuni ko Kohala.* Kohala has a **statue** of the conqueror.]

steadfast *ʻonipaʻa*. Note: This is the motto of Hawaiʻi's last queen, Liliʻuokalani.

steal *ʻaihue*.

steer *[n] pipi poʻa* (*lit.* castrated cattle). (bull = *pipi kāne*) *[v] hoʻokele* (also means **to navigate, navigator, leader**).

stem 1. *ʻau* (also means **handle, shaft, bone of lower arm, leg**). [*Kukū ke* **ʻau** *o ka loke.* The **stem** of a rose is thorny.] 2. *hā* (of *kalo* plant).

step *[n] ʻānuʻu*. *[v]* 1. *hehi*. 2. *keʻehi*. [**Keʻehi** *ka mahiʻai kalo i ka ʻūkele i ka loʻi hou.* The taro farmer **steps** in the mud in the new taro patch.]

stevedore 1. *poʻolā*. 2. *kipikoa* (from English). [*ʻO Tui ka luna* **kipikoa** *e hehi ana ma nā moku ma Kawaihae.* Tui is the **stevedore** supervisor stepping on the boats at Kawaiahae.]

stick *[n]* 1. *lāʻau* (also means **bush, medicinal herb**). 2. *ʻōʻō* (digging stick). 3. *ʻauamo* (carrying stick). *[v]* 1. *pili* (to adhere). 2. *hoʻopili* (to adhere).

sticker 1. *mea pipili*. 2. *pepa pipili*. [*He mau* **pepa pipili** *kaʻa Hawaiʻi ko kona wane.* His van has Hawaiian bumper **stickers**.]

sticky *pipili*.

stiff 1. *ʻoʻoleʻa* (rigid). 2. *māloʻeloʻe* (tight-muscled, stiff from exercise).

still 1. *mālie*. 2. *lana*.

stingy *pī*. [*ʻAno* **pī** *kāna moʻopuna?* Is his grandchild kind of **stingy**?]

stir 1. *'oni* (move). 2. *hō'eu'eu* (to animate, encourage). 3. *kāwili* (to mix, as ingredients).

stomach *'ōpū*. [*'O'ole'a ko ke kinai ahi 'ōpū.* The firefighter's **stomach** is hard.]

stone *pōhaku*.

stop 1. *kū* (stop moving). [*E kū a e hāpai i kou mau lima!* **Stop** and put your hands up!] 2. *ho'okū* (stop a car or machinery). 3. *ho'opau* (to finish). (Stop it! = *Uoki!*)

store *hale kū'ai*.

storm *pō'ino*.

stormy 1. *'ino* (also means **bad**). 2. *'ino'ino* (also means **bad**).

story (tale) 1. *ka'ao* (story considered to be fictitious). [*He mau kinolau ko nā kupua o nā ka'ao kahiko.* The demigods of the old **stories** have lots of body forms.] 2. *mo'olelo* (can also mean history, story considered to be true).

stout 1. *pu'ipu'i* (also means **plump, stocky, sturdy**). 2. *poupou* (short and stocky).

straight *pololei* (also means **correct**). [*E kalaiwa pololei a hiki i ka huina alanui a laila, e huli hema.* Drive **straight** ahead until the intersection, then turn left.]

strange *'ano 'ē* (also means **odd behavior, bizarre**).

stranger *malihini* (also means **newcomer, guest**). [*He malihini a i 'ole he kama'āina 'o ia nei?* Is this person here a **newcomer** or a local?]

strangle *'u'umi*.

stream *kahawai*.

street *alanui*. [*'O wai ka inoa o kou alanui?* What is the name of your **street**?]

strength *ikaika*.

stretch *kīko'o* (also means **to stick out**).

strike 1. *ku'i* (hit). 2. *'olohana* (work stoppage).

string *kaula* (also means **chain, rope**). [*E huki i nā kaula.* Pull the **ropes**.] (string a *lei* = *kui*)

['*Elima a 'olua lei i **kui** ai?* Did you two **string**
five *lei*?]

strip *[n] 'āpana* (also means **piece, section**). *[v]* 1.
    'u'u (to strip *maile*). 2. *māihi* (to peel). 3. *hole* (to
    peel). 4. *kīhae* (to strip thorns from *lauhala*). (to
    strip until naked = *wehe a kohana*)

stripe *kaha*.

striped *kahakaha*. [*He i'a **kahakaha** ka manini.* The
    manini is a **striped** fish.]

stroke *huki* (also means **cramp**).

strong *ikaika*.

struggle *'ā'ume'ume*.

stubborn *po'o pa'akikī*. [*He **po'o pa'akikī** ko kāna
    wahine.* His wife is **stubborn**.]

stuck *pa'a* (also means **closed, firm, completed**).
    [***Pa'a** ka pukaaniani.* The window is **stuck**.]

student *haumāna*.

study *ho'opa'a ha'awina*.

stumble *'ōkupe* (also means **to trip**). [*E **'ōkupe** ana
    ka mea 'oki mau'u i ka 'ili'ili.* The person cutting
    the grass will **stumble** on the pebbles.]

stump *'ōmuku*.

stunted 1. *'i'i*. [***I'i** ke kumu 'ōhi'a ma uka loa.* The
    'ōhi'a tree far up in the mountains is **stunted**.] 2.
    'ōkumu (implies stumpiness, shortness). 3.
    kanali'i (small growth).

stupid 1. *hūpō*. 2. *na'aupō* (ignorant).

style *kaila* (from English).

stylish *kaila*. [***Kaila** nā lole i hō'ike 'ia ma ka
    ho'olaha.* The clothes shown in the advertise-
    ment are **stylish**.]

submarine *mokulu'u*. [*'A'ohe ona hoi e holo ma loko
    o ka **mokulu'u**.* She has no desire to travel on a
    submarine.]

substitute *pani hakahaka*. [*Hiki anei iā 'oe ke **pani
    hakahaka** nāna ma kēia Pō'aono a'e?* Can you
    substitute for him next Saturday?]

subtract *lawe* (also means **to take away**). [*'Elima **lawe** 'elua 'o ia 'ekolu?* Is five **subtract** two three?]

succeed *holomua*. [*E **holomua** ana paha anei kā kāu keiki 'oihana hou?* Will your son's new business **succeed**?]

suck *omo*.

suction *omo*. [*He **omo** ikaika ko ka mīkini ho'oma'ema'e moena*. The carpet cleaning machine has strong **suction**.]

suddenly *'emo 'ole* (without delay). [***Emo 'ole** ka pi'o o ke ānuenue*. A rainbow **suddenly** appeared.]

suffering *'īnea* (also means distress, hardship, to suffer). [*'A'ole paha hiki ke ho'onā i ka **'īnea** o ka mea ma'i*. It may not be possible to quiet the **suffering** of the patient.]

sugar plantation *mahikō*.

suit (of clothes) *pa'a lole*.

suitcase *paiki*. [*He mau **paiki** a he mau ukana 'ē a'e kā ka malihini*. The guest has some **suitcases** and other baggage.]

sulky 1. *nuha*. 2. *mumule*.

summer *kauwela*. [*Ma ke **kauwela** e waele ana nā hoaaloha i nā lo'i*. It is in **summer** that the friends will weed the taro patches.]

sun *lā* (also means **day**).

sunbathe *'ōlala*.

sunburned *pāpa'a lā*. [*Inā he 'ili **pāpa'a lā** kou, e hele i ke kauka 'ili*. If you have **sunburned** skin, go to the skin doctor.]

sunglasses *makaaniani pale lā*.

sunglasses

sunrise 1. *kaiao*. 2. *wana'ao*. (Both words also mean **dawn**.)

sunset *napo'o ka lā.* [*Makemake nō lāua e noho ma ke one a* **napo'o ka lā***.* They (two) like to sit on the sand until **sunset**.]

superior *'oi a'e.* [*'O ka hale holoi lole hea ka hale holoi lole* **'oi a'e** *i kou mana'o?* Which launderette is the **superior** launderette in your opinion?]

supervisor *luna.*

support *kāko'o.*

supreme *po'okela.*

surf *he'e nalu.*

surface 1. *'ili* (skin, bark, surface of sea). 2. *papa* (flat surface).

surfboard *papa he'e nalu.*

surfer *mea he'e nalu.*

surge 1. *hū.* 2. *hānupanupa.* [*Ka* **hānupanupa** *o ke kai.* The **surging** of the sea. (a description of rough seas, fig. surging emotions)]

surplus *koena.* [*Loa'a nā hale kū'ai e kū'ai aku ana i ke* **koena** *pū'ali koa ma Kapalakiko.* There are stores that sell army **surplus** in San Francisco.]

surprised *pū'iwa.*

surrender *hā'awi pio* (also means **to give up**). [*Mai* **hā'awi pio***!* Don't **give up**!]

surround *kaiapuni.* (Hawaiian Immersion school = *kula* Kaiapuni Hawai'i)

survey *ana 'āina* (land). (to measure = *ana*)

suspect *huoi.* [*Ho'omaka anei kou hoahānau e* **huoi** *i ka hana malū a kāna kāne?* Has your cousin begun to **suspect** her husband's secretive activity?]

swallow 1. *ale.* 2. *moni.*

swamp *pohō* (also means **bog, mire, useless, in vain**).

swear 1. *'ōlelo pelapela* (also means swearing). [*He hana a ka palaualelo ka* **'ōlelo pelapela***.* **Swearing** is what a lazy windbag does.] 2. *ho'ohiki* (a vow, promise, oath).

sweat 1. *hou* (perspiration). 2. *kahe ka hou.*

sweater *kueka.* [*Pono e komo i ke **kueka** mehana a me ka lakeke ke pi'i 'oe i nā hale kilo hōkū ma Mauna Kea.* You have to put on a warm **sweater** and a jacket when you go up to the observatories on Mauna Kea.]

sweep *pūlumi.*

sweetheart *ipo.* [*E **ipo** nohea kou?* Do you have a handsome **sweetheart**?]

sweet-smelling 1. *'a'ala.* 2. *onaona* (alluring, attractive, sweet-scented).

swept away *lilo* (has many other meanings). [*E akahele o **lilo** kāu ukana i ke kahawai i pehu i ka ua nui i helele'i i ka pō nei.* Be careful or else your baggage will be **swept away** by the stream swollen with the heavy rain that fell last night.]

swim *'au'au* (also means **to bathe**). (to give a bath to someone/an animal = *hō'au'au*)

swim

swimming pool *loko 'au'au.*

swimsuit *lole 'au'au.*

swing [n] *paiō.* [v] *lele koali* (so called because one could swing on the twined vines of the *koali*, native morning glory).

swollen *pehu.*

symbol *hō'ailona* (also means **sign**). [*He hō'ailona ke ānue-nue.* The rainbow is a **symbol**.]

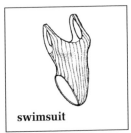

swimsuit

sympathy 1. *aloha.* [*Mai poina e ho'ouna aku i ke kāleka **aloha**.* Don't forget to send a **sympathy** card.] 2. *aloha menemene.*

table *pākaukau.*

tablespoon *puna pākaukau.* [*Loaʻa ke **puna pākaukau** i kou lumi kuke?* Does your kitchen have a **tablespoon**?]

table

taboo *kapu* (also means **sacred**). [*ʻO ka māpele ka heiau **kapu** no Lono.* The agricultural *heiau* is the religious site **sacred** to Lono.]

tack *[n] kui* (also means **nail**). *[v] pūnini* (as a sailboat; also means **to drift here and there**).

tackle *[v] lālau* (also means **to grab, seize**). *[n] lako lawaiʻa* (fishing).

Tahiti *Polapola.* (Kahiki is an ancestral homeland to the east, not Tahiti.)

tail 1. *huelo* (animal). 2. *puapua* (bird). 3. *hiʻu* (fish). [*He **hiʻu** iʻa ko ka wahine hiʻu iʻa.* The mermaid has a fish **tail**.]

take *lawe aku.* [*Nāu e **lawe aku** iā ia i ke kauka niho?* Are you the one who will **take** him to the dentist?]

take care of *mālama* (also means **keep**). [*E **mālama** i kou ola kino.* **Take care of** your health.]

tale 1. *kaʻao* (considered fictitious). [*Ua unuhi ʻia ke **kaʻao** ʻo Tazana i ka ʻōlelo Hawaiʻi.* The **tale** Tarzan was translated into Hawaiian.] 2. *moʻolelo* (considered true).

talent *kālena.*

talented *noʻeau* (also means **clever, skilled**).

talk 1. '*ōlelo*. 2. *kama'ilio* (to converse). [***Kama'ilio**
nā hoa hānau ma ka hui 'ohana*. The cousins
converse at the family reunion.]

tall *lō'ihi*.

tame *laka*. ['*A'ole **laka** ka tika*. The tiger isn't **tame**.]

tangerine '*alani pākē*.

tap *[v]* *kīkēkē*. [*Na wai i **kīkēkē** i ka puka ma ka pō
nei?* Who **tapped** on the door last night?]

tapa *kapa*. ['*O ke kilohana ke **kapa** mua o ke kapa
moe*. The *kilohana* is the top **tapa** of the
Hawaiian blanket. (In old Hawai'i, five pieces of
tapa were bound together to make a "blanket,"
with the top piece beautifully decorated. When
foreign merchants introduced cotton cloth, pieces
of cotton were beaten into the *kilohana*, resulting
in strikingly beautiful colors in the *kapa moe*.
Kilohana became a word for anything excellently
made or of highest quality.)]

tape 1. *lipine* (recording tape). 2. *leki* (cellophane
tape). [*E ho'opa'a i ka pelaha i ka paia i ka **leki**.
Put the poster on the wall with the **tape**.]

taro patch *lo'i*. (terrace of taro patches = *papa lo'i*)
[*Nui nā **lo'i** ma ka **papa lo'i***. There are lots of
taro patches in a **taro patch terrace**.]

task *hana*. [*Ma'alahi ka **hana** i ka laulima*. The **task**
is easy due to many people working together.]

taste '*ono*. [*Pehea ka '**ono** o ka ula maka?* How does
the fresh lobster **taste**?]

tasteful *kohu* (also means **tastefully**). [***Kohu** kāna
hana ho'onaninani i ka pākaukau a 'ono ho'i ka
'aina awakea*. Her decorating the table was **tastefully** done and the lunch was also delicious.]

tattoo 1. *kākau 'ili*. [*He hō'ailona ke **kākau 'ili**
Hawai'i no ka 'aumakua?* Are Hawaiian **tattoos**
symbols of guardian spirits?] 2. *kākau*. 3. *uhi*
(solid tattoo, like a covering).

taxes '*auhau*. [*No ke aha e uku ai 'o Pāpā i nā*

'auhau 'ehā manawa o ka makahiki? Why does Daddy pay **taxes** four times a year?]

taxi *ka'a ho'olimalima* (also means **rental car**). [*Āhea e hiki mai ai ke **ka'a ho'olimalima** āu i kelepona aku ai?* When will the **taxi** that you phoned arrive?]

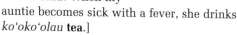
tea

tea *kī* (also means *tī* **leaf plant, key**). [*Ke hele ko'u 'anakē a ma'i i ka piwa, inu 'o ia i ke **kī** ko'oko'olau.* When my auntie becomes sick with a fever, she drinks ko'oko'olau **tea**.]

teach *a'o aku.*

teacher *kumu.* [*A'o aku ke **kumu** i ka 'ōlelo no'eau i kēlā pule kēia pule.* The **teacher** teaches a wise saying every week.]

team 1. *kimi* (from English). 2. *kime* (from English). [*E lanakila ana ka mākou **kime** ma luna o 'oukou!* Our **team** will beat you folks!]

tear (rip) 1. *hae.* 2. *hahae.* [*E **hahae** ana nā kānaka 'ohi kikiki i kā 'olua mau kikiki.* The ticket takers will **tear** your (two) tickets.]

tease *ho'ohenehene* (also means **ridicule**). [*Iā ia e uē ana, **ho'ohenehene** kona kaikuahine iā ia.* While he cried, his sister **teased** him.]

teaspoon *puna kī.*

telephone *kelepona.*

television *kīwī.*

tell 1. *ha'i.* [*E **ha'i** aku ana ka māka'ikiu i ka ha'ina i kēia lā.* The detective is going to **tell** the solution today.] 2. *'ōlelo.*

temper *na'au.* [*Ua nā ko ka ho'okele **na'au**.* The steersman's **temper** has been soothed.]

temperature 1. *wela* (hot). [*'Ehia kekele ka **wela** o* *kēia lā 'ino?* How high is the **temperature** of this stormy day?] 2. *anu* (cold).

temple 1. *heiau.* 2. *luakini* (a specific kind of large religious site, a place of human sacrifice).

temporary *kūikawā.* [*E hai 'ia ana kekahi mea ho'okipa **kūikawā** e a'u.* A **temporary** receptionist will be hired by me.]

tempt *ho'owalewale.* [*'A'ole 'oukou e **ho'owalewale** iā ia e inu i 'ole 'o Kale e hele a 'ona.* You all shouldn't **tempt** Kale to drink so that he doesn't become drunk.]

temptation *ho'owalewale.*

tent *hale pe'a.* [*'A'ole i kūkulu 'ia ka **hale pe'a** ma ka lihi kai. Aia ia ma ke kahua ho'omoana.* The **tent** wasn't set up at the edge of the sea. It's on the campground.]

tent

terrace 1. *lānai.* 2. *'anu'u* (also means **stairs, ledge, to strain, sprain**). 3. *papa lo'i* (terrace of taro patches).

terrible *weliweli* (also means **horrible, terrifying, horrifying**). [*He pōpilikia **weliweli** ko kona mau mākua.* His parents had a **terrible** misfortune.]

territory *panalā'au.*

test *hō'ike* (also means **demonstration of knowledge, skill**).

testimony *'ōlelo hō'ike.* [*'Oiai e heluhelu ana ke kiule i ka **'ōlelo hō'ike**, e helele'i iho ana nā waimaka.* While the jury was reading the **testimony**, their tears were falling.]

thanks *mahalo* (also means **admiration, respect**). [***Mahalo** nui iā 'oukou!* Many **thanks** to you all!] [***Mahalo** ka mea ho'okani 'ukulele i kā kāna kumu 'ukulele kahiko.* The 'ukulele player **admires** his teacher's old 'ukulele.]

Thanksgiving Day Lā Hoʻomaikaʻi.

that 1. *kēlā* (far away). 2. *kēnā* (near person being addressed). [*He naonao **kēnā** ma kāu kanuwika?* Is **that** (near you) an ant on your sandwich?]

the 1. *ka* (used with most words). 2. *ke* (used with words that begin with k, e, a, o). [*Mālie **ke** kahu hipa akā ʻeleu **ka** hipa.* **The** shepherd is slow, but **the** sheep is nimble.]

theater *hale keaka.* (movie theater = *hale kiʻi ʻoniʻoni*)

their (two people): 1. *ko lāua.* 2. *kā lāua.* (three or more people): 1. *ko lākou.* 2. *kā lākou. Ko lāua* and *ko lākou* are used in front of nouns that are things you can't help having, such as family born before you and including your generation, your name, land, friends, chiefs, gods, feelings, illnesses. Also used for anything one can enter into or put on, including any building, mode of transportation, clothes. *Kā lāua* and *kā lākou* are used in front of nouns that are things that can be acquired, including family born after you, your husband or wife, your work or any action, any tool [including computers and televisions], money, anything you make or create, food, drink, books.

them 1. *lāua* (two). 2. *lākou* (three or more).

theory *kumu manaʻo.* [*He **kumu manaʻo** ko ka mea kilo hōkū no ka hoʻokumu honua.* The astronomer has a **theory** about the creation of the world.]

there 1. *ʻō* (unspecified location). 2. *laila* (location known). (all over [*lit.* over there and over here] = *i ʻō a i ʻaneʻi*) [*Holo kaʻu mau ʻīlio pēpē **i ʻō a i ʻaneʻi**.* My puppies run **all over**.]

thermometer *ana wela.* [*Ma ka lā ikīki, piʻi aʻe nā kekele ma ke **ana wela**.* On hot and humid days, the temperature rises on the **thermometer**.]

they 1. *lāua* (two). 2. *lākou* (three or more).

thick *mānoanoa*. [*'Ano **mānoanoa** ka puke a ke kumu e heluhelu ana i nā keiki.* The book that the teacher is reading to the children is kind of **thick**.]

thief *'aihue*.

thigh *'ūhā* (also means **lap**). [*Eia nei, e noho iho ma ko'u **'ūhā**.* Dearie, sit on my **lap**.]

thimble *komo humuhumu*.

thin 1. *wīwī* (human body). 2. *waliwali* (poi).

thing *mea* (also means **person**). [*He 'ano pono hana hou anei kēlā **mea**?* Is that **thing** a new kind of tool?]

think 1. *mana'o*. 2. *no'ono'o*.

thirsty *makewai*. [***Makewai** wale mākou keiki, e ke kahu ma'i.* We kids are really **thirsty**, nurse.]

this *kēia*.

thought *mana'o* (also means **opinion, idea**). [*'A'ole 'ae nā Hawai'i a pau i nā 'ano **mana'o** like 'ole no ke ea, akā 'ae kākou e a'o mai a e holomua.* All Hawaiians don't agree with the various **thoughts** about sovereignty, but we all agree to learn and to go forward.]

thread *lopi*. [*Aia iā wai ka **lopi** ke'oke'o a me ka mānai? Makemake au e kui lei.* Who has the white **thread** and the *lei* needle? I want to string a *lei*.]

thread

three *'ekolu*. (syn. *'akolu, kolu*)

thrifty *makauli'i*. [*Mālama ka wahine **makauli'i** i ka lopi.* The **thrifty** woman saves thread.]

throat 1. *pu'u* (also means **hill, pimple, bump**, many other meanings).

throb 1. *konikoni*. [***Konikoni** ka pana o kona pu'uwai i ke a'a koko*. Her heart beat is **throbbing** in her vein.] 2. *kapalili*.

throw 1. *ho'olei*. [***Ho'olei** aku ka paniolo i ke kaula 'ili*. The cowboy **throws** the lasso.] 2. *nou*.

throw away 1. *kiloi*. 2. *kiola*. [*Mai **kiola** i nā nūpepa. E ho'ohana hou ana au iā lākou ma ke 'ano he pulu i ka māla pua*. Don't **throw away** the newspapers. I'll use them again as mulch in the flower garden.]

throw up *lua'i*. [*Pehea ka pēpē ma'i? Ua **lūa'i** 'o ia?* How is the sick baby? Did he **throw up**?]

thumb *manamanalima nui*.

thunder *hekili*. [*'Ōlapa ka uila, ku'i ka **hekili**, nāueue ka honua*. Lightning flashes, **thunder** roars, the earth shakes. (common line in chants)]

ticket 1. *likiki*. 2. *kikiki*. [*He mau **kikiki** kā 'olua no ka mokulele?* Do you (two) have **tickets** for the airplane?]

tickle *ho'omane'o*. [*E **ho'omane'o** 'oe i ko ka pēpē wāwae a hū kona 'aka*. **Tickle** the baby's foot until he laughs.]

tidal wave *kai e'e*. [*'Ehia hale i lilo i ke **kai e'e**?* How many houses were swept away in the **tidal wave**?]

tide 1. *kai*. 2. *au*. (low tide = *kai emi/kai malo'o*) (high tide = *kai piha*)

tidepool *kāheka*.

tidy 1. *'auli'i*. [***'Auli'i** kā kēia makua kāne holoi 'ana i nā pā*. The father's washing dishes is **tidy**.] 2. *maiau*.

tie *nāki'i*. [*E **nāki'i** i ka hoe 'ē a'e i ka 'iako*. **Tie** the other paddle to the outrigger boom.]

tight *mālo'elo'e* (taut; also means **stiff from physical labor, tired**). [*Ua **mālo'elo'e** ko'u kua ma mua o ka lomilomi 'ia 'ana*. My back was **tight** before being massaged.]

time 1. *manawa*. [*'O ka **manawa** pā'ani kēia*. This is play **time**.] (It's your turn = *'O kou manawa kēia*) 2. *hola* (telling time, o'clock). [*'O ka **hola** 'ehia kēia? 'O ka hapalua **hola** 'ekolu*. What **time** is it? It's half past three.] 3. *wā* (era, epoch). [*I ka **wā** o 'Umi*. In the **time** of 'Umi.]

tin *kini* (also means **tin can, gin** [from English], **many, multitude**).

tiny *'u'uku*. [*'**U'uku** kēia 'ano 'iole*. This type of rodent is **tiny**.]

tip 1. *wēlau* (top, edge). 2. *uku lawelawe* (gratuity).

tired *māluhiluhi*.

tobacco *paka*. (to smoke a cigarette = *puhi paka*) [*Mai **puhi paka**, ke 'olu'olu*. Don't **smoke**, please.]

today *i kēia lā*. [*E pikiniki kāua i kahakai **i kēia lā**!* Let's picnic at the beach **today**!]

toe *manamana wāwae*. [*'Ehia ou **manamana wāwae**, e ka pēpē?* How many **toes** do you have, baby?] (big toe = *manamana nui*)

toenail *miki'ao* (also means **fingernail**).

together 1. *pū*. [*Hana **pū** kēia mau hoakula*. These schoolmates work **together**.] 2. *like*.

toilet *lua*.

toilet paper *pepa hēleu*. (syn. *pepa hāleu*) [*Aia nō a loa'a ka **pepa hēleu**, pono 'o ia nei e ho'opau pilikia*. As soon as you find **toilet paper**, she has to use the bathroom.]

toilet paper

tolerant *mana'o laulā* (*lit.* broadminded; also means **main idea**).

tomato *'ōhi'a lomi*.

tomb *hē* (also means **grave**).

tomorrow *i ka lā 'apōpō*. [*I ka lā 'apōpō kāua e holo* *moku pe'a ai.* It's **tomorrow** that we (you and I) may sail on the sailboat.]

tongue *alelo.* [*Mai kīko'o i ke **alelo**!* Don't stick out your **tongue!**]

tonight *i kēia ahiahi.*

too 1. *nō ho'i.* 2. *pū.* [*Mālo'elo'e kou kua? 'O au **pū**!* Is your back tight and sore? Mine **too**!] 3. *kekahi.*

tool 1. *pono hana.* [*He **pono hana** i ho'ohana mau 'ia e ka mekanika ka mea 'ōwili.* The screwdriver is a **tool** that is always used by the mechanic.] 2. *mea ho'ohana.*

tooth *niho.* [*He mau **niho** hou kā ka luahine, akā pa'a 'ole ka 'ao'ao "mauka."* The old woman has new **teeth**, but the "mauka" (upper) teeth aren't firmly in place.]

toothbrush *palaki niho.*

toothless *niho 'ole.*

toothpaste *pauka niho.* [*Mai pakū i ka **pauka niho** mai luna i lalo.* Don't squeeze out the **tooth-paste** from top to bottom.]

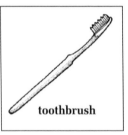

toothbrush

top 1. *luna* (top section). 2. *hū* (spinning toy).

torch *lamakū.*

toss 1. *ho'olei.* 2. *kiola.* 3. *kiloi* (toss out).

total 1. *huina.* 2. *heluna* (sum).

touch *ho'opā* (also means **to influence**).

tough 1. *uaua* (tough to chew). 2. *pa'akikī* (difficult). [*Uaua ka 'i'o kao a **pa'akikī** ka naunau 'ana no ka 'elemakule niho 'ole.* The goat meat is **tough** and chewing (it) is **difficult** for the toothless old man.] 3. *'o'ole'a* (strong condition).

tour *māka'ika'i.* [*Ua **māka'ika'i** lākou i nā mokupuni 'o nā Tuamotu.* They **toured** the Tuamotu islands.]

tourist 1. *mea māka'ika'i*. 2. *kanaka māka'ika'i*.

tow *kaualakō* (also means **to drag**). [*Kaualakō ke kalaka i ke ka'a*. The truck **tows** the car.]

towel *kāwele* (also means **to dry, wipe off**). (paper towel = *kāwele pepa*)

town 1. *kūlanakauhale* (also means **city, village**). 2. *kaona* (from English). [*Aia i hea ma Kaua'i ke kaona 'o Kalāheo?* Where on Kaua'i is the **town** of Kalāheo?]

trace *ho'okolokolo* (also means **to investigate**). [*E hiki ana iā 'oe ke ho'okolokolo i ko kou 'ohana mo'okū'auhau?* Will you be able to **trace** your family's genealogy?]

trade 1. *kālepa* (also means **merchant, salesman, to barter**). 2. *'oihana* (occupation).

tradition 1. *loina* (also means **custom, rule**). [*He mau loina ko ka holo kai ma nā wa'a?* Does ocean traveling on canoes have **traditions**?] 2. *kuluma*.

trail *alahele*.

train *ka'aahi*. [*Ua halihali ke ka'aahi i nā 'ōhua mai 'Iwilei a i Hale'iwa ma mua*. Previously, the **train** transported passengers from 'Iwilei to Hale'iwa.]

tramp *[n]* *kuewa* (vagabond). *[v]* 1. *hehi* (also means **to step, tread on, trample**). 2. *ke'ehi* (also means **to step, tread on, trample**).

trample 1. *hehi*. [*Hehi ka lehulehu i ka hinahina ma ka pu'e one*. The public **tramples** the *hinahina* plant at the sand dune.] 2. *ke'ehi*.

transform *ho'ololi*.

transformed *loli* (also means **changed**). [*Ua loli ka waiho'olu'u o ka pua hau kahiko a 'ula'ula*. The color of the old *hau* flower **changed** to red.]

translate *unuhi*.

transparent *aniani*.

transport *halihali*. [*Mai loko mai e halihali 'ia mai ka hapanui o ko Hawai'i mea 'ai*. Most of Hawai'i's food is **transported** here from the mainland.]

trap 1. *'ūmi'i* (also means **clamp, clutch, to clamp, choke,** many other meanings). 2. *pahele* (also means **deceit, snare, noose, to ensnare**). [*Loa'a nā pahele* pua'a ma ka wao kele. There are pig **traps** in the rain forest.]

trash *'ōpala* (also means **garbage**).

travel *huaka'i* (also means **trip, voyage**).

tray *pā halihali.*

treason *kipi* (also means **rebellion, treachery, rebel**). [*'O ke kipi paha, 'a'ole paha kā Wilikoki mā hana?* Were Wilcox folks doings **treason** or not?]

treasure [n] *mea makamae.* [*He mea makamae ka na'auao.* Wisdom is a **treasure.**] [v] *pūlama.* [*Pūlama 'ia nā lei pua 'a'ala.* Fragrant flower *lei* are **treasured.**]

treasurer *pu'ukū.*

treaty 1. *ku'ikahi.* 2. *palapala 'aelike.*

tree *kumulā'au.*

tree fern 1. *hāpu'u.* 2. *'ama'u.*

tremble 1. *ha'ukeke* (also means **shiver, quiver**). [*Ha'ukeke ke keiki i ke anu o ke kai, kahi āna e kāpeku nei.* The child is **shivering** due to the cold of the sea, where she is splashing around now.] 2. *ha'alulu.*

tree

trespass *komohewa.* [*Mai komohewa i ko ha'i pā hale.* Don't **trespass** in other people's yards.]

trial 1. *'aha ho'okolokolo* (court). 2. *ho'ā'o* (experiment). 3. *pōpilikia* (trouble).

triangle *huinakolu.*

tribute *ho'okupu* (also means **offerings**). [*He ho'okupu kūpono kāna mea i ha'i ai.* What he said is an appropriate **tribute.**]

trick *hana ma'alea.*

trim 1. *'oki* (to cut). 2. *'auli'i* (neat).

trip *[n] huaka'i. [v]* 'ōkupe. [*Ke* **'ōkupe** *hou ka 'ele-makule, e kōkua aku iā ia.* Whenever the old man **trips** again, help him.]

troop *hālau* (hula). 2. *pū'ali koa* (army).

trouble *pilikia.* [*Nalukai kēia luahine no ka mea ua 'ike i nā 'ano* **pilikia** *like 'ole.* This old lady is weatherworn because she has experienced all kinds of **trouble**.]

truck *kalaka* (from English).

true *'oia'i'o.* [*Eia nei,* **'oia'i'o** *ka'u i lohe ai, ua ho'omaha loa kāu kāne?* Darling, is it **true** what I've heard, that your husband retired?]

trunk 1. *kumu* (tree). 2. *pahu* (chest, box). 3. *ihu loloa* (elephant; *lit.* very long nose).

trust *hilina'i.* [*Mai* **hilina'i** *i nā kānaka e noi aku ana i kāu kālā.* Don't **trust** those who ask for your money.]

truth *'oia'i'o.* [*He aha ka* **'oia'i'o**? What is the **truth**?]

try *ho'ā'o.*

T-shirt 1. *pālule* T. 2. *pale 'ili* (undershirt).

tug *hiuhiu.* [**Hiuhiu** *ka pōpoki pēpē i ka mea pā'ani palupalu.* The kitten **tugs** at the soft toy.]

tune *[n] leo mele* (also means **melody**). [*Pehea ka* **leo mele** *o "Alekoki"? 'Āwīwī anei ka pana?* How about the **tune** of "Alekoki"? Is the beat fast?] *[v] ho'okani pono.*

turn 1. *huli.* [*E* **huli** *hema i ke kukui 'ula'ula.* **Turn** left at the red light.]

turn off machine *ho'opio.*

turn on machine *ho'ā.* [*E* **ho'ā** *ana ka pailaka i ka lolouila? Ua 'ā mua!* Will the pilot **turn on** the computer? It's already on!]

turtle 1. *honu* (common green turtle). [*Ulu nā pu'u ma nā* **honu** *a puni ka honua akā 'a'ole i maopopo 'ia ke kumu o ia ma'i weli.* Tumors grow on **turtles** around the world, but the reason for that dreadful disease is not understood.]

2. ʻea (hawksbill turtle; ʻea has many other meanings).

tusk niho (also means **tooth**).

TV kīwī.

twilight mōlehu. [*Ma ka mōlehu e kau mai ʻo ʻIao a me Venuse.* At **twilight** Jupiter and Venus appear.]

twine [n] 1. kaula. 2. kaula kuaina (from English). [v] wili.

twirl koali.

twist wili (also means **entwined, bound together**). [**wili** ʻia me ka maile lau liʻiliʻi, **twisted** with small-leaf maile (song, "Aloha Kauaʻi," by M. A. Lake)]

two ʻelua. (syn. ʻalua, lua)

type ʻano.

ugly *pupuka*. [*Inā ma'ema'e 'ole ke kino, 'o ia ka
    mea **pupuka**. A inā ma'ema'e, nani*. If the body
    isn't clean, that's an **ugly** thing. And if it's clean,
    that's beautiful.]

ukulele *'ukulele* (*lit.* "jumping flea," evolved from
    instrument introduced
    by Portuguese immi-
    grants).

ulcer *pūhā* (also means
    abscess, to burst).

ultimate *hope loa* (also
    means **very last**). [*'O ka
    he'e nalu 'ana ma
    Ko'olauloa ka pahuhopu*
    hope loa *o nā mea he'e*

ukulele

    nalu. Surfing in the Ko'olauloa area is the **ulti-
    mate** goal of surfers.]

umbilical *piko*.

umbrella *māmalu*. [*'Oiai ke helele'i nei ka ua, e
    wehe i kēnā **māmalu** āu*. Since the rain is falling,
    open up that (by you) **umbrella** of yours.]

uncle *'anakala*. [*'Akahi nō a ho'omaka nā **'anakala**
    e wehe i ka pulu niu a aia nō a nahā nā niu, e
    wa'u ana nā 'anakē i ka 'i'o*. The **uncles** have
    finally started to remove the coconut husks and
    as soon as the coconuts are cracked open, the
    aunties will scrape out the meat.]

uncover *wehe* (also means **to open, take off**).

undecided *kānalua* (also means **doubt, doubtful**).

under *lalo*. [*'Ano kānalua ka haku inā he uku
    kaulele kā nā limahana ma **lalo** ona*. The boss is

kind of doubtful whether the employees **under** him have overtime pay.]

underhanded *poholalo.*

underpants *pale maʻi.* [*He aha ke ʻano o kou **pale maʻi** e komo nei?* What kind of **underpants** are you wearing?]

understand *maopopo.* [*ʻAʻole **maopopo** iā ia pehea e hoʻopiha ai i ka palapala ʻauhau.* He doesn't **understand** how to fill out the tax form.]

undulate *hoʻānuʻunuʻu.* [*Hoʻānuʻunuʻu nā ʻupena i ke kai piʻi.* The nets **undulate** on the incoming tide.]

unequaled 1. *lua ʻole.* [*He nani **lua ʻole** ko Nāpali.* The Nāpali coast has **unequaled** beauty.] 2. *ana ʻole.*

uneven 1. *kaulike ʻole* (also means **unjust**). 2. *lualua* (also means **rough, bumpy**).

unfair *kaulike ʻole.* [***Kaulike ʻole** ka hoʻēmi ʻana i ka uku hana a nā wāhine e hana e like nō me nā kāne.* Reducing the salaries of women who do the same work as men is **unfair**.]

unfamiliar *kamaʻāina ʻole.* [*Ua kāhāhā ke anaina i ko ka hui hīmeni **kamaʻāina ʻole** i ka mele i noi ʻia ʻo "Pua Lililehua."* The audience was surprised at the singing group's being **unfamiliar** with the song which was requested, "Pua Lililehua."]

unfavorable *kūpono ʻole.* [*Kūpono a **kūpono ʻole** paha ka hopena o ka ʻolohana?* Are the results of the strike favorable or **unfavorable**?]

unfold 1. *lole* (also means **clothes, to turn inside out**). 2. *mōhala* (as a flower).

uniform *[n] makalike.* [*Komo ko ka hōkele mau limahana i nā **makalike**.* The hotel's employees wear **uniforms**.] *[adj] like.* (syn. *kohu like*)

unimportant *mea ʻole.* [***Mea ʻole** ka loa o Kaimukī lā.* The distance to Kaimukī is **unimportant**. (song, "Kaimukī Hula," by A. Richart)]

unintelligible *maopopo ʻole*. [***Maopopo ʻole** kāna ʻōlelo ma hope o ka maʻi huki*. His speech is **unintelligible** after the stroke.]

uninteresting *manakā* (also means **dull, boring, uninterested**). [***Manakā** ka helu ʻana i nā ʻaoʻao*. Counting pages is **uninteresting**.]

union 1. *hui* (group, meeting). 2. *pilina* (close relationship). 3. *uniona* (from English; labor union).

unique *laha ʻole* (also means **rare**).

united *hui pūʻia*. (United States of America = ʻAmelika Hui Pūʻia)

unity *lōkahi*. [*ʻO ka laulima a me ka **lōkahi** nā mea e hoʻomaluhia mai ai*. Sharing work and **unity** are the things that bring peace.]

universe *ao holoʻokoʻa*. [*ʻO ka Iʻa ka inoa o ko kākou māhele o ke **ao holoʻokoʻa***. The Milky Way is the name of our section of the **universe**.]

university *kula nui*.

unkind *loko ʻino* (also means **merciless, heartless, cruel**). [***Loko ʻino** maoli ʻoe e ke hoa*. You are truly **unkind**, friend. (song, "Latitu," by S. Kainoa)]

unlucky *pakalaki*. [*Manaʻo kekahi poʻe, he hōʻailona **pakalaki** ke ao pouli*. Some people think a dark cloud is an **unlucky** sign.]

unprepared 1. *hemahema* (also means **awkward**). 2. *mākaukau ʻole*.

unsafe *makaʻu* (also means **risk, danger, fear, dangerous, afraid**). [*I kēia mau lā, he hana **makaʻu** ka moe ipo*. These days, having an affair is **unsafe**.]

upland *uka*. [*Aia ke kula waiwai loa o ʻAmelika ma Kalihi **uka***. The richest school in America is in **upper** Kalihi.]

upper *luna* (also means **above**).

urge 1. *koi*. [*E **koi** ana ka pelikikena i nā lālā o ka Hui Kīwila Hawaiʻi e ʻimi kālā*. The president of

the Hawaiian Civic Club will **urge** the members
to fund-raise.] 2. *ha'akoi*.

urgent *ko'iko'i* (also means **emphatic, prominent,
harsh, stressed, weight**). [*He hana **ko'iko'i** ka
ho'ona'auao 'ana i ka hanauna hou.* Educating
the new generation is an **urgent** thing.]

urinate *mimi*. [*Aia ia hea ka lua?* Pono au e **mimi**.
Where is the toilet? I have to **urinate**.]

urine *mimi*.

us 1. *kāua* (you and I). *2. māua* (we two, not you). *3.
kākou* (us all, three or more). 4. *mākou* (we all,
not you). Note: *Māua* and *kāua* include two people only. *Māua* refers to "us" in the sense of "me
and my buddy," not including the person being
addressed. *Kāua* includes only the person speaking and the one being addressed, "us" here meaning "you and me." *Mākou* and *kākou* refer to
three or more people. *Mākou* has the same meaning as *māua*, only now it means "me and my
buddies." *Kākou* includes the speaker and everyone she is talking to.

use *ho'ohana*. [*E **ho'ohana** i ka hamale e ku'i i ke
kui.* **Use** the hammer to hit the nail.]

used to *ma'a* (also means **skilled at**). [*Ma'a ka
ho'okele wa'a i ka hākilo 'ana i ka 'alihi lani.*
Navigators are **used to** staring at the horizon.]

useless 1. *makehewa*. [***Makehewa** kou ku'i 'ana i ka
'opihi. Pono 'oe e noi iā 'Anakē e a'o mai iā 'oe.*
Your pounding *'opihi* is **useless**. You should ask
Aunty to teach you.] 2. *waiwai 'ole*.

usual *ma'amau*.

vacant *hakahaka* (also means **empty**). [*Hakahaka ka hale hoʻolimalima*. The rental house is **vacant**.]

vacate *haʻalele*.

vacation *wā hoʻomaha*. [*Ma kona hale hoʻomaha mākou e kipa mai nei i ka **wā hoʻomaha** Pakoa*. It's at her vacation home that we all are visiting now during Easter **vacation**.]

vagina *kohe*.

vague *powehi*. (syn. *poehi*)

vain 1. *makehewa* (useless, unsuccessful effort). 2. *pohō* (useless, unsuccessful effort). 3. *hoʻokano* (proud).

valley *awāwa*. [*Laukanaka ke **awāwa** ʻo Hālawa na Molokaʻi i ke au kahiko*. The **valley** of Hālawa on Molokaʻi was densely populated in ancient days.]

valuable *waiwai* (also means **wealth**, many other meanings).

vanish *nalowale* (also means **to disappear, lose something, lost, disappeared**). [*Pono nā Hawaiʻi e makaʻala o **nalowale** ko kākou hoʻoilina*. Hawaiians have to be vigilant or our heritage will **vanish**.]

vapor *ea* (also means **gas**, many other meanings).

variable *lolelua* (also means **inconsistent, unstable**). [*Lolelua ko ka moho manaʻo i kāna haʻi ʻōlelo*. The candidate's thoughts are **variable** in his speech.]

various *like ʻole*. [*Hō ka nani o nā pua poni **like ʻole** i wili ʻia i ka lei poʻo!* My goodness, how beautiful are the **various** purple flowers that have been bound together in the head *lei*!]

vegetable 1. *lau ʻai.* 2. *mea kanu.*

vegetarian 1. *mea ʻai lau ʻai.* 2. *hamu lau.*

vein *aʻa koko.*

velvet *weleweka.*

verdict *ʻōlelohoʻoholo.* [*Hiki anei ke kūkala ʻia ka ʻōlelohoʻoholo ʻo "hewa"?* Can the "guilty" **verdict** be broadcast?]

verify 1. *hōʻoiaʻiʻo.* 2. *hōʻoia* (also means **to confirm, validate**). [*Ma o ka hoʻopaʻa ʻana i ka wikiō e hōʻoia ai ke kauka holoholona i ka hana ʻino i nā lio.* (It is) by making a video that the vet should **verify** the abuse of the horses.]

verse *paukū.*

very 1. *loa.* [*Hauʻoli loa ka paʻa male hou.* The newly married couple is **very** happy.] 2. *nui.* 3. *nō.*

veterinarian *kauka holoholona.* [*Aloha kaʻu kauka holoholona i nā ʻano pōpoki like ʻole.* My **vet** loves all kinds of cats.]

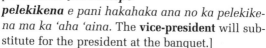
veterinarian

veto *hōʻole* (also means **to deny, refuse, negate**).

vice-president *hope pelekikena.* [*Na ka hope pelekikena e pani hakahaka ana no ka pelekikena ma ka ʻaha ʻaina.* The **vice-president** will substitute for the president at the banquet.]

vicious *ʻino.*

victim *luaahi.* [*E makaʻala o lilo ʻoe i luaahi.* Be alert so you don't become a **victim.**]

victorious *lanakila.* [*Ua lanakila ʻo Kamehameha ma luna o Kiwalaʻō ma ke kaua ʻo Mokuʻōhai.* Kamehameha was **victorious** over Kiwalaʻō at the battle of Mokuʻōhai.]

victory *lanakila.*

video *[n] wikiō.* [*E kiʻi kāua i wikiō e nānā ai ma ka* *hopenapule.* Let's you and me go get a **video** to watch on the weekend.] *[v] hoʻopaʻa wikiō.*

view *ʻikena* (also means **scenic view point**).

vigilant *makaʻala* (also means **watchful, alert**).

vine *lāʻauhihi.* [*E ʻuʻu pono i ka maile i onaona ka lāʻauhihi.* Strip the *maile* carefully so that the **vine** will be sweetly fragrant.]

violence *hana ʻino.* [*Ma muli o ka nui o ka* **hana ʻino** *e hōʻike ʻia ma ke kīwī, hōʻole pinepine ko koʻu mau hoahānau mau mākua iā lāua e nānā.* Due to the great amount of **violence** that is shown on TV, my cousins' parents often don't allow them to watch.]

VIP 1. *maka nui.* 2. *mea nui.*

virtue *hemolele.*

visible *kūmaka* (also means **seen, eyewitness**). [*Kūmaka ka uluwehi o ke kuahiwi i ka noe.* The verdant beauty of the mountain in the mist is **visible**.]

vision 1. *ʻike* (sight; also means **to see, to know**). 2. *akakū* (extra-sensory perception; also means **reflection, trance, hallucination**).

visit *kipa.* [*Kipa aku, kipa mai ka ʻohana ma ka lā nui.* The family **visits** back and (visits) forth on the holiday.]

voice *leo.* [*A he* **leo** *wale nō, ʻae.* And it is only a **voice**, (saying) yes. (line from chant granting permission to enter)]

volcano *lua pele.*

volunteer *ʻaʻa* (also means **to dare, to challenge**). [*E* **ʻaʻa** *ana ʻoe e kōkua i nā kānaka ʻōmaʻimaʻi?* Will you **volunteer** to help the chronically ill?]

vomit *luaʻi.*

vote *koho pāloka* (also means **election, voting**; *lit.* choose ballot). [*Pehea lā e loaʻa ai ke ea ma ke* **koho pāloka** *ʻana?* How indeed will sovereignty be obtained through a **vote**?]

vow *ho‘ohiki* (also means **promise, to swear an oath**).

voyage *huaka‘i* (also means **trip, tour**). [*E huaka‘i maika‘i ma ka Pākīpika.* Have a good **voyage** on the Pacific.]

wade *helekū*. [**Helekū** *'o Holoua i loko o ke kāheka.* Holoua **wades** in the tidepool.]

waft *māpu* (also means **bubbling, surging [emotions], wind-borne fragrance**). [*He 'ala nei e **māpu** mai nei.* Here is a fragrance that is being **wafted** here on the wind. (song, "Ahe Lau Makani," by Lili'uokalani)]

wag *luli* (also means **to shake, sway unsteadily**). [**Luli** *ke kanaka mū i kona po'o a pēlā 'o ia e hō'ike nei i kona maopopo.* The mute person **wags** her head, and that's how she's showing that she understands.]

wage (pay) *uku* (also means **reward, revenge**, many other meanings). [*Ua loa'a ka **uku** iā 'oe i kēia kakahiaka?* Did you receive your **wages** this morning?]

wagon *ka'a*.

wail 1. *uē*. 2. *kanikau*.

wait 1. *kali*. 2. *alia*. ["*E **alia** iki*" *wahi a ke kuene.* The waitress said, "**Wait** a little."]

waiter *kuene* (also means **waitress, flight attendant**).

waitress

wake someone up *ho'āla*. [*'Akahi nō a hiamoe ka'u kāne akā pono au e **ho'āla** iā ia.* My husband is finally sleeping but I have to **wake him up**.]

wake up *ala* (also means **to rise up, awake**). [*E **ala** mai, e ka maka hiamoe!* **Wake up**, sleepyhead!]

walk *hele wāwae.* [**Hele wāwae** *ko Likolehua hoaku-la a puni ka pāka i nā kakahiaka a pau.* Likolehua's classmate **walks** around the park every morning.]

wall 1. *paia* (wall of a building). 2. *pā* (an outside wall or fence).

wander *'auana.* [*Mai kahi pae a kahi pae o ka 'āina i* **'auana** *ai nā kuewa.* From one end of the land to the other the tramps **wandered.**]

wane 1. *manono* (moon). [**Manono** *ka mahina i kēia pule.* The moon **wanes** this week.] 2. *emi.*

want *makemake* (also means **need, desire**). [*He aha kou* **makemake,** *e ke keiki?* What do you **want,** child?]

war *kaua.* [*Hiki anei i ka hanauna hou ke ho'opau i ke* **kaua**? Can the new generation put an end to **war**?]

warehouse *hale ho'āhu.* [*Mehana nā pahu i waiho 'ia ma ka* **hale ho'āhu.** The boxes which were deposited in the **warehouse** are warm.]

warm *mehana.*

warn *a'o.*

warrior *koa* (also means **courage, brave, martial, native tree** whose wood is prized for furniture, canoes). [*E ola* **koa.** (*'ōlelo no'eau*) Live long and like a **warrior**, with courage.]

warrior

wary *'e'ena.*

wash *holoi* (also means **to erase**).

washing machine (clothes) *mīkini holoi lole.* [*'O nā lole ke'oke'o wale nō nā lole āna e ho'okomo nei i ka* **mīkini holoi lole**? Is it only white clothes that he is putting into the **washing machine**?]

washing machine (dishes) *mīkini holoi pā.*

waste *hoʻomāuna.* [*ʻAʻole kākou e **hoʻomāuna** i nā waiwai o ka ʻāina o hewa loa kā kākou hana ma mua o nā kūpuna.* We shouldn't **waste** the resources of the land or else our actions will be very wrong to our ancestors.]

watch *[n] uaki* (also means **clock**). *[v]* 1. *nānā* (also means **to observe, look at**). 2. *mālama* (also means **to keep, take care of**). 3. *kiaʻi* (watch over, protect).

watch out *makaʻala* (also means **alert, vigilant**). [*E **makaʻala** o lilo ke keiki i ka pāʻani lolouila.* **Watch out** or else the child will become absorbed in the computer game.]

water *wai.*

water ditch *ʻauwai.* [*Holo ka wai ma ka **ʻauwai** a hiki i ka papa loʻi.* Water flows in the **water ditch** to the taro patch terrace.] (sewer = *ʻauwai lawe mea ʻino*)

waterfall *wailele.* [***Wailele** hune nā pali, ko kāhiko nō ia.* **Waterfall** sprinkling the cliffs, it is your adornment. (song, "Molokaʻi Waltz," by M. Kāne)]

watermelon *ipu haole.*

wave (ocean) 1. *nalu* (breaks close to shore). 2. *ʻale* (ocean swell).

way *alahele.*

we 1. *kāua* (you and I). 2. *māua* (us two, not you). 3. *kākou* (all of us; three or more). 4. *mākou* (all of us [three or more], not you).

weak *nāwaliwali.* [*ʻAno **nāwaliwali** paha ka pēpē i hānau ʻia i nehinei.* The baby which was born yesterday is possibly a bit **weak**.]

wealth *waiwai* (also means **property, benefit, valuable**, many other meanings).

weapon *mea kaua.* [*ʻAʻole ka pahi kaua he **mea kaua** kahiko ma kēia pae ʻāina.* The sword was not an ancient **weapon** in this island chain.]

weapon

wear *komo* (also means **to enter**). [***Komo** mau ka'u luna i ka lei pua.* My supervisor always **wears** a flower *lei.*]

wearisome *ho'oluhi* (also means **burdensome**). [*He hana **ho'oluhi** kā ke kauka.* Doctors have a **wearisome** job.]

weary *luhi.*

weather 1. (phrase) *ke 'ano o ka manawa.* 2. *aniau* (climate). 3. *[v] nalukai* (weathered).

weave *ulana.* [*No ka hapalua kālā wale nō i kū'ai aku ai kona kupuna wahine i nā pāpale lauhala a kona 'ohana i **ulana** ai i ka hale kū'ai ma Kona i kona wā kamali'i.* It was for only a half dollar that his grandmother sold the *lauhala* hats her family **wove** to the store in Kona in her childhood.]

web *'upena* (also means **net**). [*'Ehia 'īniha ka lōloa o ka maka **'upena**?* How many inches long is the eye of the **net**?] (spider web = *'upena nananana;* syn. *pūnāwelewele*)

wedding *male 'ana.* [*Aia ka **male 'ana** ma waho, ma ka māla pua.* The **wedding** is outside, in the flower garden.]

weed *[n] nāhelehele.* [*Pono e waele i nā **nāhelehele** i ka lo'i i 'ole e uluwale ka lo'i.* The **weeds** in the taro patch have to be pulled so that the patch won't be overgrown.] *[v] waele.*

week *pule.* [*'Ehia **pule** āna e holopeki ai a mākaukau no ka heihei?* How many **weeks** should she jog until she is prepared for the race?]

weep 1. *uē.* 2. *kulu waimaka.* [*Ke lohe au i ia mele, **kulu waimaka**.* Whenever I hear that song, **tears fall**.]

weight *kaumaha* (also means **sad, depressed**). [*'Ehia paona ke **kaumaha** o kou kino?* How much do you **weigh**? (*lit.* How many pounds is the weight of your body?)]

weightlifting 1. *hāpai hao*. 2. *hāpai paona*.

welcome 1. *ho'okipa* (to welcome, entertain as guest). [***Ho'okipa** 'o Malia i kona mau hoaaloha ma ke kahua mokulele.* Malia **welcomes** her friends at the airport.] 2. *aloha aku* (give greeting). [*E **aloha aku** iā Kīhei.* **Give my love** to Kīhei.]

well *maika'i*.

well supplied *lako*.

west *komohana* (where the sun enters the sea [*komo*] at sunset).

wet *pulu* (soaked with rain).

whale 1. *koholā* (humpback whale). 2. *palaoa* (sperm whale; also means **ivory**, especially whale ivory used to make whale-tooth pendants (*lei niho palaoa*), a symbol of high rank).

whale

wharf *uapo* (also means **bridge**).

what *he aha*. [***He aha** kēnā? He mau pūpū nani kēia.* **What**'s that (by you)? These are pretty shells.]

wheel *huila*. [*ke 'oni nei ka **huila**,* **wheels** turning (song, "Holoholoka'a," by C. Kinney)]

wheelchair *noho huila*.

when *i ka manawa* (at the time). [*I ka manawa āu i pae ai i ka nalu, ua 'ike paha 'oe i ka manō?* **When** you caught the wave, did you maybe see a shark?] Note: Unlike in English, there are a variety of ways to say "when" in Hawaiian, depending on the type of sentence pattern being used.

where 1. *kahi* (the place where). 2. *Aia i hea...?* (Where is...?)

which 1. *hea* (used in questions). [*'O ka lā **hea** kou lā male?* **Which** day is your wedding day?]

whirlpool 1. *mimilo.* 2. *wiliwai* (also means **eddy**).

whiskers *'umi'umi* (also means **mustache, beard**). [*Kahi ke kāne i kona mau pāpālina i 'ole e ulu ka **'umi'umi**.* The man shaves his cheeks so **whiskers** don't grow.]

whisper *hāwanawana.*

whispering *hāwanawana.* [*Kawaihae, i ke kai, i ke kai **hāwanawana**,* Kawaihae, the sea, the **whispering** sea (traditional song, "Hilo Hanakahi")]

whistle *hōkio.*

white *ke'oke'o.* (white hair on head = *po'o hina*)

whiz by *pūhalahio.* [*Ua **pūhalahio** a'e 'o Wala'au ma kona wa'a pe'a.* Wala'au **whizzed by** on his sailing canoe.]

who *'o wai.* [*'O wai kēlā?* **Who**'s that?]

whole *holo'oko'a* (also means **entire**). [*Ua 'oki'oki 'ia ka 'ulu **holo'oko'a**.* The **whole** breadfruit was chopped into small pieces.]

why *no ke aha.* [***No ke aha** i ho'ohūnā'ia ai ka hula kahiko ma mua?* **Why** was ancient hula hidden in the past?]

wide 1. *ākea* (also means **spacious, unobstructed, broad, public**). 2. *laulā* (also means **liberal, publicly**).

widespread *laha.* [*Ua **laha** ke aloha 'āina.* Patriotism (love for the land) is **widespread**.]

width 1. *ākea.* 2. *laulā.* [*'Ehā kapua'i ka **laulā** o ka pākaukau koa. 'Ehia kapua'i ka lō'ihi?* Four feet is the **width** of the *koa* table. How many feet is its length?]

wife *wahine* (also means **woman, female, feminine**).

wild *'āhiu* (also means **shy**). [*'A'ole **'āhiu** kēia manu. Laka ia.* This bird is not **wild**. It's tame.]

will *[n]* 1. *palapala ho'oili-na.* 2. *palapala kauoha.* [*I kona unuhi 'ana i nā* **palapala kauoha** *kahiko, kolokolo ka loio i ka ho'oilina 'āina.* When she translates old **wills**, the lawyer traces the inheritance of land.]

will

wilt *mae* (also means **wilted**). [*Mae nā lei pua i ka wela o ka lā.* The flower leis **wilted** in the heat of the sun.]

win *lanakila.* [*'O wai ka inoa o ka mea oli i* **lanakila** *i ke kūlana 'ekahi?* What is the name of the chanter who **won** first place?]

wind *makani* (also means **breeze**). [*Pā aheahe mai ana ka* **makani.** The **wind** is gently blowing.]

window *pukaaniani.*

wind surf *he'e nalu makani.*

wing *'ēheu.* [*'Elua* **'ēheu** *o ka manu.* Birds have two **wings**.]

wink *'imo* (also means to **twinkle**, as stars). [**'Imo**'imo *kou maka, kou le'ale'a paha.* Your eyes **wink**, you're maybe having fun. (song, "He Mea Ma'a Mau Ia," by J. Almeida)]

wink

winter *ho'oilo* (*lit.* rainy season; ancient Hawaiians had no word for winter).

wipe *kāwele* (also means **towel, to dry**).

wire *uea* (also means **cable**). [*E nāki'i i ka* **uea** *a puni ka pou.* Tie the **wire** around the post.]

wisdom *na'auao* (also means **enlightenment, knowledge**).

wise *na'auao* (also means **enlightened, educated, intelligent**).

wish *makemake*. [*Ua ho'okō ka'u ipo i ko māua* **makemake** *e kipa aku i Kaho'olawe.* My sweetheart fulfilled our (her and my) **wish** to visit Kaho'olawe.]

with *me*. [*Me wai i komo ai ka mea ma'i i ka haukapila? Me ia?* **With** whom did the patient enter the hospital? **With** him?]

without *'ole*. [*Niho 'ole ka pēpē.* The baby is **without** teeth.]

witness *'ike maka*. [*Ua 'ike maka ko'u kupuna wahine i ka ho'opahūpahū iā Pu'uloa.* My grandmother **witnessed** the bombing of Pearl Harbor.]

woman *wahine*.

wonder *[n]* 1. *mea kupaianaha* (amazing or astonishing thing). 2. *hana kupaianaha* (amazing event). *[v] nune* (speculate, ponder). [*Nune nā kilo hōkū inā loa'a ke ola ma nā hōkūhele 'ē a'e.* Astronomers **wonder** if there's life on other planets.]

wonderful *kupaianaha* (also means **astonishing, mysterious, surprising**). [*Kupaianaha ka hū 'ana o ka pele.* The spouting up of lava is **astonishing**.]

wood *lā'au* (also means **bush, medicine**). [*'Ai wale nā mū i nā hale* **lā'au**. Insects and bugs eat **wood** houses.]

wool *hulu hipa*.

word *hua 'ōlelo*. [*He aha ka mana'o o kēia* **hua 'ōlelo**? What's the meaning of this **word**?]

work *[n] hana* (refers to any activity; *'oihana* refers specifically to job, profession). [*He aha kāu* **hana** *ma hope o ka hola 'elima?* What (activity) do you do after five o'clock?] *[v] hana* (also means **to make something**). [*Hana kāna mo'opuna wahine kuakahi ma ko kāna kāne hale kū'ai.* His greatgranddaughter **works** at her husband's store.]

worker *limahana* (also means **employee, laborer**).

work together 1. *hana like.* 2. *alu like.* 3. *laulima.*

world 1. *honua.* (globe = *poepoe honua*) 2. *ao.*

worm *koʻe.*

worried *hopohopo.*

worry *hopohopo.* [*Mai hopo-hopo, e hauʻoli!* Don't **worry**, be happy!]

worship 1. *hoʻomana.* 2. *haipule.* [*Mālama ʻia kekahi hana **haipule** ma Mauna ʻAla i ka mahina ʻo Pepeluali.* A **worship**

worried

service is held at Mauna ʻAla (Royal Mausoleum) in the month of February.]

worthless 1. *waiwai ʻole.* 2. *lapuwale* (also means **foolishness, vanity, scoundrel**). 3. *ʻalaʻuka* (also means **vile conduct, dregs of society**). [***ʻAlaʻuka** a poholalo kā nā kānaka loko ʻino hana ʻāpuka.* Nasty people's fraudulent activities are **worthless**.]

worthy *kūpono* (also means **proper, favorable, appropriate**).

wound *palapū.* [*E loaʻa ana paha ka **palapū** i ke koa ma ka hoʻouka kaua.* The soldier might receive a **wound** in the battle.]

wrap *wahī* (also means **envelope, covering, case, to bundle up, cover up, dress wound**). [*E **wahī** i nā pua melia a me nā kiele i ka lāʻī.* **Wrap** the plumerias and gardenias in the *tī* leaf.]

wreck *wāwahi* (also means **to demolish, tear down, shatter**). [*He hana kūpono ka **wāwahi** wale ʻana i nā hale kahiko?* Is it a proper thing to just **wreck** old houses?]

wring *ʻuī.* [*Ua **ʻuī** ʻia nā welu pulu.* The wet rags were **wrung** out.]

wrinkled *minomino.* [*He hōʻailona ko kuʻu kupuna*

*lae **minomino** i ka nui o kona naʻauao.* The **wrinkled** brow of my beloved grandparent is a sign of the breadth of her wisdom.]

wrinkles *ʻuka.*

wrist *pūlima* (also means **to sign your name**). [*ʻEha pinepine ko ka laweleka **pūlima**.* The mail carrier's **wrist** is often sore.]

write *kākau* (also means **tattoo**).

writer *mea kākau.*

writing 1. *palapala.* 2. *kākau.*

wrong *hewa* (also means **guilt, sin**). [***Hewa** paha nā ʻōlelo kuhikuhi i hāʻawi ʻia mai iaʻu.* Perhaps the directions which were given to me are **wrong**.]

yam *uhi* (also means **cover, lid, veil, solid tattooing, to cover**).

yam

yard 1. *pā hale* (of a house). [*He mau kumuniu a he mau kumumaiʻa kāna ma kona **pā hale**.* She has coconut trees and banana trees in her **yard**.] 2. *iā* (measurement). [*ʻEhia **iā** ka lōʻihi kūpono no ka holokū?* How many **yards** is the proper length for a *holokū* (formal, figure-hugging *muʻumuʻu* worn for balls and special occasions, with a long train)?

yawn *hoʻohāmama.* [*Ke **hoʻohāmama** ʻoe, piha ke akemāmā i ke ea.* When you **yawn**, the lungs fill with air.]

year *makahiki.* (last year = *i kēlā makahiki aku nei*) (next year = *i kēia makahiki aʻe*) [*I kēlā makahiki aku nei, ʻaʻole i hiki iā Laʻakea ke heʻe nalu makani, akā naʻe, i kēia makahiki aʻe ana ʻo ia e heʻe nalu makani ai ma Hoʻokipa, Maui.* **Last year**, Laʻakea couldn't wind surf; however, it is **next year** that he will windsurf at Hoʻokipa, Maui.]

yearn *ake.* [*Ke **ake** inu wai o ka Maluakiʻiwai.* The Maluakiʻiwai wind **yearns** to drink water. (song, "Kalamaʻula," by H. Dudoit)]

yearning *ʻiʻini.* [*I loko nō o ka lōʻihi o ke kaʻawale ʻana, ulu mau ko ke keiki **ʻiʻini** e ʻike hou i kona māu mākua.* In spite of the length of separation, the **yearning** of a child to see his parents again always grows.]

yell 1. *hoʻōho.* [*Mai* **hoʻōho** *i koʻu wahi pepeiao!* Don't **yell** in my dear little ear!] 2. *ʻuā.*

yellow 1. *melemele* (light yellow). 2. *lenalena* (orange yellow).

yes *ʻae* (also means **to yield, allow**). [*E* **ʻae** *paha ana kaʻu haku ʻāina i kaʻu noi e loaʻa i ka hānaiāhuhu.* My landlord may say **yes** to my request to have a pet.]

yesterday *i nehinei.* [*I* **nehinei** *i mālama ʻia ka hoʻomaikaʻi ʻana i ka hale.* **Yesterday** was when the house blessing was held.]

yet 1. *naʻe* (also means **however**). [*Ua luhi loa koʻu hoahānau a ua hiki* **naʻe** *iā ia ke humuhumu i nā pāʻū hula me ka maiau.* My cousin was really tired, **yet** she could sew the hula skirts skillfully.] 2. *akā naʻe.*

yield *ʻae.*

you 1. *ʻoe* (one person). 2. *ʻolua* (you two). 3. *ʻoukou* (you all, three or more).

young *ʻōpiopio.* [*Kōkua nā kāne* **ʻōpiopio** *i nā kānaka makua.* The **young** men help the adults.]

your (one person): 1. *kou.* 2. *kāu.* (two people): 1. *ko ʻolua.* 2. *kā ʻolua.* (three or more people): *ko ʻoukou.* 2. *kā ʻoukou. Kou, ko ʻolua,* and *ko ʻoukou* are used in front of nouns that are things that are things you can't help having, such as family born before you and including your generation, your name, land, friends, chiefs, gods, feelings, illnesses. Also used for anything one can enter into or put on, including any building, mode of transportation, clothes. *Kāu, kā ʻolua,* and *kā ʻoukou* are used in front of nouns that are things that can be acquired, including family born after you, your husband or wife, your work or any action, any tool [including computers and televisions], money, anything you make or create, food, drink, books.

youth *'ōpio.* [*Ha'aheo ka lāhui i nā* **'ōpio** *e ho'ōla nei i kā kākou 'ōlelo.* The Hawaiian people are proud of the **youth** who are reviving our language.]

zeal *mana'o ikaika.*

zero *'ole.* [*'O ko lākou helu kelepona 'o 'eiwa 'ehā 'eiwa 'elima **'ole** 'elua 'ehiku.* Their (three) phone number is nine four nine five **zero** two seven.]

zigzag *kīke'eke'e* (also means **twisting, crooked**).

zigzag

zipper *huka.* [*Mai huki ikaika i ka **huka** o poloke paha.* Don't pull strongly on the **zipper** or else it might break.]

zone 1. *māhele* (also means **portion, piece**). 2. *wao* (refers to biogeographic zones such as *wao kanaka*, the section of fertile lands where people lived).

zoo *kahua holoholona.* [*'Aka'aka aku au i nā keko ma ke **kahua holoholona**.* I laugh at the monkeys in the **zoo**.]